THE
GREENS
COOK
BOOK

THE
GREENS

COOK

BOOK

Extraordinary Vegetarian Cuisine

from the Celebrated Restaurant

BY DEBORAH MADISON

with Edward Espe Brown

BROADWAY BOOKS

NEW YORK

This book is affectionately dedicated
to our mothers

First Broadway Books trade paperback edition published 2001.

Designed by David Bullen
Illustrated by Laurie Anderson

The Cataloging-in-Publication Data is on file with the Library of Congress.

ISBN 0-7679-0823-6

10 9 8 7 6 5

ALSO BY DEBORAH MADISON

The Savory Way

Vegetarian Cooking for Everyone

This Can't Be Tofu!

Table of Contents

SOUPS AND STOCKS

SANDWICHES AND BREADS

PIZZAS

PASTA

GRATINS, STEWS, AND CASSEROLES

TARTS AND TIMBALES

FILO PASTRIES, FRITTATAS, CREPES, AND ROULADES

COMPANION DISHES

SAUCES, RELISHES, AND BUTTERS

DESSERTS

APPENDIX

Foreword

I clearly remember the first time I visited Greens at Fort Mason. Although I had heard many enthusiastic reports about it, I still had my doubts because of the rather dismal, lackluster meals I'd had in other vegetarian restaurants.

But I was immediately impressed when I entered Greens. The large dining room with its lofty ceiling, polished wood paneling, redwood sculpture, and bold, bright murals was dramatic—a balancing contrast to the wall of glass overlooking an expansive view of San Francisco Bay, the Golden Gate Bridge, and Marin hills in the background. The tables were neatly set and had a simple, clean look. Everything was polished and bright, and the food turned out to be better than I could have possibly imagined. Beautiful, delicious, and pleasing, this vegetarian food had sparkle and character and was obviously prepared with skill, imagination, and taste, as well as restraint—they weren't adding one more pine nut than was needed.

Over many visits for both lunch and dinner, I noticed a high level of consistency with everything that came to the table. The appetizers and accompaniments were as carefully presented as the main dishes. There was a marvelous variety of freshly baked breads, including an attractive focaccia with rock salt and sage or rosemary; the Black Bean Chili was a hearty eye-opener; the Wilted Spinach Salad with feta cheese and olives was often lunch for me, as were the sandwiches such as the Grilled Tofu Sandwich—simple but so good.

Deborah Madison is the person chiefly responsible for developing the menus and the wonderful food. She is truly an American cook, her dishes reflective of our melting-pot country. She has gathered dishes from Mexico, Italy, Greece, and France, as well as an occasional Asian recipe. Her knowledge of gardening adds another helpful dimension to her sense of season and freshness.

While there are many good cooks who write cookbooks, there are only a few good cooks who are good teachers, and Deborah and Ed Brown are among them. Ed is the author of three previous cookbooks, including *The Tassajara Bread Book*. He worked at Greens for four and a half years in a variety of positions including waiter, host, manager, and wine buyer. Together, he and Deborah make a fine team. Their chapter on soups, for instance, readily demonstrates their ability to show step by step how to make vegetarian stocks, and a variety of satisfying soups. Many times the recipes contain useful instructions and sensible pointers that are often left unsaid or taken for granted in other cookbooks. The attentiveness which made the Greens food such a great success has produced a book with equal clarity and delight.

The Greens Cookbook is a treasure house of dishes which can be made without meat. The breadth and scope of these recipes clearly demonstrates that the absence of meat can spur creativity rather than rein it in, and this book proves to be an invaluable resource for any cook who would like to expand his or her repertoire of dishes. Additionally, I found the book to be fine reading, a comfortable bedside book that has, at times, the feeling of poetry.

It has been well worth waiting a long time for this book!

Marion Cunningham, 1986

Acknowledgments

The making of Greens and of *The Greens Cookbook* happened with the support, encouragement, and hard work of many people whom the authors wish to thank. During the time we were writing this book, the staff at Greens patiently allowed our inquiries and intrusions, and we particularly thank Annie Somerville, Camille Convey, Michael Sawyer, Laurie Schley, Jay Simoneaux, and Jito Yumaka; also John Birdsall and Mick Sopko, who helped with the recipes, and Pam Dixon, who tested many of them. Sibella Kraus kept us up-to-date on the names and availability of new varieties of produce; Stephen Singer gave us helpful words on wine; and Patti Sullivan lent her warm support and assistance. Elizabeth Tuomi undertook the typing of the manuscript; Elaine Ginger pruned it into shape; and Jane Hirshfield generously lent her skills as both an editor and cook. We are also grateful to David Bullen, who worked patiently with us and succeeded in giving the book its graceful design.

Our heartfelt thanks are given to Alice Waters and the staff at Chez Panisse, particularly Paul Bertolli, Pat Curtan, Lindsey Shere, and Peggy Smith, who have worked with us over the years. Alice's keen sense of food and willingness to share her knowledge with others have been deeply inspiring, as have the beautiful vegetable dishes we have seen and tasted at Chez Panisse.

Many others have helped shape our cooking through their writings and their cooking. Among them we wish to express our gratitude to Giuliano Bugialli, Marion Cunningham, Elizabeth David, M. F. K. Fisher, Jane Grigson, Marcella Hazan, Madelaine Kamman, Diana Kennedy, Richard Olney, Julie Sahni, Jeremiah Tower, Barbara Tropp, and Paula Wolfert.

Greens would not have existed without the San Francisco Zen Center and the wider community of friends and supporters who encouraged the Zen Center to establish such a restaurant. Among the many who participated in creating Greens, we wish to thank Richard Baker, the abbot of Zen Center at the time, and Karin Gjording, who gave her organizing skills and critical good taste to the innumerable decisions which bring the vision of a restaurant into a smoothly functioning reality. Elaine Maisner and Jim Phalen helped shape the kitchen with their energy, enthusiasm, and creative talents. Dan Welch tirelessly supported the sometimes flagging spirit of the founding chef with his own good spirit and encouragement. Peter Overton and the Zen Center's Tassajara Bread Bakery supplied our bread and many of our desserts. Dick Graff gave us his wines, his generous advice, and baskets of spring-grown watercress. Farmers Clay Calhoun, Wendy Johnson, and Peter Rudnick of Zen Center's Green Gulch Farm, and Dorothy Coil from Trethaway Farm in Lodi, supplied us with the beautifully grown produce, flowers, eggs, and honey which so inspired our cooking.

Lastly, we are deeply grateful to and appreciative of our agent, Michael Katz, who worked closely with us from beginning to end with much patience and humor, and to our editor at Bantam Books, Tobi Sanders, whose efforts and faith in our work made all this possible.

Introduction

We opened Greens at Fort Mason in 1979 to offer lively and enjoyable vegetarian food to a public accustomed to eating meat. The setting is ideal—the large airy restaurant sits on a dock that juts into San Francisco Bay. A wall of high windows faces the Golden Gate Bridge and the hills of the Marin headlands. Foghorns, ships' bells, and sea gulls fill the air with sound, and often, as dinner begins, the setting sun floods the dining room with light.

We set out to create a cuisine whose complexity and interest left the diner feeling that nothing was missing. We drew upon a wide variety of traditions—the Mediterranean cooking of southern France and Italy, dishes from Mexico and the American Southwest, a few adaptations from the cuisines of Asia, and others—but what pulled it all together was our reliance on the freshest vegetables, herbs, and spices. Anyone who knows the fragrance of tomatoes ripening in the sun, the sweetness of berries so ripe they practically fall into the hand, or the flavor of asparagus and corn when picked and cooked right away knows food at its pleasurable best. This quality is what we wanted to be able to offer in our restaurant.

From the start we worked closely with Green Gulch Farm in Marin County, which has made it possible for us to experiment with new varieties of foods and to stay in touch with what is in season locally. The cool, foggy climate of Green Gulch is well suited to growing all sorts of lettuces, potatoes, winter squash, flowers, and many kinds of herbs, but for hot-weather vegetables and fruit we had to drive to nearby inland farms. We spent many mornings on our knees pulling tomatoes, peppers, and eggplants from the vine, or, in late summer, picking figs, persimmons, and quince. These farm runs added hours to an already long day of cooking, but the time spent was always generously repaid with the inspiration we gained. The menus seemed to plan themselves as we walked through the fields allowing the smell, touch, and feel of the plants to make their own suggestions for a dish or a meal. It was a very different experience from thinking up a recipe and then seeing if the ingredients were available.

We hope that readers of this book will also plan their meals by first finding out which foods are at their prime and then choosing recipes that make use of them. This has become much easier to do in the last few years, during which increased interest and demand has brought fine produce closer to hand. Greens no longer has to go to great lengths to secure its supplies, thanks to improvements in the distribution of small farmers' crops, and when we tested the recipes for this book we were able to purchase all of the ingredients at local supermarkets and groceries. We do, however, encourage urban shoppers to seek out the farmer's or green markets that have opened in most cities as well as in many small towns across the country. Also, local ethnic grocery stores, especially Asian and Mexican markets, can be good sources of the kinds of produce we like to use.

After determining what is good and available, the cook must then decide how to structure the meal. Over many years of planning vegetarian menus we have devoted a great deal of attention to developing a wide range of ideas for entrées—main dishes that can be confidently served in the central place normally occupied by a meat course. The tradition of having a focus, a point to which a meal leads and from which it tapers away, remains important to many of us. This book includes a selection of seasonal menus as well as many examples of recipes that have been enthusiastically received as main courses by our customers at the restaurant.

An entrée at Greens is not so much a meatlike food as it is one that commands attention by its form and appearance. Frequently, the more complicated dishes succeed best in providing focus and interest by their visual complexity, the diversity of their tastes, and their textures. A cake of layered crepes and fillings, a molded timbale with a sauce, or a rolled soufflé sliced to show its spiraled pattern are ideal as entrées. Even a shapeless dish, such as a stew or a casserole, can take on the character appropriate for a main dish when baked and served in small individual crocks, or ramekins. Vegetable gratins, especially when baked in handsome earthenware casseroles, make beautiful entrées with their golden crusts and layers of flavors and colors.

Those who don't mind breaking with tradition may want to try an entirely different way of arranging a meal. A series of foods can be offered one after another—some grilled vegetables, a small bowl of pasta with aromatic herbs, bread and butter, a sauté of peppers followed by thickly sliced tomatoes baked in cream, a salad, some fresh figs and sheep's milk ricotta, a little pastry, a fragrant tea or coffee—or the main parts of the meal can be brought to the table all at once, an assortment of platters and bowls in different shapes, colors, and styles, holding various foods that do not necessarily relate to one another in a traditional way.

A meal engages all the senses. Although we tend to consider the taste of the food to be primary, our enjoyment is made up of many parts: the aroma of cooking food that can fill a room, the colors of the various dishes, subtle or bright, and the different textures, soft and silky or chewy and dense. Even sounds can be enticing, such as the crackling of parchment-wrapped vegetables or the sizzling of a sauté. The food itself, its presentation, the sequence of courses—all these elements work together to capture the attention of those eating and to involve them in the pleasures of the table. The meal should do just that and no more, so that conversation and conviviality are not overwhelmed by food that requires homage. The perfect meal is one that draws people together with dishes that may be delicious, even gorgeous, but then lets them go so they can enjoy one another's company.

We know we are offering *The Greens Cookbook* to a busy world and have considered the need for meals that are both satisfying and simple to make. We also realize that there are those occasions when one wants to take the time to enjoy the process of giving form to a dish or a meal. Choosing and handling produce, smelling, tasting, using your hands to cut, chop, and toss, joining with family or friends to prepare a festive meal can be as nourishing to body and mind as the food itself. Through these recipes we want to pass on some of the delights and discoveries that have come out of our work. We hope that they will become departure points for your own explorations and your own style of cooking.

Deborah Madison

Preface to the Recipes

Cooking is a matter of trusting your own sensibilities. It is observing, tasting, touching, smelling, and experiencing the ingredients for yourself, and noticing what happens to them as they are cooked. When we give extensive directions in this book, our intention is to explain how the recipe works, not to dictate an exact, right way. You decide what you like, how to cook it, and how much time and energy you are willing to commit. Though you may refer to various clues and reference points in this book, you will sense for yourself, finally, when something is tender, when something is chewy. There is no secret outside of trusting your own sensibilities.

One thing this means is to work closely with the ingredients you have in front of you. It means to understand the equipment and the stove you have; to know, for example, whether your oven is "fast" or "slow." You are not cooking carrots in general, but specifically *these* carrots, in *this* pot, on *this* stove. Cooking times vary according to the ingredients—their freshness, their size, how they are cut—the kind of pot, the heat from the stove, and your own taste. So although the directions give a general guide, the cook must observe what is happening in this particular instance, right now, and then respond accordingly by, for example, letting something cook longer or taking it off the stove.

Similarly, seasoning is essentially a matter of personal taste, whether it is salt, pepper, chili pepper, vinegar, herbs, spices, or sugar. Be careful not to get caught up in comparing how something tastes with an imaginary, arbitrary standard. Instead, simply observe how each seasoning affects the flavor and choose the level of seasoning you like. When seasoning, be prudent and cautious, as heavy-handed seasoning cannot be undone. Especially if you are not familiar with the effects of a particular seasoning, be patient and add just a little at a time. Keep in mind that freshly ground peppers and spices will be stronger than those ground previously and that dried herbs lose their potency while sitting on the shelf over a period of months. The basic guideline for seasoning is to make it light enough that the overall flavors are heightened. Generally speaking, if you can taste the seasoning as a separate element, you have put in too much, whether it is salt in a soup, sugar or vinegar in a sauce, or nutmeg in a custard.

Most of the individual steps in cooking—washing, cutting, cooking, seasoning, and cleaning up—are simple and straightforward. Yet the thoroughness with which the activity is done can make a world of difference to a dish: grit left in the spinach or a stone hidden in the beans will ruin the most delicious meal. Even for the unfamiliar task of making pasta, there is no help for it but to plunge in and learn from the doing. Skill and confidence come through practice.

The fundamentals of the Greens cuisine are the same as those of fine cooking anywhere: selecting ingredients seasonally, seeking out and encouraging local sources of produce, building flavors with stocks, using fresh herbs and freshly ground dried herbs and spices, choosing good quality oils and other staples, adapting recipes and ideas to one's own circumstances, and harmonizing tastes, textures, and colors.

A cook's mind is supple and flexible enough to do justice to the beauty and particularity of fruits and vegetables and is always ready to warm to the task. There is a lot to think about and a lot to get done, but to be efficient does not mean to be hurried, and to be unhurried does not mean to sit in a lawn chair. Take the time to give each task its due—it comes out in the food: a generosity of spirit. Call it rejoicing, tenderness, graciousness, or simple attention to detail, the quality of caring is an ingredient everyone can taste.

Edward Espe Brown

SALADS

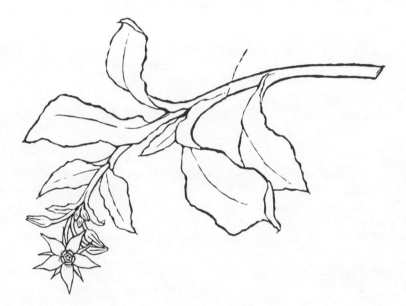

Notes on Lettuces, Vinegars, and Oils

Lettuces and other salad plants deserve an entire chapter to themselves, especially now that produce markets are carrying more varieties of lettuce, chicories, and herbs, which display delightful variations in taste, form, and color. Most varieties of greens and herbs are available in seed form, and they are easy to grow (a very helpful book, devoted specifically to growing salad plants, is *The Salad Garden* by Joy Larkcom). The considerable pleasure these plants give in growing, harvesting, and eating will unquestionably repay the efforts involved in tending a small garden plot.

Lettuces and chicories can fill a salad bowl with colors that range from bright chartreuse to deep bronze. In between are all shades of green, solid, striped, or streaked with washes of color from rose to dark red. The textures range from creamy, soft, and buttery to crisp and crinkled; the leaf shapes can be broad and upright, or low and so highly indented as to be lacelike. Flavor goes from sweet to bitter, hot, and peppery. Taken from your garden, plants can be harvested a leaf at a time or a plant at a time, in either case picked when they are most tender and succulent.

The leaves, branches, and flowers of herbs make pretty and aromatic additions to salads, particularly in the summer when they are at their best. Other kinds of cultivated greens to include in a salad are lamb's-quarters, rocket (arugula), lamb's-lettuce, purslane, field cress, and watercress, while some useful wild greens include dandelion, chickweed, and miner's lettuce, which can be counted on to give strong, vigorous character to salads.

The opportunity to choose from such a wide range of plants can make a green salad a wonderfully complex and colorful event. Its composition depends on your taste and what is available. Sometimes a wild array of greens, flowers, and herbs is suitable; at other times something more simple or austere may best complement a meal.

A large assortment of vinegars is available, and they differ widely in flavor, strength, and character. You might want to use a soft, mild vinegar, such as a Champagne vinegar or a white wine vinegar, with tender, delicate lettuces. Greens that have stronger leaf structure and taste can better support and are complemented by a strong vinegar, such as an aged red wine vinegar or a sherry vinegar, used with a heavier, fruitier olive oil. The chicories, which include the mildly bitter escarole, curly endive, and radicchio, take especially well to strong vinegars used alone or sweetened with balsamic vinegar, the flavorful nut oils, and other ingredients, such as mustard and cream.

You need not be limited to a single vinegar per salad. Vinegars can be combined, using one as a base and another for its particular sharpness, sweetness, or flavor. Lemon, orange, tangerine, grapefruit, and lime juices add an acidic quality that is sparkly, clean, and fresh, and they can also be combined with vinegars.

Oils can also be mixed together to good effect. Walnut and hazelnut oils can be blended with olive oil or used alone. (Nut oils should always be refrigerated because they are unstable and easily turn rancid.) Dark sesame oil is too strong to use alone, but a small amount added to a light sesame vegetable oil is enough to convey its toasty, warm flavor.

The correct proportion of oil to vinegar is commonly assumed to be three parts oil to one part vinegar, and this can be used as a loose guide to follow, given the range of tastes and strengths among oils and vinegars. In addition, there is your own palate to consider and what you find to be an acceptable level of acidity. This is why all the recipes for vinaigrettes suggest a final taste to check the balance of the dressing.

Green Salad

Our everyday green salad is served with a wide variety of foods, so we make it on the simple side with a modest number of seasonal greens, mostly lettuces. A few chicories or other greens, such as lamb's-lettuce, rocket (arugula), or wild greens, depending on the season, and a dressing of flavorful olive oil, a few fresh herbs, and vinegar complete the salad.

6 handfuls mixed greens
1 shallot, finely diced
1 ½ tablespoons red wine vinegar, sherry vinegar, or Champagne vinegar
¼ teaspoon salt
5 to 6 tablespoons virgin or extra virgin olive oil
Fresh herbs: parsley, chervil, marjoram, thyme leaves, basil or lovage, finely chopped
Pepper (optional)

Make a selection of greens from what is available, combining a variety of tastes, colors, and textures. If possible, use small, tender heads of lettuce. Wash them in a large bowl of water and dry them in a salad spinner. If they aren't to be used for a while, roll them loosely in a kitchen towel and refrigerate until needed.

Combine the shallot, vinegar, and salt in a bowl; then whisk in the olive oil. Taste and adjust for tartness, and add more vinegar or oil if needed. When ready to dress the salad, toss the leaves with the herbs; then pour the dressing over the greens and toss gently and thoroughly. Serve with freshly ground pepper if you wish.

MAKES FOUR SMALL SALADS

Butter Lettuce and Spinach with Citrus and Avocado

Light and dark greens, the mildly acid fruit, and the creamy avocado provide a lively dynamic in this simple salad. Aromatic Szechuan peppercorns, roasted, then ground with salt, have a flowery fragrance, but if you use them, omit the fruit vinegar and substitute sherry vinegar.

1 head butter, limestone, or Bibb lettuce
1 small bunch young spinach leaves
2 ruby grapefruit
2 avocados
4 teaspoons sherry vinegar
2 teaspoons raspberry or other fruit vinegar
1 shallot, finely diced
¼ teaspoon salt
6 to 7 tablespoons virgin olive oil or a mixture of virgin and light olive oil
1 teaspoon mint, finely chopped
2 teaspoons chives, finely sliced
Black pepper or Szechuan peppercorns

Separate the leaves of the lettuce and remove the spinach stems. Discard any leaves that are bruised or yellow, wash the greens—the spinach in two changes of water—and dry them in a spinner. If the spinach leaves are small, leave them whole. If they are large, layer several leaves together, roll them up, and slice them into wide or narrow ribbons. Place them loosely in a kitchen towel and refrigerate until needed.

Use a very sharp knife to peel the grapefruit. Slice a piece off the top and the bottom of each, then work down the sides, removing the white pith as well as the peel. Holding the grapefruit over a bowl to catch the juice, cut each section loose from its membrane and turn it into the bowl. (Later you can drink the juice.)

Peel the avocados, slice them in half, and remove the seeds. Lay the halves cut side down and slice them crosswise at an angle.

Combine the vinegars, shallot, and salt in a bowl. Whisk in the oil or mixture of oils. Taste, and adjust the balance of vinegar and oil if necessary. Stir in the mint and chives.

Pour the juice off the grapefruit sections, combine them with the avocado slices, and dress them carefully with some of the vinaigrette. Toss the greens with the rest of the vinaigrette and lay them on salad plates. Set the grapefruit and avocado slices in and among the leaves. Add a grinding of black pepper (or roasted Szechuan pepper) and serve.

MAKES FOUR TO SIX SMALL SALADS

Belgian Endive and Watercress with Roasted Walnuts

This is a little more unusual than the regular lettuce salad; yet endives and watercress are available almost anywhere. The endive is crisp, wet, and slightly bitter, and is very refreshing with the peppery watercress.

12 walnuts, cracked and shelled
1 teaspoon walnut oil
Salt
Pepper
2 bunches watercress with large, smooth leaves
Walnut-Shallot Vinaigrette (see below)
2 or 3 firm white Belgian endives

Preheat the oven to 350°F. Toss the walnuts in the oil with the salt and freshly ground black pepper and bake them for 5 to 7 minutes, or until they smell toasty. Set them aside to cool.

Break apart the branches of the watercress into smaller leafy stems and discard the thick trunks. Wash and dry it.

Prepare the vinaigrette.

Just before serving, quarter the endives, cut out the cores, and slice the wedges diagonally. Combine the two greens, toss them with the walnuts and the vinaigrette, and serve.

WALNUT-SHALLOT VINAIGRETTE
1 tablespoon sherry vinegar or strong red wine vinegar
¼ teaspoon salt
1 small shallot, finely diced
4 tablespoons virgin olive oil
1 teaspoon walnut oil, or more, to taste

Combine the vinegar, salt, and shallot in a bowl, and stir to dissolve the salt. Whisk in the oils. Taste, and adjust the ingredients if necessary.

Variations: Sliced blood oranges or ruby grapefruit tossed with the greens and the walnuts make a lovely winter salad to serve as a first course. Or, served with small pieces of a good blue cheese—Roquefort, Maytag Blue, or Gorgonzola—and slices of red Comice pear or a flavorful apple, this would make a nice finish to a meal.

SERVES FOUR TO SIX

Romaine and Summer Vegetable Salad and Lime Vinaigrette

The multiplicity of colors and shapes in this salad is best shown when it is served in a wide shallow bowl. It goes well with the Black Bean Chili, or can be served by itself as a light meal.

1 head romaine lettuce or several heads red and green garden romaines
1 small red onion, quartered and thinly sliced
2 small yellow pattypan squash or zucchini, sliced ¼ inch thick
16 yellow pear or cherry tomatoes, halved
1 small red bell pepper or a mixture of different-colored peppers (long, slender Gypsy peppers
*   are ideal), thinly sliced into rounds or strips*
1 jalapeño pepper, seeded and diced (optional)
4 large red radishes, thinly sliced
1 cup jicama, cut into ½-inch cubes
1 large avocado, peeled and sliced
2 lemon cucumbers, sliced into wedges
Lime Vinaigrette (see below)
½ cup dry jack cheese, grated
1 to 2 tablespoons chives, sliced into small rounds, for garnish
Long sprigs of cilantro, for garnish

Remove the large outer leaves of the romaine, and cut the crisp heart leaves into pieces about 1-inch square. Wash and dry them, wrap them lightly in a kitchen towel, and put them in the refrigerator until needed. Cover the onion slices with cold water and refrigerate.

Bring a quart of water to a boil and add a teaspoon of salt. Add the squash, boil 30 seconds, and then remove it to a bowl of cold water to stop the cooking. Set it aside on a kitchen towel to drain.

Cut and prepare all the vegetables. If lemon cucumbers aren't available, use another kind of cucumber and slice it into rounds.

Prepare the vinaigrette.

Just before serving, drain the onion slices and add them to the rest of the vegetables. Pour most of the vinaigrette onto the vegetables and gently mix it in with your hands. Dress the lettuce with the remaining vinaigrette. Lay the lettuce around the sides of the bowl and set the vegetables in the middle. Grate the cheese over the top, garnish with the chives and the cilantro, and serve.

LIME VINAIGRETTE

Grated peel and juice of two limes
1 tablespoon sherry vinegar
2 to 3 tablespoons cilantro, chopped
¼ teaspoon ground cumin seeds
¼ teaspoon ground cardamom
1 clove garlic, finely chopped
½ teaspoon salt
6 tablespoons olive oil

Combine the lime peel and juice, vinegar, and herbs and seasonings in a bowl, and then whisk in the olive oil. Taste, and adjust for salt and tartness.

SERVES FOUR TO SIX

Romaine Hearts with Buttered Croutons and Roquefort Vinaigrette

This salad is a response to too many complicated, exotic salads. It consists of quartered romaine hearts, two to a plate, covered with blue cheese dressing and a garnish of croutons, pepper, and chives. The dressing won't cover all the leaf surfaces as well as if the leaves were torn and tossed, but if you enjoy tackling a large piece of lettuce with a knife and fork, this is the way to do it.

2 heads romaine lettuce
Roquefort Vinaigrette (see below)
3 to 4 slices firm, good-quality white bread or Cottage Cheese-Dill Bread
2 tablespoons butter
Pepper
Chives, thinly sliced into rounds

Remove the large outer leaves of the lettuce until you get to the hearts, which should be well shaped, firm, and pale green. (Use the outer leaves in another salad or for soup stock.) Cut them lengthwise into quarters, rinse, and dry; then wrap them in a damp kitchen towel and refrigerate until needed.

Prepare the vinaigrette.

Preheat the oven to 400°F. Slice the crusts off the bread and cut it into small cubes. Melt the butter, pour it over the bread cubes, and toss well. Bake them in the oven until they are crisp and golden. Croutons can also be fried in the butter on top of the stove, stirring occasionally to keep them from burning.

Set two quarters of romaine heart on each plate, ladle the dressing over each, scatter the croutons on top, and finish with plenty of coarsely ground black pepper and the chives.

ROQUEFORT VINAIGRETTE
2 to 3 ounces Roquefort cheese
6 tablespoons olive oil
2 tablespoons crème fraîche or sour cream
4 teaspoons sherry vinegar
Salt

Combine the cheese, oil, and crème fraîche or sour cream in a blender jar and blend until fairly smooth. Scrape the mixture into a bowl and stir in the vinegar. Season to taste with salt, and adjust the vinegar if necessary.

SERVES FOUR

Wilted Spinach Salad

This salad has been on the menu since the restaurant opened and is still a favorite we make every day. The spinach is tossed with *very* hot olive oil, which cooks it slightly, sweetening and softening the leaves. As the feta cheese and the olives are both salty, no additional salt is needed.

1 small red onion, quartered and thinly sliced
3 to 4 slices baguette per person, for croutons
6 tablespoons olive oil
8 to 12 Kalamata olives
1-pound bunch spinach
1 clove garlic, finely chopped
1 tablespoon mint leaves, finely chopped
2 tablespoons sherry vinegar
6 ounces feta cheese

Preheat the oven to 400°F. Cover the onion slices with cold water and refrigerate until needed. Brush the bread with some of the olive oil and toast it in the oven until it is crisp and lightly browned, 6 to 8 minutes. Press the olives to split them open, take out the pits, and cut or tear the meats in two.

Remove the spinach stems (or not, as you prefer) and discard any bruised or yellow leaves. Cut the large leaves into halves or thirds; small leaves can be left whole. Wash the spinach, using two changes of water if the spinach is very sandy, and spin dry.

When you are ready to make the salad, drain the onions. Put the spinach in a large metal bowl and toss it with the onions, garlic, mint, olives, and vinegar. Break up the cheese and crumble it over the spinach. Heat the rest of the olive oil until it is very hot but just short of smoking. Immediately pour it over the salad, turning the leaves with a pair of metal tongs so that the hot oil coats and wilts as many leaves as possible. Taste, and season with more vinegar if needed. Serve the salad with the croutons tucked in and around the leaves.

This salad could be accompanied with a moderately dry riesling, or perhaps a zinfandel or Beaujolais.

Variations: Instead of using only spinach, combine it with curly endive, escarole, or thinly sliced red cabbage—all greens that respond well to being prepared in this way.

MAKES TWO LARGE, OR FOUR TO SIX SMALL SALADS

Wilted Endive and Potato Salad with Sieved Egg Garnish

Use just the inner leaves of curly endive and escarole, or mix them with spinach and radicchio. The sweetness of the shallots and the delicate, earthy flavor of the potatoes contrast well with these strong-tasting greens.

THE POTATOES

1 pound Rose Fir or other small, smooth-skinned red potatoes
4 large shallots, thinly sliced into rounds
3½ tablespoons virgin olive oil
1½ tablespoons sherry vinegar
Salt
Pepper

If the potatoes are firm and fresh, leave the skins on and slice them into ¼-inch-thick rounds. Cook them in a vegetable steamer until they are tender, 8 to 10 minutes; then put them in a bowl with the shallots and toss them, while hot, with the oil and the vinegar. Season with salt and freshly ground black pepper.

THE GREENS

6 handfuls (about 12 cups) loosely packed greens:
*   the pale inner leaves of curly endive and escarole, spinach, radicchio*
2 eggs
1½ tablespoons sherry vinegar
½ tablespoon balsamic vinegar
1 clove garlic, finely chopped
½ teaspoon salt
4 tablespoons virgin olive oil
Pepper

Wash the greens, giving special attention to the curly endive and escarole, which often hold quite a bit of fine silt at the base of the leaves, and tear them into pieces. Cut the spinach and radicchio leaves, if using, into strips ½ to 1 inch wide. Bring the eggs to a boil, then turn off the heat and let them sit in the water for 6½ minutes before draining. Separate the whites and the yolks, and chop the whites finely. Set the yolks aside to use as a final garnish.

Put the greens in a large bowl and toss them with the vinegars, garlic, and salt. Heat the olive oil in a skillet until it is very hot and nearly smoking. Bring the salad to the stove and pour the hot oil over the leaves while tossing them with a pair of tongs. As soon as all the oil has been added, pick up the leaves in clumps and swish them around in the hot skillet to wilt them further. Taste, add salt if necessary, and season with plenty of freshly ground black pepper.

To serve the salad, arrange the greens on plates, distribute the potatoes and shallots over them, and then the chopped egg whites. Rub the yolks through a sieve, letting them fall over the salad.

Variation: In place of shallots, use a small red onion, sliced very thinly into rounds or quarter rounds. The color is very pretty with the greens and the white and yellow of the eggs.

SERVES FOUR TO SIX

Warm Red Cabbage Salad

The cabbage is cooked just enough to soften it, then tossed with apples, goat cheese, and roasted walnuts. This is a very nice salad for fall when both walnuts and apples are newly harvested. For variation in flavor and color, mix the cabbage with other greens, such as spinach or curly endive.

15 to 20 walnuts, enough to make ³/₄ cup, shelled
2 teaspoons walnut oil
Salt
Pepper
1 small red cabbage (about 18 ounces)
1 crisp red apple
1 clove garlic, finely chopped
2 tablespoons balsamic vinegar
2¹/₂ tablespoons olive oil
1 red onion, quartered and thinly sliced
3 to 4 ounces goat cheese, broken into large pieces
1 tablespoon parsley, chopped
¹/₂ teaspoon marjoram, finely chopped

Preheat the oven to 350°F. Crack the walnuts, leave the meats in large pieces, and toss them with the walnut oil and some salt and freshly ground black pepper. Toast them in the oven for 5 to 7 minutes, or until they begin to smell nutty. Then remove them from the oven and let them cool.

Quarter the cabbage and remove the core. Cut the wedges into thin pieces, 2 to 3 inches long, and set them aside.

Cut the apple lengthwise into sixths, cut out the core, then slice the pieces thinly, crosswise.

Put the garlic, vinegar, and oil in a wide sauté pan over a medium-high flame. As soon as they are hot, add the onion and sauté for 30 seconds. Next add the cabbage and continue to cook, stirring it with a pair of tongs for approximately 2 minutes, or until just wilted. The leaves will begin to soften and the color will change from bright purple-red to pink. Season with salt, plenty of freshly ground black pepper, and more vinegar, if necessary, to sharpen the flavors. Add the goat cheese, apple slices, herbs, and walnuts. Toss briefly and carefully before serving.

For a white wine with this salad, consider a sauvignon blanc or a vin gris; for a red, a pinot noir.

This salad was inspired by Jeremiah Tower. His version uses plenty of pancetta; we use apples.

SERVES FOUR TO SIX

Warm Pasta Salad with Peppers, Tomatoes, and Purple Basil

Colorful and aromatic with masses of herbs, red and yellow vegetables, and the deep purple opal basil, this salad is highly perfumed and tastes delicious when served warm. Use a dry pasta with a good shape for catching the sauce, such as a shell, the twisted fusili, or the ruffled cockscombs.

6 ounces Sweet 100s or other cherry tomatoes, halved or quartered
6 ounces yellow pear tomatoes, halved
½ cup finely chopped herbs: marjoram, parsley, thyme, lemon thyme, green or opal basil
2 to 3 tablespoons small capers, rinsed
3 tablespoons shallots, finely diced
1½ cups red, yellow, and green peppers, thinly sliced
½ cup Niçoise or Gaeta olives, pits removed
6 tablespoons virgin olive oil
2 narrow strips of lemon peel, slivered into fine threads
Salt
Pepper
8 to 12 ounces dry pasta shapes
Lemon juice or red wine vinegar to taste
4 tablespoons Parmesan Reggiano, freshly grated
Small whole purple basil leaves, for garnish

Combine the tomatoes, herbs, capers, shallots, peppers, olives, olive oil, and lemon peel in a large bowl. Season with salt and some freshly ground black pepper, stir, and let stand while you cook the pasta.

Bring a large pot of water to a boil and add a tablespoon of salt. Add the pasta and give it a stir so the pieces don't clump together on the bottom of the pot. Cook until it is al dente; then drain it in a colander and shake off the extra water. Add the hot pasta to the vegetables and herbs, and gently fold everything together with a rubber spatula. Season with additional salt, if needed, and lemon juice or vinegar to taste. Just before serving, garnish with the cheese and basil leaves. Serve hot, warm, or at room temperature.

SERVES FOUR TO SIX

Escarole and White Bean Salad with Fennel and Gruyère Cheese

A seasonal salad for winter and early spring, this can make an entire meal for four. A perfect dessert would be cool juicy pears and some walnuts. All the preparations can be done while the beans are cooking.

½ cup small dry white beans
¼ teaspoon salt
Mustard Vinaigrette (see below)
1 tablespoon chives, sliced into narrow rounds
1 to 2 tablespoons Italian parsley, chopped
1 teaspoon fresh tarragon or 1 tablespoon chervil, finely chopped
1 small fennel bulb or several celery stalks, sliced into ¼-inch pieces
3 ounces Gruyère cheese, cut into narrow matchsticks
Pepper
6 handfuls (about 12 cups) escarole leaves or a mixture of escarole,
*   curly endive, romaine hearts, and radicchio*
2 tablespoons butter
2 slices rye bread or Country French Bread, cut into cubes for croutons

Sort through the beans and rinse them well. Cover them with boiling water and let them soak for 1 hour; then pour off the soaking liquid. Cover them generously with fresh water, bring them to a boil, add the salt, and lower the heat to a simmer. Cook until the beans are tender but still hold their shape, 45 minutes or longer, as needed. Drain, and save the liquid to use in a soup stock.

While the beans are cooking, prepare the vinaigrette. When the beans have cooled down so that they are warm but no longer hot, toss them with half the vinaigrette and the herbs, fennel, and cheese. Season to taste with salt, if needed, and freshly ground black pepper, and set aside.

Prepare the greens. Use the pale inner leaves of the escarole and endive, torn or cut into pieces; tear or slice the radicchio into smaller pieces. Wash the greens carefully, giving special attention to the bases of the escarole and endive leaves, which often hold a lot of silt. Spin them dry and if they are not to be used right away, wrap them in a kitchen towel and store them in the refrigerator.

Melt the butter in a skillet, add the bread cubes, and toss them well. Fry them over low heat until they are brown and crisp all over, shaking the pan every so often so they don't burn.

To assemble the salad, toss the greens with the remaining vinaigrette; then add the beans and the croutons and toss again. Arrange the salad in a shallow, flat bowl with the beans distributed evenly among the greens. If chives are in bloom, pick a head of blossoms, swish it in cold water, then separate the florets and scatter them over the salad for a garnish.

MUSTARD VINAIGRETTE
¼ teaspoon dried tarragon
¼ teaspoon fennel seeds
1½ tablespoons sherry vinegar
¼ teaspoon salt
1½ teaspoons Dijon mustard
2 tablespoons crème fraîche or sour cream
6 tablespoons virgin olive oil

Grind the tarragon and the fennel seeds with a pestle to bruise them and partially break them up. Put them in a bowl with the vinegar, salt, mustard, and crème fraîche or sour cream, and stir until the mixture is smooth. Whisk in the olive oil vigorously until the ingredients are completely amalgamated into a thick sauce. The dressing will be very strong.

SERVES FOUR TO SIX

Black Bean and Pepper Salad

The glossy squares of red and yellow peppers mixed with the black beans make this a pretty salad. It is good eaten by itself and combines well with other salads on composed salad plates.

1¼ cups dried black beans
1 bay leaf
½ teaspoon dried thyme
½ teaspoon dried oregano
½ onion, finely chopped
1 teaspoon salt
Vinaigrette with Cumin and Mint (see below)
½ cup each, red, yellow, and green peppers, seeded and diced into small squares
1 small red onion, cut into small squares
1 stalk celery, cut into small squares
Sprigs of cilantro, for garnish

Sort through the beans and remove any stones or chaff. Cover them with water and soak them overnight. The next day, drain the beans and cover them generously with fresh water; add the herbs and the finely chopped onion. Bring the beans to a boil and add the salt; then lower the heat and simmer until the beans are tender but still hold their shape (about 45 minutes to 1 hour). Drain the beans.

Prepare the vinaigrette and add it to the cooked beans while they are still warm, along with the peppers, red onion, and celery. Fold everything together. Taste, and correct the seasoning. Add more salt, if needed, and some minced chilies and cilantro if you like a spicier flavor. Serve warm or at room temperature, garnished with sprigs of cilantro.

VINAIGRETTE WITH CUMIN AND MINT
1 tablespoon lemon or orange juice
1 teaspoon lemon or orange peel, grated
1 tablespoon sherry vinegar
½ teaspoon salt
1 clove garlic, finely chopped
½ teaspoon cumin seeds
½ teaspoon coriander seeds
¼ teaspoon paprika
5 to 6 tablespoons olive oil
1 tablespoon mint leaves, chopped
1 tablespoon cilantro, chopped
1 jalapeño pepper, seeded and finely diced (optional)

Combine the juice, peel, vinegar, salt, and garlic in a bowl. Bruise the cumin and coriander seeds by smashing them in a mortar, or grind them in a spice grinder. Add them, with the paprika, to the combined ingredients, and then whisk in the oil. Taste, and balance the proportion of acid and oil; then add the fresh herbs and jalapeño pepper, if using.

Variations: In the summer we often make a tossed romaine salad with these black beans, sweet red onions, and avocados, adding the black beans at the very end so they remain visually distinct without coloring the other ingredients. The beans are also useful as part of a composed salad, served with fresh tomatoes, the Jicama-Orange Salad, pickled onions, fresh white cheese, and tortillas.

SERVES FOUR TO SIX

Lentil Salad with Mint, Roasted Peppers, and Feta Cheese

The tiny French lentils are best for this salad—they hold their shape and cook through without becoming mushy. Serve small portions as an appetizer or make this salad the main focus of a composed salad plate with a variety of garnishes, such as hard-cooked eggs, olives, tomatoes, and garden lettuces. This is a good picnic food—it is easy to carry and the flavors develop as it sits.

1½ cups small French lentils
1 medium carrot, peeled and diced into ⅛-inch squares
½ small onion, finely diced
1 bay leaf
1 clove garlic, finely chopped
½ teaspoon salt
2 medium red bell peppers
Lemon Vinaigrette (see below)
2 teaspoons mint, chopped
3 tablespoons chopped mixed herbs: parsley, marjoram or cilantro, thyme
Pepper
Sherry vinegar or red wine vinegar to taste
8 ounces feta cheese
Olive oil, for garnish

Rinse the lentils, cover them generously with water, and bring them to a boil with the carrot, onion, bay leaf, garlic, and salt. Simmer them until they are cooked, about 20 to 25 minutes. They should be tender, just a little firm, and still hold their shape. Drain the lentils and save the liquid for soup stock.

While the lentils are cooking, roast the peppers over a flame until they are evenly charred, and put them in a covered bowl to steam for 10 minutes or so; then scrape off the charred skins with a knife. Do not rinse them under water, or the flavorful juices will be lost. Slit them open, remove the veins and seeds, and cut them into squares.

Prepare the vinaigrette and fold it into the warm lentils. Add the mint, herbs, and most of the peppers. Taste, and season with freshly ground black pepper and additional salt, if needed. Taste again just before serving and add a little more vinegar to brighten the flavors. Crumble the feta cheese and gently stir it into the lentils. Garnish with the remaining peppers and drizzle some olive oil over the surface. A Rhône wine would nicely complement this salad. Either a zinfandel or a chardonnay would also be good.

LEMON VINAIGRETTE

Juice and peel of one large lemon
¼ teaspoon paprika
Pinch cayenne pepper
1 clove garlic, minced
¼ teaspoon salt
6 to 8 tablespoons virgin olive oil

Remove two wide strips of peel from the lemon with a vegetable peeler, and slice them into narrow slivers. Put 3 tablespoons of the lemon juice in a bowl with the lemon peel, paprika, cayenne, garlic, and salt. Whisk in 6 tablespoons of the olive oil and taste. Adjust for tartness, adding more lemon juice or oil, whichever is needed.

SERVES FOUR TO SIX

Chinese Noodle Salad with Roasted Eggplant

This salad is very popular at the restaurant. The use of fragrant sesame oil, toasted sesame seeds, and cilantro are a pleasant departure from our more usual habit of cooking with olive oil. Not only is this salad delicious, it is also easy to prepare, and the noodles and eggplant will keep well for several days in the refrigerator. It is an excellent salad to bring to parties. The Chinese ingredients are easy to find in large supermarkets as well as in oriental food stores.

THE NOODLES AND THE MARINADE

7 tablespoons dark sesame oil
7 tablespoons soy sauce
3 tablespoons balsamic vinegar
3 to 4 tablespoons sugar
2½ teaspoons salt
1 tablespoon red pepper oil
8 to 10 scallions, the white parts plus some of the firm greens, thinly sliced into rounds
3 tablespoons cilantro, chopped
One 14-ounce package fresh Chinese egg noodles, preferably the thinnest ones available

Begin by making the marinade. Combine all the ingredients (except the noodles) in a bowl, and stir them together until the sugar is dissolved. Next, bring a large pot of water to a boil for the noodles. While it is heating, gently pull apart the strands of noodles with your fingers, loosening and fluffing them as you do so. Add the noodles to the boiling water without any salt, and give them a quick stir with a fork or a pair of chopsticks. Cook briefly until they are done but not overly soft, a few minutes at most. Immediately pour them into a colander and rinse them in cold water to stop the cooking. Shake the colander vigorously to get rid of as much water as possible, and put the noodles into a bowl.

Stir the marinade again; then pour half of it over the noodles and toss them with your hands to distribute the marinade. Set the remaining marinade aside. If the noodles aren't to be used for a while, cover them with plastic and refrigerate them. The flavors, as well as the heat in the red pepper oil, will develop as the noodles sit.

THE EGGPLANT AND THE VEGETABLE GARNISHES

1 pound firm, shiny Japanese eggplants
1 tablespoon fresh ginger root (about 1½ ounces), peeled and minced
1 clove garlic, finely chopped
Reserved Marinade
1 cup snow peas, strings removed, and cut into narrow strips
½ pound mung bean sprouts
3 tablespoons sesame seeds
1 medium carrot, peeled, sliced thinly on the diagonal, and then cut into fine, thin strips
Cilantro leaves, for garnish

Preheat the oven to 400°F. Pierce the eggplants in several places and bake them until they are soft and their skins have shriveled, about 20 minutes, depending on their size. Turn them over after 10 minutes so they will bake evenly. When the eggplants are done, remove them to a cutting board and slice them in half lengthwise. When they are cool enough to handle, peel the skin away from the flesh. Don't worry about any small pieces of skin that are difficult to remove—the flecks of dark purple-brown are pretty. Shred the eggplants, gently tearing them into ¼-inch strips. Add the ginger and garlic to the reserved marinade, then the eggplant strips. Turn the pieces over several times to make sure all the surfaces are well coated, and set them aside.

Bring a quart of water to a boil with a teaspoon of salt. Blanch the snow peas until they are bright green; then remove them with a strainer and rinse them in cool water. Cut them into long, narrow strips and set them aside. Next, put the sprouts in the water and cook them for about 30 seconds. Pour them into a colander, rinse them with cold water, and lay them on a clean kitchen towel to dry.

Roast the sesame seeds in a pan until they are lightly colored and smell toasty.

If the noodles have been refrigerated, allow them to come to room temperature; then toss them with the eggplant strips and half the sesame seeds. Mound them on a platter, distribute the carrots, snow peas, and mung bean sprouts over the noodles, and garnish with the remaining sesame seeds and the leafy branches of cilantro. Present the salad like this, layered and laced with the colorful garnishes, either on a single large platter or on individual plates. Once served, guests can toss the noodles and vegetables together to thoroughly mingle the different colors, textures, and tastes.

This salad is a combination of recipes that were suggested to us by the China scholar and cook, Barbara Tropp, author of *The Modern Art of Chinese Cooking*. She thought they would be particularly well suited to our vegetarian menu, and they are.

Variations: Instead of sesame seeds, use roasted peanuts or cashew nuts. Black sesame seeds can also be mixed with the white. In spring, blanched asparagus tips can be used in place of the eggplants, and long red or white radishes, thinly sliced, then slivered, can be included among the garnishes.

SERVES FOUR TO SIX

Wild Rice and Hazelnut Salad

Earthy flavors and good, chewy texture characterize this salad. Serve it tucked in the curl of a lettuce leaf surrounded with rose-red radicchio, or simply by itself. This salad would contribute well to a Thanksgiving or holiday dinner.

¾ cup wild rice
½ teaspoon salt
½ cup hazelnuts
5 tablespoons currants
Juice of 1 large orange
Citrus Vinaigrette with Hazelnut Oil (see below)
1 small fennel bulb, cut into small squares
1 crisp apple

Rinse the wild rice, and soak it in water for ½ hour; then drain. Add 4 cups fresh water and the salt, and bring to a boil. Cook, covered, at a simmer until the grains are swollen and tender, but still chewy, about 30 to 35 minutes. Pour the cooked rice into a colander and let it drain briefly.

Preheat the oven to 350°F. While the rice is cooking, toast the hazelnuts in the oven 7 to 10 minutes, or until they smell toasty. Let them cool a few minutes; then rub them in a kitchen towel to remove most of the skins. Don't worry about any flecks of skin that won't come off. Roughly chop the hazelnuts, leaving the pieces fairly large.

Rinse the currants in warm water and squeeze them dry; then cover them with the orange juice and let them soak until needed.

Prepare the vinaigrette.

Add the soaked currants and the fennel to the warm rice, and toss with the dressing. Just before serving, cut the apple into small pieces, add it to the rice, along with the hazelnuts, and toss. Season with freshly ground black pepper, and additional salt if needed, and serve.

CITRUS VINAIGRETTE WITH HAZELNUT OIL

Grated peel of 1 orange
4 tablespoons fresh orange juice
4 teaspoons lemon juice
1 teaspoon balsamic vinegar
½ teaspoon salt
3 scallions, white parts only, minced
¼ teaspoon fennel seeds, crushed in a mortar or under a spoon
5 tablespoons olive oil
1 tablespoon hazelnut oil
1 tablespoon chives, sliced into narrow rounds
1 tablespoon chervil or fennel leaves, chopped
1 tablespoon parsley, finely chopped

Put the orange peel, orange juice, lemon juice, and vinegar in a bowl with the salt, scallions, and crushed fennel seeds. Whisk in the oils, then the herbs. Taste, and adjust any of the ingredients if necessary. The dressing should be fresh and sparkly.

SERVES FOUR TO SIX

Warm Spring Vegetable Salad

Similar to a ragout or vegetable stew, but lightly handled so that the flavors remain separate and clean, this salad is lovely to make when asparagus, peas, zucchini, and the first hothouse basil are in the market. In addition to the vegetables, young spinach greens might also be included. Blanch them last, dress them with oil, and place them around the edge of the plate.

Plan to use about 1 cup of vegetables per person. Keep the pieces large enough so that each vegetable is visually distinct, or cut everything small to make a mosaic of color, as you prefer. This kind of salad usually works best with no more than four or five vegetables, but the choices are many: asparagus, snow peas, English peas, carrots, tiny spring turnips, fava beans, zucchini, fennel, and baby corn; later in the year, use new potatoes, red and yellow peppers, and tomatoes. Choose for taste, color, and balance of texture. The following is a sample recipe.

1 or 2 strips of lemon peel, finely chopped
1 tablespoon Italian parsley, roughly chopped
2 tablespoons mixed herbs, chopped, or basil leaves, torn or cut into strips
½ bunch scallions, white parts only, finely sliced
3 to 4 tablespoons virgin olive oil
8 very small carrots or 2 medium carrots
8 to 12 ounces asparagus
4 ounces snow peas or sugar snap peas
2 small zucchini
1 pound fresh fava beans
Salt
Pepper
Juice of 1 lemon

Combine the lemon peel, parsley, mixed herbs, and scallions with the olive oil in a large bowl and set it aside.

Peel the carrots and slice them in half lengthwise if they are tiny. If they are large, cut them diagonally into long thin pieces, then into narrow matchsticks. Break off the tough lower ends of the asparagus and discard them. Leave the tips 2 to 3 inches long and slice the stalks diagonally into pieces about ¼ inch thick. Remove the strings from the peas and leave them whole. Cut the zucchini in half lengthwise and section them into 1½-inch lengths; then slice them into thin strips. Remove the fava beans from their pods and parboil them; then slip off their outer skins.

Bring 3 quarts of water to a boil and add 1 tablespoon salt. Add the carrots and asparagus and boil for 2 minutes. Scoop them out, shake off the water, and add them to the herbs and oil. Next, cook the peas and zucchini for 1½ minutes, scoop them out, shake off the water, and add them to the other vegetables along with the peeled fava beans. Use a rubber scraper to fold everything together. Add lemon juice to taste and season with salt and freshly ground black pepper. Serve the salad right away, while it is warm.

This can be served as a first course with the Olive Oil Bread or as a side dish with something soft and creamy, such as a timbale or a gratin.

SERVES FOUR TO SIX

Moroccan Carrot Salad

This unusual carrot salad is fresh and colorful. Serve it alone, garnished with some black oil-cured olives, or as part of a large salad plate. Except for the hour in the refrigerator, this salad is made very quickly.

1 pound carrots
2 tablespoons lemon juice
1 teaspoon olive oil
1 tablespoon sugar
⅛ teaspoon salt
Orange flower water

Peel the carrots and discard the peels. Continuing to use the peeler, scrape the carrots, working your way around them, removing strips of carrot about ⅜ inch wide. Set them aside in a bowl. Mix together the lemon juice, olive oil, sugar, salt, and orange flower water to taste. Pour this dressing over the carrots and toss them very lightly with your fingers. Cover and refrigerate 1 hour before serving.

This salad is based on one of Paula Wolfert's recipes from *Couscous and Other Good Foods from Morocco*. Other surprising and refreshing salads are in her book—herb beet salads and various orange salads, flavored with rose water and cinnamon.

MAKES 4 CUPS; SERVES FOUR TO SIX

Snow Peas and Beets with Szechuan Pepper

This is a colorful little salad with crisp and tender textures, which we often serve alongside baked dishes such as filo pastries, tarts, or frittatas. The fragrant Szechuan pepper, which can be found in Chinese markets, goes well with both the beets and the peas, and adds an unusual, pleasant taste.

8 ounces trimmed beets, red or golden, or both
6 ounces snow peas
Salt
1 tablespoon Szechuan peppercorns
6 black peppercorns
½ bunch scallions
2 teaspoons chives, sliced into narrow rounds
Chive blossoms (optional), for garnish
1 tablespoon rice wine vinegar or Champagne vinegar
3 tablespoons light olive or light sesame oil

Put the beets in a baking dish with ¼ inch of water; cover and bake until they are tender but still somewhat firm. Red and golden beets should be baked in separate dishes or the colors will bleed. This will take 25 to 45 minutes, depending on the size of the beets. Set them aside to cool.

Trim both ends of the peas and pull off the strings. Bring a pan of water to a boil, add 1 teaspoon salt, drop in the peas, and blanch for 1 minute. Drain them in a colander, and rinse them briefly in cool water; then lay them out on a clean kitchen towel to dry.

Roast both types of peppercorns together in a small heavy frying pan over low heat until they are fragrant and begin to smoke, about 4 to 5 minutes. Immediately remove the peppercorns from the pan so they don't scorch, and grind them to a powder with a mortar and pestle or a spice grinder or a food processor. Use as needed for seasoning the dish.

Slice the scallions, or if they are very thick, mince them. If you have chive blossoms, swish the heads in a bowl of water; then cut them at the base to separate the individual flowers.

Combine the vinegar and oil and season to taste with salt.

When the beets are cool, skin them, trim the ends, and slice them into wedges or rounds. If using both red and golden beets, remember to keep them separate, or the golden beets will soon be red. Toss them with part of the dressing, add half the scallions, and season to taste with the ground peppers. Dress the peas with the remaining vinaigrette just before serving so they don't lose their color, and season with the remaining scallions, half the chives, and ground peppers to taste. Serve the two vegetables in separate mounds and garnish with the remaining chives and chive blossoms.

MAKES FOUR TO SIX SMALL SALADS

Jicama-Orange Salad

More a relish than a salad, this combination is very refreshing and clean tasting with a wash of citrus and no oil. It is just the dish to serve before, or alongside, enchiladas or chilaquiles. The flavor of the jicama will benefit from sitting at least an hour before serving, and can sit even longer, tossed occasionally in the juices. Add the oranges and radishes just before serving.

8 to 12 ounces jicama
5 tablespoons orange juice
6 tablespoons grapefruit juice
3 tablespoons lemon juice
½ teaspoon grated grapefruit peel
¼ teaspoon salt
2 pinches cayenne pepper
1 tablespoon cilantro leaves, roughly chopped
1 or 2 oranges
4 large red radishes
Sprigs of cilantro, for garnish

Peel the jicama with a knife or a vegetable peeler, cut it in half, and slice each half into pieces ⅛ inch thick. Cut the slices into small cubes, and put them in a large shallow bowl.

Combine the juices, grapefruit peel, salt, cayenne, and cilantro in a bowl; then pour them over the jicama. Let it sit for an hour, and toss once or twice to distribute the juice. If it is to sit longer, cover the bowl and refrigerate.

Just before serving, peel the orange, and remove each section from the fine membrane that surrounds it. You may leave the sections whole or cut them into smaller pieces. Slice the radishes into paper-thin rounds, then into narrow strips—each piece will be tipped with red. Combine the radishes and the orange sections with the jicama and toss them together. Serve garnished with long fresh sprigs of cilantro.

Cutting the jicama and radishes into small pieces makes a relishlike salad. For a different effect, cut the jicama into larger ½-inch cubes or long strips, or slice the radishes and oranges into rounds.

The inspiration for this recipe came from Diana Kennedy's *Cuisines of Mexico*. We have included radishes and often use Champagne vinegar or rice wine vinegar instead of the citrus juices.

SERVES FOUR TO SIX

Marinated Eggplant

A delicious salad to serve as an appetizer, the flavors are even better when it is made ahead of time. Slices of eggplant are grilled, then layered with garlic and basil, and splashed with vinegar. If you are grilling outside, make this salad at the same time; then set it aside in the refrigerator. As an alternative to grilling, the eggplant can be fried or broiled. The long, narrow oriental eggplants are preferable—they needn't be salted first—and they are the perfect size.

About 2 pounds firm Japanese eggplants
Olive or vegetable oil
Salt
Pepper
About 2 to 3 tablespoons balsamic vinegar
3 plump garlic cloves, sliced
1 bunch (or 1 cup) basil leaves, torn into penny-size pieces

For grilling the eggplant: Wipe the eggplants; then slice them either lengthwise or diagonally into pieces about ½ inch thick. Discard those end pieces that are mostly skin. Brush each slice generously with oil and grill over a charcoal fire. To make a crisscrossing of grill marks, turn each slice once 45 degrees. Cook on both sides until the eggplant is nicely colored and tender.

Remove the eggplant slices and begin layering them in a non-corrosive dish while they are still warm. Season each layer with salt, freshly ground black pepper, and vinegar splashed from the bottle, and then scatter a few slices of garlic and several pieces of basil on top. Add the next layer of eggplant and continue until everything is used. Cover the dish and refrigerate for several hours, or preferably overnight, before serving.

For frying the eggplant: Heat 6 tablespoons of light olive or peanut oil in a 10-inch skillet. When it is hot enough to sizzle a drop of water, add a layer of eggplant and immediately turn each slice over so that both sides pick up the oil. Cook until both sides are golden brown; then briefly drain on paper towels before layering.

For broiling the eggplant: Preheat the broiler. Brush both sides of the eggplant slices generously with oil; then broil them under the flame, turning once, until both sides are browned and the flesh is tender. If you put the eggplant in a Pyrex dish, it will cook faster and the skins won't dry out.

SERVES FOUR TO SIX

Roasted Eggplant with Garlic Purée

Serve this simply prepared seasoned eggplant purée on a salad plate to spread on croutons or tuck inside fresh pita bread. The large globe eggplant is easier to handle in this recipe than the narrow oriental variety.

1 eggplant, weighing about 1½ pounds
2 large cloves garlic, thinly sliced
Grated peel and juice of 1 lemon
1 tablespoon virgin olive oil
1 teaspoon cilantro or parsley, chopped, or more, to taste
1 tablespoon thick unsweetened yogurt
Salt
Pepper
Cilantro or parsley leaves, for garnish

Preheat the oven to 350°F. With a sharp knife, make incisions all over the eggplant and insert a sliver of garlic into each one. Bake the eggplant until it is thoroughly soft and wrinkled all over, about 1 hour; then set it in a colander to drain for 30 minutes.

After the eggplant has drained, slice it open and scrape the meat and the garlic slivers out of the skin. Chop it finely with a knife or work it in a food processor to make a coarse purée. Stir in the lemon peel, olive oil, herbs, and yogurt. Season to taste with lemon juice, salt, and freshly ground black pepper. Mound it in a bowl, and garnish with some whole cilantro or parsley leaves.

MAKES 1 CUP

Cucumber-Feta Salad with Red Onions and Mint

This cool-looking and cool-tasting salad is lovely when made with the pale Armenian cucumbers with their fluted edges. Any variety of cucumber, however, or even a mixture of types, can be used. Once you slice the cucumbers, let them sit in the refrigerator for a half hour so they will be crunchy and cold when served.

2 pounds cucumbers, such as Armenian, English, Japanese
1 small onion: a red onion, or torpedo onion, or one of the very sweet varieties, such as the Walla
  Walla
Salt
White pepper
8 ounces feta cheese (preferably Bulgarian, which is less salty), thinly sliced or crumbled
3 tablespoons mixed herbs: mint, parsley, marjoram, and chives, finely chopped
2 teaspoons Champagne vinegar or rice wine vinegar
2 tablespoons virgin olive oil
Whole mint leaves, for garnish

Peel the cucumbers if the skins have been waxed or have a bitter taste. Otherwise, leave them on, or peel most of the skins away, leaving a few narrow strips, which will make the slices pretty. Peel Armenian cucumbers only if the skins are tough. Slice the cucumbers thinly (if they are very mature with large seeds, halve them lengthwise, scoop out the seeds, and thinly slice the halves). Put the slices in a bowl; cover and refrigerate for at least ½ hour.

Peel the onion, keeping it whole, and then slice it into rounds as thinly as possible. Cover with cold water and refrigerate, also for ½ hour.

Just before serving, remove the cucumbers and the onion from the refrigerator. Drain the onion and shake off the excess water. Layer the cucumber and onion slices informally on a platter or in a large shallow bowl. Season with a little salt and freshly ground white pepper, and scatter the cheese and herbs on top. Whisk together the vinegar and oil with a fork, and pour it over the salad. Garnish with the mint leaves and serve.

Variation: The addition of finely chopped green chilies will make this a salad with both cool and hot tastes.

SERVES FOUR TO SIX

Broccoli with Roasted Peppers, Capers, and Olives

When you long for a big plateful of colorful, brightly seasoned vegetables, here is the salad to make. The broccoli stems as well as the flowers are used; their crispness contrasts with the tender flowers and soft roasted peppers. Broccoli salad is good served with creamy-textured foods, such as tarts and timbales.

1 red and 1 yellow bell pepper
Light olive oil, for the peppers
1 clove garlic, finely chopped
4 tablespoons virgin olive oil
1 tablespoon small capers
12 Niçoise or Gaeta olives, pits removed
3 scallions, white parts with some green, finely sliced
1 tablespoon parsley, chopped
1 teaspoon marjoram, chopped
¼ teaspoon red pepper flakes
Balsamic vinegar to taste
Salt and pepper
1 bunch broccoli (about 1½ to 2 pounds)

Preheat the oven to 400°F. Halve the peppers lengthwise, remove the veins and seeds, and brush both sides with the light olive oil. Set them on a baking tray skin side up and bake them until the skins are wrinkled and lightly colored. When cool enough to handle, scrape off the skins. Slice the peppers into strips ¼ to ½ inch wide, and mix them with the garlic, virgin olive oil, capers, olives, scallions, parsley, marjoram, red pepper flakes, and the balsamic vinegar to taste. Season with salt.

Bring 3 quarts of water to a boil. While it is heating, divide the broccoli into florets of equal size. Trim the stalks by cutting off the tough, dried ends and removing the thick fibrous skins with a paring knife. Slice the stalks diagonally into pieces about ¼ inch wide. When the water is boiling, add a tablespoon of salt, and cook the broccoli in two or three separate batches for about 30 seconds. Scoop out each batch and set it in a colander or on a tea towel to drain.

Combine the broccoli with the rest of the ingredients and toss them together. Taste for salt, add more oil or vinegar, if needed, and a grinding of black pepper. If you don't plan to serve the salad right away, wait to add the final vinegar until just before serving to prevent the colors from fading.

Variations: Use lemon juice and finely slivered lemon peel instead of vinegar. Sun-dried tomatoes, thinly sliced into strips, may also be added to this salad.

SERVES FOUR TO SIX

Beets, Apples, and Cress with Walnuts and Curry Vinaigrette

With red and golden beets, green apples, and dark green cress, this is a colorful salad, perfect to make in the fall when the walnuts have just been harvested and the apples are fresh and crisp. Use watercress by itself, or mix it with peppery field cress.

Curry Vinaigrette (see below)
1 pound beets, mixed red and golden
6 scallions, white parts only, minced
Lemon juice or red wine vinegar to taste
½ cup currants
2 large bunches watercress or a mixture of water and field cress
2 firm apples, sweet or tart, as you prefer
1 celery heart, sliced into pieces ¼ inch wide
¾ cup walnut meats, freshly cracked if possible

Prepare the vinaigrette and set it aside.

Preheat the oven to 400°F. Leaving the tails and an inch of the stems on the beets, rinse them, put them in a baking pan with ¼ inch of water, cover, and bake them until they are tender when pierced with a knife, 25 to 40 minutes, depending on the size of the beets. Take care not to overcook them. When cool enough to handle, peel the beets, slice them in half, then into wedges, and toss them with 2 tablespoons of the vinaigrette and half the scallions. Add lemon juice or vinegar to taste to make the beets a little tart. Set them aside.

Cover the currants with hot water and let them stand to soften for 15 minutes. Then drain, gently squeeze them to remove extra water, and add them to the cooked beets.

Go through the watercress and break off the small branches from the thick main stems. Discard any yellow leaves. Wash and spin dry. If you are using field cress, wash and dry it also. Quarter the apples and slice them into thin pieces. Combine them with the celery, walnuts, and the rest of the scallions; toss with 2 tablespoons of the dressing. If you are using both kinds, combine the two cresses, dress them with the rest of the vinaigrette, and set them out on salad plates or a large platter. Arrange the beets on top of the greens with the celery, apples, and walnuts scattered over and around them.

CURRY VINAIGRETTE

1 clove garlic
½ teaspoon coarse sea salt
2 teaspoons curry powder
½ teaspoon fresh ginger (about ½ ounce), peeled and grated
1½ tablespoons lemon juice or red wine vinegar, or more to taste
6 tablespoons olive oil

Pound the garlic in a mortar with the sea salt until it forms a smooth paste. Add the curry powder (use a commercially prepared powder or make one using the recipe on page 328) and the ginger, and work them into the garlic. Stir in the lemon juice or vinegar, then whisk in the oil.

SERVES FOUR TO SIX

Fennel, Mushroom, and Parmesan Salad

A good first course for a fall or winter dinner, this salad is best if you use the most flavorful extra virgin olive oil and a good piece of young Parmesan Reggiano.

1 clove garlic
¼ teaspoon coarse sea salt
2 to 2½ tablespoons lemon juice
2 strips of lemon peel, minced
⅛ teaspoon fennel seeds, crushed under a spoon or in a mortar
4 to 5 tablespoons extra virgin olive oil
8 ounces large, firm mushrooms, wiped clean
Pepper
1 fennel bulb
1 tablespoon fennel greens, chopped
1 tablespoon Italian parsley, coarsely chopped
Salt
2 to 3 ounces Parmesan Reggiano, shaved into paper-thin slices

Pound the garlic and the salt in a mortar until completely smooth. Stir in the lemon juice, lemon peel, fennel seeds, and olive oil to make a tart, lemony vinaigrette.

Thinly slice the mushrooms, carefully dress them with a few tablespoons of the vinaigrette, and season them with plenty of freshly ground black pepper. Lay a damp kitchen towel or a piece of plastic wrap directly over them to keep them from browning, and set them aside for 1 hour to marinate.

Trim the fennel bulb and cut it into quarters. Remove most of the core; then slice it lengthwise, very thinly, leaving the pieces joined together. Dress it with most of the remaining vinaigrette and half the herbs, and season with salt and pepper. Add the rest of the herbs to the mushrooms.

Layer the mushrooms, cheese, and fennel on each plate and spoon the remaining vinaigrette over the top.

SERVES FOUR TO SIX

Fennel and Blood Orange Salad

Peppery dark green cress, crisp fennel, black olives, and crimson blood oranges give this salad a complexity of textures, colors, and tastes.

12 to 18 almonds
Orange Vinaigrette (see below)
1 fennel bulb, 8 to 10 ounces trimmed
1 teaspoon fennel greens or parsley, finely chopped
3 blood oranges or navel oranges
2 large bunches (or 4 or 5 handfuls) watercress
12 to 18 small brine-cured or oil-cured black olives

Preheat the oven to 350°F. To blanch the almonds, bring a few cups of water to a boil, drop the almonds in, turn off the heat, and let them sit for about 1 minute. Pour the water off; then pinch off the skins with your fingers. Slice the almonds in half lengthwise and put them in the oven to dry for 10 to 12 minutes.

Prepare the vinaigrette.

Slice the bottom off the fennel bulb and remove the tough outer leaves. Then quarter the bulb, cut out the core, and slice the bulb as thinly as possible. Toss with 2 tablespoons of the dressing and the fennel greens or parsley.

Using a very sharp knife, peel the oranges: Remove a slice from each end and stand the oranges upright on the cutting board. Remove the skin from each, including the white pith, with several downward sawing strokes, working your way around the orange. Cut the peeled oranges into thin rounds, and set them in a dish with 2 table-spoons of the vinaigrette.

Pick the small branches off the large center stems of the watercress, and discard any yellow leaves. Wash, dry, and set them aside.

To compose the salad, dress the greens with the remaining vinaigrette and layer them loosely with the oranges, fennel, almonds, and olives.

ORANGE VINAIGRETTE
Grated peel and juice of 1 orange
1 shallot, minced
1 tablespoon Champagne vinegar
1 teaspoon balsamic vinegar
½ teaspoon salt
6 tablespoons extra virgin olive oil

Grate enough orange peel to make 1 teaspoon. Combine it with 4 tablespoons orange juice, the shallot, vinegars, and salt. Whisk in the olive oil. Adjust the tartness with additional Champagne vinegar or balsamic vinegar if needed.

SERVES FOUR TO SIX

Winter Vegetables with Parsley Sauce

The direct, clean taste of fresh herbs and simply prepared vegetables can be enjoyed in winter as well as in summer, and is perhaps even more welcome in winter, when foods tend to be richer and want the contrast of something fresh. The green sauce, made with the most commonly available herb, parsley, could certainly include other fresh herbs, such as chervil or tarragon, chives, marjoram, or thyme.

Even in winter a generous selection of vegetables is available. Rather than give a specific recipe, here are some suggestions as to what can be used. Choose many vegetables or just a few, keeping in mind their colors as well as their flavors; allow about 1 cup of vegetables per person. Some whole leaves of Belgian endive or some radishes will make a crisp contrast to the softer cooked vegetables.

Artichokes, the hearts cooked in water with olive oil, lemon, and thyme
Small whole carrots, steamed
Red or golden beets, baked separately and quartered
Yellow Finnish, Rose Fir, or red potatoes, steamed or roasted
Cauliflower or broccoli, in florets, steamed or blanched
Leeks, the white parts, cut lengthwise and blanched
Slices of raw fennel or small fennel bulbs, quartered and blanched
Belgian endive, the leaves separated and served raw
Red radishes with their small green leaves
Baby turnips, blanched
Winter squash, peeled and cubed or sliced, fried or blanched

PARSLEY SAUCE
2 small cloves garlic
¼ teaspoon coarse sea salt
8 black peppercorns
¼ teaspoon fennel seeds
¼ teaspoon dried tarragon
¾ cup finely chopped parsley (preferably Italian parsley)
1 large shallot or 4 scallions, finely chopped
Grated peel of 1 lemon
¾ to 1 cup virgin olive oil
Champagne vinegar or red wine vinegar to taste
Salt

Pound the garlic in a mortar with the sea salt, peppercorns, fennel seeds, and tarragon to make a smooth paste. Add about 2 tablespoons of the parsley, and work it into the paste. Stir in the rest of the parsley with the shallot or scallions, the lemon peel, and the olive oil. Let this mixture stand covered while the flavors infuse for an hour or more. Just before serving, add the vinegar to taste, and season with salt if desired. Ladle the sauce onto serving plates and loosely arrange the vegetables on top.

Serve this salad at the beginning of a meal with a good bread, perhaps a warm loaf of Olive Oil Bread, and follow it with something simple, such as a creamy squash soup or an uncomplicated pasta dish.

MAKES 1 CUP SAUCE, ENOUGH FOR FOUR TO SIX SERVINGS

Winter Vegetables with Mixed Winter Greens

This winter salad brings together flavors that are earthy and sweet, tart and bitter. Because it has many elements and flavors, serve it with something rather simple, such as a puréed soup.

Mustard-Tarragon Vinaigrette (see below)
3 to 4 beets, red, golden, or both, about 8 ounces
Balsamic vinegar to taste
8 to 12 ounces Rose Fir or red potatoes, cut into ¼-inch rounds or ½-inch cubes
1½ tablespoons small capers
12 to 18 whole baby carrots or 3 regular carrots, peeled and cut diagonally
1 celery root
2 tablespoons lemon juice
Salt
Pepper
6 large handfuls (about 12 cups) mixed greens, such as spinach, curly endive,
    watercress or field cress, radicchio, romaine lettuce
4 to 6 hard-cooked eggs

Prepare the vinaigrette and set it aside.

Preheat the oven to 400°F. Leave the tails and an inch of the stems on the beets, rinse them well, and put them with ¼ inch of water into a covered pan. Red and golden beets should be baked in separate pans; otherwise the golden ones will be stained. Bake them until they are tender when pierced with a knife, about 30 to 45 minutes, depending on the size of the beets. Let them cool, slip off the skins, cut them into ½-inch wedges or strips, and toss them with 2 tablespoons of the dressing. Taste, and season with balsamic vinegar to taste.

Bring several quarts of water to a boil and add a tablespoon of salt. Add the potatoes and cook them until they are tender. Scoop them out with a strainer, shake off the excess water, and put them in a bowl with the capers and 2 tablespoons of the dressing.

Let the water return to a boil and cook the carrots until they are tender but still firm. Remove them with a strainer, shake them dry, and add them to the potatoes.

Peel the celery root, cut it into ¼-inch slices, then into cubes or strips. Put the cut pieces into a bowl of water with the lemon juice to keep them from turning brown. Once the celery root is all cut, pour the acidulated water off, and cook the celery root briefly in the boiling water, a half minute or so. Drain it into a colander and add it to the potatoes and carrots with another 4 tablespoons vinaigrette; gently toss everything together. Season to taste with salt and freshly ground black pepper.

Wash and dry the greens, toss them with the remaining dressing, and set them on serving plates or a large platter. Put the vegetables over the greens, adding the beets last so that they don't stain everything pink. Halve or quarter the eggs and set them on the salad with a twist of pepper on each one.

MUSTARD TARRAGON VINAIGRETTE

1 large clove garlic, roughly chopped
½ teaspoon salt, preferably coarse sea salt
½ teaspoon dried tarragon
Yolk of 1 small egg
2 teaspoons mustard, Dijon or coarse mustard
1 large shallot, finely diced
2 tablespoons red wine vinegar
2 tablespoons crème fraîche or sour cream
4 tablespoons virgin olive oil
¼ cup mixed fresh herbs: tarragon, parsley, chives, or chervil, chopped

Pound the garlic in a mortar with the salt and the dried tarragon until it forms a smooth paste. Then work in the egg yolk and mustard. Stir in the shallots and vinegar, then gradually add the cream and olive oil, stirring until the sauce is smooth. Add the herbs, and season with more vinegar or salt, if necessary.

SERVES FOUR TO SIX

Farm Salad

Ultimately, the greatest inspiration to anyone cooking is the material one has to work with, and in this way we have been very fortunate to have Green Gulch Farm. Located just across San Francisco Bay from the restaurant (it would be visible from the dining room except for a few hills), the farm has consistently provided us with carefully grown, unusual varieties of produce.

One dish we make that closely reflects the harvest of the hour is the Farm Salad. It begins taking shape around eight in the morning when the produce, still wet with coastal fog, arrives from the farm and is stacked at the back door of the kitchen: boxes of red and golden beets, their leaves still on; big cans filled with herbs and herb flowers; crates of deep red and pale green lettuces; small white cauliflower still wreathed with blue-green foliage; new potatoes smelling of earth; slender long leeks, the bloom still on the leaves; a basket of green and purple bush beans; a few cartons of eggs. Perhaps not a lot of any one thing, but in all, there is a beautiful collection of fragrant, young vegetables. After looking over what is there, we plan a plate of little salads so that each vegetable is presented to its best advantage with an enhancing herb or vinaigrette. One such plate might include beets in a walnut vinaigrette, cauliflower and potatoes in a mustardy sauce with rocket greens, little green beans with tarragon, and summer squash in a Champagne vinaigrette, all set on a bed of dressed red lettuces with quarters of hard-cooked eggs tucked in. Something completely fresh and undressed, such as a freshly pulled radish or carrot, or something pickled, such as onions or olives, might also be included, as well as colorful garnishes of blue borage blossoms.

The Farm Salad reflects what is close at hand, fresh, and exciting, whether it is from a nearby farm or farmer's market, a backyard garden in the city, or the supermarket. Because the ingredients are so variable, rather than giving a single recipe, we have included several very simple single-vegetable salad recipes that can be made individually and brought together on one plate in various combinations. Preparing a Farm Salad can be time consuming, since each vegetable is cooked separately and dressed with its own vinaigrette. Here are a few suggestions to help you organize your work.

☞ Begin with those things that take the most time, like baking beets and bringing a large pot of water to boil. Other things can be done while the beets are baking and the water is heating, like tipping the beans, making the vinaigrette, paring artichokes, and so forth.

☞ Mince all the shallots, garlic, and herbs that will be used in the different salads at one time and set them aside in separate bowls. They will be ready when you need them and you won't have to stop and chop shallots three or four different times.

☞ End with those things that are best done at the last minute: dressing beans, so they retain their bright color; quartering hard-cooked eggs, so the yolks stay moist; dressing lettuces, so they stay crisp; and salting tomatoes, to keep in their juices.

☞ Always handle red beets last and place them right where you want them on the plate—they will stain everything they touch.

ALLOW ¾ TO 1 CUP VEGETABLES PER SERVING

Beets with Walnut Vinaigrette

This is a choice but simple way to prepare beets in the autumn.

1 pound small beets, trimmed
1 tablespoon sherry vinegar
1 to 2 teaspoons balsamic vinegar
¼ teaspoon salt
1 tablespoon walnut oil
3 to 4 tablespoons olive oil
Italian parsley, chopped
Pepper

Preheat the oven to 400°F. Leave about an inch of the stems as well as the tails on the beets. Scrub them and put them in a baking dish with ¼ inch of water. Cover, and bake the beets until they are tender but still offer a little resistance when pierced with a knife, about 25 to 45 minutes. Let cool; then peel and quarter the beets.

While the beets are baking, prepare the vinaigrette. Combine the vinegars and salt, and add the oils. While the beets are still warm, dress them with the vinaigrette and the parsley. Taste, and if they need to be more tart, add a little more balsamic vinegar. Season with freshly ground black pepper.

SERVES FOUR

Bush Beans with Tarragon

All kinds of bush beans and pole beans are delicious picked when they are tender and small. Choose among *haricots verts,* Blue Lakes, Kentucky Wonders, or yellow wax beans, or make a salad with a mixture of beans. The blossoms of scarlet runner beans would make a brilliant garnish.

1 pound beans, about 3 inches long
3 to 4 tablespoons extra virgin olive oil
1 shallot, finely diced
Fresh tarragon to taste, finely chopped
Salt
Pepper
Champagne vinegar or tarragon vinegar to taste

Tip the stem ends of the beans. Bring 4 quarts of water to a boil and add 1½ tablespoons salt. Cook the beans in two batches until they are tender but still a little firm. Taste them as they are cooking to determine when they are done; then lift them out with a scoop and lay them on a kitchen towel to dry for a minute or so. Transfer them to a bowl and toss them with the olive oil, shallot, and tarragon. Season to taste with salt and freshly ground black pepper, and just before serving, add the vinegar, also to taste. Adding the vinegar just before serving will prevent the bright green color of the beans from fading.

MAKES FOUR SMALL SALADS

Late Summer Tomatoes with Fresh Herbs

Vine ripened in the sun, late summer tomatoes are incomparable, especially when they are from your backyard, a local farm, or a farmer's market. Basil is always right with tomatoes, but other herbs are delicious too—lovage, tarragon, Italian parsley, or hyssop leaves and blossoms. Use a good olive oil and freshly ground black pepper.

1½ pounds juicy vine-ripened tomatoes
4 to 5 tablespoons extra virgin olive oil
2 to 3 tablespoons fresh herbs, chopped
Salt
Pepper
Balsamic or wine vinegar to taste

Use a serrated knife—a steak knife or bread knife—and slice a plateful of tomatoes. Pour some olive oil over the tomatoes, a scattering of herbs, and salt and pepper. Add a little vinegar, or not, as you prefer.

If the tomatoes are going to sit very long before serving, wait to add the salt until the last minute, as the salt will draw the juice out of the tomatoes, diminishing their flavor and texture.

SERVES FOUR TO SIX

Summer Squash and Shallots with Champagne Vinaigrette

Summer squash picked when they are only two or three inches long, cooked whole, and dressed with a Champagne vinaigrette make a delicate element on a Farm Salad plate. This should be of special interest to those who have a plethora of summer squash in their gardens.

2 small shallots, thinly sliced into rings
2½ tablespoons Champagne vinegar
Salt
1 pound small summer squash, green or golden zucchini, pattypans, or crooknecks
4 to 5 tablespoons olive oil
Pepper
Parsley or chervil, finely chopped

Put the shallots, vinegar, and ¼ teaspoon salt together in a bowl, and let them sit at least 10 minutes while you prepare the squash.

Bring 3 quarts of water to a boil; add a tablespoon of salt and the squash. Cook them until they are tender but still a little firm when pierced with a knife. Pierce as few squash as possible while testing them for doneness so that they don't become waterlogged. When they are done, set them on a clean kitchen towel to drain. Whisk the olive oil into the shallot and vinegar mixture. Season to taste with salt and freshly ground black pepper, and stir in the parsley or chervil. Cut off the stems and slice the squash in two lengthwise, and pour the dressing over them while they are still warm.

MAKES FOUR SMALL SALADS

Composed Salad Plates

A collection of little salads, combined with other edibles, extends the idea of the Farm Salad, bringing together on one plate an interesting and harmonious grouping of tastes, textures, and colors. These plates can serve as a simple antipasto dish or a complete meal, depending on their complexity and scale.

Many different composed salads can be assembled with the recipes given here in addition to recipes you already know. As a general guideline, avoid having so much diversity that the plate ends up being a confusion of small tastes that are quickly lost. More satisfying, particularly when served as a meal, is a plate that includes one or two principal salads from which one eats seriously, with lively accents coming from a few other striking foods. For example, a composed salad might have the Black Bean and Pepper Salad and Guacamole as a focus, while pickled red onions, tiny, sweet tomatoes, and some salty, crisp tortilla chips provide accents of taste and color. A piece of cheese or a hard-cooked egg might be included for additional protein, and good bread or crackers always have a place.

After considering the composition and balance of flavors and textures, one of the special pleasures of making these plates is putting together elements of color. And each season brings its own particular hue. Winter colors are soft and muted, with accents of red from beets and radicchio; spring colors are fresh and delicate; the strong, vibrant colors of summer parallel such summer garden flowers as zinnias and marigolds. As always, the seasons themselves, as expressed in your garden or market, are the best source of inspiration. Nonetheless, here are a few combinations we have enjoyed assembling for composed salad plates.

GUACAMOLE SALAD PLATE
Guacamole (page 50)
Jicama-Orange Salad (page 29)
Potato and Lovage Frittata (page 267) or Summer Roulade with
Tomatoes, Cream Cheese, and Herbs (page 279)
Herb Cream Cheese (page 53)
Easy Onion Pickles (page 49)
Red lettuce salad
Fresh corn tortillas or wheat tortillas

MEDITERRANEAN SALAD PLATE
Lentil Salad with Mint, Roasted Peppers, and Feta Cheese (page 20)
Moroccan Carrot Salad (page 27)
Roasted Eggplant with Garlic Purée (page 31)
Oil-cured olives
Pita bread
Radishes or slices of blood oranges
Fresh figs and almonds

SUMMER SALAD PLATE

Cucumber-Feta Salad with Red Onions and Mint (page 32)

Hummous (page 52)

Whole Baked Eggplants (page 295)

Grilled Country French Bread (page 130) or Cottage Cheese-Dill Bread (page 127)

Herb Cream Cheese (page 53) (if using, omit feta cheese from cucumber salad)

ANOTHER SUMMER SALAD PLATE

Marinated Eggplant (page 30) or Charcoal-Grilled Leeks (page 305)

Summer Squash Frittata with Green Sauce (page 266)

Sliced tomatoes

Mixed black olives

Summer lettuce salad

Olive Oil Bread with Rosemary (page 147)

BLACK BEAN SALAD PLATE

Black Bean and Pepper Salad (page 18)

Sliced Avocados with Sweet Pepper Relish (page 319)

Easy Onion Pickles (page 49)

Quartered lemon cucumbers

Fresh radishes

Feta or other crumbly dry white cheese

Kumquats

Fresh tortillas or tortilla chips

FALL SALAD PLATE

Beets, Apples, and Cress with Walnuts and Curry Vinaigrette (page 34)

Hard-Cooked Eggs (page 50)

Walnuts roasted with walnut oil

Salad of curly endive and radicchio with Walnut Vinaigrette

Baguette croutons

Sour pickles (cornichons)

Easy Onion Pickles

Quick to make, these onion pickles turn completely pink as they sit. Serve them with sandwiches or as part of a salad plate. Their tart, fresh quality goes well with the Black Bean and Pepper Salad, and they can also be very effective and pretty when diced and added to other vegetable salads. They will keep a week or so covered and refrigerated.

3 small or 2 medium red onions, about 1 pound
1 quart boiling water
²/₃ cup rice wine vinegar
²/₃ cup cold water
10 black peppercorns
2 to 3 bay leaves

Peel the onions and slice them into very thin rounds (to make the pieces paper thin, use a well-sharpened knife and brace it against your knuckles as you slice).

Separate the rings and put them in a colander. When the water comes to a boil, pour it over the sliced onions. Rinse them under cold water; then put them in a bowl with the vinegar, water, peppercorns, and bay leaves. Cover and refrigerate at least 1 hour before using.

MAKES 2 CUPS

Guacamole

Many recipes for guacamole already exist, but there are so many uses for this delicious sauce that we include a recipe here. Wonderful with warm tortillas or fresh tortilla chips, guacamole is also good in pita bread or on a plate with other salads, some fresh vegetables, and cheese. However you choose to use it, serve the guacamole as freshly made as possible.

2 to 3 medium avocados
½ small red onion, finely diced
1 to 2 teaspoons cilantro, chopped
1 to 2 serrano chilies, seeded and finely chopped
1 tomato, seeded and chopped (optional)
Juice of 1 lime
Salt to taste

Peel the avocados, remove the seeds, and mash the flesh in a bowl or stone mortar until it makes a fairly smooth mass but still retains some texture. Stir in the onion, cilantro, chilies, tomatos, if using, and lime juice, and season to taste with salt.

MAKES 2 CUPS

Hard-Cooked Eggs

Regardless of the number of eggs being cooked, this method always works, and produces a beautifully cooked egg. The yolk will still be slightly moist, and when fresh farm eggs are used, they will be a bright yellow-orange color.

Use large eggs; put them in a pan and cover them with cold water. Bring the water to a boil; then immediately turn off the heat and cover the pan. Let the eggs sit for exactly 6 minutes; then pour off the hot water and cover the eggs with cold running water until they are cool, or put them in a bowl of cold water with plenty of ice. Peel the eggs, but wait to slice them until just before serving so the yolks will stay moist. If the eggs are part of a salad plate, spoon a little of the vinaigrette and grind some pepper over the yolks.

Grilled Peppers

There are many uses for these delicious grilled peppers. Whether grilled over a charcoal fire or indoors over a gas flame, the aroma of the charring skins is wonderfully smoky and autumnal—even a fog-bound San Franciscan can imagine piles of maple leaves burning in a backyard nearby. Use these peppers by themselves or as an ingredient in other salads; for example, dice them and add them to the Lentil Salad with Mint, Roasted Peppers, and Feta Cheese. They will keep, covered, in the refrigerator for several days, but, like most things, are best when used fresh.

3 to 4 red or yellow bell peppers, weighing about 1 pound in all
1 clove garlic, thinly sliced
1 shallot, finely diced (optional)
1 tablespoon extra virgin olive oil
Balsamic vinegar to taste
Salt
Pepper

Roast the peppers directly over a gas flame or grill them over a charcoal fire, turning them until the skin is charred all over. The charred peppers will be fairly soft. While roasting, the easiest way to pick them up and turn them is to use a pair of short tongs—you will avoid both burning yourself and poking holes in the peppers, which lets the delicious juices run out. When the peppers are thoroughly charred, put them in a bowl, cover them with a plate, and let them steam in their own heat for 20 minutes or so.

Take them out and scrape off the burned skin with the dull edge of a knife. Save any of the juices that come out or collect in the bottom of the bowl, and resist the temptation to clean the peppers by running them under water, or you will wash away much of the good flavor that comes from grilling. Cut the peppers open and scrape out the seeds; then cut them into strips of any width you want. Put the strips in a bowl, add the rest of the ingredients, and season to taste. Include fresh chopped herbs, olives, capers, and other such ingredients to build a little salad, or keep the peppers on the plain side. Serve at room temperature.

Oven-roasted peppers: A quicker method than grilling is to cut the peppers in half, remove the seeds, and brush both sides with oil. Preheat the oven to 475°F. Bake them cut side down until the skins are loose and puckered, about 15 minutes. They will not have a smoky flavor, but they will be succulent and soft.

MAKES 1 CUP

Hummous

A smooth and nourishing filling for the Pita Salad Sandwich, hummous can also be included as part of a composed salad plate. The flavors are earthy and bright with lemon and garlic.

1 cup dried chick peas (garbanzo beans), soaked overnight
Salt
6 tablespoons tahini or sesame butter
2 cloves garlic, roughly chopped
5 tablespoons lemon juice
3 tablespoons virgin olive oil
Cayenne pepper
½ cup cooking liquid from the beans or water, as needed

Pour off the soaking water from the chick peas, cover them generously with fresh water, and bring them to a boil. Lower the heat to a slow boil, add ¼ teaspoon salt, and cook until the beans are completely soft, about 1½ hours, or more. Or cook the chick peas in a pressure cooker at 15 pounds for 45 minutes.

Drain the cooked beans, reserving the liquid. Put them in a food processor or a blender with the tahini or sesame butter, garlic, lemon juice, olive oil, salt, and a pinch of cayenne pepper, and process or blend until smooth. When the beans are puréed in a blender, extra liquid may be necessary; use the cooking water from the beans, water, or additional olive oil. Taste and adjust the salt, pepper, lemon, and oil to your liking.

MAKES 3 CUPS

Herb Cream Cheese

Though not really a salad, this fragrant, herbaceous cheese can be included on a salad plate along with a good bread and various vegetable salads. It also makes a good filling for sandwiches. Try to use a natural cream cheese, which is lighter, more delicate, and less cloying than cream cheese that has gelatin added to it. Use a bouquet of herbs or a single herb, as you wish.

8 ounces cream cheese
4 to 6 tablespoons yogurt, milk, crème fraîche, or cream
1 small clove garlic
4 to 6 tablespoons herbs: parsley, chives, marjoram, tarragon or chervil, a little lovage or basil,
  finely chopped
Salt
Pepper

Soften the cream cheese and work in the yogurt (or milk, etc.) a little at a time until the mixture is soft and easy to spread. Pound the garlic in a mortar until it breaks into a smooth paste, or mince it finely. Fold the garlic and the herbs into the cream cheese and season with salt and freshly ground black pepper. If the cheese will not be used right away, cover and refrigerate until needed.

Variation: For a lighter, less caloric cheese, use ricotta in place of some or all of the cream cheese.

MAKES 1 CUP, ENOUGH FOR FOUR SANDWICHES

SOUPS *and*

STOCKS

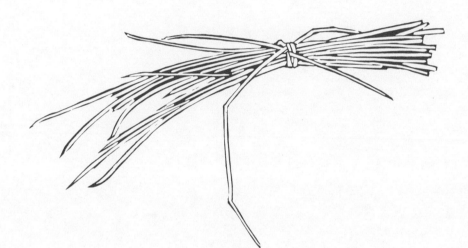

Soup Making

At Greens, we do not have a single, all-purpose stock to use interchangeably in soups, stews, pastas, and other dishes that require a liquid more flavorful than water. Though we make stocks on a regular basis, they are adapted to reflect the dishes in which they are used. Thus, careful attention and consideration must be paid to the distinct characteristics of the vegetables and herbs utilized in developing each stock.

Think of parsnips, rosemary, asparagus, cilantro, sorrel, mushrooms, potatoes, ginger. The range of tastes includes sweet, acid, pungent, grassy, and earthy, with high and low fragrances. Though these would not work especially well together to build one strong flavor, some elements might be combined to produce specific stocks complementary to particular dishes. For example, dried mushrooms, tomatoes, and rosemary could be ingredients in a stock for the Tomato and Wild Mushroom Soup served with croutons fried in rosemary-flavored oil. Parsnip parings, cilantro, and ginger might be the basis of a stock for the Parsnip Soup with Curry Spices. The tough ends of asparagus, simmered in water, would help accentuate the flavor of Asparagus Soup.

A stock is not always necessary. In recipes with many ingredients, such as the Lima Bean and Winter Vegetable Soup, or ones that are strong and spicy, such as the Spicy Red Pepper Soup, water is used and the soup makes its own stock as it cooks. However, a soup that has only one or two elements, such as the Leek and Chervil Soup, requires a carefully developed stock that is both complex and balanced so that depth is provided without a dominance of any one flavor. Several stocks come close to being all-purpose, good for their many uses as broth for simple soups and liquid in pastas and ragouts. We have given recipes for these on pages 64–67.

Making vegetable stock is not as time-consuming as is often believed. Only several minutes are needed to peel and dice a few vegetables, rinse some parsley, add a handful of lentils, and cover it all with water. While the stock cooks, you can prepare the soup vegetables, and the final straining takes but a moment. When stock making becomes habitual, extra onions, carrots, and celery will be kept on hand, and vegetable trimmings, like pumpkin seeds and parsnip cores, will be regarded as sources of flavor. Making stock becomes a timeless, simple event, as much a part of the cooking process as washing vegetables or wiping the counter.

The key element to preparing good stock is to know your ingredients and understand how they work. Each vegetable and herb is an unexpected source of flavor. By mining these sources, you will become adept at building a range of tastes and flavors.

Guidelines

Here are some basic guidelines that apply to the making of all stocks.

☞ Wash all your ingredients before using them.

☞ If you are not sure about how a particular ingredient works in a stock, cook it by itself, taste the water as it simmers, and notice how the flavor changes. Does it turn grassy after ten minutes? Bitter after thirty?

☞ Roughly cut all the vegetables into small pieces about ½ to 1 inch square. This increases the exposed surface area, and the flavors will come out more quickly and completely.

☞ Begin cooking the stock in cold water. Bring it to a boil; then simmer 30 to 45 minutes. Stop the cooking when the vegetables have no more flavor to give. If you want a more concentrated flavor, strain the stock; then reduce it by boiling it slowly, uncovered, until it has the desired strength.

☞ Strain the stock soon after it has finished cooking. Certain vegetables and herbs can turn a stock bitter if they sit and steep too long.

☞ Stewing the stock vegetables and herbs first in butter or oil before adding the water helps bring out and strengthen the flavors, but this step can be omitted if you wish to reduce the use of fat. Or the stock can be chilled and the hardened butter or oil removed from the top.

☞ Most important, don't put anything in a stock that is not clean and fresh. A stock can't taste any better than what goes in it, and tired, bruised, lifeless vegetables can give no more vitality than they possess.

Elements of Stocks—How They Work and What They Do

This list includes only those vegetables most frequently used in stock making and general cooking. It is by no means complete, particularly in regard to the new and unfamiliar varieties of vegetables that are being introduced in produce markets.

Vegetables

ONIONS AND LEEKS

Onions or leeks are basic to every stock. We use onions most frequently, sometimes in combination with leeks. Red, yellow, and white onions can be used more or less interchangeably, red onions and yellow onions both being slightly sweeter than white. Although onion skins can beautifully color water, their taste is unpleasant, and they shouldn't be used. If you want a stock with darker color and deeper flavor, caramelize the onions first: Cut them into ½-inch squares and cook them slowly in butter or oil until they are quite brown; then add the water and other ingredients.

Leeks have a slightly sweeter, more delicate flavor than onions. They are expensive, but the root ends and the leaves can be used for stocks. When using the leaves, discard the ragged outer ones and use the palest inner leaves, chopped into 1-inch pieces. One to 1½ cups are sufficient for 8 cups of water.

CARROTS AND CELERY

Along with onions and leeks, these two vegetables are nearly always included in stock. Carrots give an earthy, sweet flavor as well as a golden color, although too many carrots can overwhelm a stock with sweetness. Mature, medium-sized, and sometimes even large carrots generally have more flavor than tiny, immature carrots. Whatever the size, they should be peeled, then cut into small pieces. Do not use carrot tops in stocks.

Celery is not as sweet as carrots, but it gives the important quality of body to a stock. Use the stringy outer ribs in stock and use the tender hearts for salads and other dishes. Celery seeds can be used in place of, or in addition to, fresh celery.

POTATOES
The skins, in particular, give stock a good strong flavor, which is earthy, but unlike other root vegetables, not pronouncedly sweet. Avoid using skins that look old; they should be smooth and firm with a fresh appearance. The starchy flesh of the potato can break down and cloud the stock, so if a clear broth is called for, use the washed skins only. Thick parings with some flesh attached are ideal.

WINTER SQUASH—BANANA, PERFECTION, ACORN, BUTTERNUT, DELICATA
All of these squashes have a clear, sweet flavor that makes a nice addition to soups and stews that include squash, cabbage, and leeks. The seeds and the stringy matter attached to them, as well as the skins, contain a lot of flavor. The flesh, though flavorful, will fall apart and cloud the stock.

SUMMER SQUASH—ZUCCHINI, CROOKNECK, PATTYPAN
These squashes have a very particular, delicate flavor, and they can always be included in stocks featuring summer produce. The flesh is watery, so be generous with them. They needn't be peeled, but they should be sliced or diced before using.

CHARD, CHARD STEMS, KALE, AND BEET GREENS
These greens have an earthy, meaty quality, particulary chard and chard stems, and they won't turn grassy when cooked in a stock, as does spinach. Red chard and red beet greens will definitely produce a rose-colored stock.

TOMATOES
Tomatoes provide both flavor and tartness, or acidity, which is often preferred in summer stocks. Use ripe, flavorful tomatoes. Grilling them first and leaving the charred skins on lends a faintly smoky flavor to the stock.

MUSHROOMS
Mushrooms can be a valuable source of flavor in a stock, particulary if they are sautéed in butter or oil with garlic. Domestic cultivated mushrooms, especially those that are still tightly closed, will not deliver an enormous amount of flavor, but what they do provide is earthy and meaty. Mushrooms that are already open will generally have a more pronounced mushroom flavor. When using fresh wild mushrooms, use the stems, parings, and odd broken pieces in a stock, or simmer them alone to make a pure mushroom broth, which is wonderful for use in pastas as well as in soups using mushrooms. Dried mushrooms, shiitake, porcini or cèpes, various Chinese mushrooms, morels, etc., are very flavorful and unique in their tastes. They are expensive, but even a few added to a stock will contribute an earthy, woodsy flavor.

CELERIAC

This is a wonderful vegetable. Dirt and sand fill its rough, gnarled crevices, but the vegetable underneath this rough exterior is white, sweet, and aromatic. Scrub the roots well with a vegetable brush, remove the skins, and use them in a stock for flavor that is both earthy and sweet. The flesh can be used in the stock as well, but because celery root is expensive, it may be better to use it directly in a soup, salad, or stew. Remember that once the root is peeled it should be put in acidulated water to keep it from turning brown.

EGGPLANT

Surprisingly, eggplant contributes a soft, meaty flavor to a stock, particularly when it has first been stewed in oil along with some onions, garlic, and thyme. If the eggplant is young and firm, it is not necessary either to peel it or salt it before use.

LETTUCE

Although fragile and delicate, lettuce leaves have a surprisingly deep flavor and can be included in any stock. Make use of the outer leaves that are too large or tough for salads.

FENNEL BULB

This bulb has an anise flavor that will generally remain recognizable above the other elements in a stock. Hence, it is best used when the flavor is going to reappear, as in a fennel soup. The stalks and thick outer leaves, which are often scarred, can be used for the stock; use the pale inner bulb for cooking.

ASPARAGUS AND PEAS

The flavor of both these vegetables is quite pronounced and clearly identifiable. This makes them most suitable for stocks that will be used in dishes that include these ingredients.

TURNIPS, RUTABAGAS, AND CABBAGES

Cooked turnips, rutabagas, and cabbages are sweet and delicious, but they can carry overtones of flavor common to all the brassica, which are not necessarily pleasant when used in excess. These vegetables benefit from being stewed first in butter. Use them in moderation and do not overcook them.

GREEN BEANS

Green beans contribute an earthy and grounding flavor to summer vegetable stocks. Use the overgrown, tougher beans for stocks, and keep the tender small ones for eating.

PROBLEMATIC VEGETABLES

Of the vegetables commonly available, a few are problematic. Cauliflower and brussels sprouts tend to give off a strong unpleasant odor when cooked. Artichokes can be acrid and at best would complement only an artichoke soup. Beets and beet greens are flavorful, but turn everything red. Spinach can turn grassy when overcooked. Some parts of other vegetables can be bitter, such as carrot tops and onion skins.

Herbs and Aromatics

GARLIC

The sharp, pungent flavor of garlic softens and sweetens as it cooks. It contributes depth to any stock and can be used generously, peeled or unpeeled. Try to use firm ivory-colored cloves that are not bruised or pitted with brownish spots.

PARSLEY

This is a very important ingredient in vegetable stocks. It has a grounding effect for all the sweet, high tastes, as its flavor is dark and deep. Use parsley generously—entire stems with their leaves—or, if your supply is low, use just the long stems. Used whole or roughly chopped, 5 to 10 branches are not too much for 8 cups of water.

MARJORAM, OREGANO, AND BASIL

These delicious herbs give a light, bright quality to stock. They are best with summer stocks. Use fresh or dry herbs.

THYME

Like parsley, thyme is valuable for its ability to bring the high, sweet flavors down to earth, while contributing a distinctive flavor of its own. Use it fairly generously if it is fresh, but ½ teaspoon of dried thyme will be ample for 8 cups of water. The dried herb, in quantity, can become bitter as it steeps, which is one of the reasons for straining a stock as soon as it has finished cooking.

BAY LEAVES

Bay leaves have a strong, deep taste. Use 1 or 2 good-sized leaves in almost any stock for added depth of flavor. Warming them slowly in oil or steeping them 15 minutes or so in hot water will help bring out their flavor.

LOVAGE

This is not yet a common herb, but plants and seeds are becoming more available in nurseries and seed catalogs. It is a lovely plant with a flavor very similar to celery. Its leaves, which resemble a giant Italian parsley, are powerfully scented. Use only a small branch—3 to 4 leaves—at a time, and only where you want a pronounced celerylike flavor. Delicious with potatoes, lovage can be used, for example, in a stock for a potato soup. It is also good with carrots and celery. The tender young leaves are fresh and unusual in salads.

BORAGE

This herb is easy to grow and lovely to have in the garden for its beautiful blue flowers, which have become quite popular for use in salads and as garnishes. The leaves are generally too prickly to eat raw, but they lend a good, straightforward, earthy flavor to stocks. If you have a borage plant, you can make a habit of using the leaves in stock, much as you would use parsley.

Other Sources of Flavor in Stocks

LENTILS

Lentils are a good source for a deep, meaty flavor. A handful, or about ¼ cup, added to a stock will be plenty. Other dried beans and legumes do not work well in stocks because they absorb too much water before giving any flavor back. However, the broth formed from cooking beans will contribute both flavor and body to a soup.

STINGING NETTLES

These prickly greens are usually volunteers in the garden that make themselves known with their sharp, surprising sting when you are trying to weed. They are a wonderfully strong green herb with great nutritional value. Boiled in water, the stinging properties disappear, and the broth is rich, smooth, and an astounding shade of green. The taste is hearty and deep and does, in fact, give the impression it could sustain one through an otherwise foodless winter. Use nettles in moderation—1 or 2 handfuls for 8 cups of water. Nettle broth itself, with the addition of a few potatoes and cream, makes a robust and tasty soup. Soups made from the broth of boiled nettles have been known to support the lives of at least two saints—the Irish saint Columba and the Tibetan, Milarepa.

CORN COBS

Corn cobs, what remains after the kernels have been sliced off, are filled with a sweet milky liquid that has plenty of corn flavor. Boil the cobs in water, either by themselves or with other vegetables, for ½ hour or so.

MUNG BEAN SPROUTS

Like lentils, these sprouted legumes have a pleasant earthy flavor. Use 1 or 2 handfuls for 8 cups of water.

NUTRITIONAL YEAST

Nutritional yeast has a rich, almost fatty quality that adds fullness and roundness to stocks and soups. It works best if cooked first in butter or oil for a minute or so; when cooking onions for the stock, add nutritional yeast to the onions toward the end of their cooking. Nutritional yeast varies a great deal among brands and is not to everyone's liking. For these reasons, begin by using it in small amounts, a teaspoon or so in a soup for six, and work up from there. It is a valuable source of vitamins, particularly B vitamins, phosphorus, and iron, which are sometimes elusive in a vegetarian diet. It is most easily incorporated in soups that have strong flavors, where its flavor disappears into the background. Nutritional yeast, available in natural food stores, is not the same as brewer's yeast or baking yeast.

MISO, TAMARI, AND SOY SAUCE

These fermented soy products have distinct, strong flavors. Red miso, diluted in warm water and stirred into a stock, adds a deep, beefy quality, and a little tamari or regular soy sauce will help heighten flavors. White miso is too sweet to use in stocks unless you are making a white miso soup. All these products are salty, so if you plan to use them you might want to reduce the salt in your stock.

SALT

We have found that 1 teaspoon of salt in 8 cups of water is sufficient in these stocks. You might want to add less, or more, depending on how much salt you are accustomed to using and whether you are trying to cut back on consumption. If a stock will be reduced considerably, use less salt because the concentration will eventually be greater. As mentioned before, if you rely on substantial amounts of miso and tamari for flavoring, less salt will be required.

BUTTER AND OIL

Stocks do not have to be made with butter or oil, especially if reducing the use of fats is a concern. They can consist of vegetables and herbs boiled in water. However, first stewing the vegetables in a little butter or oil until they begin to wilt and give up their juices adds a certain amount of flavor. Butter or oils also make it possible to caramelize onions, which give a stock deeper flavor and a rich, dark color.

Summer Vegetable Stock

1 tablespoon butter
1 tablespoon olive oil
1 onion, chopped into ½-inch squares
8 branches parsley
2 bay leaves
Several large basil leaves or 1 teaspoon dried basil
Several branches marjoram or 1 teaspoon dried marjoram
Other fresh summer herbs, such as savory, lovage, borage leaves
1 teaspoon nutritional yeast (optional)
1 potato, diced
2 medium carrots, peeled and diced
2 celery stalks, diced
4 tomatoes, coarsely chopped
4 summer squash, sliced
1 handful green beans, roughly chopped
4 chard leaves and their stems, chopped
1 cup eggplant, diced
4 ounces mushrooms, chopped
1 teaspoon salt
8 cups cold water

Heat the butter and oil in a soup pot; add the onion, herbs, and nutritional yeast, if using. Cook briskly over a medium-high flame for several minutes to lightly color the onion, stirring as needed; then add the other vegetables. Cook them for 12 to 15 minutes; then add the water, bring to a boil, and simmer for 45 minutes. Strain the stock. If the stock is to be used in a pasta or ragout, reduce it further to strengthen the flavor.

MAKES 6 CUPS

Winter Vegetable Stock

No one flavor dominates in this complex, full-bodied stock, so it can be used unobtrusively in simple soups such as the Leek and Chervil Soup or Fennel and Celeriac Soup, or as a broth in stews and rice dishes. The proportions are roughly 7 cups vegetables to 8 cups water to yield 4 to 6 cups of stock, depending on how long it is cooked or reduced. Use different vegetables from those suggested if they would better complement the dish in which the stock will be used.

2 tablespoons butter or olive oil
1 onion, diced into ½-inch squares
1 cup leek greens, roughly chopped
2 medium carrots, peeled and diced
3 to 4 outer stalks of celery, plus some celery leaves, diced
1 cup winter squash, cubed, or squash seeds and skins
1 cup chard stems, cut into 1-inch lengths
1 medium potato or 1 cup thick potato parings
½ celery root, scrubbed and diced
¼ cup lentils, rinsed
6 branches thyme or ¼ teaspoon dried thyme
2 bay leaves
2 handfuls borage leaves, chard leaves, lettuce, or nettles
3 sage leaves
10 branches parsley, roughly chopped
4 cloves garlic, peeled
1 teaspoon salt
2 teaspoons nutritional yeast (optional)
8 cups cold water

Heat the butter or oil in a wide pot, add the vegetables, herbs, garlic, salt, nutritional yeast, if using, and ½ cup water, and stew over medium-low heat for 15 to 20 minutes. Pour in the 8 cups cold water and bring to a boil; then simmer, partially covered, for 30 to 40 minutes. Pour the stock through a sieve and press out as much of the liquid as possible. Use it as is, or reduce it further for a richer flavor. Taste, and season with more salt if needed.

MAKES 4 TO 6 CUPS

Wild Mushroom Stock

The full, dense flavor of dried wild mushrooms makes this stock a frequently used ingredient in our repertoire. We use it to enrich and strengthen mushroom soups and, in reduced form, to provide a rich broth for vegetable ragouts, mushroom pastas, and pilafs. It is also used as the base of several sauces in place of milk or cream, such as the Sorrel Sauce and Wild Mushroom Sauce.

We usually use cèpes or porcini (*Boletus eduli*), but other varieties of mushrooms could be used with different results in the final flavor, for instance, shiitake or morels. Porcini have a woodsy, wild taste. Those imported from South America are less expensive than those from France or Italy. Although their poor texture makes them unsuitable for eating, they have plenty of flavor.

1 ounce dried porcini mushrooms
1½ tablespoons olive oil
4 ounces fresh mushrooms, sliced or chopped (optional)
2 medium carrots, peeled and diced
2 celery stalks, diced
1 medium onion, chopped into ½-inch squares
½ cup leek greens, roughly chopped into 1-inch pieces (optional)
4 to 6 thyme branches or ¼ teaspoon dried thyme
2 bay leaves
6 branches parsley, roughly chopped
3 sage leaves or large pinch dried sage
2 cloves garlic, chopped
1 teaspoon salt
9 cups cold water

Cover the dried mushrooms with 1 cup hot water and set them aside. Heat the olive oil in a soup pot, add the vegetables, herbs, garlic, salt, and cook over medium-high heat, stirring frequently, for about 5 minutes. Next add the dried mushrooms and their soaking liquid plus the 9 cups cold water, and bring to a boil; then simmer for 45 minutes. Strain the stock through a fine-meshed sieve. Use it as is or return it to the stove and reduce it further to intensify the flavor as much as desired. Generally it takes about 15 minutes at a slow boil to reduce the volume of liquid by 1 cup.

Variation: For a darker-colored stock, caramelize the onion separately first. Heat the oil, add the onion, and cook it until it has turned a very dark brown, stirring occasionally at first, then more frequently as it gets darker. Add the remaining ingredients plus the water, bring to a boil, cook as above, and strain.

MAKES 6 TO 8 CUPS

Stock for Curried Soups and Dishes

2 to 3 tablespoons clarified butter (page 325)
2 carrots, peeled and diced
3 zucchini or yellow squash, diced
1 celery stalk with leaves, diced
1 large red onion, sliced
1 small potato, chopped
5 parsley branches
3 garlic cloves, peeled and roughly chopped
3-inch piece cinnamon stick
6 cloves
2 teaspoons coriander seeds
1 teaspoon cumin seeds
¼ teaspoon cardamom seeds
1½ teaspoons salt
8 cups cold water

Heat the clarified butter in a soup pot and add the vegetables, herbs, spices, and salt, giving the vegetables a stir to coat them well with the butter. Cook over medium heat, stirring frequently, until the onion begins to color, about 10 minutes; then add the water. Bring to a boil, lower the heat, and simmer about 30 minutes. Strain the stock, and use it in soups seasoned with Indian spices. If you wish to use it in a vegetable stew, return the strained stock to the stove and reduce it, simmering it for another half hour or so to strengthen the flavor.

MAKES 6 CUPS

Early Spring Vegetable Soup

This healthful-tasting soup is like a satisfying tonic. No vegetable seems to taste as fresh as peas do, and their flavor shines through the tastes of the other vegetables in this soup. Snow peas are the first to appear in early spring, but if they're not available, use frozen English peas.

THE STOCK
Use water or boil 8 cups water with some of the leek greens, chard stems, and parsley. This would be a good occasion to use nettles if you have them.

THE SOUP
3 tablespoons butter or olive oil
4 to 5 small leeks, white parts only (about 8 ounces), sliced
1 medium potato, scrubbed and sliced
3 to 4 celery stalks (about 1 cup), diced
Salt
¼ pound snow peas, strings removed, roughly chopped, or ½ cup frozen peas
8 branches parsley or chervil
3 lovage leaves or 1 handful sorrel leaves, roughly chopped
1 small bunch spinach or chard (about 12 ounces), stems removed, roughly chopped
6 cups water or light stock
Nutmeg
Lemon juice or Champagne vinegar to taste
Cream or crème fraîche (optional)
Pepper (optional)

Warm the butter or oil in a soup pot, add the leeks, potato, and celery, 1 teaspoon salt, and 1 cup water. Cover the pot, and stew the vegetables over medium-low heat for 15 minutes. Stir once or twice to make sure the vegetables aren't sticking to the bottom of the pot; if they are, add more water. Next add the peas, herbs, and greens, cover, and continue to cook until the greens have wilted, about 5 minutes. Add the 6 cups water or stock and bring to a boil; then simmer for 10 minutes.

Let the soup cool briefly; then transfer it to a blender and purée. If all the strings have not been removed from the peas, the soup may be fibrous. Check to see if it is smooth, and if not, pass the soup through a food mill or chinoise.

Season the soup to taste with a few scrapings of nutmeg, and lemon juice or vinegar. Add salt if needed. Thin it with cream, if desired, or serve it with crème fraîche and freshly ground black pepper. Gently reheat the soup before serving. Little croutons fried in butter or a garnish of chive blossoms make a nice finish to this soup.

SERVES FOUR TO SIX

Asparagus Soup

Asparagus soup is always welcome in spring. The tips are left whole for a garnish, the middle parts of the stalks are puréed, and the tougher ends go into the stock.

THE STOCK

1 pound thin asparagus, lower ends only
1 cup leek greens, roughly chopped
1 bay leaf
1 carrot, peeled and chopped
1 celery stalk, chopped
4 parsley branches
½ teaspoon salt
8 cups cold water

Snap the lower ends off the asparagus where they break easily when bent. Rinse the ends well and roughly chop them into 1-inch pieces. Combine all the ingredients in a stock pot, bring to a boil, simmer 20 to 25 minutes, and then strain.

THE SOUP

1 pound thin asparagus (about 12 ounces after the ends are removed)
3 tablespoons butter
2 to 3 leeks, white parts only (about 8 ounces), sliced
½ teaspoon salt
1 tablespoon parsley, chopped
5 to 7 cups stock
¼ to ½ cup light or heavy cream (optional)
Pepper
½ to 1 teaspoon grated lemon peel
Parmesan, grated, for garnish

Cut off the tips of the asparagus and set them aside. Roughly chop the stems into 1-inch pieces. Melt the butter in a soup pot, add the leeks, and cook them over medium-high heat for 2 or 3 minutes, stirring as needed. Add the asparagus stems, salt, and parsley. Pour in 5 cups of the stock and bring to a boil; then cook at a simmer until the asparagus are just tender, about 6 minutes. Blend the soup well; then work it through the fine screen of a food mill or through a chinoise to remove any fibers. Return it to the stove, stir in the cream, if using, and thin it with more stock, if necessary. Season to taste with salt, freshly ground black pepper, and the lemon peel.

In another pot bring a few cups of water to a boil with a little salt. Cook the asparagus tips 1½ to 2 minutes until they are done; then pour them into a colander.

Garnish the soup with Parmesan and a few asparagus tips in each bowl.

SERVES FOUR TO SIX

Fresh Pea Soup with Mint Cream

Filled with the sweet flavor of fresh peas, this soup makes a light, delicate first course. Small tender peas are most delicious, and their pods are used to flavor the stock.

THE STOCK
2 to 3 cups pea pods, roughly chopped, taken from 3 pounds peas
10 lettuce leaves
1 carrot, peeled and chopped
1 celery stalk, chopped
1 bunch green onions, including the firm greens, chopped
1 bay leaf
1½ teaspoons salt
7 cups cold water

Shell the peas and use 2 to 3 cups roughly chopped pods for the stock, setting aside the peas for the soup. Combine all the ingredients together in a stock pot, and bring to a boil. Lower the heat and simmer 25 to 30 minutes; then strain.

THE SOUP
3 tablespoons butter
Stock
4 shallots, thinly sliced
3 pounds peas (from The Stock)
½ teaspoon salt
White pepper
⅓ cup heavy cream
2 to 3 teaspoons mint leaves, finely chopped

Melt the butter in a soup pot with ½ cup stock. Add the shallots and gently stew them for 5 to 7 minutes, until soft. Set aside a handful or two of peas, and add the rest, the salt, and enough stock to cover. Bring to a boil; then simmer until the peas are tender but still retain their bright color. Add the rest of the stock, and blend until the soup is smooth. Return it to the pot and season to taste with salt, if needed, and freshly ground white pepper.

Bring a small pot of water to a boil, add salt, and cook the remaining peas until tender. Pour them into a colander and rinse them in cool water to stop the cooking.

Whip the cream until it forms soft peaks. Add a pinch of salt and stir in the chopped mint. Serve the soup with a few whole peas and a spoonful of the cream in each bowl. The cream will melt, leaving behind the fragrant flecks of mint.

SERVES FOUR TO SIX

Spinach Soup with Indian Spices

The pairing of Indian spices with spinach may seem unusual, but it works very well, making a fragrant, delicate soup. The flavor is developed, in part, by making a vegetable stock seasoned with clove and cumin. Serve the soup with little croutons made with white bread and fried in clarified butter until crisp and golden.

THE STOCK
Prepare the Stock for Curried Soups and Dishes (page 67).

THE SOUP
6 tablespoons clarified butter (page 325)
1 large red onion, sliced
1 clove garlic, chopped
3 tablespoons white rice
½ teaspoon salt
4 cloves
1 teaspoon cumin seeds
¼ teaspoon freshly grated nutmeg
7 cups stock
1 bunch spinach weighing at least 1 pound (about 4 cups leaves)
½ cup light cream
Grated peel and juice of 1 lemon
Pepper
1 cup small bread cubes, for croutons

Warm 3 tablespoons of the clarified butter in a soup pot and add the onion, garlic, rice, and salt. Grind the cloves and the cumin seeds to a powder in an electric spice mill or with a mortar and pestle, and add them with the nutmeg to the onion, garlic, and rice. Cook everything together over medium-low heat, stirring occasionally, for about 5 minutes. Add 1½ cups stock and simmer for 10 minutes.

Slice the stems off the spinach, remove the bruised and wilted leaves, and wash the rest in two changes of water. Add the spinach leaves to the pot, cover, let them wilt down, and add another 5½ cups stock. Bring to a boil and simmer 5 minutes. Cool the soup briefly; then purée it in a blender. Return it to the pot and stir in the cream and grated lemon peel. Season to taste with the lemon juice, freshly ground black pepper, and more salt, if needed. If necessary, thin the soup with stock or water.

Heat the remaining clarified butter, add the squares of bread, and fry them until they are crisp and golden. Serve the soup with the croutons and additional pepper.

SERVES FOUR TO SIX

Lentil-Spinach Soup

Dried beans are frequently cooked in soups with fresh greens. Both ingredients are always available, making this an easy to prepare soup that can be served any time of year. Consider using chard or sorrel in place of the spinach.

THE STOCK
Use water plus any juice reserved from the tomatoes called for in The Soup ingredients.

THE SOUP
1 cup green or brown lentils, cleaned and rinsed
1 bay leaf
1 celery stalk, diced into ¼-inch squares
7 cups water
Salt
3 tablespoons olive oil
1 large red onion, finely diced
2 cloves garlic, minced
3 tablespoons parsley, chopped
3 medium tomatoes, fresh or canned, peeled, seeded, and chopped; juice reserved
1 bunch spinach (about 1 pound), stems removed and leaves washed
Red wine vinegar or sherry vinegar to taste
Pepper
Asiago or Parmesan cheese, grated, or crème fraîche

Put the lentils, bay leaf, and celery in a soup pot with the water, the reserved juice from the tomatoes, and ½ teaspoon salt. Bring to a boil and scoop off any foam that forms on the surface; then lower the heat to a slow boil. While the lentils are cooking, heat the oil in a skillet and add the onion and ½ teaspoon salt; cook briskly for a few minutes, lower the heat, and stir in the garlic and parsley. Continue cooking until the onion is soft. Add the tomatoes and cook for 5 minutes; then combine with the cooking lentils.

Cut the spinach leaves into ½-inch strips; there should be about 4 cups. When the lentils are soft, stir in the spinach by handfuls. Once it has cooked down, thin the soup, if necessary, by adding more water, and taste for salt.

Simmer the soup 5 minutes; then add vinegar to taste, to brighten the flavors. Serve with freshly ground black pepper and Asiago or Parmesan cheese, or a spoonful of crème fraîche.

This soup would be nicely complimented by a chardonnay.

SERVES FOUR TO SIX

Potato-Sorrel Soup

This soup is easy to prepare and comforting, the way things made with potatoes often are. The potatoes fall apart into a coarse purée as they cook, and the sorrel brightens the flavor just enough. This soup goes well with many of the vegetable salads as well as with the Winter Squash Gratin or an egg dish, such as the Escarole Frittata.

THE STOCK
Water is fine for this soup.

THE SOUP
5 tablespoons butter
7 cups water
3 leeks, white parts only (about 8 ounces), cut into ¼-inch rounds or strips
4 to 6 ounces sorrel leaves (about 8 cups), stems removed and roughly sliced or chopped
½ teaspoon salt
1½ pounds red potatoes, quartered lengthwise and thinly sliced
Pepper
Sour cream or crème fraîche (optional)
1 tablespoon chives, thinly sliced, for garnish

Melt the butter in a soup pot with ½ cup of the water. Add the leeks, sorrel, and salt, and stew, covered, for 5 minutes over medium-low heat. Add the potatoes and cook another 10 minutes, stirring occasionally. Pour in the rest of the water and gradually bring it to a boil. Lower the heat and simmer until the potatoes are tender, about 30 minutes.

Taste the soup and add more salt if necessary. Serve the soup with a grinding of black pepper, a spoonful of sour cream or crème fraîche, if desired, and the chives.

SERVES FOUR TO SIX

Yellow Summer Squash Soup with Curry Spices

Yellow crookneck squash go particularly well with these spices, but golden zucchini, Sunburst pattypans, or any summer squash can also be used with good effect. If you are picking squash from your garden and have squash blossoms, use one or two, finely chopped, along with the cilantro, as a garnish.

THE STOCK
Use water or make the Stock for Curried Soups and Dishes (page 67).

THE SOUP
3 tablespoons clarified butter (page 325)
1 large yellow onion, sliced
1½ pounds yellow summer squash, sliced
1 teaspoon cumin seeds
1 teaspoon coriander seeds
1 teaspoon yellow mustard seeds
4 cloves
¼ teaspoon cardamom seeds
½ teaspoon ground cinnamon or 1-inch piece cinnamon stick
½ teaspoon turmeric
¼ teaspoon cayenne pepper, or more, to taste
1½ teaspoons fresh ginger root, peeled and minced
½ teaspoon salt
6 cups water or stock
½ cup light or heavy cream
3 tablespoons cilantro leaves, chopped, for garnish
Squash blossoms, for garnish (optional)

Heat the clarified butter, add the onion and the squash, and cook over medium heat for 5 to 10 minutes, stirring as needed. Gather all the whole dried spices together and grind them to a powder in an electric spice mill. Add them to the onion and squash, along with the cinnamon, turmeric, cayenne, ginger root, salt, and ½ cup water or stock, and continue to cook over medium heat for 5 minutes.

Pour in the rest of the water or stock and bring to a boil; then lower the heat and simmer for 15 minutes. Pass the soup through a food mill or purée it in a blender. Return the soup to the stove and stir in the cream.

Taste for salt and add more if necessary. Because some squash are less watery than others, the soup may need thinning with additional water or cream. Serve the soup garnished with the chopped cilantro and squash blossoms if available.

SERVES FOUR TO SIX

Mexican Vegetable Soup with Lime and Avocado

This soup was inspired by Diana Kennedy's recipe for Caldo Tlalpeño, which caught our attention partly because it was subtitled "vegetable broth from Tlalpán." In fact, a closer look revealed both shredded chicken and chicken broth, which this version omits. A light and spicy soup with a smoky flavor, this is one of our favorites. It is an ideal accompaniment to the potato frittata and any of the fritters.

THE STOCK
Make the Summer Vegetable Stock (page 64) and include ½ teaspoon dried oregano. If you are cooking chick peas, some of the cooking liquid can also be used in the soup.

THE SOUP
1 tablespoon light olive oil or vegetable oil
1 medium red onion, finely diced or sliced
1 clove garlic, finely chopped
½ teaspoon dried oregano
½ teaspoon salt
2 carrots, cut into ¼-inch-thick rounds
8 ounces green beans, tipped and cut into 1½-inch pieces
1 large or 2 medium tomatoes, peeled, seeded, and chopped
6 cups stock, heated
¾ cup cooked chick peas or hominy
1 or 2 teaspoons chilpotle chilies, minced
1 avocado, peeled and sliced, for garnish
Cilantro leaves, for garnish
6 wedges lime

Warm the oil in a soup pot, add the onion, garlic, oregano, and salt, and cook over medium-low heat until the onion softens. Add the carrots, beans, and tomatoes; pour in the heated stock and simmer. After 20 minutes add the chick peas or hominy and then gradually stir in the chilpotle chilies to taste. Cook another 5 minutes; then taste for salt. Ladle the soup into bowls; garnish with the avocado and the cilantro leaves. Serve the lime on the side.

SERVES FOUR TO SIX

Corn and Green Chili Chowder

This corn chowder is made with mild roasted chilies and tomatillos, the Mexican green tomatoes. Both the poblano chilies and tomatillos can be found in Mexican markets and frequently in supermarkets. If they aren't available where you live, substitute another type of pepper, such as a bell pepper or Anaheim, and use canned tomatillos.

THE STOCK
Milk, heated with herbs, provides the liquid for the soup.

THE SOUP
3½ cups milk
1 medium yellow onion, diced into ¼-inch squares
1 bay leaf
4 branches parsley
1 branch thyme
One 4-inch branch marjoram
8 peppercorns
3 poblano or Anaheim chilies or 1 large bell pepper
8 ounces tomatillos
5 to 6 ears white or yellow corn
1 cup water
2 tablespoons butter
½ teaspoon salt
4 ounces muenster cheese, cut into small cubes
Cilantro leaves, coarsely chopped, for garnish

Slowly heat the milk with half the diced onion and the bay leaf, parsley, thyme, marjoram, and peppercorns. Just before it comes to a boil, turn off the heat, and cover. Let the milk steep with the herbs until needed; then strain.

Roast the chilies or bell pepper over a flame until the skins are blistered and charred. Put them in a bowl, cover them with a dish, and set them aside to steam for 10 minutes. Then scrape the skins, remove the seeds and veins, and cut the chilies into strips or squares.

Bring several cups of water to a boil; then lower the heat to a simmer. Remove the papery husks from the tomatillos, rinse them, and drop them into the simmering water and cook slowly for 10 minutes. Remove them to a blender and purée. If using canned tomatillos, drain them first, then purée.

Slice the corn kernels off the cob. As you do so, press hard with your knife against the cobs to force out the milky liquid, and add it to the corn in a bowl. Set aside 1 cup of the kernels and blend the rest with the 1 cup water in two batches at the highest speed for at least 2 minutes. Work the resulting purée through a fine-meshed sieve, using the back of a spoon or rubber scraper to press out all the liquid.

Melt the butter in a soup pot with a little water; add the remaining onion and cook over medium-low heat until it is soft. Add the puréed tomatillos, corn kernels, peppers, and salt. Cook for 2 to 3 minutes; then stir in the puréed corn and the strained milk. Cook the soup over low heat for about ½ hour, stirring frequently. Check the seasonings and add salt if necessary.

Serve the soup over the cubes of cheese, and garnish with cilantro.

SERVES FOUR TO SIX

Roasted Eggplant Soup with Saffron Mayonnaise

Eggplant can be prepared in various ways for use in a soup. At the restaurant we grill it first over a charcoal fire, along with the peppers, onions, and tomatoes, then stew it in olive oil with herbs and stock. A simpler method for cooking at home, which also produces a full flavor, is to roast the vegetables in a hot oven, then cook them in water or stock. The resulting soup will be thick and flavorful. This is a good soup for the crisp days of early autumn—the spicy yellow-orange mayonnaise gives brightness and piquancy; and the croutons, a welcome textural contrast.

THE STOCK
Use water, a simple vegetable stock, or the Summer Vegetable Stock (page 64) seasoned with basil and thyme.

THE SOUP
1 to 2 firm, shiny eggplants, weighing in all 1½ pounds
About 4 tablespoons virgin olive oil
1 large red or torpedo onion, halved but not peeled
1 large or 2 medium red peppers, halved and seeded
2 medium ripe tomatoes
4 to 5 thyme branches or ½ teaspoon dried thyme
1 bay leaf
2 cloves garlic, chopped
1 teaspoon dried basil
1 teaspoon salt
2 tablespoons basil leaves, chopped (optional)
7 cups water or stock
Juice of 1 lemon
1 cup diced bread tossed with 2 tablespoons olive oil
Saffron Mayonnaise (see below)
Basil leaves, for garnish

Preheat the oven to 400°F. Wipe the outside of the eggplants, halve them length-wise, and brush the entire surface with olive oil. Salt and pepper the cut surfaces, set the halves on a baking sheet or large earthenware dish, and start them baking. Brush olive oil on the cut sides of the onion, both sides of the peppers, and the tomatoes, and add them to the pan with the eggplant after it has baked 20 minutes. Continue baking another 20 minutes or so, until the eggplant is soft and is beginning to col-lapse, and the skins of all the vegetables are loose and wrinkled. Remove the vege-tables from the oven and cool briefly. Take off what you can of the pepper skins and peel the onions; then roughly chop all the vegetables into large pieces.

Slowly warm 2 tablespoons of olive oil with the thyme, bay leaf, garlic, and dried basil. After several minutes add the baked vegetables, salt, and the chopped basil, if using. Pour in the water or stock, bring to a boil, cover, and simmer slowly for 25 minutes.

Cool the soup briefly; then purée it in a blender at a low speed, preserving some texture and small flecks of the pepper and eggplant skins. Return it to the pot and season to taste with salt and lemon juice. Thin with additional water or stock if needed. If the soup stands for very long before serving, it may be necessary to thin it further.

Prepare the Saffron Mayonnaise. Just before serving, toast the croutons in the oven until they are crisp and golden brown. Serve the soup with a spoonful of the mayonnaise in each bowl, along with a handful of croutons. A scattering of chopped basil leaves will give additional color and freshness to the soup.

For a wine with this soup try a light- to medium-bodied pinot noir or a Beaujolais.

SAFFRON MAYONNAISE

1 egg yolk, room temperature
2 cloves garlic, roughly chopped
½ teaspoon salt, preferably coarse sea salt
½ cup light olive oil or peanut oil
½ teaspoon cayenne pepper
⅛ teaspoon saffron threads dissolved in 1 tablespoon hot water
Lemon juice or vinegar to taste

If the egg is cold from the refrigerator, set it in a bowl of hot water for 1 minute or so to warm it up.

Pound the garlic with the salt in a mortar—the coarse grains of sea salt work especially well for breaking down the garlic—until it forms a smooth paste. Add the egg yolk, and stir briskly for about 1 minute with the pestle. Whisk in the olive or peanut oil as for a mayonnaise, drop by drop at first, then adding it in larger amounts as you go along. When all the oil is incorporated, add the cayenne and the dissolved saffron. Season to taste with lemon juice or vinegar.

Thin the mayonnaise by stirring in hot water by the spoonful until you have the consistency you want. If it is not to be used right away, cover and refrigerate until needed; then bring it to room temperature before serving.

SERVES FOUR TO SIX

Summer Potato Soup with Tomatoes and Basil

New potatoes are sweet and delicate with soft, paper-thin skins. Neither starchy nor stodgy, they are a delightful summer vegetable, and here they make a light soup flecked with pink and green. If you have a garden with small leeks that are ready to harvest, use them instead of the onion in the soup.

THE STOCK
Water alone is fine for this soup.

THE SOUP
2 tablespoons butter
6½ cups water
1 large white onion or 10 small leeks, thinly sliced, then chopped
1 bay leaf
5 branches lemon thyme or culinary thyme
1½ pounds new potatoes, washed and roughly chopped
1 teaspoon salt
4 tablespoons olive oil
1 pound ripe tomatoes, peeled, seeded, and finely chopped
1 cup basil leaves, loosely packed
Champagne vinegar or red wine vinegar to taste
White or black pepper

Melt the butter in a soup pot with ½ cup of the water and add the onion, bay leaf, and thyme. Cook over medium-low heat 4 to 5 minutes; add the potatoes and salt. Cover the pot and stew for 5 minutes. Pour in the rest of the water and bring to a boil; then simmer, covered, until the potatoes are tender and falling apart.

Pass the soup through a food mill, and return it to the soup pot. Avoid using a blender, which will tend to make the soup gummy and glutinous. Taste for salt and add more if needed.

Warm a tablespoon of the olive oil in a skillet, add the tomatoes, and cook over medium-high heat until the juice has evaporated and the tomatoes have thickened slightly. Break them up with a spoon to make a semi-smooth sauce, and season to taste with salt. Once the potatoes have been passed through the food mill, stir in the tomatoes.

Combine the remaining oil and the basil in a blender jar and purée. Season with salt and vinegar to taste.

Serve the soup with a spoonful of the basil purée swirled into each bowl and a generous grinding of pepper. If the soup thickens between the time it is made and served, thin it with additional water or, if you prefer, milk or cream.

SERVES FOUR TO SIX

Spicy Red Pepper Soup

This slow-cooking red pepper soup is based on Elizabeth David's recipe for the Catalán soup, *majorquina*. This spicier version includes ground or puréed ancho chili. Serve the soup alone or with a spoonful of crème fraîche or Saffron Mayonnaise.

THE STOCK
Water is fine for this soup.

THE SOUP
1 or 2 ancho chilies
3 tablespoons virgin olive oil
½ teaspoon Herbes de Provence or ½ teaspoon mixed marjoram, thyme, and savory
2 bay leaves
2 cloves
4 cloves garlic, roughly chopped
1 medium red onion, sliced
1 leek, white part only, sliced
1 pound pimentos or red bell peppers, seeded and sliced
1 teaspoon salt
1 pound ripe tomatoes, peeled, seeded, and chopped; juice reserved
6 cups water
8 ounces savoy or smooth green cabbage, chopped
Fresh herbs: parsley, marjoram, thyme, for garnish

Remove the stems, seeds, and veins from the chilies. Tear the flesh into a few large pieces. Cover them with water, bring to a boil, and simmer for 20 minutes; then purée them in a blender.

Slowly warm the olive oil in a soup pot with the Herbes de Provence or mixed herbs, bay leaves, and cloves until they are aromatic. Add the garlic and cook about ½ minute, without letting it brown; then stir in the onion, leek, peppers, and salt. Stir well to coat the vegetables with the oil, cover the pot, and leave on a flame-tamer over very low heat.

Check the pot after 5 minutes and give a stir. If the vegetables are sticking at all, add ½ cup water, and continue cooking another 5 to 10 minutes. Add the tomatoes, 4 tablespoons of the chili purée, and 6 cups of water. Bring to a boil; then lower the heat to a slow simmer. Add the cabbage, cover with a lid, and cook as slowly as possible for 40 minutes.

Let the soup cool briefly; then purée it for 1 minute or longer so that it is fully blended, or it will separate in the bowls. Return the soup to the pot and season to taste with salt, and more chili if desired. Serve the soup with a fresh garnish of chopped parsley, marjoram, or thyme leaves.

SERVES FOUR TO SIX

White Bean and Fresh Tomato Soup with Parsley Sauce

A bean soup for warmer weather, the beans are left whole and the broth is richly flavored with sage. The flavor develops as the soup sits, so it can be made a day ahead. The parsley sauce is added just before serving.

THE STOCK
Use the broth from the beans alone or in combination with the Summer Vegetable Stock (page 64).

THE SOUP
¾ cup dry navy beans
10 cups water
10 fresh sage leaves or 1 teaspoon dried sage
4 cloves garlic
3 bay leaves
6 thyme branches or ¼ teaspoon dried thyme
3 tablespoons virgin olive oil
Salt
1 medium red or yellow onion, finely chopped
1 pound ripe tomatoes, peeled, seeded, and chopped
Pepper
Parsley Sauce (see below)

Sort through the beans and remove any small stones and chaff. Rinse them well, cover them generously with water, and set them aside to soak overnight.

Next day, pour off the soaking water and cover the beans with 10 cups fresh water. Add half the sage, 3 of the garlic cloves (peeled and left whole), 2 of the bay leaves, the thyme, and 1 tablespoon of the olive oil. Bring to a boil, add 1 teaspoon salt, lower the heat, and cook the beans at a simmer or slow boil until they are tender but not mushy, about 1 hour. Remove them from the heat and strain, reserving the broth.

Slowly warm the rest of the oil in a soup pot with the remaining sage, garlic (roughly chopped), and bay leaf for 1 or 2 minutes; then add the onion and cook until it is soft, about 8 to 10 minutes. Stir in the tomatoes; then add 6 to 7 cups of the bean broth and ½ teaspoon salt. Bring to a boil and simmer for 20 minutes. Add the beans and cook another 10 minutes.

Season to taste with salt and freshly ground black pepper. The soup may be served immediately or set aside for later. Just before serving, prepare the sauce. Reheat the soup and garnish each bowl with a generous spoonful of sauce.

PARSLEY SAUCE

1 cup Italian parsley leaves, loosely packed
2 cloves garlic
¼ teaspoon salt, preferably coarse sea salt
3 tablespoons virgin olive oil
3 tablespoons Parmesan, grated
Red wine vinegar to taste

Chop the parsley fairly fine. Pound the garlic with the salt in a mortar until it is broken into a smooth paste. Add a tablespoon or so of the parsley and work it vigorously into the garlic; then stir in the olive oil, cheese, and remaining parsley. Add the vinegar to taste, and season with salt if necessary.

SERVES FOUR TO SIX

Basque Pumpkin and White Bean Soup

The pumpkin melts into a soft, smooth background and binds together the beans and vegetables. This soup is substantial enough to make a meal. Some planning ahead is needed, as the beans require time for soaking and cooking.

THE STOCK

Use the cooking water from the beans combined with a light stock made with the following
ingredients:
Seeds and parings from a 1-pound pumpkin or winter squash
1½ cups leek greens, chopped and washed
5 parsley branches
4 cloves garlic, peeled and left whole
½ teaspoon salt
6 cups cold water

First cut the pumpkin in half; then scoop out the seeds and stringy fibers with a metal spoon. Next cut the halves into slices an inch or so thick, and cut the skins off each slice with a paring knife and set them aside. Put the seeds and parings in a pot with the rest of the stock ingredients, bring to a boil, simmer for 30 minutes, and then strain.

THE BEANS

½ cup small white beans
3 fresh sage leaves or ½ teaspoon dried sage
1 large clove garlic, peeled and left whole
1 bay leaf
2 thyme branches
½ teaspoon salt
5 to 6 cups water

Cover the beans with water and soak them overnight or, alternatively, cover them with boiling water and soak them for 1 hour. Pour off the soaking water and put the beans in a pot with the rest of the ingredients and bring them to a boil. Skim off any foam that rises to the surface, lower the heat, and cook the beans at a slow boil until they are tender, 45 minutes to 1 hour. Drain the beans and reserve the cooking water.

THE VEGETABLES

Peeled and seeded pumpkin slices (from The Stock)
2 tablespoons virgin olive oil
3 leeks, white parts only, quartered and cut into ¼-inch pieces
2 carrots, peeled and cut into ¼-inch cubes
1 celery heart or 2 outer stalks, cut into ¼-inch dice
1 large clove garlic, finely minced
1 to 2 teaspoons nutritional yeast (optional)
2 large sage leaves or ¼ teaspoon dried sage, crumbled
½ teaspoon salt
Stock
Reserved cooking water from the beans
Pepper
2 tablespoons parsley, chopped
Additional olive oil, for garnish

Cut the pumpkin slices into ½-inch squares. Warm the oil in a soup pot and add the pumpkin, vegetables, garlic, nutritional yeast, if using, sage, and salt. Stir to coat everything with a film of oil, and cook over medium-low heat for 10 minutes, stirring occasionally. Pour in the stock and the cooking water from the beans, about 8 cups in all. Bring to a boil; then lower the heat and simmer for about ½ hour, until the pumpkin begins to soften and fall apart.

Add the beans, and continue cooking until the pumpkin has broken into a smooth purée.

Taste for salt and season with more, if needed, and a generous grinding of black pepper. Serve the soup with the parsley and a small spoonful of olive oil stirred into each bowl. As this soup sits, the flavors will develop, so it can be made one or even two days before serving.

This soup could be warmly contrasted with a pinot noir or perhaps a wood-aged chardonnay.

SERVES FOUR TO SIX

Pumpkin Soup with Gruyère Cheese

For this soup use Sugar pumpkins or Perfection squash—both are sweet and full-flavored without being stringy and watery. Delicata and butternut squash, though milder, are also delicious. The stock is a simple one, using the seeds and scrapings of the pumpkin or squash, a few vegetables, and herbs.

THE STOCK

Seeds and scrapings from the pumpkin or squash
2 carrots, peeled and diced
1 celery stalk, plus some leaves, chopped into small pieces
1 turnip, peeled and diced
2 bay leaves
½ teaspoon dried sage leaves or 5 to 6 fresh sage leaves
4 parsley branches
3 thyme branches
½ teaspoon salt
8 cups cold water

Cut the pumpkin or squash in half and scrape out all the seeds and stringy material with a large metal spoon. Put them in a pot with the remaining ingredients, bring to a boil, simmer for 25 minutes, and then strain.

THE SOUP

1 pumpkin or squash, weighing about 2½ pounds, halved and scooped out
3 tablespoons butter
1 medium yellow onion, cut into ¼-inch dice
½ to 1 teaspoon salt
6 to 7 cups stock
½ to 1 cup light cream
White pepper
3 ounces Gruyère cheese, finely grated
Thyme leaves, finely chopped, for garnish

Preheat the oven to 400°F. Bake the pumpkin or squash halves, face down, on a lightly oiled baking sheet until the skin is wrinkled and the flesh is soft, about 1 hour. Remove them from the oven and, when cool enough to handle, peel off the skin. Reserve any caramelized juices that may have collected on the pan.

Melt the butter in a soup pot, add the onion, and cook over medium heat for about

5 minutes. Add the cooked pumpkin, the juices, if any, the salt, and 6 cups of the stock. Bring to a boil; then simmer, covered, for 25 minutes.

Pass the soup through a food mill, which will smooth it out while leaving some texture. Return the soup to the pot and add the cream and more stock, if necessary, to thin it.

Taste for salt and season with the freshly ground white pepper. Stir in the grated cheese and serve the soup with the thyme leaves scattered over it.

Variation: Another way to make this soup is to bake pumpkins with the cream and the cheese inside their hollowed-out shells. The cooked flesh is scraped into the hot cream and melted cheese and served right from the pumpkin—a satisfying and fun way to cook and eat.

SERVES FOUR TO SIX

Winter Squash Soup with Red Chili and Mint

The warm colors of the squash and tomatoes and the heat of the chili make this soup especially pleasing on cool autumn days or cold winter ones. If good fresh tomatoes are available, grill them with the peppers to give the soup a smoky flavor.

THE STOCK
The seeds and inner fibers of 2½ pounds winter squash
2 celery stalks, diced
1 onion, roughly chopped or sliced
1 bay leaf
5 branches parsley
½ teaspoon dried sage leaves
1 teaspoon salt
8 cups cold water

Halve the squash, scrape out the seeds and stringy fibers with a metal spoon, and put them in a pot with the rest of the ingredients. Save the flesh for the soup. Bring to a boil, turn the heat down, and simmer 25 to 35 minutes; then strain.

THE SOUP
2½ pounds winter squash—butternut, Perfection, Sugar pumpkin, or other
1 red bell pepper or 2 pimentos
1 pound fresh or canned tomatoes, peeled, seeded, and chopped; juice reserved
1 ancho chili for chili purée or 1 to 2 tablespoons New Mexican chili powder
1 tablespoon butter
1 tablespoon sunflower or olive oil
1 large yellow onion, finely chopped
1 clove garlic, minced
1 to 2 teaspoons nutritional yeast (optional)
1 teaspoon salt
6 to 7 cups stock
1 tablespoon parsley, chopped
1 tablespoon mint, chopped

After halving the squash and removing the seeds and fibers for the stock, cut the halves into smaller, more manageable pieces for peeling. Then remove the skins and add them to the simmering stock. (In the case of large, smooth squash, like butternut, the skins can be easily removed with a vegetable peeler.) Cut the peeled squash into pieces, roughly ½ inch square.

To give the peppers a smoky flavor, roast them directly over the flame or in the broiler until the skin is charred, and then set them aside in a covered bowl to steam for 10 minutes or so. Scrape off the charred skin with a knife, remove the seeds, and dice the peppers into ¼-inch squares.

If using an ancho chili, first remove the stem, seeds, and veins. Cover it with boiling water and soak it for 20 minutes; then blend until smooth.

Heat the butter and oil in a soup pot, add the onion, garlic, and nutritional yeast, if using, and cook over medium-low heat until the onion is soft, about 10 minutes. Stir in the tomatoes, half the chili, and the salt, and stew for 5 minutes. Add the cubed squash, grilled peppers, reserved tomato juice, and 6 cups of the stock. Simmer until the squash has melted into a purée, about 25 to 40 minutes.

Thin with more liquid, if needed, season with salt, and add more chili purée if desired. Serve the soup with the parsley and the mint stirred in at the last minute.

If the soup sits before serving, the sweet and hot flavors will deepen and merge. This soup, a salad of crisp, tart greens, and cornbread make a satisfying simple meal.

Try a lighter zinfandel with this soup, or if you'd prefer a white, serve a sauvignon blanc.

SERVES FOUR TO SIX

Tomato and Wild Mushroom Soup

Fresh wild mushrooms fill this soup with the perfume of leaves and woods damp with rain. It is especially delicious made with porcini (cèpes) and the very last tomatoes found on vines already beginning to wither. These small tomatoes have thickish, shriveled skins, and a very concentrated flavor. Although fresh wild mushrooms are not commonly available, dried mushrooms will make a flavorful soup, and good quality canned tomatoes can be substituted for the fresh, their taste strengthened with some puréed sun-dried tomato if you wish.

THE STOCK
Prepare the Wild Mushroom Stock (page 66).

THE SOUP
1 large red onion
4 tablespoons virgin olive oil
6 branches thyme or ½ teaspoon dried thyme
2 teaspoons fresh marjoram leaves, chopped, or ½ teaspoon dried marjoram
14 ounces mushrooms: porcini or cultivated field mushrooms, sliced ¼ inch thick
Salt
1 large clove garlic, pounded in a mortar
1 pound ripe tomatoes or 1 pound canned pear tomatoes, peeled, seeded, and chopped; juice
* reserved*
6 to 7 cups stock
2 sun-dried tomatoes, puréed (optional)
Pepper
Thinly sliced baguette, 2 slices per person
Fresh thyme or marjoram leaves, chopped, for garnish
Parmesan Reggiano, freshly grated, for garnish

Halve the onion and divide each half lengthwise into thirds. Slice each third crosswise into thin pieces (this size will sit comfortably in a soup spoon). Warm 2 tablespoons of the olive oil in a soup pot, and slowly cook the onion over low heat with the thyme and marjoram until the onion is melted.

While the onion is cooking, heat the remaining 2 tablespoons of oil in a large skillet and when hot, add the mushrooms. Toss them immediately to distribute the oil. Salt lightly and cook them over medium-high heat until they begin to release their juices.

Add the mushrooms to the onion along with the garlic, tomatoes, salt, and a cup of the stock. Cover and stew slowly for 20 minutes. Add the remaining stock, any reserved tomato juice, and the puréed sun-dried tomato, if using. Bring to a boil and simmer 25 minutes.

If possible, let the soup sit an hour or more before serving to allow the flavors to soften and merge. Taste for salt and season with freshly ground black pepper. Brush the bread with olive oil and toast in a hot oven. Serve the soup over the bread garnished with the fresh herbs, and pass the Parmesan cheese.

Variations: If you have chanterelle mushrooms, clean them and boil the parings in the water and use that for the stock, seasoned with thyme and bay leaves as in the Wild Mushroom Stock. For a soup with a different kind of mushroom flavor, use a combination of fresh and dried shiitake. Use the dried shiitake in place of the porcini in the stock; then remove them, slice them into pieces, and cook them with the fresh mushrooms in the soup.

SERVES FOUR TO SIX

Bresse Mushroom Soup

Adapted from a recipe of Jane Grigson's, this soup has long been a favorite at Greens. The flavor is full-bodied and deep, particularly when it is made with the Wild Mushroom Stock. Thickened with bread, it can be puréed coarsely, leaving chewy pieces of mushrooms, or puréed finely to make a silky cream.

THE STOCK
Use the Wild Mushroom Stock (page 66) or water.

THE SOUP
2 tablespoons butter
1 yellow onion, sliced
1 teaspoon salt
2 cloves garlic, roughly chopped
2 tablespoons parsley, chopped
1 teaspoon nutritional yeast (optional)
½ cup dry white wine
1 pound mushrooms, roughly sliced or chopped
6 cups stock or water
2 slices bread, any kind
½ cup light cream
Pepper
Chives, parsley, or tarragon, chopped, for garnish

Heat the butter in a soup pot until it foams; then add the onion and salt. Cook over medium-high heat for 3 minutes to soften the onion, stirring frequently. Add the garlic, parsley, and yeast, if using, and cook 2 minutes more. Pour in the wine, raise the heat, and reduce it for another 3 minutes.

Add the mushrooms and stew them with the onion over medium-low heat for 6 to 8 minutes, giving them a stir partway through the cooking. Pour in the stock or water, and bring it to a boil. Lower the heat, add the bread, and simmer for 20 minutes.

Let the soup cool slightly; then either briefly purée it in a blender, leaving small pieces of mushroom, or purée it longer, making a smooth, creamy soup. Heat the soup again and stir in the cream. Taste it and season with more salt, if needed, and freshly ground black pepper. Serve with the fresh herbs. This soup is also nice served with a spoonful of crème fraîche in each bowl.

SERVES FOUR TO SIX

Mushroom, Leek, and Potato Soup

The Wild Mushroom Stock gives this simple potato and leek soup a deep, woodsy flavor.

THE STOCK

Prepare the Wild Mushroom Stock (page 66). In place of the onion, use 1½ cups chopped leek greens. If you don't want skins on your soup potatoes, use them in the stock. Fresh wild mushroom stems and trimmings can be used instead of dried mushrooms.

THE SOUP

3 tablespoons butter
1 small red onion, cut into ½-inch squares
3 leeks, white parts only (8 ounces), sliced into ¼-inch rounds or half-rounds
1 pound potatoes, quartered and thinly sliced
Salt
6 cups stock
1 tablespoon olive oil
8 to 12 ounces mushrooms, irregularly sliced
½ cup dry white wine
Pepper
½ to 1 cup light or heavy cream (optional)
Fresh herbs: parsley, chervil, tarragon, thyme, finely chopped, for garnish

Melt 2 tablespoons of the butter in a soup pot and add the onion and leeks. Cook them over high heat for several minutes, stirring frequently; then lower the heat and add the potatoes, 1 teaspoon salt, and 2 cups of the stock. Cover the pot and stew the vegetables over low heat for about 10 minutes.

Heat the remaining tablespoon butter and the olive oil in a wide skillet. Add the mushrooms and sauté them over high heat until they begin to release their juices, stirring as needed. Add ½ teaspoon salt and the wine, and cook until the wine is reduced and syrupy. Scrape the mushrooms into the soup pot, and add the remaining 4 cups of the stock. Bring to a boil; then simmer slowly, covered, until the potatoes are completely soft, about 25 minutes.

Taste the soup and season with more salt, if needed, and freshly ground black pepper. Add the cream, if using, and heat through. Serve the soup garnished with the fresh herbs.

SERVES FOUR TO SIX

Kale and Potato Soup with Red Chili

A vigorous and deeply satisfying winter soup, this is full of dense green kale, an abundant quantity of garlic cooked until it is soft and sweet, and a small red chili for piquancy and warmth.

THE STOCK

The ingredients of this soup supply plenty of flavor, so use water to prepare a simple stock using the stems of the kale.

THE SOUP

1 bunch kale
3 tablespoons virgin olive oil
1 medium red or yellow onion, diced into ½-inch squares
6 cloves garlic, peeled and sliced
1 small dried red chili, seeded and chopped, or ½ teaspoon chili flakes
1 bay leaf
1 teaspoon salt
4 medium red potatoes (about 1 pound), scrubbed and diced into ½-inch cubes
2 teaspoons nutritional yeast (optional)
7 cups water or stock
Pepper
Crème fraîche or sour cream (optional)

Using a sharp knife, cut the ruffled kale leaves off their stems, which are very tough and take a long time to cook. Cut the leaves into pieces roughly 2 inches square, wash them well, and set them aside.

Heat the olive oil in a soup pot, add the onion, garlic, chili, bay leaf, and salt, and cook over medium-high heat for 3 or 4 minutes, stirring frequently. Add the potatoes and the yeast, if using, plus a cup of the water or stock. Stir together, cover, and cook slowly for 5 minutes.

Add the kale, cover, and steam until it is wilted, stirring occasionally. Pour in the rest of the water or stock, bring to a boil, then simmer slowly, covered, until the potatoes are quite soft, 30 to 40 minutes.

Use the back of a wooden spoon to break up the potatoes by pressing them against the sides of the pot, or purée a cup or two of the soup in a blender and return it to the pot. This will make a unifying background for the other elements.

Taste the soup for salt and add a generous grinding of black pepper. If possible, let the soup sit for an hour or so before serving to allow the flavors to further develop. Serve the soup hot without any garnish, or with a spoonful of crème fraîche or sour cream if desired.

SERVES FOUR TO SIX

Turnip Soup with Turnip Greens

People often think of turnip soup as bitter and thin, but this one, made with young delicate turnips, is creamy and sweet. Blanching the turnips first removes any bitterness, and the sharpness of the greens makes a delicious counterpoint to the sweetness of the turnips.

THE STOCK
None is needed for this soup.

THE SOUP
1½ pounds small turnips (about 1 to 2 inches across), weighed without their greens
Salt
5 tablespoons butter, in all
2 to 3 leeks, white parts only (about 8 ounces), sliced
6 branches thyme or ¼ teaspoon dried thyme
4 cups milk
White or black pepper
About 2 to 3 cups turnip greens
Fresh chopped thyme for garnish (optional)

Peel the turnips (thickly, if they are large and mature) and slice them into rounds about ¼ inch thick. Bring 3 quarts of water to a boil; then add 2 teaspoons salt and the turnips. Cover the pot and cook for 1 minute; then drain.

Melt 3 tablespoons of the butter in a soup pot with ½ cup water. Add the leeks, the blanched turnips, the thyme, and 1 teaspoon salt. Stew them, covered, over medium-low heat for 5 minutes, and then add the milk. Slowly heat it without bringing it to a boil, and cook, stirring occasionally, until the turnips are completely tender.

Cool the soup briefly; then purée it in a blender. If necessary, thin it with additional milk or water. Season to taste with salt, if needed, and freshly ground pepper.

Sort through the turnip greens and remove any that are bruised or especially tough looking, and wash them. Melt the remaining 2 tablespoons of butter in a pan, add the turnip greens, and cook them over medium heat until they are tender, about 5 to 10 minutes. Season with salt and pepper. Remove the cooked greens to a cutting board and chop them, roughly or fine, as you prefer; then add them to the soup and serve. Or garnish with fresh chopped thyme.

SERVES FOUR TO SIX

Fennel and Celeriac Soup

Winter bulbs and roots have a sweetness and delicacy that pervade this soothing soup. Serve it with other seasonal foods, such as a plate of winter vegetables with Parsley Sauce, or the Buckwheat Linguine with French Lentils, Carrots, and Chard.

THE STOCK
2 cups leek greens, sliced and washed well
The thick outer leaves of the fennel bulb
Parings from the celery root
2 carrots, peeled and diced
1 bay leaf
5 parsley branches
½ teaspoon fennel seed
½ teaspoon celery seed
½ teaspoon salt
8 cups cold water

Discard the ragged outer leaves of the leeks, and use the lighter inner greens. Chop the thick outer fennel leaves, and if they are available, use some of the upper stalks and greens. Scrub the celery root well, take a slice off the top and the bottom, and then cut down the sides, removing all the gnarly skin. Use the parings in the stock, and put the trimmed celery root in a bowl of water acidulated with lemon juice or white vinegar. Combine the leek, fennel, and celery root parings with the remaining ingredients, bring to a boil, simmer 25 to 35 minutes, and then strain.

THE SOUP
2 tablespoons butter
½ cup water
3 leeks, white parts only (about 8 ounces), sliced into rounds
1 fennel bulb, weighing about 1 pound, trimmed, quartered, and sliced
1 celery root, weighing about 1 pound, trimmed, quartered, and sliced
1 to 2 teaspoons nutritional yeast (optional)
½ teaspoon salt
6 to 7 cups stock
½ to 1 cup light cream
Pepper
Inner fennel leaves, finely chopped, plus a good handful watercress,
*   or rocket leaves (arugula), chopped*

Melt the butter with the ½ cup water and add the leeks, fennel, celery root, nutritional yeast, if using, and salt. Give everything a stir; then cover and stew very slowly for 20 minutes. Check once during the cooking to make sure there is ample moisture in the pot, and add a little water or stock if there is not.

Pour the strained stock over the vegetables, bring to a boil, and then simmer, covered, for 15 minutes. Let cool briefly before blending the soup for a full minute, in two or more batches, to make it smooth. The soup may have quite a bit of air in it at first, but after a while it will settle down to a more creamy, less fluffy, consistency.

Stir in the cream. If the soup is too thick—and celery root will cause it to thicken as it sits—thin it with additional stock or water. Taste for salt, and add more if necessary. Season with pepper. Stir the chopped greens into the soup to cook them briefly, and then serve.

A Côtes-du-Rhône wine would be complementary with this soup.

SERVES FOUR TO SIX

Split Pea and Celeriac Soup

This pea soup is not so thick that it will support the proverbial standing spoon. Light but full-bodied, it is served with crisp croutons fried in rosemary oil.

THE STOCK
Use water, or for a richer soup, the Winter Vegetable Stock (page 65) cooked with a small branch of rosemary and the trimmings of the celeriac.

THE SOUP
1 cup green split peas
½ cup light olive oil
3 bay leaves
1 teaspoon rosemary, coarsely chopped
1 clove garlic, sliced
1 large yellow onion, cut into ½-inch squares
3 inner stalks celery, cut into a small dice
1 celeriac, trimmed and cut into small cubes
1 teaspoon salt
1 tablespoon nutritional yeast (optional)
½ cup dry white wine
8 cups water or stock
Pepper
1 rosemary branch, about 3 inches long
2 or 3 slices of white bread, cut into squares, for croutons
Parsley or chervil, finely chopped, for garnish
Grated Parmesan or Romano cheese (optional)

Sort through the peas and pick out any chaff and small stones you might find. Rinse them well, cover them generously with water, and set them aside to soak overnight, or 6 hours. Alternatively, cover them with boiling water and soak them for an hour. (Soaking the peas contributes both to the texture and flavor of the soup. However, if you do not have time to pre-soak them, plan to use more liquid in the soup, as the dry peas will absorb a great deal before they begin to soften and cook.)

Gradually warm 3 tablespoons of the olive oil in a soup pot with the bay leaves and the rosemary, and cook slowly for 3 minutes to flavor the oil. Add the garlic and cook another ½ minute without letting it brown. Next add the vegetables along with the salt and the nutritional yeast, if using, and cook 5 minutes, stirring occasionally, over medium heat. Pour in the wine, raise the heat, and reduce. Drain the peas and add them, with the water or stock, to the pot. Bring to a boil, cover, and simmer until the peas are completely soft, about 1½ hours.

Blend a few cups of the soup, or work it through a food mill, and return it to the pot. Taste for salt and season the soup with freshly ground black pepper.

Warm the remaining 5 tablespoons oil in a small skillet with the rosemary branch. When the oil is hot and fragrant with rosemary, remove the herb branch and add the bread squares, frying them until they are crisp and golden. Remove them from the oil to some toweling or a plate, and use the extra oil to flavor the soup. Serve the soup with the croutons and some fresh parsley or chervil. If you wish, pass around a bowl of freshly grated Parmesan or Romano cheese.

SERVES FOUR TO SIX

Yellow Split Pea Soup with Spiced Yogurt

This smooth yellow soup is seasoned with fresh ginger, cumin, and lemon.
The peas benefit from being soaked at least 2 hours—they will break down more
quickly and absorb less liquid when cooked.

THE STOCK
Use water or the Stock for Curried Soups and Dishes (page 67).

THE SOUP
2 tablespoons clarified butter or 1 tablespoon each butter and olive oil
1 large yellow onion, diced into ¼-inch pieces
2 cloves garlic, finely chopped
1-inch piece fresh ginger root, peeled and minced
1 bay leaf
1 teaspoon salt
½ teaspoon cumin seeds or ground cumin
3 cloves
1⅔ cups yellow split peas, soaked 2 hours or longer
1 celery heart or 2 outer stalks, diced
2 medium carrots, peeled and cut into small squares
7 cups water or stock
Grated peel and juice of 1 lemon
Spiced Yogurt (see below)
Cilantro or parsley, chopped, for garnish

Warm the clarified butter, or butter and oil, in a soup pot and add the onion, garlic,
ginger, bay leaf, and salt. Grind the cumin seeds and the cloves in a spice mill, and
add them to the onion. Stir everything together and cook over medium-low heat for
3 to 4 minutes. Drain the peas, and add them to the onions along with the celery,
carrots, and 7 cups water or stock. Bring to a boil; then simmer until the peas have
completely fallen apart, about 45 to 60 minutes.

Pass the soup through a food mill or purée it in a blender; then return it to the
stove. Add more water or stock, as needed, to achieve the consistency you like. Season to taste with additional salt, the lemon peel, and the lemon juice. Serve the soup
in warm bowls with a spoonful of spiced yogurt and a sprinkling of cilantro or
parsley.

SPICED YOGURT
½ cup plain yogurt
½ teaspoon turmeric
½ teaspoon paprika
¼ teaspoon cayenne pepper, or more, to taste
¼ teaspoon ground cumin seed
Pinch salt

Whisk the yogurt until it is smooth; then stir in the spices.

SERVES FOUR TO SIX

Lima Bean and Winter Vegetable Soup

The limas are large, soft, and plump—pleasing in the mouth. In spite of their size, the beans need only an hour or so to cook, whether they have been soaked overnight or for just an hour in boiling water. Don't let them overcook and become too soft— a little texture is nice.

THE STOCK

Use the cooking liquid from the beans combined with extra water if necessary. Or make the Winter Vegetable Stock (page 65), using a cup of the cabbage leaves, sliced and stewed, ¼ teaspoon fennel seeds, and the stems from the mushrooms.

THE SOUP

1 cup dry lima beans
8 cups water
1 bay leaf
2 tablespoons olive oil
Salt
3 tablespoons butter
1 large yellow onion, cut into ½-inch squares
2 teaspoons nutritional yeast (optional)
½ teaspoon dried thyme
½ teaspoon dried marjoram
¼ teaspoon fennel seeds
2 cloves garlic, finely chopped
½ cup dry white wine
2 carrots, peeled and cut into ½-inch pieces
¼ small head savoy cabbage, shredded
1 small fennel bulb, diced into ½-inch pieces
One 4-ounce turnip or rutabaga, peeled and cut into ½-inch squares
4 ounces mushrooms, stems removed, caps roughly chopped
6½ cups stock or bean broth
Pepper
Fresh herbs: marjoram, thyme, fennel greens, parsley, or a mixture, finely chopped, for garnish
Parmesan (optional)

Rinse the beans well, cover them generously with water, and let them soak 6 hours or overnight; or cover them with boiling water and soak 1 hour. Pour off the soaking water and put the beans in a pot with the 8 cups water, the bay leaf, and 1 tablespoon of the olive oil. Bring to a boil, add 1 teaspoon salt, lower the heat, and simmer slowly until the beans are nearly tender. (They will continue cooking in the soup.) Remove any of the skins that have become detached and have floated to the surface. Drain the beans and set them aside. Save the broth to use in the soup, or for another purpose.

Using a large soup pot with a heavy bottom, melt the butter and the remaining 1 tablespoon oil, and add the onion. Cook over medium-high heat, stirring occasionally at first, and more frequently later, until the onion is a rich, dark brown, 15 to 20 minutes. Add ½ teaspoon salt, the nutritional yeast, if using, and the dried herbs and garlic, and cook together for a minute. Pour in the wine, reduce by half, then add all the vegetables and ½ cup stock or bean broth. Cover, and stew slowly for 10 minutes; then add 6 more cups liquid. Simmer 15 minutes, add the beans, and cook another 15 minutes.

Taste the soup and season with additional salt, if needed, and freshly ground black pepper. Serve with a garnish of fresh herbs and, if desired, grated Parmesan.

This soup will taste even better a day or two after it is made, when the flavors have more thoroughly developed and merged. Served with an honest piece of bread, it makes a wholesome meal.

SERVES FOUR TO SIX

Parsnip Soup with Curry Spices

Warm curry spices balance the apple-sweet flavor of parsnip, a delicious winter vegetable that is often overlooked. Serve the soup by itself or with a few spoonfuls of cooked rice added to each bowl.

THE STOCK
The parings and fibrous inner cores of the parsnips (from The Soup)
1½ cups leek greens, chopped
2 carrots, peeled and chopped
2 celery stalks with some leaves, diced
5 whole branches cilantro
1 ounce ginger root, peeled and sliced (optional)
½ teaspoon salt
7 cups cold water

Put everything together in a pot and slowly bring to a boil; then cover and simmer for 25 minutes. Strain immediately. There should be 5 to 6 cups.

THE SOUP
3 to 4 parsnips, about 7 inches long
4 tablespoons clarified butter (page 325)
1 medium yellow onion, cut into ½-inch squares
1 tablespoon curry powder (page 328)
4 tablespoons cilantro leaves, chopped
2 to 3 leeks, white parts only (8 ounces), chopped
2 carrots, peeled and diced
2 celery stalks, diced
1 teaspoon salt
5 to 6 cups stock
1 cup light cream
Whole cilantro leaves, for garnish
3 radishes, very thinly sliced, for garnish

Scrub the parsnips, trim the tops, and peel them. Quarter them lengthwise and cut out most of the fibrous inner core. Use both the parings and the cores for the soup stock. Chop the pared parsnips roughly into pieces.

Heat the clarified butter in a soup pot and add the onion. Cook it over medium heat, stirring frequently, until it turns a rich golden color, about 15 minutes. Stir in the curry powder and half the chopped cilantro, and cook for 1 minute; then add the parsnips, leek, carrots, celery, salt, and the stock. Bring to a boil, lower the heat, cover, and cook until the vegetables are soft.

Cool the soup briefly; then pass it through a food mill or blend it at a low speed to leave a little texture and flecks of color. Return the soup to the pot, stir in the cream, and taste for salt.

Serve the soup garnished with the remaining chopped cilantro, a few whole leaves of cilantro, and a cluster of thinly sliced radishes in each bowl.

Although we usually serve this soup hot, it makes a good cold soup as well, perhaps for an especially warm day in early spring.

SERVES FOUR TO SIX

Red Onion and Red Wine Soup
with Tomatoes and Thyme

Hearty and invigorating, this winter soup is a good one to pair with those winter gratins and stews that are rich and creamy and need the balance of something acidic. The stock is made only with herbs to add depth without the sweetness or varied flavors of other vegetables.

THE STOCK
½ teaspoon dried thyme or several branches fresh thyme
8 branches parsley
3 bay leaves
3 cloves garlic
6 large borage leaves (optional)
½ teaspoon salt
8 cups cold water

Put all the ingredients in a pot, bring to a boil, and simmer 25 minutes. Pour through a sieve lined with paper toweling or cheesecloth to screen out any tiny pieces of thyme, which become bitter as they steep.

THE SOUP
4 tablespoons virgin olive oil
2 pounds red onions, cut into thirds, then sliced thinly across
4 cloves garlic, coarsely chopped
½ teaspoon coarse sea salt
1 pound fresh tomatoes or 2 cups canned whole tomatoes, juice reserved
½ teaspoon salt
The Stock
1 cup full-bodied red wine
Pepper
Baguette for croutons, 2 or 3 slices per person
About 4 tablespoons virgin olive oil, for croutons and garnish
Fresh thyme leaves, for garnish

Warm the olive oil in a heavy wide soup pot that will comfortably hold the onions. Add the onions and stir to coat them with oil. Cook them slowly over low heat until they are wilted and soft, stirring occasionally, about 25 to 30 minutes.

While the onions are cooking, pound the garlic to a paste in a mortar with the sea salt. Peel, seed, and chop the fresh tomatoes. If the tomatoes are canned, squeeze out the seeds before chopping them. Strain the juice and set it aside to use in the soup.

When the onions are soft, stir in the garlic, tomatoes, the ½ teaspoon salt, and 1 cup of the strained tomato juice or stock. Cover the pot and stew for 15 minutes; then raise the heat, add the wine, and cook until reduced by half.

Pour the remaining stock over the onions and tomatoes, bring to a boil, and simmer, partially covered, for 25 minutes. Taste for salt and season with freshly ground black pepper.

Slice the baguette and brush the pieces with olive oil. Toast them in the oven until they are crisp and golden on both sides. Serve the soup over the croutons; then stir a small spoonful of oil into each bowl and garnish with the thyme leaves.

This soup could use the warmth and fruitiness of a Beaujolais. For a white wine, consider trying a sauvignon blanc.

SERVES FOUR TO SIX

Leek and Chervil Soup

A clear, simple soup or broth that contains a single vegetable, and perhaps some rice or pasta, has an invaluable place at the beginning of a large dinner. Its very simplicity makes it satisfying in the way that chicken soup or broth can be. What is necessary, though, is a stock with a well-developed, balanced flavor, such as the Winter Vegetable Stock. This version is thickened slightly with a small amount of flour. If you prefer a thinner, clear soup, omit it.

THE STOCK
Prepare the Winter Vegetable Stock (page 65).

THE SOUP
6 cups stock
4 to 5 leeks, white parts only (10 to 12 ounces)
4 tablespoons butter
1 teaspoon salt
1½ tablespoons flour
Pepper
Several tablespoons chopped chervil (if not available, use Italian parsley or fennel greens)
Parmesan

If the stock is cold, heat it on the stove while preparing the leeks. Cut the leeks into rounds and wash them well. Melt the butter in a wide soup pot; add the leeks and the salt. Cook them slowly over low heat for about 15 minutes, stirring frequently. Add a little water or stock to keep the leeks from sticking to the pot. Stir in the flour, cook for a minute, then pour in the warmed stock. Simmer the soup for 25 minutes.

Taste, add more salt if needed, and season with freshly ground black pepper. Garnish with the chervil and freshly grated Parmesan.

Variations

LEEK AND CHERVIL SOUP WITH RICE OR PASTA
Prepare the soup according to the recipe, but omit the flour. Cook 4 tablespoons rice or tiny pasta shapes separately in salted water, and add them to the soup just before serving.

LEEK AND CHERVIL SOUP WITH GRILLED BREAD AND CHEESE
Reduce the amount of flour in the soup to 1 tablespoon. Brush melted butter or olive oil on thinly sliced pieces of Country French Bread or baguette, and then toast them in the oven 6 to 10 minutes, until they are crisp and golden. Lay the bread in the soup bowls, cover it with finely grated Gruyère or Fontina cheese, and ladle the soup over.

SERVES FOUR TO SIX

Black Bean Chili

Black Bean Chili has been served every day since Greens opened in 1979. It has a woodsy campfire quality and a complexity of tastes from the various smoked and roasted chilies. In addition to serving these beans as chili, we also use them as an ingredient in the Black Bean Enchiladas and the Black Bean Chilaquiles. It is worth making double the amount and freezing half to have it available to use in other recipes.

2 cups black turtle beans, soaked overnight
1 bay leaf
4 teaspoons cumin seeds
4 teaspoons dried oregano leaves
4 teaspoons paprika
½ teaspoon cayenne pepper
1 chili negro or ancho chili, for chili powder, or 2 to 3 tablespoons chili powder
3 tablespoons corn or peanut oil
3 medium yellow onions, diced into ¼-inch squares
4 cloves garlic, coarsely chopped
½ teaspoon salt
1½ pounds ripe or canned tomatoes, peeled, seeded, and chopped; juice reserved
1 to 2 teaspoons chopped chilpotle chili
About 1 tablespoon rice wine vinegar
4 tablespoons cilantro, chopped
Garnishes:
   ½ to ¾ cup muenster cheese, grated
   Green chilies: 2 poblano or Anaheim, roasted, peeled, and diced, or 2 ounces canned
      green chilies, rinsed well and diced
   ½ cup crème fraîche or sour cream
   6 sprigs cilantro

Sort through the beans and remove any small stones. Rinse them well, cover them generously with water, and let them soak overnight. Next day, drain the beans, cover them with fresh water by a couple of inches, and bring them to a boil with the bay leaf. Lower the heat and let the beans simmer while you prepare the rest of the ingredients.

Heat a small heavy skillet over medium heat. Add the cumin seeds, and when they begin to color, add the oregano leaves, shaking the pan frequently so the herbs don't scorch. As soon as the fragrance is strong and robust, remove the pan from the heat and add the paprika and the cayenne. Give everything a quick stir; then remove from the pan—the paprika and the cayenne only need a few seconds to toast. Grind in a mortar or a spice mill to make a coarse powder.

Preheat the oven to 375°F. To make the chili powder, put the dried chili in the oven for 3 to 5 minutes to dry it out. Cool it briefly; then remove the stem, seeds, and veins. Tear the pod into small pieces and grind it into a powder in a blender or spice mill.

Heat the oil in a large skillet, and sauté the onions over medium heat until they soften. Add the garlic, salt, and the ground herbs and chili powder, and cook another 5 minutes. Add the tomatoes, their juice, and about 1 teaspoon of the chilpotle chili. Simmer everything together for 15 minutes; then add this mixture to the beans, and, if necessary, enough water so the beans are covered by at least 1 inch. Continue cooking the beans slowly until they are soft, an hour or longer, or pressure cook them for 30 minutes at 15 pounds' pressure. Keep an eye on the water level and add more, if needed, to keep the beans amply covered.

When the beans are cooked, taste them, and add more chilpotle chili if desired. Season to taste with the vinegar, additional salt if needed, and the chopped cilantro.

Prepare the garnishes. If you are using fresh green chilies, roast them over a flame until they are evenly charred. Let them steam 10 minutes in a bowl covered with a dish; then scrape off the skins, discard the seeds, and dice.

Serve the chili ladled over a large spoonful of grated cheese, and garnish it with the crème fraîche or sour cream, the green chilies, and a sprig of fresh cilantro.

Though served in a bowl and eaten with a spoon, this chili is a great deal thicker than most soups—thick enough in fact to be served on a plate right alongside fritters or cornbread. It also, however, can be thinned considerably with stock, water, or tomato juice, to make a much thinner but still very flavorful black bean soup. When thinned to make a soup, it can be served as part of a meal rather than a meal in itself.

MAKES 8 CUPS

SANDWICHES *and*

BREADS

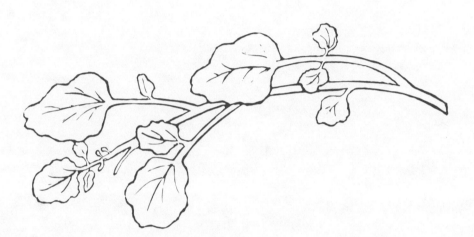

There is something very satisfying about eating with one's hands. Even pizzas have become a knife-and-fork food, but sandwiches are still picked up, handheld, and carried places—to work, on picnics, or maybe just to the kitchen table. Served with a soup or salad, or eaten with vegetables or fresh fruits, sandwiches make a wholesome, informal meal. These recipes offer a wide range of possibilities for sandwich ingredients, including some you may not have previously encountered, such as grilled, marinated tofu and Cheese and Nut Loaf.

Good bread is a large part of what makes a sandwich wholesome and delicious, and fortunately it is not so difficult to find small bakeries that make good, quality breads. But for those who enjoy making their own, we've included a few recipes for the sandwich breads we like to use.

Herb Cream Cheese and Cucumbers on Toast

A nutty wheat bread or other whole grain bread is a good choice for this open-faced sandwich. The toast is crisp, the cheese creamy, and the cucumbers wet and cool. If you like, include a peppery green, such as nasturtium leaves, watercress, or rocket (arugula), between the cream cheese and the cucumbers.

Whole grain bread, 8 slices
Herb Cream Cheese (page 53)
1 tablespoon chives, sliced into narrow rounds
1 cucumber, very thinly sliced
Salt
Pepper

Toast or grill the bread on both sides; then thickly spread on the cream cheese. Sprinkle the chives over the cream cheese, and lay the cucumbers on top, overlapping one another. Finish with salt and freshly ground pepper.

MAKES FOUR SANDWICHES

Tomato and Cheddar Sandwich
with Basil Mayonnaise

This is a classic summertime sandwich made with vine-ripened tomatoes.

3 to 4 ounces sharp cheddar cheese
1 large or 2 medium ripe tomatoes
½ cucumber
4 slices bread
Basil Mayonnaise (see below)
Thin slices of sweet red onion
Salt
Pepper

Slice the cheese, tomatoes, and cucumber. Prepare the basil mayonnaise and spread it generously on the bread. Layer the cheese, onion, tomatoes, and cucumber slices over the mayonnaise. Season with salt and freshly ground black pepper, top with bread, and slice in two.

BASIL MAYONNAISE
Basic mayonnaise (page 324)
1 clove garlic
4 to 6 tablespoons basil leaves, chopped

Mash the garlic in a mortar until it has broken down into a fine paste. Stir it into the mayonnaise, then add the basil and combine.

MAKES TWO SANDWICHES

Red Onion, Tomato, and Herb Cream Cheese

A moist, chewy whole grain bread seems just right with the herb cream cheese in this sandwich.

Several thin slices red onion
Herb Cream Cheese (page 53)
Whole grain bread, 8 slices
Vine-ripened tomatoes, thickly sliced
Salt
Pepper

To make the onion milder, cover it with cold water and refrigerate for half an hour before using.

Spread the cream cheese thickly on the bread. Arrange the tomato and onion slices over the cheese. Season with salt and freshly ground black pepper, and cover with the second slice of bread. Cut in half and serve.

MAKES FOUR SANDWICHES

Stilton with Cucumbers and Cress

A dark whole grain bread sets off the crisp, pungent, and buttery elements in this sandwich.

3 ounces Stilton cheese
2 ounces natural cream cheese
Milk or cream
Handful watercress or garden cress
2 teaspoons chives, cut into narrow rounds
Salt
Bread, 4 slices
½ cucumber, sliced very thin
White pepper

Work the Stilton cheese and cream cheese together with enough milk or cream to make the mixture soft and spreadable. Discard the thick stalks of the cress, and chop the leaves coarsely. Stir them into the cheese mixture with half the chives, and salt to taste. Toast the bread, or not, as you wish, and spread the cheese thickly over it. Set the cucumber slices on top in overlapping layers. Sprinkle with salt, add a twist of white pepper, and garnish with the remaining chives.

MAKES TWO SANDWICHES

Pita Salad Sandwich

This is a wet, juicy sandwich. Serve it as soon as it is made, with plenty of napkins.

Lemon Vinaigrette (see below)
½ small red onion, thinly sliced
½ small bell pepper, any color, seeded and thinly sliced
1 small cucumber, peeled, seeded, and diced
2½ ounces feta cheese, crumbled
10 Kalamata olives, pitted and chopped
Salt
Pepper
2 whole wheat or white flour pita breads (6 inches across)
1 cup Hummous (page 52)
4 tablespoons basic mayonnaise (page 324)
Lettuce leaves for lining the bread
Sprigs of borage blossoms, for garnish (optional)

Prepare the lemon vinaigrette.

Mix the onion, pepper, cucumber, feta, and olives together, and dress them with the vinaigrette. Season to taste with salt and freshly ground black pepper if necessary.

Cut the pita breads in half and open them up. Spread about a quarter of the hummous and a tablespoon of mayonnaise on each half; lay one or two lettuce leaves on top, and a quarter of the vegetables over the lettuce.

Set the sandwiches hummous side down on the plate, to keep the pita from getting soggy. Serve right away. Sprigs of borage blossoms make a pretty garnish.

LEMON VINAIGRETTE
2½ teaspoons lemon juice
½ teaspoon lemon peel, grated
1 teaspoon sherry vinegar
1 small clove garlic, minced
Large pinch cayenne pepper
1 teaspoon fresh mint, chopped
3 tablespoons virgin olive oil

Mix together the first 6 ingredients; then whisk in the olive oil. Do not season with salt, as the feta cheese and olives in the pita salad are salty already.

MAKES TWO PITAS OR FOUR HALVES

Pan Bagnat

A pan bagnat—a hard roll hollowed out and filled—has limitless possibilities. This version has vegetables, fresh or smoked mozzarella cheese, pickled artichokes, and a basil vinaigrette. It makes a sturdy sandwich to take on a picnic or to work. As it sits, the flavors merge, and the bread soaks up the dressing.

Basil Vinaigrette (see below)
1 large or 2 medium ripe tomatoes
1 cucumber, peeled, seeded, and diced
Several inner stalks of celery, diced
4 scallions, white parts plus a few greens, minced
4 to 6 marinated artichoke hearts, quartered and roughly chopped
1 large red bell pepper, grilled, peeled, and diced
15 to 20 Niçoise olives, pitted and chopped
3 tablespoons pine nuts, pan roasted until lightly browned
Four 6-ounce hard rolls
4 ounces fresh or smoked mozzarella cheese, sliced

Prepare the vinaigrette and set it aside.

Cut the cores out of the tomatoes, slice them in half horizontally, and gently squeeze out the seeds and juice. Chop them coarsely into pieces about ½ inch square.

Combine the tomatoes with the other vegetables and the pine nuts, and dress with the vinaigrette. Taste and adjust the seasonings.

Slice off the top third of each roll. Pull out the soft bread inside the save it for bread crumbs. Take care to leave the bottom of the roll intact. Layer the vegetables and the cheese into the hollowed rolls and replace the tops. Press down the sandwich; then wrap it and set it aside. The sandwich can be served right away, but after an hour or so the roll will have soaked up the flavorful dressing and the various tastes will have merged and developed.

BASIL VINAIGRETTE
1 cup basil leaves (loosely packed), roughly chopped
2 cloves garlic, roughly chopped
6 tablespoons virgin olive oil
2 tablespoons Parmesan or Romano cheese, freshly grated
1 tablespoon red wine vinegar
Salt
Pepper

Purée the basil and garlic in a blender with the olive oil. Scrape it into a bowl, stir in the cheese, and then add the vinegar, salt, and freshly ground black pepper to taste.

MAKES FOUR SANDWICHES

Grilled Cheese with Smoked Chilies and Cilantro

A sandwich with verve, this has clean, strong flavors, hot with smoked jalapeños. The Jicama–Orange Salad would be a cool and sweet side dish.

Soft butter
4 slices white or wheat bread
2 teaspoons or more Chilpotle Purée (page 327)
5 ounces Fontina or cheddar cheese, thinly sliced
1 large tomato, thinly sliced
½ small red onion, very thinly sliced into rounds
1 tablespoon cilantro, coarsely chopped

Butter the outsides of the bread for grilling. Then spread the insides with the chilpotle purée, putting a scant ½ teaspoon on each slice, or more if you like your sandwich very hot. Layer the cheese, tomato, onion, and cilantro on a slice of bread, and place the other on top.

Grill the sandwich over moderate heat in a skillet or on a griddle; turn to brown it on each side. Use a lid over the sandwich to help the cheese melt. The sandwich will be nicely browned and the cheese melted in about 8 minutes. Cut in half diagonally and serve.

MAKES TWO SANDWICHES

Grilled Tofu Sandwich

Marinating and grilling tofu gives it a meaty, chewy texture and flavor, which makes this a very satisfying sandwich. Plan to marinate the tofu for at least 24 hours so that the flavors of the marinade take well.

2 to 3 one-inch slabs (14 to 18 ounces) Marinated Tofu (page 304)
4 slices white or whole wheat bread
Basic mayonnaise (page 324)
Horseradish to taste
1 large tomato, sliced
Salt
Pepper
Lettuce
Thinly sliced red onions (optional)

Prepare a fire if you are grilling the tofu, and grill it on both sides, about 6 inches above the coals, until it is well browned and a little crispy. Otherwise, broil the tofu on both sides.

Spread the bread with mayonnaise and horseradish to taste. Slice the tofu in half, crosswise, to make pieces ½ inch thick, and cut the pieces to fit the bread. Arrange the tomato slices on the tofu, and salt and pepper them; add the onion if you wish. Cover with the lettuce and the top piece of bread.

MAKES TWO SANDWICHES

Tofu Salad Sandwich

Like the Grilled Tofu Sandwich, this has been on the menu since Greens opened. The tofu is seasoned with fresh herbs, mustard, capers, scallions, and finely diced vegetables, which also give it texture. This makes a light, moist, satisfying sandwich filling, especially good on whole wheat bread.

18 ounces firm tofu
5 tablespoons bell pepper, finely diced
5 tablespoons celery, finely diced
4 tablespoons carrot, finely diced
2 tablespoons scallion or red onion, minced
2 tablespoons fresh herbs: parsley, thyme, marjoram, and, if possible, some hyssop or
  summer savory, finely chopped
½ cup basic mayonnaise (page 324)
2 teaspoons capers or sour pickles, chopped
1 teaspoon nutritional yeast (optional)
Mustard to taste
Salt
Pepper
Red wine vinegar or sherry vinegar
Whole wheat bread
1 large tomato, sliced
Lettuce

Rinse the tofu in cool water. To dry and crumble the tofu, place it in a clean kitchen towel, gather the corners together, and twist the towel until all the water has been squeezed out. Put the tofu in a bowl with the vegetables, herbs, 4 tablespoons mayonnaise, capers, nutritional yeast, if using, and mustard to taste. Lightly mix everything together with a fork; then season with salt, freshly ground black pepper, and vinegar. Although the taste may be bland at first, the flavors of the vegetables and herbs will strengthen and gradually permeate the salad as it sits. If possible, let it sit at least half an hour before using.

Spread the tofu salad thickly on a slice of bread, and add the tomato and lettuce. Spread mayonnaise on the other slice of bread before placing it on top.

Homemade pickled vegetables, marinated artichokes, green olives, and other tart, pickled things are good served alongside.

MAKES TWO TO THREE SANDWICHES

Creole Egg Salad Sandwich

This egg salad, salmon colored and peppery with cayenne, is served on charcoal-grilled or toasted bread. Watercress is layered in the middle. A version of the creole egg salad, using just the yolks, can be used for filling deviled eggs.

4 large eggs
Basic mayonnaise (page 324)
4 tablespoons celery, finely diced
2 tablespoons red onion, minced
3 tablespoons sour French pickles (cornichons) or other sour pickle, finely chopped
1 clove garlic, minced
2 teaspoons paprika
½ teaspoon cayenne pepper
1½ teaspoons sherry vinegar
1 teaspoon lime or lemon juice
1 teaspoon capers, chopped
Salt
Bunch watercress
8 slices bread

Put the eggs in a pan, cover them with cold water, and bring them to a boil. Immediately turn off the heat and cover the pan. After they sit for 6½ minutes, pour the water off the eggs, and run them under cold water until they have cooled.

Prepare the mayonnaise and stir in the celery, onion, pickles, and seasonings. Peel and chop the eggs, add the mayonnaise, and season with salt. Break off the smaller branches of watercress from the thick stems; wash and dry them.

Assemble the sandwiches. Spread some egg salad on each slice of bread, and put them together with several sprigs of cress in the middle. Cut in half and serve.

MAKES FOUR SANDWICHES

Cheese and Nut Loaf Sandwich

Like a meat loaf sandwich, this is hearty and reassuring. We make it when we have leftover Cheese and Nut Loaf.

Cheese and Nut Loaf (page 227)
Bread
Mustard
Mayonnaise
Horseradish
Sliced tomato
Salt
Pepper
Fresh herbs: parsley or chives, finely chopped
Lettuce leaf or sprigs of watercress

Preheat the oven to 400°F. Slice the cheese and nut loaf a little less than ½ inch thick. Wrap it in foil and warm it in the oven for 10 to 12 minutes. Spread one slice of bread with mustard, the other with mayonnaise and horseradish. Put the warm nut loaf over the slice with mustard; add the tomato slices and sprinkle them with salt, a grinding of black pepper, and the fresh herbs. Add the lettuce or watercress and put the bread with mayonnaise on top. Slice and serve with a garnish of sour pickles and a little red cabbage salad.

Goat Cheese and Sun-Dried Tomato Toasts

These simple, colorful little cheese toasts can be served as an appetizer or alongside a green salad.

5 ounces mild goat cheese
1 to 2 tablespoons crème fraîche or cream
1 tablespoon fresh herbs: thyme, hyssop, a little rosemary, chopped
Olive oil
12 long slices of baguette, cut diagonally about ¼ inch thick
3 to 4 sun-dried tomatoes, packed in olive oil, sliced into narrow strips
Pepper

Preheat the oven to 425°F. Work the cheese and crème fraîche or cream together, using enough crème fraîche or cream to make the cheese soft and easy to spread. Mix in half the herbs and set it aside. Brush one side of the bread slices with olive oil, and toast them in the oven or under the broiler so that both sides are lightly colored. Remove them from the oven and spread the cheese over the oiled sides. Lay the strips of tomato in a crisscross or diagonal pattern over the top and return the bread to the oven. Bake until the cheese is warm and soft, about 3 minutes. Garnish with the remaining herbs and a grinding of black pepper over the top.

MAKES TWELVE LITTLE TOASTS

Potato Bread

This is a white bread with body and flavor, one that makes good toast and sandwiches. The potatoes make it moist and tender.

1 cup warm whole milk
1 cup warm water
1½ packages active dry yeast (3½ teaspoons)
2 tablespoons honey or sugar
6 to 7 cups unbleached white flour
½ pound small red potatoes
3 tablespoons corn or safflower oil
1 tablespoon salt
1 egg plus 1 tablespoon milk or water, beaten, for egg wash

Combine the milk and water in a large bowl, stir in the yeast, and let it dissolve; then add the honey or sugar and 3 cups of the flour. Beat vigorously with a spoon to form a thick, smooth batter. Cover and let rise in a warm place until doubled in size, about 45 minutes.

While the dough is rising, boil or steam the potatoes, leaving the skins on if you like. Mash the cooked potatoes with a fork, and set them aside to cool. Once the dough has risen, add the potatoes, oil, and salt, and mix well.

Fold in about 2 more cups flour, ½ cup at a time, turning the bowl a quarter turn between folds to approximate the action of kneading. When the dough becomes too thick to handle in this way, turn it out onto a floured surface, and begin kneading. Knead the dough until the surface is smooth and satiny, 5 to 8 minutes, adding only enough flour to keep it from sticking.

Place the dough in an oiled bowl, turn it over so the top is coated, then cover and let rise in a warm place until doubled in size, about 45 minutes. Punch it down, and let it rise again, 35 to 40 minutes.

Shape the dough into two loaves, place them in oiled pans, and let them rise until doubled, about 25 minutes. Preheat the oven to 350°F. Brush the tops with the egg wash. Bake for 50 to 60 minutes, until golden brown on all sides. Remove the loaves from the oven and turn them out onto a rack to cool.

MAKES TWO LOAVES

Cottage Cheese-Dill Bread

A light herbaceous bread flecked with dill, this goes well with many soups, is an excellent sandwich bread, and makes delicious croutons.

1½ packages active dry yeast (3½ teaspoons)
1¾ cups warm water
2 tablespoons honey or sugar
6½ to 7½ cups unbleached white flour
4 tablespoons corn oil
½ medium yellow onion, finely diced
2 eggs, beaten
½ cup cottage cheese
¼ cup dry dill weed
1 tablespoon salt
1 egg plus 1 tablespoon milk or water, beaten, for egg wash

Dissolve the yeast in the warm water in a large bowl; then stir in the honey or sugar and 2½ cups of the flour. Beat vigorously with a spoon to form a smooth, thick batter. Cover and set aside in a warm place to rise until doubled in bulk, about 45 minutes.

While the dough is rising, heat 1 tablespoon of the oil, and sauté the onion until it softens; then set it aside to cool. Once the dough has risen, stir in the onion, eggs, cottage cheese, dill weed, salt, and the remaining 3 tablespoons oil. Mix well. Fold in 3 cups flour, ½ cup at a time, turning the bowl a quarter turn between folds, which will approximate the action of kneading. When the dough is too thick to fold in any more flour, turn it out onto a floured surface.

Knead the dough until the surface is smooth and satiny, about 5 to 8 minutes, adding only enough flour to keep it from sticking. Put the dough into an oiled bowl, turn it over so that the top is coated with oil, cover, and let rise in a warm place until doubled in size, about 40 minutes. Punch it down, and let it rise again, about 30 minutes.

Shape the dough into two loaves, place them in oiled pans, and let them rise to the tops of the pans, about 20 to 25 minutes. Preheat the oven to 350°F. Brush the tops with the egg wash. Bake for 50 to 60 minutes, until nicely browned. Remove the loaves from the oven and turn them out onto racks until cool.

MAKES TWO LOAVES

Whole Wheat Bread

Here is a straightforward whole wheat bread with just enough white flour to give it a light but firm, even texture.

2 packages active dry yeast (4½ to 5 teaspoons)
3 cups warm water
2 tablespoons honey
1 cup unbleached white flour
6 to 7 cups whole wheat flour
3 tablespoons safflower oil
1 tablespoon salt
1 egg plus 1 tablespoon milk or water, beaten, for egg wash

Dissolve the yeast in the water in a large bowl; then stir in the honey, white flour, and 2 cups of the whole wheat flour. Beat vigorously with a spoon to form a thick, smooth batter; then cover and set aside to rise in a warm place for 40 minutes.

Stir in the oil and the salt. Then fold in about 3½ cups whole wheat flour, ½ cup at a time, turning the bowl a quarter turn between folds to approximate the action of kneading. When the dough is too thick to add any more flour, turn it out onto a floured work surface, and knead it for 5 to 8 minutes, adding only enough flour to make a smooth, elastic dough.

Place the dough in an oiled bowl, and turn it over so that the top is coated with oil. Cover and let rise until doubled in size, about 45 to 50 minutes. Punch the dough down, and let it rise again, about 35 to 40 minutes.

Shape the dough into two loaves and let them rise in oiled pans until they have doubled in size, about 25 to 30 minutes. Preheat the oven to 350°F. Brush the tops with the egg wash. Bake for about 1 hour, or until nicely browned on the top, sides, and bottom. Remove the loaves from the oven and turn them out onto a rack to cool.

MAKES TWO LOAVES

Millet Bread

The whole kernels of millet give this wheat bread a crunchy texture and a grainy sweetness. It makes exceptionally good toast; the grains of millet take on a nutty flavor.

2 cups whole millet
1¼ cups hot water, for soaking the millet
3 packages dry yeast (2 tablespoons)
2 cups warm water
2 tablespoons honey
1 cup unbleached white flour
6 to 7 cups whole wheat flour
3 tablespoons corn oil
1 tablespoon salt
1 egg plus 1 tablespoon milk or water, beaten, for egg wash

Start the millet soaking in the hot water. Use very hot tap water, but not boiling water, which will make the millet too soft.

Dissolve the yeast in the warm water in a large bowl; then stir in the honey, white flour, and 1½ cups of the whole wheat flour. Beat vigorously with a spoon to form a smooth, thin batter. Cover and set aside to rise in a warm place until doubled in size, about 40 minutes.

Stir in the corn oil, salt, and millet, including any of the water that has not been absorbed. Then fold in about 3 cups whole wheat flour, ½ cup at a time, turning the bowl a quarter turn between folds to approximate the action of kneading. When the dough is too thick to fold in any more flour, turn it out onto a floured work surface, and knead, adding only enough flour to keep it from sticking.

When the dough is smooth and elastic, after 5 to 8 minutes of kneading, place it in a clean, oiled bowl, and turn it over so the top is coated with oil. Cover and let rise until doubled in size, about 45 minutes. Punch the dough down, and let it rise again, about 35 minutes.

Shape the dough into loaves and place them in oiled bread pans. Let them rise until they have doubled in size, about 25 minutes. Preheat the oven to 350°F. Brush the tops of the loaves with the egg wash. Bake until nicely browned on the top and sides, about 50 to 60 minutes.

MAKES TWO LOAVES

Country French Bread

This sturdy bread, which has a distinct, mildly sour flavor, uses both a sourdough starter and yeast for leavening. The starter, which can be made at home (a recipe is given here and others are available in bread books) or commercially bought, is mixed with fresh flour and water to form a thick batter, which sits overnight. The fermentation that takes place at this time is what gives the bread its sour flavor and smell. In the morning a portion of the batter is removed to provide starter for future use.

Both whole wheat and white flour are used so that the bread has an ample wheat flavor without being too heavy. If you like, the proportions can be varied, using less whole wheat flour for a lighter bread. A baking stone is excellent for this bread, especially for the texture of the crust, although you may have to bake just one round loaf on the stone at a time or change the shape of the loaves so that two can fit. Instructions for using the stone and peel (wooden paddle) are given at the end of the recipe.

THE BREAD
2 cups sourdough starter (see below)
3½ cups warm water
4 to 4½ cups whole wheat flour
2 packages active dry yeast (4½ to 5 teaspoons)
¼ cup warm water
4 teaspoons salt
4 to 6 cups unbleached white flour
Coarse cornmeal

Put the sourdough starter into a bowl with the warm water; add 2 cups of the whole wheat flour, and mix well. Stir in another 2 to 2½ cups whole wheat flour to form a thick batter, or "sponge," and beat it with a spoon to incorporate lots of air. Cover and let it sit overnight, 8 to 10 hours, in a moderately warm place such as a gas oven with the pilot light on. Without the warmth the sponge will take a bit longer to sour.

In the morning remove 2 cups of the sponge and use it to replenish your supply of starter.

Dissolve the yeast in the warm water, and stir it into the remaining batter along with the salt. Fold in the white flour ½ cup at a time, turning the bowl a quarter turn between folds to approximate the action of kneading. When the dough is too thick to continue working in this way, turn it out onto a floured board, and knead it for 5 to 8 minutes, until the surface is smooth and satiny. Place the dough in an oiled bowl, and turn it over once so the top is coated with oil; then cover and set aside in a warm place to rise until it has more than doubled in size, about 1½ hours.

Sprinkle cornmeal on a baking sheet. Punch the dough down, shape it into two round loaves, and place them on the baking sheet with several inches of space between them to give them room to rise. Brush or spray the tops with water, and let the loaves rise until they have more than doubled in size, about 40 minutes.

Preheat the oven to 425°F and place an empty pan on the bottom shelf, so that it will be hot when the bread is ready to bake. Make several cuts in the surface of the dough to allow the bread to expand without tearing during baking—we often make a "tic-tac-toe" cross-hatching of cuts, about ½ inch deep and an inch apart, across the entire surface. Place the bread in the oven, and pour a cup of hot water into the hot, empty pan, being mindful that it will immediately start to steam. Close the oven door to keep the steam in. Bake the bread for 35 to 40 minutes, until a solid crust is formed, well-browned on the bottom and lighter brown on the top. The loaves will sound hollow when thumped. The water in the pan should steam away, so the bread finishes baking in a dry oven. If the water has not steamed away after 25 minutes, remove the water pan from the oven. Take the finished loaves from the oven and turn them out onto a rack to cool.

Using a stone and peel: If using a pizza stone and peel, put the stone in the oven on the upper shelf at the same time as the empty pan goes on the lower shelf, and allow both to preheat for 20 minutes. Dust the wooden peel generously with flour, then scatter cornmeal over the flour. Set the loaves on the peel to let them rise. When they are ready to bake, slide them onto the heated stone, add the water to the pan below, and close the oven door to trap the steam. It may take a little less time for the bread to bake on the stone than on a metal baking sheet.

THE SOURDOUGH STARTER

Foods, including wheat, sour because of the action of microorganisms, which are always present in the air. The basic principle of making a sourdough starter, then, is simply to let some flour "sour" or "spoil" over the course of a few days. To do this, mix 1 cup water with 1½ cups whole wheat flour. Put the mixture in a plastic, ceramic, or glass (but not metal) bowl, and leave it open to the air for two to three days. If a crust forms, stir it in. Add more flour to make a soft dough, cover, and let it sit another couple of days. By this time the dough should have a distinctly sour smell. To promote the souring, use water in which potatoes, pasta, rice, or other grains have been cooked. Some bakers like to add a small amount of active dry yeast to the initial batter.

MAKES TWO ROUND LOAVES, ABOUT 2 POUNDS EACH

PIZZAS

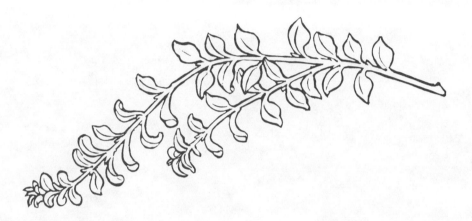

Pizza can be the center of an informal meal or a bright beginning to several courses when it is made as small individual pizzettas or served in thin wedges. Whenever we have begun a dinner with an appetizer of pizza, the dining room seems to come alive and quicken with energy and conversation. Whether it is the irresistible aroma, the prettiness, or the familiarity of pizza, there is a timeless and satisfying quality about a simple bread dough pressed out thin and baked with tasty, fragrant cheeses and vegetables.

All of these pizza recipes make a light meal for one or two, or appetizers for four. They can be completed, from start to finish, including the yeasted dough, in little more than an hour, and the preparations are simple and straightforward. The amount of dough made by one recipe is small and very easy to handle. A single recipe will make a thin-crusted 10-inch pizza, and a double recipe will make a 14-inch pizza. The dough can also be fashioned into small, individual pizzas, or fitted onto rectangular baking sheets and the finished pizza cut into squares. Both the dough and fillings are easy to multiply, and doubling the quantities adds very little time to the preparations. Although the recipes included all contain cheese, this can be omitted or reduced if you desire a lighter pizza.

A pizza stone and peel, or wooden paddle, are well worth buying if you make pizza frequently. The direct heat of the stone makes a wonderfully crisp crust, and the pizza bakes very quickly. The stone can also be used for baking breads that do not require a pan, such as the Country French Bread or any of the olive oil breads. If you use this method, it is important to have the peel well floured before laying down the dough so that it will slide easily onto the stone. It may take a little practice to develop confidence in this maneuver (our first few tries missed by more than an inch), but this is a skill that doesn't take long to acquire. Baking the pizzas in the upper third of a very hot oven (500°F) allows the crust to bake quickly without overcooking the cheese and vegetables.

Pizza Dough

For texture and flavor, a small amount of whole wheat flour and rye flour are combined with the white flour in this pizza dough. However, it can also be made entirely with white flour. You can prepare the ingredients for the topping while the dough is rising.

3 tablespoons hot water
3 tablespoons milk
½ package (about 1¼ teaspoons) active dry yeast
Pinch of sugar
1 tablespoon olive oil
¼ teaspoon salt
1 tablespoon rye flour
2 tablespoons whole wheat flour
⅝ cup unbleached white flour

Combine the water and the milk—the mixture should be not much warmer than body temperature. Add the yeast and the sugar, and stir to dissolve the yeast; then mix in the olive oil, salt, rye flour, and whole wheat flour. Gradually add the white flour, stirring to make a soft, workable dough. Add only enough flour to keep the dough from sticking—the dough should be a little moist. Turn it out onto a lightly floured surface and knead it for about 5 minutes. Put the dough into an oiled bowl, and turn it once so the surface is coated with oil. Cover the bowl and let the dough rise in a warm place until it has doubled in bulk, about 35 to 40 minutes.

Preheat the oven to 500°F and warm the pizza stone, if using, for 20 minutes.

To shape the pizza, first form the dough into a ball, and then roll it out on a floured surface. Pick up the dough and stretch it, shaping it with your hands to form a circle, and roll out more, as necessary. The 10-inch round will be about ⅛ inch thick, at most, and slightly thicker around the edge. Set the dough on a pan or on a well-floured wooden peel, brush it with garlic oil, if desired, and cover it with the topping you have chosen.

Bake the pizza on its pan, or slide it from the peel onto the heated pizza stone.

MAKES ONE 10-INCH PIZZA

Garlic Oil

Cover finely minced garlic amply with olive oil, and use it to brush over the surface of pizza dough before adding the toppings if you like extra garlic. In addition to the flavor, the garlic oil makes a kind of protective seal that keeps the crust crisp and dry.

Niçoise Pizza

This was the first, and for a long time, the only pizza we made. We wanted a pizza that was simple and light, somewhat in the style of the Niçoise pissaladière, an onion tart seasoned with herbs and olives. Gradually cheese and tomatoes were added, then capers, peppers, and fresh lemon. Though it now bears little resemblance to a simple onion tart, the name has remained.

1 recipe Pizza Dough (page 136)
4 to 6 tablespoons virgin olive oil
1 medium yellow onion, thinly sliced
2 cloves garlic, chopped
1 teaspoon Herbes de Provence or mixed marjoram, thyme, and savory
½ teaspoon salt
3 medium tomatoes, peeled, seeded, and chopped
1 thin wedge of lemon
1 tablespoon small capers
24 Niçoise olives, pitted and chopped
3 ounces Provolone cheese, grated
1 tomato, sliced crosswise
1 small green or yellow bell pepper, seeded and thinly sliced
Parmesan
Fresh herbs: lemon thyme, marjoram, summer savory, chopped

Prepare the pizza dough and set it in a warm place to rise.

Warm 2 tablespoons of the olive oil in a skillet, add the onion, garlic, Herbes de Provence or mixed herbs, and the salt, and cook over medium-low heat. The salt should draw enough water out of the onion so that it stews, rather than fries, but if the pan is dry, add a little water. Cook the onion until it is soft; then stir in the chopped tomatoes and raise the heat. Continue cooking until the juices evaporate. Taste, and adjust the seasoning. Slice the lemon wedge thinly crosswise (peel and flesh both), and cut each slice into 2 or 3 pieces, making 18 to 24 small pieces in all.

Preheat the oven to 500°F and if using a pizza stone, warm it for 20 minutes.

Roll out the pizza dough, and place it on a well-floured peel or on a pizza pan. Brush the dough with olive oil, spread on the onion-tomato mixture, and then distribute the lemon, capers, most of the olives, and then the cheese. Arrange the tomato and pepper slices on top, and generously brush them with olive oil.

Bake the pizza on its pan or slide it from the peel onto the heated stone and bake in the upper third of the oven for about 8 to 12 minutes, or until the edges and bottom are nicely browned. Remove the pizza from the oven and garnish it with the rest of the olives, the Parmesan, and the fresh herbs.

This pizza would be good with a Beaujolais or light zinfandel.

MAKES ONE 10-INCH PIZZA

New Potato and Grilled Pepper Pizza

Delicate and sweet new potatoes are thinly sliced and stewed with olive oil, garlic, and herbs. Lemon thyme and lovage, delicious with potatoes, could be used here to good effect. Serve this pizza with one or two little vegetable salads such as the bush bean or summer squash salads.

1 recipe Pizza Dough (page 136)
1 red bell pepper
3 to 4 tablespoons virgin olive oil
1½ teaspoons balsamic vinegar
Salt and pepper
8 ounces small new potatoes or red potatoes, very thinly sliced
1 clove garlic, chopped
4 to 6 teaspoons fresh herbs: parsley with lemon thyme, marjoram, or lovage, coarsely chopped
4 to 6 Kalamata or 12 Niçoise olives, pitted and chopped
1 small red onion, thinly sliced
2 ounces smoked cheese: smoked mozzarella, Brüder Basil, or smoked Gruyère, grated
2 ounces Provolone cheese, grated
Parmesan

Prepare the pizza dough and set it in a warm place to rise.

Roast the pepper over a flame or under the broiler until it is evenly charred. Put the pepper in a covered bowl to steam for 5 to 10 minutes so that the skin loosens; then scrape off the skin and remove the seeds and stem. Cut it into narrow strips, and season it with 1 teaspoon of the olive oil, the vinegar, salt, and freshly ground black pepper. Set aside.

Warm 2 tablespoons olive oil in a large skillet, then add the potatoes, the garlic, 1 teaspoon of the herbs, and salt to taste. Cook for a minute or two, stirring frequently, and then add 2 to 3 tablespoons of water. Cover, reduce the heat, and cook until the potatoes are tender, about 5 to 6 minutes. Remove the lid and raise the heat to reduce any excess liquid. Combine the potatoes with the pepper and add the olives. Season to taste with pepper, and additional salt if necessary.

Preheat the oven to 500°F and if using a pizza stone, warm it for 20 minutes.

Shape the dough, and place it on a well-floured pizza peel or on a pizza pan. Brush the surface with olive oil and cover with the red onion. Distribute about two thirds of the smoked cheese and Provolone, then the potatoes and pepper, and the remaining smoked cheese and Provolone.

Slide the pizza onto the stone or bake it on its pan in the upper third of the oven for about 12 minutes, or until the edges and bottom are nicely browned. After removing the pizza from the oven, sprinkle it with the remaining herbs and freshly grated Parmesan.

MAKES ONE 10-INCH PIZZA

Eggplant and Zucchini Pizza with Basil and Cherry Tomatoes

This summer pizza presents seasonal vegetables in a colorful and delicious way. Use a total of 10 to 12 ounces of eggplant and zucchini.

1 recipe Pizza Dough (page 136)
1 medium zucchini
1 Japanese eggplant
4 to 6 tablespoons virgin olive oil
Salt
Pepper
12 cherry tomatoes, halved or quartered
1 clove garlic, finely chopped
2 ounces mozzarella cheese, grated or thinly sliced
2 ounces Fontina cheese, grated
3 tablespoons basil, finely chopped
Parmesan
Fresh thyme and basil, finely chopped

Prepare the pizza dough and let it rise in a warm place.

Slice the zucchini and the eggplant diagonally into pieces 3 to 4 inches long and ¼ inch thick. Heat 2 tablespoons of the olive oil in a large skillet, add a layer of the vegetables, and turn them over immediately to coat both sides with oil. Fry on each side until lightly browned—the eggplant will take longer than the zucchini—then set them on paper toweling to drain. Cook all the zucchini and eggplant in this way, making sure the oil is hot at the start of each batch. Season well with salt and freshly ground black pepper.

Dress the tomatoes with a tablespoon of the oil, the garlic, and salt and pepper. Drain the tomatoes before putting them on the pizza.

Preheat the oven to 500°F and if using a pizza stone, warm it for 20 minutes.

Shape the dough and place it on a well-floured peel or on a pizza pan, and brush it with olive oil. Distribute most of the mozzarella and Fontina, then the basil. Arrange the zucchini and eggplant slices in overlapping layers with the tomatoes in and among them. Finish with the rest of the mozzarella and Fontina cheese.

Slide the pizza onto the stone or bake on its pan in the upper third of the oven for about 8 to 12 minutes, or until the edges and bottom are well browned. Remove the pizza from the oven and garnish it with freshly grated Parmesan and the herbs.

Variation: Pesto (page 140) can also be used to garnish the pizza in place of the Parmesan and herbs.

MAKES ONE 10-INCH PIZZA

Tomato and Pesto Pizza with Mozzarella

This pizza takes very little time to put together. The flavors and colors are summery and pretty, particularly if you can include a yellow tomato along with the red ones. Fresh mozzarella, if it is available, adds a soft, creamy texture and a mild taste.

1 recipe Pizza Dough (page 136)
3 medium tomatoes, yellow and red
2 tablespoons virgin olive oil
1 clove garlic, finely chopped
Salt and pepper
½ to ¾ cup Pesto (see below)
½ small red onion, thinly sliced
3 ounces mozzarella cheese, thinly sliced
18 Niçoise olives or other small black olives, pits removed

Prepare the pizza dough and set it in a warm place to rise.

Slice the tomatoes thinly crosswise, and season them with 1 tablespoon of the oil, the garlic, salt, and freshly ground black pepper.

Prepare the pesto.

Preheat the oven to 500°F and if using a pizza stone, warm it for 20 minutes.

Shape the dough, set it on a well-floured peel or on a pizza pan, and brush it with oil. Lay the sliced onion on the dough, and arrange the tomatoes and the cheese in overlapping layers.

Slide the pizza onto the stone or bake it on its pan in the upper third of the oven for about 8 to 12 minutes, or until the edges and bottom are well browned. Remove the pizza from the oven, spoon the pesto over the tomatoes, and garnish with the olives.

PESTO (*Makes about ¾ cup*)
⅓ cup basil leaves, chopped
6 tablespoons olive oil
2 tablespoons Parmesan, grated
3 tablespoons walnuts, chopped
1 clove garlic, sliced
Salt

Put the basil in the blender with the olive oil, cheese, walnuts, and garlic. Blend until smooth; then season with salt.

This pesto can also be used to garnish other pizzas, soups, or vegetable dishes. If it is to be spooned over pizza, be sure it isn't too thick—if it is, thin with additional oil.

MAKES ONE 10-INCH PIZZA

Pizza Mexicana

This pizza is hot with chilpotle chilies and brightly seasoned with garlic and cilantro. For fresh peppers, use the mild Anaheims, colorful Gypsy peppers, or a bell pepper.

1 recipe Pizza Dough (page 136)
2 tablespoons Garlic Oil (page 136)
2 tablespoons Chilpotle Purée (page 327)
1 small red onion, thinly sliced
2 ounces muenster or smoked cheese, grated
2 ounces sharp cheddar cheese, grated
2 ounces Monterey Jack cheese, grated
1 Anaheim or Gypsy pepper, or a small green bell pepper, cut into thin strips
1 medium tomato, sliced crosswise, or 12 cherry tomatoes, halved
Salt
Cilantro, coarsely chopped

Prepare the pizza dough, and set it in a warm place to rise.

Preheat the oven to 500°F and if using a pizza stone, warm it for 20 minutes.

Shape the dough, and place it on a well-floured peel or on a pizza pan. Brush it with half the garlic oil; then spread on the chilpotle purée and the red onion. Combine the cheeses, reserving ¼ cup for the top, and put the rest on the pizza. Toss the pepper with the remaining garlic oil, and then arrange it on the cheese along with the tomato. Season with salt and finish with the reserved cheese.

Slide the pizza onto the stone or bake it on its pan in the upper third of the oven for 8 to 12 minutes, or until the crust and bottom are nicely browned. Remove it from the oven and garnish with the cilantro.

For a wine with this pizza, try a sauvignon blanc, vin gris, or zinfandel.

MAKES ONE 10-INCH PIZZA

Peperonata Pizza

Peperonata, an Italian dish of pimentos stewed with tomatoes and onions, is wonderful in its own right and a dish we make often in later summer when peppers are plentiful. It is very good served cold as well as warm, and leftovers can be used to make a delicious pizza. If pimentos aren't available, use red or yellow bell peppers.

1 recipe Pizza Dough (page 136)
1 tablespoon virgin olive oil
3 pimentos or 2 red bell peppers, or 1 red and 1 yellow, cut into thin strips
2 small tomatoes, peeled, seeded, and chopped, or ½ pound canned tomatoes, chopped
1 bay leaf
1 teaspoon fresh thyme, chopped, or ¼ teaspoon dried thyme
3 cloves garlic, finely chopped
Salt
Pepper
2 tablespoons Garlic Oil (page 136)
2 to 3 ounces mozzarella cheese, grated
2 to 3 ounces Provolone cheese, grated
6 to 8 yellow pear tomatoes, sliced into halves or quarters
Parmesan
4 tablespoons basil, cut into narrow ribbons

Prepare the pizza dough and set it aside to rise in a warm place.

Heat the olive oil in a large skillet, and sauté the pimentos or the peppers for 3 to 4 minutes, stirring over high heat. Add the tomatoes, bay leaf, thyme, and garlic. Once the tomato is bubbling, reduce the heat, and simmer for 10 to 15 minutes. Season with salt and freshly ground pepper. Raise the heat at the end of the cooking time to reduce any extra liquid, if necessary.

Preheat the oven to 500°F and if using a pizza stone, warm it for 20 minutes.

Shape the dough, place it on a well-floured peel or on a pizza pan. Brush it with the garlic oil, and then add the peperonata. Distribute the mozzarella and Provolone; then arrange the pear tomatoes on top and season them with salt and freshly ground pepper.

Slide the pizza onto the stone or bake it on its pan on the top shelf of the oven for 8 to 12 minutes, or until the edges and bottom are browned and the cheeses are melted. Remove the pizza from the oven, and garnish it with some freshly grated Parmesan and the basil. Purple opal basil can be used with, or in place of, the green basil.

This pizza could be complemented with a cabernet, or for something more lively, a zinfandel or Beaujolais.

MAKES ONE 10-INCH PIZZA

Mushroom Pizza with Jack and Dry Jack Cheese

The dried mushrooms, richly flavored with a meaty texture, heighten the flavor of the fresh mushrooms. Fresh wild mushrooms would be wonderful to use as well.

1 recipe Pizza Dough (page 136)
½ ounce dried porcini mushrooms
2 tablespoons butter
2 medium leeks, white parts only, quartered and sliced
Salt and pepper
2 tablespoons virgin olive oil
6 to 8 ounces fresh mushrooms, thinly sliced
2 cloves garlic, finely chopped
About 1 tablespoon thyme, marjoram, and parsley, chopped
2 tablespoons white wine or water
3 ounces Monterey Jack cheese, grated
1 ounce dry jack cheese, grated

Prepare the pizza dough and set it in a warm place to rise.

Pour boiling water over the dried mushrooms, just enough to cover, and set them aside to soak for 15 minutes. Rub your fingers over the mushrooms to remove any sand, squeeze out the liquid, and coarsely chop them. Strain the soaking liquid and set it aside.

Heat 1 tablespoon of the butter in a small skillet and add the leeks. Sauté briskly for a minute or so; then add a few spoonfuls of water and lower the heat. Cook until they are tender and the liquid has evaporated; then season with salt and freshly ground black pepper, and set aside.

Heat the remaining butter and the olive oil in a wide skillet. Add the chopped dried mushrooms and cook over high heat for a minute. Add the fresh mushrooms and ½ teaspoon salt, and continue cooking. Add the garlic when the mushrooms have begun to give up their juices.

Cook a few minutes more until the mushrooms taste done; then season with salt, pepper, and half the herbs. Remove the mushrooms from the pan with a slotted spoon, leaving behind any juices. Raise the heat; add the wine and soaking water from the mushrooms, and reduce to a tablespoon or so of syrupy juice.

Preheat the oven to 500°F for 20 minutes and heat the stone, if using.

Shape the pizza dough, and set it on a well-floured peel or on a pizza pan. Brush it with olive oil, and cover it with the leeks, about two-thirds of the cheese, and the mushrooms; then add the rest of the cheese.

Slide the pizza onto the stone or bake it on its pan in the top third of the oven for 8 to 12 minutes. Remove it from the oven, pour the mushroom juices over the top, and garnish it with the remaining fresh herbs.

MAKES ONE 10-INCH PIZZA

Pizza with Escarole, Fontina, and Walnuts

Sautéed with onions, garlic, and chili, the cooked escarole is delicious on this pizza. It is especially well suited for the cooler months when escarole is in season. This preparation of escarole would also make a tasty side dish.

1 recipe Pizza Dough (page 136)
4 walnuts, cracked and coarsely chopped
Walnut oil
2 tablespoons olive oil
1 small red onion, diced
3 cloves garlic, finely chopped
1 small head (8 to 10 ounces) escarole, washed and cut into 1-inch pieces
Salt
Pepper
Balsamic or red wine vinegar to taste
1 or 2 pinches chili flakes
4 or 5 ounces Fontina cheese, grated

Prepare the pizza dough and set it in a warm place to rise.

Preheat the oven to 350°F. Toss the walnuts with a little walnut oil and roast them in the oven for about 5 to 6 minutes, until they are fragrant.

Heat 1½ tablespoons of the olive oil in a large skillet, and sauté the onion for 3 to 4 minutes, until it begins to soften. Stir in the garlic, add the escarole, salt lightly, and cover. Let the escarole cook down for 3 to 4 minutes. Adjust the salt and season to taste with freshly ground black pepper, vinegar, and chili flakes.

Preheat the oven to 500°F and if using a pizza stone, warm it for 20 minutes.

Shape the dough, place it on a well-floured peel or on a pizza pan, and brush it with olive oil. Distribute all but a couple of tablespoons of the Fontina cheese over the dough. Cover with the escarole, the walnuts, and then the rest of the cheese.

Slide the pizza onto the stone or bake it on its pan in the upper third of the oven for about 8 to 12 minutes, or until the edges are nicely browned.

MAKES ONE 10-INCH PIZZA

Goat Cheese Pizza with Red Onions and Green Olives

The goat cheese melts over the red onions, which have been cooked until soft and sweet. Use a creamy goat cheese, either a mild California cheese, or a more strongly flavored French variety, such as Boucheron or Lezay.

1 recipe Pizza Dough (page 136)
3 tablespoons virgin olive oil
2 small red onions, thinly sliced
2 cloves garlic, finely chopped
Salt
Pepper
2 ounces mozzarella cheese, grated or thinly sliced
4 ounces goat cheese
12 to 18 Niçoise or California green olives, pitted and halved
2 sun-dried tomatoes packed in oil, cut into narrow strips
Fresh herbs: mostly parsley and thyme with some rosemary, finely chopped

Prepare the pizza dough and set it aside to rise in a warm place.

Heat 2 tablespoons of the olive oil in a wide skillet and sauté the onions for 3 minutes, or until they turn translucent. Add the garlic, season with salt and freshly ground black pepper, lower the heat, and continue to cook another 3 minutes. Check the seasoning and set the onions aside.

Preheat the oven to 500°F and if using a pizza stone, warm it for 20 minutes.

Shape the dough, and place it on a well-floured peel or on a pizza pan. Brush it with olive oil, and cover it with the sautéed onions and the mozzarella cheese. Distribute the lumps of the soft goat cheese, the olives, and the sun-dried tomatoes over the pizza.

Slide the pizza onto the stone or bake it on its pan in the upper third of the oven for about 8 to 12 minutes, or until the edges and bottom are well browned. Remove it from the oven and sprinkle it with the fresh herbs.

Variation: Rather than sprinkling the pizza with herbs after baking, finish with Pesto (page 140).

MAKES ONE 10-INCH PIZZA

Pizza with Four Cheeses

This is one of the easiest and most quickly assembled pizzas, and the aroma of melting cheeses is irresistible. Rich and cheesy, serve it cut in thin slices as an appetizer, or baked as small, individual pizzas.

1 recipe Pizza Dough (page 136)
2 tablespoons Garlic Oil (page 136)
½ small red onion, thinly sliced
1 ounce (⅓ cup) Gorgonzola cheese, crumbled
2½ ounces Fontina cheese
2½ ounces Provolone cheese
1 ounce Parmesan
1 medium tomato, thinly sliced
Salt
Pepper
1 to 2 teaspoons fresh marjoram, finely chopped

Prepare the pizza dough and set it in a warm place to rise.

Preheat the oven to 500°F and if using a pizza stone, warm it for 20 minutes.

Shape the dough, and place it on a well-floured peel or on a pizza pan. Brush it with the garlic oil, and top with the red onion. Add the cheeses, then the tomato slices. Season the tomato with a little salt and freshly ground black pepper.

Bake the pizza in the upper third of the oven until the edges and bottom are nicely browned and the cheeses are melted, about 8 to 12 minutes. Remove it from the oven and sprinkle it with the fresh marjoram. The cheeses will be quite runny, so let the pizza sit a minute or two before slicing.

MAKES ONE 10-INCH PIZZA

Olive Oil Bread (Focaccia)

We always make this bread for weekend dinners, varying it with additions of rosemary or sage leaves, olives, onions, and coarse sea salt. A flattish bread with toppings, it is like a very simple pizza. The dough, tender and fragrant with olive oil, is a pleasure to make. It is easy to handle and requires only a single rising, making it fairly quick to prepare for lunch or dinner.

Olive oil bread can be shaped in a variety of attractive ways. Usually we roll the dough into an oval, make a number of decorative cuts, then pull the edges of the dough to open the cuts to reveal a pattern. The dough can also be left uncut, covered with onions or studded with green olives. If you have a pizza stone, bake the bread right on it for a good toasty crust.

1 package active dry yeast (2½ teaspoons)
1 cup warm water
1 teaspoon salt
3 tablespoons virgin olive oil
Pinch sugar
2½ cups unbleached white flour or a mixture of whole wheat and white
Coarse sea salt

Dissolve the yeast in the warm water with the salt, olive oil, and sugar. Stir in the flour in two or three additions. Once a dough has formed, turn it out onto a board dusted with flour, and knead it for several minutes, adding only enough flour to keep the dough from sticking. When the dough is smooth and shiny, set it in a lightly oiled bowl, turn it over once, cover, and put it in a warm place to rise, until it is doubled in bulk, about 30 to 40 minutes.

After the dough has risen, turn it onto the counter and shape it with a rolling pin into one large or two small ovals, about ½ inch thick. Make several cuts in the dough in the center of the oval—parallel or fan-shaped cuts, or many little diagonal slices—then pull the edges of the dough apart, opening the cuts to give the loaf a latticed appearance. If you are going to bake the bread on a pizza stone, transfer the loaf to a well-floured peel. Otherwise, put it on an oiled baking sheet. Brush the bread with olive oil, sprinkle it lightly with coarse sea salt, and set it aside to rise for 20 minutes.

Preheat the oven to 450°F and if using a pizza stone, warm it for 20 minutes.

After it has risen, slide the dough onto the stone, or put the baking sheet in the oven. Bake in the top third of the oven for 20 to 30 minutes, or until the bread is nicely browned. You can spray the bread and oven with a fine mist of water two or three times during the first 10 minutes of the baking to help give the bread a good crust. Serve hot from the oven, with or without butter.

Variations

OLIVE OIL BREAD WITH GREEN OLIVES

Use about 2 dozen green Niçoise olives. After the dough has been rolled out into an oval, place it on a baking sheet or a floured pizza peel. Use your fingertips to make firm indentations over the surface of the dough, and place an olive in each indentation. Brush it with olive oil, let it rise for 20 minutes, then bake according to the recipe.

OLIVE OIL BREAD WITH ONIONS

Use about a cup of thinly sliced red or yellow onions. Toss them with olive oil and season them with salt and freshly ground black pepper. After the dough has been shaped into an oval, place it on a baking sheet or on a floured pizza peel. Spread the onions over the top and press them lightly into the dough. Let the bread rise for 20 minutes, then bake according to the recipe.

OLIVE OIL BREAD WITH ROSEMARY

Coarsely chop enough rosemary leaves to measure about a tablespoon. When the dough has risen for the first time, turn it out onto the counter and roll it in the rosemary, or simply scatter the chopped herb over the top. Shape the loaf, lightly pressing or rolling the rosemary into it. Make decorative cuts over the top, brush it with oil, sprinkle with coarse sea salt, if you like, and set the dough on a baking sheet or a floured pizza peel to rise for 20 minutes. Bake according to the recipe.

OLIVE OIL BREAD WITH SAGE LEAVES

Take about a dozen fresh sage leaves, coarsely chop half of them, and knead them lightly into the dough or scatter them over the surface of the oval. Press the whole leaves onto the surface, brush with olive oil, and sprinkle with coarse sea salt. Set the dough on a baking sheet or floured pizza peel and let it rise for 20 minutes. Bake according to the recipe.

SERVES FOUR

PASTA

The taste and texture of fresh pasta is always delightful, and transforming a few basic ingredients into supple sheets of pasta dough can be as relaxing and satisfying an activity as baking bread. Although ready-made fresh noodles are now more available, they are never as fresh as those you can make yourself, nor do they have the diversity of pasta made at home, which can incorporate different herbs and flours.

Once learned, pasta making is easy and quick, which makes it very useful for good, but more or less last-minute, meals that are as suitable for company as for the family. Only 10 minutes are needed to make the dough, which then needs to rest for about an hour, but can be left to rest for several hours. While the dough is resting, the remainder of the ingredients for the pasta, and the meal, can be prepared. Rolling out the dough and cutting the noodles take little time.

Only a few ingredients are needed for pasta dough—the basic recipes simply require good unbleached all-purpose white flour, salt, large eggs, and olive oil or water. If the eggs are from chickens that have been allowed to range and scratch for their food, the yolks will have a brilliant color, which gives the noodles a pale yellow-gold hue, the true color of egg pasta. Variations on the basic dough include the use of other flours, particularly buckwheat and whole wheat flours mixed with the white; the addition of finely chopped herbs, used singly or in a mixture; and spinach, which colors the dough a bright green. Other aromatics can be used in pasta as well, such as saffron or pepper.

Making the Dough

The basic process in pasta making is the even distribution of the egg and a small amount of water or oil throughout the flour. The dough is then gathered into a ball and kneaded well. This is similar to the making of pastry dough, in which the butter is cut into the flour in finer and finer increments until the whole mixture resembles a coarse meal, at which point a little liquid is added and the whole gathered together. This can be done in a food processor quite easily, or by hand. Getting the knack of making dough by hand takes practice. The most commonly made error is attempting to form the dough before the egg is well distributed throughout the flour, which makes it very difficult to incorporate the remainder of the flour. The usual response is to add more and more water to bring the dough together and eventually to quit in frustration. Have some dried pasta on hand for those occasions, but keep trying and suddenly you'll get the hang of it.

Although many pasta instructions illustrate the flour heaped on a board with a well in the middle for the egg, we have found it easier to use a bowl when making small quantities of pasta. Combine the flour and the salt in a bowl and make a well. Break the egg first into a cup and lightly beat it; then pour it into the well and add the oil. If you are using any extra water, put it in the cup and use it to wash out any remaining egg. Gradually, and very lightly, work the egg into the flour, using your fingertips. Continue this process until the egg is well distributed and an even, fine-textured meal is formed; then turn the mixture out onto the counter and begin to knead. If the dough is too dry and won't hold together, add water a few drops at a time, and keep working, adding more water in small amounts if necessary. It is far better to make the dough on the dry side because a wet dough, though easier to handle at first, can produce noodles that stick together disastrously in the end.

Knead the dough until it is smooth and shiny, 5 to 10 minutes. It may be stiffer than other doughs you are accustomed to, but as you get more practice making pasta, your hands will become stronger, and it will become easier. If you cannot bring the dough together into a smooth mass, go ahead and wrap it in plastic, or put it in a plastic bag to rest for an hour or so. After the dough has rested, flatten it out as best you can; then feed it through the widest setting on your pasta machine four or five times—this will help complete the kneading process and will smooth out the dough. The machines that are the most popular, economical, and easiest to come by are the small metal ones that clamp onto a counter and are rolled by hand.

Using a Food Processor

A food processor can be used to very good effect to distribute the egg throughout the flour. Put the flour, salt, herbs, or spinach, if using, in the work bowl and briefly mix them together. Stop the motor, add the egg and the oil or water, then process for about 10 seconds and stop—you will see tiny pearls of amalgamated egg and flour. Turn them out onto the work surface, and then gather them together to form a ball. Knead the dough until it is smooth and satiny. If herbs or spinach have been included, and the dough feels a little wet, knead in more flour at this point. Wrap the dough in plastic, or put it in a plastic bag, and set it aside to rest for at least an hour.

Rolling the Dough and Shaping the Noodles

After the dough has rested, press on it to flatten it out so that it will go easily through the pasta machine. Open your machine to the widest aperture and roll the dough through several times. It is useless at this point to attempt to dry out a wet dough by kneading more flour into it—most of the flour will stay on the surface and not enough can be absorbed to make a helpful difference. If the dough is only a little too damp, dusting the counter, as well as the dough, lightly with flour or semolina will help keep the sheets from sticking to one another.

Roll the dough to the desired thinness. The setting used depends on the type of machine you have. Sometimes the narrowest setting is too thin, making a dough that is nearly transparent and far too fragile. On the other hand, the next-to-the-last setting may not be narrow enough. If this is the case, send the dough through the next-to-the-last setting several times, until it is as thin as you want. Experiment with your machine to find out what works best. When passing it through for the final time, cut the dough into 12-inch lengths, which are easier to handle than one long sheet. Lightly dust each sheet with semolina or flour, and stack the sheets on top of one another.

To cut the dough into noodles, use either of the two sizes available on your machine, or cut them by hand. To do this, either cut the strip of dough straight across the width to make noodles that are about 6 inches long, or roll a length of dough loosely from the short end; then cut across the desired width. Take care not to make the noodles so long that they are difficult to manage on the plate. Once the noodles are cut, toss them with semolina or flour, making sure they are well separated, and let them sit for a few minutes on the counter to dry. If you are not going to cook them within a quarter hour or so, put them on a lightly floured baking sheet, cover them with plastic wrap, and refrigerate until needed. This will keep the noodles soft and fresh.

If you have made more noodles than you want to cook, allow them to dry; then store them in a plastic bag for another meal.

Pasta can be cut in any width, but various standard sizes have been suggested in most recipes, largely to indicate whether a wide or narrow noodle is best suited to the other ingredients.

The sizes we have used most often are:

Taglierini ($\frac{1}{16}$ inch)
Linguine ($\frac{1}{8}$ inch)
Tagliatelle ($\frac{1}{4}$ inch)
Fettuccine ($\frac{3}{8}$ inch)
Pappardelle (1 inch)

Cooking Pasta

Always use plenty of boiling water, 5 to 6 quarts, or more, and add the salt just before adding the pasta—about a teaspoon per quart. Shake any excess flour off the noodles, add them to the water all at once, and stir them with a fork (rather than a spoon) to separate them from one another. Thin fresh pasta will cook in less than 1 minute—even as little as ½ minute, so stay close to the pot and check the noodles frequently. Fresh noodles are cooked when they no longer have a floury taste and are still a little firm. Only dried pasta can be cooked really *al dente*, as it is made with the harder semolina. When the noodles are ready, lift them out all at once with a strainer, let most of the water drain off, and add them directly to the sauce or vegetables. (It is neither necessary nor useful to rinse noodles in cold water.) Removing the noodles with a strainer takes less time than carrying the pot to the sink and pouring the noodles into a colander. The easiest kinds of strainer to use are an oval-shaped basket strainer or a Chinese skimmer, which is, essentially, a flattish woven wire basket attached to a bamboo handle. Chinese skimmers are inexpensive and easy to find in oriental markets that sell basic cookware supplies.

Finishing and Serving the Pasta

For most of the recipes in this section, the cooked noodles are added to a pan with the vegetables or sauce and tossed repeatedly by lifting the noodles with a pair of tongs until they are coated with the sauce. Metal tongs, which can be found in restaurant supply houses or good hardware stores, are a very useful tool for this job. They allow you to be very dexterous in portioning, and they can be held in one hand while the pan is held in the other. They come in various lengths—a shorter length is easier to manage.

Pasta should be served on heated plates or bowls because it cools quickly. In addition, sauces of reduced cream will soon thicken on a cold plate, but will better retain their liquid qualities on a heated one.

Portions

The portion size, whether it is large or small, depends on who is eating, the richness of the dish, and what else is being served. We prefer to serve moderate portions of 2½ to 3 ounces, even when the pasta is the main part of the meal. Not only is this an ample amount of food, it is also a small enough portion to stay hot while being eaten, provided the plates are heated. Also, unless a pasta dish has a fairly complex array of textures and tastes, large servings can become tiresome after a certain point.

A recipe using 1 cup of flour will make about 7 ounces of pasta dough. This will make two large, or three or four moderately large, servings. It is easy to double the recipe, and 2 cups of flour are, in some ways, easier to knead than one, as there is more to get hold of. Three cups of flour, or three times a recipe, may be a little difficult to knead if your hands are not used to it. In this case, make the dough, divide it in half, and knead half at a time. Leftover noodles, as mentioned before, can be allowed to dry, then stored and used at another time.

Egg Pasta*

1 cup unbleached all-purpose flour
Good pinch salt
1 large egg
1 teaspoon olive oil
A few drops water, if necessary

Combine the flour and the salt in a bowl, make a well in the middle, and add the egg and the olive oil. Using your fingers, lightly and gradually work the egg into the flour so that it is completely distributed throughout. When it is well combined, press the mixture together to form a dough. Turn it out onto a counter and begin to work it together. If it is too dry, add drops of water, a few at a time, to moisten the dough and help it come together. Knead the dough for about 10 minutes, until it feels smooth and supple. Put it in a plastic bag or wrap it in plastic, and set it aside to rest at least a half hour, preferably an hour, before rolling it out.

MAKES 7 OUNCES PASTA DOUGH

Fresh Herb Pasta

Use a single herb, such as basil, marjoram, or Italian parsley, or a mixture of herbs, such as savory, hyssop, thyme, and lovage, or a mixture of leaves, such as borage, sorrel, and chard. Chop them very finely and add them to the flour.

1 cup loosely packed herb leaves
1 cup unbleached all-purpose flour
Good pinch salt
1 large egg
1 teaspoon olive oil

Wash the herbs and dry them as thoroughly as possible, blotting them in a kitchen towel. Chop them very finely and measure out no more than 3 tablespoons (if there are extra herbs, set them aside to use in your pasta dish). Combine the herbs with the flour and the salt, add the egg and the oil, and proceed according to the basic recipe. If the dough is wetter than usual, knead in a little extra flour to make it dry.

MAKES 7 OUNCES PASTA DOUGH

*If you are unfamiliar with making pasta dough, first read the detailed instructions on pages 151–153.

Spinach Pasta

Spinach makes this dough a bright, uniform green. It is especially handsome in layered dishes of lasagne. The spinach contains a lot of moisture, so it may be necessary to knead in an additional ½ cup or more of flour to make the pasta sufficiently dry.

1 cup spinach leaves without stems, loosely packed
1 large egg
1 to 1½ cups unbleached all-purpose flour
Pinch salt

Wash the spinach leaves and dry them as well as you can by blotting them in a kitchen towel. Chop them very finely to make a coarse purée; then gently squeeze out the water and set it aside. Mix the chopped spinach with the egg; then stir it into 1 cup of flour mixed with the salt. Proceed to make the dough as usual. If it is very moist, knead in as much flour as it will hold. If the spinach was squeezed so thoroughly dry that extra moisture is needed, use the juice from the spinach.

MAKES 7 OUNCES PASTA DOUGH

Rosemary Pasta

Proceed as with the herb pasta, using just the long, narrow leaves of the rosemary that have been finely chopped. Because the flavor is particularly strong, use 1 tablespoon rather than 3 tablespoons.

Whole Wheat Pasta

Use equal parts of whole wheat and unbleached white flour, or less whole wheat, depending on the flavor you want. A little extra water may be required in order to bring the dough together.

Buckwheat Pasta

Replace ¼ or ⅓ cup of the white flour with buckwheat flour, and use at least a teaspoon of water because buckwheat is very absorbent. Do not be surprised if even more water is required to bring the dough together. The dough will be dark and flecked with brown and gray.

Spring Pasta with Artichokes, Mushrooms, and Peas

The colors of this pasta are soft and delicate, as tentative as mild days in February. Make this in springtime with morels or the more strongly flavored shaggy parasols (or *Lepiota rachodes*). If wild mushrooms aren't available, use the cultivated ones.

1 recipe Egg Pasta (page 155)
1 lemon
2 large artichokes
5 tablespoons butter
3 tablespoons virgin olive oil
4 shallots or 2 newly pulled red onions, thinly sliced
1 clove garlic, finely chopped
½ teaspoon fresh thyme leaves, chopped
6 to 8 ounces mushrooms, cut into irregular pieces or slices
Salt and pepper
2 stalks celery, cut into small squares
1 pound tender pod peas, shelled
1 tablespoon parsley, chopped
2 teaspoons chervil or tarragon, chopped
Parmesan

Prepare the pasta dough and let it rest; then roll it out and cut it into strips ⅛ inch wide to make linguine. Bring a large pot of water to a boil.

Squeeze the lemon into 1½ cups water. Then trim the artichokes: Snap off the tough outer leaves and trim around the base. Slice off the remaining leaves; then cut the base into quarters and remove the choke. Dice the heart into small cubes, and put them into the acidulated water to keep them from turning brown.

Melt the butter and the olive oil in a wide skillet, add the shallots or onions, garlic, thyme, and drained artichokes, and stew them together for 1 minute. Add 1 cup of water from the pasta pot, cover, and cook over medium heat for another 2 minutes. Raise the heat, add the mushrooms, season with salt and freshly ground black pepper, and cook for 1 minute. Add the celery and the peas and more water, if the first cup has cooked off, so that there will be a little sauce at the end. Lower the heat again, cover, and cook gently for 3 to 4 minutes, or until the mushrooms are done.

Cook the pasta, scoop it out when it is done, and add it to the pan with the vegetables. Season it with the fresh herbs, and more ground pepper and salt if needed, and toss with a pair of tongs to mix everything together. Serve with the Parmesan.

SERVES TWO TO FOUR

Tagliatelle, Asparagus, and Peas with Saffron Cream

The peas are small and fresh, the asparagus, pencil thin. The fragrant saffron-flavored cream makes this pasta filling and substantial. This is a rather special dish, fine for a company dinner.

1 recipe Egg Pasta (page 155)
1 pound thin asparagus
1 pound English peas
1/8 teaspoon saffron threads
1 tablespoon butter
2 shallots, finely diced
1 1/2 cups light or heavy cream
Salt
Chervil, roughly chopped
1 thin strip lemon peel, very finely slivered
Parmesan
Pepper

Prepare the pasta dough and set it aside to rest. Then roll it out and cut it into strips 1/4 inch wide. Bring a large pot of water to a boil.

Snap off the tough ends of the asparagus and set them aside to use in a soup stock, or discard them. Cut off the tips, leaving them about 2 inches long, and slice the remaining pieces on the diagonal or into short rounds. Shell the peas. Cover the saffron with a couple of tablespoons of boiling water, to make an infusion.

Melt the butter in a wide sauté pan, and gently cook the shallots for several minutes, or until they are soft. Add the cream and the saffron infusion, bring to a boil, reduce slightly, and season with salt.

When the pasta water is boiling, add salt, and cook the asparagus, and then the peas, in the boiling water. Scoop them out when they are done and add them to the cream. Next cook the pasta; when it is done, add it to the cream, turning it over several times with a pair of tongs to coat it with the sauce. Add the chervil leaves and the lemon peel, and serve on warm plates with grated Parmesan and freshly ground pepper.

SERVES FOUR

Pappardelle and Spring Vegetable Ragout

Here we have a simple stew with a few vegetables and wide hand-cut noodles. Choose fava beans that are fairly small because the large ones tend to be dry. If favas aren't available, use English peas or sugar snap peas sliced into strips.

1 recipe Egg Pasta (page 155)
2 to 3 leeks, white parts only (about 8 ounces)
4 medium artichokes
Juice of 2 lemons
1½ pounds fava beans
3 tablespoons extra virgin olive oil
1 clove garlic, finely chopped
1 small fennel bulb, trimmed, quartered, and sliced into ¼-inch pieces
2 teaspoons tarragon, chopped
Salt
3 tablespoons butter
1 tablespoon parsley, chopped
Pepper
Parmesan

Prepare the pasta dough and set it aside to rest. Then roll it out and cut it by hand into strips about 1 inch wide. Bring a large pot of water to a boil.

Slice the leeks in half lengthwise; then cut them diagonally into strips about ¼ inch wide, and wash them well. Put the lemon juice into 2 cups water. Trim the artichokes: Remove the stem from each artichoke and discard the dark outer leaves, snapping them off at the base, until the pale inner leaves are reached. Cut off the top two thirds of the leaves and trim the base around the broken stubs. Quarter the artichokes, remove the choke with a paring knife, and then cut them into thirds. Place the pieces in the acidulated water as you work, so that they won't turn brown.

Shell the fava beans and cook them in the pasta water for about 1 minute. Remove them to a bowl of cool water, then, one by one, squeeze off the outer pale green skin; the bean underneath will be bright green. Put them aside.

Warm the olive oil in a wide skillet, add the leeks and the drained artichokes, and sauté over medium-high heat for 1 minute. Add the garlic, fennel, tarragon, and some salt; then pour in about 1½ cups of the water from the pasta pot. Cover the pan, lower the heat, and stew slowly until the artichokes are done, about 15 to 20 minutes. During the last 5 minutes, add the fava beans and the butter.

Add salt to the boiling pasta water, then the pasta, and cook until the noodles are done. Scoop the pasta out, add it to the vegetables, along with the parsley, and toss well with tongs to coat the noodles with the sauce. Season with freshly ground black pepper and serve the vegetables and pasta with the Parmesan.

SERVES TWO TO FOUR

Green Ravioli with Ricotta, Marjoram, and Cream

These large ravioli are creamy and fragrant. Serve them with something fresh and clean tasting like the Cherry Tomatoes Sautéed with Shallots and Herbs, or a salad of watercress and citrus.

2 recipes Spinach Pasta (page 156)
1 pound fresh creamy ricotta
2 egg yolks
4 tablespoons Italian parsley, chopped
4 tablespoons marjoram, chopped
1 tablespoon chives, sliced into narrow rounds
1 cup Parmesan, grated
Nutmeg
Salt
Pepper
2 tablespoons butter
6 tablespoons coarse bread crumbs
Butter
Bread crumbs
Cream with Shallots, Marjoram, and Chives (page 311)

Prepare the pasta dough, and set it aside to rest while you make the filling.

Combine the ricotta and the egg yolks so that they are well blended; then stir in the parsley, marjoram, chives, and cheese. Add a few scrapings nutmeg, enough to give a subtle fragrance, and season with salt and freshly ground black pepper to taste.

When the dough has rested and you are ready to make the ravioli, have at hand a spray bottle of water, or a bowl of water and a pastry brush, as well as a ravioli cutter. Roll the pasta to the thinnest setting on your machine, and cut the final pieces into lengths that are easy to handle, about 12 to 18 inches.

Lightly dust each strip of pasta with flour, and set the strips on top of one another. Work with one strip at a time, and cover the others with a kitchen towel. Lay the pasta on a lightly floured surface, fold the strip over on itself lengthwise, gently crease the fold to make a line, and then open it back up. Using the line as a guide, place rounded tablespoons of filling just below the line, leaving at least 2 inches between each spoonful. Spray a fine mist over the pasta or paint a strip of water around the edges and between each spoonful of filling; this will help the ravioli hold together. Fold the top half of the pasta over the filling. Press between each ravioli to form a seal, forcing out the air as you do so; then press around the bottom and sides of the strip. Use a ravioli cutter to finally seal and separate each ravioli, and set the finished squares on a floured baking sheet.

Bring a large pot of water to a boil. While it is heating, melt the butter in a small skillet; add the bread crumbs and cook until they are crisp and golden. Set them aside.

Prepare the cream sauce.

Salt the boiling water, add the ravioli, and cook them until they are done, about 2 to 4 minutes, depending on how long they have rested. Test by trying a corner of one. Gently remove the ravioli with a sieve or slotted spoon, and add them to the cream. Heat so that the cream bubbles over the ravioli, and then serve on warm plates, pouring the cream sauce over the top. Garnish with the bread crumbs. For wine, consider a dry chenin blanc or a dry pinot blanc.

MAKES 16 TO 18 RAVIOLI; SERVES FOUR TO SIX

Taglierini, Zucchini, Lemon, Pine Nuts, and Herbs

The narrow strips of zucchini, tipped with color, echo the shape of the pasta. This is a summery dish that can be enjoyed far in advance of the actual arrival of summer—an anticipatory pasta.

1 recipe Egg Pasta (page 155)
8 ounces small, firm green or golden zucchini
½ cup mixed fresh herbs: Italian parsley, marjoram, basil, chervil, hyssop, lemon thyme, and others
1 lemon
6 tablespoons virgin olive oil
5 tablespoons pine nuts
4 shallots, thinly sliced, then roughly chopped
4 teaspoons tiny capers, rinsed in water
2 sun-dried tomatoes, cut into narrow strips
Salt
Pepper
Parmesan (optional)

Prepare the pasta dough and set it aside to rest. Then roll it out, and cut it into strips ¹⁄₁₆ inch wide. Bring a large pot of water to a boil.

Slice the zucchini diagonally into pieces about the same thickness as the pasta. Line up the slices and cut them into narrow matchsticks. Each one will be tipped with green or gold.

Make a selection of fresh herbs from those suggested in the ingredients list. Pull the leaves off the stems and chop them, but not too finely. Include any flowers, such as the purple flowers of the hyssop, or pink thyme blossoms. With a vegetable peeler remove a thin strip of peel from the lemon and cut it into fine slivers.

Heat 2 tablespoons of the olive oil in a small pan and add the pine nuts. Cook them until they begin to color; then add the shallots. Cook the two together over medium-low heat until the shallots are soft and the pine nuts are browned. Transfer them to a wide bowl and add the rest of the oil, the capers, lemon peel, sun-dried tomatoes, and herbs. Season with salt, freshly ground black pepper, and ½ teaspoon, or so, lemon juice, to taste.

Add salt to the boiling water, drop in the zucchini, and cook it about 1 minute. Scoop it out, shake off the water, and add it to the bowl with the other ingredients. Next cook the pasta, scoop it out, and add it to the bowl as well. Toss with a pair of tongs so that the noodles are coated with the oil and herbs. Serve with the cheese passed separately. For a wine, serve a sauvignon blanc.

SERVES TWO TO FOUR

Fresh Egg Pasta with Tomatoes, Tarragon, and Cream

This is very nice as a first or second course. The cream is left a little thin and is tinted pink from the tomatoes. Dried noodles can also be used—they won't absorb the cream so readily—but the fresh ones have a lovely delicacy.

1 recipe Egg Pasta (page 155) or 7 to 8 ounces dried pasta shapes
2 or 3 tomatoes, about 1½ pounds in all
1½ cups heavy or light cream
2 shallots, finely diced
1 tablespoon tarragon, chopped
1 tablespoon parsley, chopped
Salt
Pepper
Parmesan

If you are using fresh pasta, prepare the egg pasta and set it aside to rest. Then roll it out and cut it into pieces ¼ inch wide.

If possible, use large, meaty tomatoes. Bring a small pan of water to a boil, immerse the tomatoes to a count of ten, or until the skins break; then remove them and immediately rinse them in cool water. Cut out the cores, peel and halve them, and gently squeeze out the juice and seeds. Cut the tomatoes into nice-looking pieces ½ inch square, and set them aside.

Bring a large pot of water to a boil. While it is heating, prepare the sauce. Heat the cream with the shallots in a wide skillet. Bring to a slow boil, and when it begins to thicken (after 30 seconds), add half the herbs and the tomatoes. Allow it to reduce to the thickness you want; then turn off the heat and season to taste with salt.

When the pasta water comes to a boil, add salt, then the pasta. Stir, then cook until done. Scoop out the pasta and add it directly to the cream. Heat for 1 minute, while turning over the strands of pasta with a pair of tongs to coat them with the cream. Add the rest of the herbs and several twists of black pepper. Serve the pasta in warm shallow bowls and top it with the cheese.

SERVES TWO TO FOUR

Cockscombs, Tomatoes, Garlic, and Parsley

This is a very simple pasta to make when really delicious little tomatoes of any variety—Sweet 100s, yellow pear, or the usual cherry tomatoes—are in season. The cockscombs (or other dried pasta shapes) catch and hold both the tomatoes and their juices, bringing all the tastes together.

2 pints (4 cups) cherry tomatoes, or mixed varieties
2 shallots or a bunch of scallions, finely chopped
4 cloves garlic, finely chopped
6 tablespoons virgin olive oil
1 small bunch Italian parsley, roughly chopped
Salt
Pepper
8 ounces cockscombs or other dried pasta shapes
Parmesan

Wash and stem the tomatoes. Then, using a serrated knife, slice them into halves or quarters. Put them in a large skillet (without heat) with the shallots or scallions, garlic, olive oil, and parsley. Season to taste with salt and freshly ground black pepper.

Bring a large pot of water to a boil; add salt and the pasta. Cook until the pasta is *al dente*. About 1 minute before the pasta is finished cooking, warm the tomatoes quickly over medium-high heat. Don't let them cook, or they will fall apart and the skins will toughen; they just need to be heated. When the pasta is finished cooking, drain it, add it to the pan, and toss well. Serve immediately, garnished with the cheese and more pepper.

Variation: This recipe also makes a good pasta salad. Add the hot pasta to the tomatoes and other ingredients, without warming them, toss well, and season to taste with red wine vinegar. Salty, vinegary things—olives and capers—can be added as well. Omit the cheese.

SERVES TWO TO FOUR

Fettuccine with Roasted Eggplant, Peppers, and Basil

We often make eggplant pastas with eggplant that has been fried in oil, then cut into strips; but in this version the small oriental eggplants are roasted whole, shredded, and marinated in olive oil with garlic and basil. While the color is not as pretty as in the fried version, the meat itself is soft and succulent, and absorbs the pure flavor of the oil beautifully. Toasted bread crumbs give the dish some crunch, and, if available, plum-colored opal basil adds both color and flavor.

1 recipe Egg Pasta (page 155)
1 to 1½ pounds Japanese eggplants
6 tablespoons virgin or extra virgin olive oil
3 cloves garlic, finely chopped
20 Niçoise or Gaeta olives, pitted and chopped
½ cup basil leaves, coarsely chopped
Salt and pepper
2 bell peppers, red or yellow
1 cup coarse bread crumbs
Balsamic vinegar to taste
Parmesan or Romano cheese

Prepare the pasta dough and set it aside to rest. Then roll it out and cut it by hand into ⅜-inch-wide strips.

Preheat the oven to 400°F. Prick the eggplants in several places, and bake them until they are wrinkled and soft, about 20 minutes. Turn them once halfway through.

Let the eggplants cool a few minutes; then slit them open and peel away the skins. Shred or tear the eggplants into pieces, and combine them with the olive oil, garlic, olives, and half the basil. Season with salt and freshly ground black pepper, and set aside.

Roast the peppers over a flame or in a very hot oven and scrape off the skins (page 51). Cut them into strips about ¼ inch wide, and add them to the eggplant. Toss the bread crumbs with enough oil to moisten them, then toast them in the hot oven until they are crisp and golden.

When you are ready to cook the pasta, bring a large pot of water to a boil. Transfer the eggplant and peppers to a wide skillet, and warm them very gently over low heat. Salt the water, cook the pasta, scoop it out, and add it to the vegetables. Add the rest of the basil leaves, toss well with a pair of tongs, and season to taste with salt, freshly ground pepper, and vinegar. Garnish each plate with the bread crumbs, and pass around grated cheese. For wines, consider a chilled Beaujolais or a dry vin gris. This could also be accompanied with a light- to medium-bodied pinot noir.

SERVES TWO TO FOUR

Fettuccine and Saffron Butter with Spinach and Roasted Peppers

The ingredients in this pasta are varied and have strong individual tastes. Make the butter first so the flavors can develop fully.

THE SAFFRON BUTTER
6 tablespoons unsalted butter
1 large shallot, finely diced
1 tablespoon marjoram or basil leaves, roughly chopped
1 tablespoon parsley leaves, roughly chopped
⅛ teaspoon saffron threads or powder soaked in 1 teaspoon hot water
Pinch cayenne pepper
Grated peel of 1 lemon or ½ orange
¼ teaspoon salt

Cream the butter with the rest of the ingredients. Cover and set aside until needed.

THE PASTA AND THE VEGETABLES
1 recipe Egg Pasta (page 155)
2 bell peppers, 1 red and 1 yellow, or both one color
1 tablespoon light olive oil
1 bunch spinach
¼ cup pine nuts
3 tablespoons virgin olive oil
1 red onion, quartered and thinly sliced
1 cup Summer Vegetable Stock (page 64) or water
3 cloves garlic, finely chopped
½ teaspoon salt
Pepper
Parmesan

Prepare the pasta dough and set it aside to rest. Then roll it out and cut it into strips ⅜ inch wide, using a cutting attachment or by hand. Bring a large pot of water to a boil.

Slice the peppers in half, remove the seeds and cores, and brush both sides with the light olive oil. Bake them cut side down in a hot oven until the skins are wrinkled and loose. When they are cool enough to handle, scrape off the skins, and cut them into narrow strips.

Stem the spinach, and wash it well to get rid of the sand. Pull out and discard any bruised and yellow leaves; then cut it into wide strips. Toast the pine nuts in a dry skillet until they are golden.

When you are ready to cook the pasta, heat the virgin olive oil in a skillet, and add the onion. Fry it over medium-high heat for about 1 minute; then add the stock or water, garlic, peppers, and salt. Cook together another minute; then add the spinach. Stir with a pair of tongs until the spinach wilts; then lower the heat and add all but a tablespoon of the saffron butter. Add a little more stock or water if the first cup has evaporated, so that the melted butter and the pan juices create a sauce.

Add salt to the boiling pasta water, cook the pasta, scoop it out, and add it to the vegetables along with the rest of the saffron butter. Mix well with a pair of tongs, letting the butter melt into the noodles. Season the dish with pepper, and lastly add the pine nuts and toss well. Serve the pasta garnished with the grated cheese, and for a wine, try a crisp sauvignon blanc.

SERVES TWO TO FOUR

Spinach, Cheese, and Tomato Lasagne

There are several steps in making this fragrant, summery lasagne, but none are difficult. Begin with making the lasagne, then the tomato sauce, the filling, and the béchamel. Time spent preparing fresh pasta is well repaid in the lightness and delicacy of the dish.

2 recipes Egg Pasta (page 155)
8 ounces mozzarella cheese, fresh, if possible
2½ pounds tomatoes, fresh or canned, peeled, seeded, chopped
3 tablespoons virgin olive oil
1 small onion, finely diced
2 cloves garlic, finely chopped
1½ teaspoons fresh marjoram or oregano, or ½ teaspoon dried
Salt and pepper
½ cup red wine
Sugar, if necessary
Red wine vinegar

Prepare the pasta dough and set it aside to rest. Grate or slice the cheese; then prepare the tomato sauce and spinach-cheese filling.

Heat the oil in a wide skillet, add the onion, garlic, and marjoram or oregano, and sauté until the onion is transparent and soft. Season with salt; then add the tomatoes and the wine. Cook slowly until the sauce is thickened. If the tomatoes are overly tart, correct the acidity by adding a pinch or two of sugar. Once they are cooked, pass them through a food mill; then season to taste with a few drops of vinegar, freshly ground black pepper, and more salt if needed.

THE SPINACH–CHEESE FILLING
3 small or 2 large bunches spinach
2 tablespoons olive oil
1 small onion, finely diced
2 cloves garlic, finely chopped
Salt, pepper, and nutmeg
2 cups ricotta
2 eggs
1 cup Parmesan, freshly grated
3 tablespoons parsley, chopped
1 teaspoon lemon peel, minced or grated

Remove the stems from the spinach; discard any bruised or yellow leaves. Wash the spinach well in two changes of water. Roughly chop the leaves into small pieces about an inch square. In a wide pan, heat the oil and sauté the onion for several minutes; then add half the garlic, the spinach leaves, and a sprinkling of salt. Cook until the spinach is wilted; then remove it to a bowl and combine it with the ricotta, eggs, Parmesan, the remaining garlic, and the parsley and lemon peel. Season to taste with salt, freshly ground pepper, and a scraping or two of nutmeg.

THE BÉCHAMEL
1 tablespoon butter
1 tablespoon flour
1 cup milk
Salt, pepper, and nutmeg

Melt the butter in a saucepan, add the flour, and cook over a low flame for 2 to 3 minutes, stirring continuously. Scald the milk in a separate pan; then pour it all at once into the flour-butter mixture, whisking as you do so. Season with salt, pepper, and a scraping of nutmeg, and continue to cook the sauce for 15 minutes over low heat, giving it an occasional stir.

Roll out the pasta dough to the thinnest setting, and cut the final strips into pieces that will fit your baking pan. Bring a pot of water to a boil and add salt. Have ready a large bowl of cold water. Cook several pieces of dough at a time. Pull them out when they rise to the surface, and put them in the cold water to cool; then spread them on a kitchen towel. Continue cooking until all are done.

Preheat the oven to 350°F. Butter a 9-by-13-inch baking dish and spread half the béchamel over the bottom. Piece together several strips of the pasta so that they cover the bottom and hang over the edges of the baking dish. (Later they will be folded over the top to make a package, effectively sealing in the fillings.)

Spread half the tomato sauce over this first layer of pasta and cover it with half the mozzarella. Put down another layer of pasta and cover these with half the spinach-cheese filling. Continue the sequence with more pasta, tomato and mozzarella, pasta and spinach-cheese filling. Finish by laying one or two strips of pasta down the center and folding the overhanging edges over the top. Cover with the remaining béchamel sauce.

Cover the lasagne with foil, and bake for 20 minutes. Remove the foil and continue baking another 15 minutes, or until the top is puffed and browned. Let the lasagne rest for a few minutes; then cut it into pieces and serve. A chilled Beaujolais or a vin gris would go well with this.

Note: Lasagne can also be made using commercial fresh pasta sheets, which will be thicker than those you make at home. These commercial pasta sheets often come in pieces about 9 by 13 inches, each weighing about 4 ounces; 1½ pounds should be more than enough. Use 4 or 5 sheets and do not try to overlap the bottom layer as in the basic recipe. Though fresh pasta makers often say the lasagne sheets need not be precooked, the lasagne will be lighter and moister if they are.

SERVES SIX

Basil Fettuccine with Green Beans, Walnuts, and Crème Fraîche

With this recipe it is necessary to use crème fraîche rather than sour cream because the latter will curdle when heated. Fresh walnuts, harvested in early September, are delicate and sweet; combining them with the cream and slender green beans makes a perfect end-of-summer pasta.

1 recipe Fresh Herb Pasta (page 155) made with 4 teaspoons chopped basil
12 to 16 ounces small green beans
½ cup walnuts, freshly shelled
3 tablespoons butter
4 shallots, finely chopped
½ cup basil leaves, cut into fine strips
2 cloves garlic, finely chopped
Salt
1½ cups Summer Vegetable Stock (page 64) or water
1½ cups crème fraîche
Pepper
Chili flakes (optional)
Parmesan

Prepare the pasta dough and set it aside to rest. Then roll it out and cut it into strips about ⅜ inch wide, by hand or with the fettuccine attachment on a machine. Bring a large pot of water to a boil.

Preheat the oven to 350°F. Cut the tips and tails from the beans. Chop the walnuts into fairly small pieces and toast them in the oven for 5 minutes.

Melt the butter in a skillet; add the shallots and cook over medium-low heat for about 1 minute. Add 2 tablespoons of the basil, the garlic, a sprinkling of salt, and 1½ cups of the stock or water. Cook over medium heat until the shallots are soft; then stir in the crème fraîche, and cook until it is slightly thickened. Taste and season with salt, freshly ground black pepper, and the chili flakes, if using.

When the pasta water has begun to boil, add salt and cook the beans for 2 to 3 minutes, or until they are tender but still a little firm. Scoop them out and add them to the shallots and cream. Using the same water, cook the pasta, scoop it out, and add it to the pan along with the rest of the basil leaves.

Toss well, add the walnuts, and toss again. Serve on heated plates and garnish with the Parmesan. Serve with a dry sauvignon blanc.

SERVES TWO TO FOUR

Spinach Noodle Pudding

This old-fashioned savory-sweet dish of spinach and noodles is baked in a custard. Easy to prepare, it looks quite handsome when unmolded. Serve it warm from the oven with sour cream and a crisp, tart salad of watercress and apples. Leftovers are good sliced and fried in butter. A fresh smooth ricotta can be used in place of the cottage cheese.

½ cup natural cream cheese
1 cup small curd cottage cheese, or ricotta
3 large eggs, beaten
1¼ cups milk
½ cup golden raisins, soaked for 10 minutes in warm water and drained
¼ teaspoon nutmeg
¼ teaspoon cinnamon or cardamom
Salt
1 bunch spinach, stems removed
4 ounces dry flat egg noodles or fettuccine
Pepper
Sour cream, for garnish

Bring a large pot of water to a boil. Combine the cream cheese with the cottage cheese or ricotta and stir in the eggs. Add the milk, raisins, spices, and ½ teaspoon salt.

When the water boils, add several teaspoons of salt, and plunge in the spinach. Cook it for 1 minute, then scoop it out with a strainer. Press out as much of the water as possible with the back of a spoon; then chop the spinach fairly fine and add it to the other ingredients.

Return the water to a boil, add the noodles, and give them a stir with a fork. Taste the noodles as they cook, and drain them when they are still somewhat under-cooked. Add the drained noodles to the custard, and stir well. Add freshly ground black pepper, and taste to make sure the seasonings are right.

Preheat the oven to 350°F. Generously butter a baking dish with a 6-cup capacity (an oval baking dish with 4-inch sides makes an especially attractive pudding). Pour in the noodle-custard mixture and bake it until it is firm and nicely browned on top, about 1 hour. Remove it from the oven, slide a knife around the sides of the baking dish, and turn the pudding onto a serving plate. Slice it with a serrated knife, and serve it warm with sour cream.

SERVES SIX

Fresh Herb Noodles with Three Cheeses

These herb noodles are aromatic, creamy, and rich. Serve them with something tart and fresh such as the Fennel and Blood Orange Salad.

1 recipe Fresh Herb Pasta (page 155)
1½ cups heavy cream
4 ounces Fontina, cut into small cubes
2 to 3 ounces Gorgonzola
1 clove garlic, finely chopped
1 teaspoon marjoram, chopped
1 teaspoon parsley, chopped
Salt
Pepper
Parmesan Reggiano

Prepare the pasta dough, using mostly marjoram and parsley with a little thyme for the herbs. Let it rest; then roll it out and cut it into tagliatelle or fettuccine. Bring a large pot of water to a boil.

In a wide sauté pan, heat the cream slowly with most of the Fontina, all the Gorgonzola, and the garlic. Cook over low heat, stirring as the cheeses melt, until the sauce is slightly thickened. Stir in the fresh herbs, and season with salt if needed—the cheeses may have contributed enough saltiness.

Salt the boiling water, cook the pasta, scoop it out, and add it directly to the pan along with the rest of the Fontina. Turn the pasta over repeatedly with a pair of tongs to distribute the sauce. Serve onto heated plates or bowls. Finish with a grinding of black pepper and a generous amount of grated Parmesan Reggiano.

SERVES TWO TO FOUR

Wide Green Noodles, Cauliflower, and Broccoli with Mustard Butter

Hand-cut silky green noodles are cooked with a mass of cauliflower and broccoli florets and a mustardy shallot butter. The flowers are tiny, so they will disperse throughout the dish. If the curiously shaped broccoli romanesco that is covered with twisted, spiraled peaks can be found, it would be perfect here, mixed with the broccoli and cauliflower. Be sure to include any small tender leaves, chopped and stewed in the butter.

1 recipe Fresh Herb Pasta (page 155) or Spinach Pasta (page 156)
7 tablespoons soft butter
2 tablespoons strong Dijon mustard
3 shallots, finely diced
2 cloves garlic, minced
2 teaspoons balsamic vinegar, or more, to taste
2 tablespoons parsley or a handful of rocket leaves (arugula), roughly chopped
1 cup bread crumbs
2 sun-dried tomatoes, cut into small pieces
3 to 4 cups broccoli and cauliflower florets, broken into tiny pieces
Thin strip lemon peel, very finely slivered
Salt
Pepper
Parmesan

Prepare the pasta dough, set it aside to rest; then roll it out and cut it by hand into strips about ½ inch wide. Bring a large pot of water to a boil.

Cream 4 tablespoons of the butter with the mustard, shallots, garlic, vinegar, and parsley or rocket. This can be done well ahead of time, then covered and set aside until needed.

Melt the remaining butter, add the bread crumbs, and fry them until they are crisp and browned.

When you are ready to cook the pasta, salt the boiling water, melt the mustard butter over a low flame and add ½ cup of the pasta water and the sun-dried tomatoes. Drop the broccoli and cauliflower into the boiling pasta water, return to a boil, and cook about 1 minute. Scoop them out, and add them to the butter.

Next cook the pasta; then add it with the lemon to the vegetables. Toss well with a pair of tongs to mix everything together, and season with salt and freshly ground black pepper. Serve on warm plates garnished with the bread crumbs and freshly grated Parmesan.

SERVES TWO TO FOUR

Cannelloni with Greens and Walnut Sauce

These cannelloni are filled with chard, or a mixture of greens, including beet greens and spinach. If red chard or beet greens are used, the stems will bleed splotches of pink through the dough, which will make it rather pretty.

2 recipes Egg Pasta (page 155)
Walnut Sauce (page 313)
3 pounds chard or mixed greens, weighed with the stems
2 cups ricotta
½ cup each grated Parmesan and Romano cheese or 1 cup grated Parmesan
3 cloves garlic, finely chopped
4 tablespoons parsley, chopped
4 eggs
Grated peel and juice of 1 lemon
Nutmeg
Salt
Pepper

Prepare the pasta dough and set it aside to rest while you make the sauce and the filling. The double recipe of egg pasta will make a little more dough than is needed, but you can cut the extra dough into noodles and set them aside to dry for use at another time.

Prepare the walnut sauce.

Bring a large pot of water to boil for the greens. Cut the leaves away from the thick center stems and wash them well. Save the chard stems to cook separately or for soup stock. If using a mixture of greens, cook them separately—some will take longer than others. When the water comes to a boil, add salt, and cook the greens until they are tender, 3 to 5 minutes. Scoop them out and set them in a colander. Press out as much moisture as possible with your hands or the back of a wooden spoon; then set the greens on a cutting board and chop them finely. Combine them with the ricotta, grated cheeses, garlic, parsley, eggs, and lemon peel, and mix well. Season to taste with a few scrapings of nutmeg, salt, freshly ground pepper, and lemon juice—make the seasoning lively and bright.

While rolling out the pasta bring a fresh pot of water to a boil. To make the cannelloni, roll the dough out to the thinnest setting and cut the final strip into squares approximately 4 by 4 inches. Most pasta machines will roll a sheet 6 inches wide. The cannelloni can be made that wide, but the smaller shape is easier to handle and better fits most baking dishes. Have ready a bowl of cold water to receive the cooked squares, and a clean kitchen towel. When the water boils, add salt; then drop the squares, several at a time, into the water. They will immediately fall to the bottom, then rise to the surface. When the pasta returns to the surface, remove it with a slotted spoon to the cold water. Once cooled, lay the squares out on the towel.

Fill the cannelloni by laying 3 to 4 tablespoons of the chard along one end of each square of pasta. Loosely roll or fold the pasta around the filling.

Preheat the oven to 375°F, and generously butter one 9-by-13-inch rectangular baking dish. Lay the cannelloni, seam side up, next to one another, and cover them with half the walnut sauce. Bake them for 20 minutes; then let them rest for 10 minutes more.

Chop a little extra parsley, and stir it into the remaining sauce. Make a pool of the sauce on the bottom of each serving plate and set the cannelloni on top, or pour the sauce over the cannelloni.

MAKES 12 TO 16 CANNELLONI; SERVES FOUR TO SIX

Winter Squash Ravioli

These delicate ravioli are served with cream reduced with brown butter and dry jack cheese. Their creamy smoothness is contrasted with the garnish of chopped nuts.

2 recipes Egg Pasta (page 155)
1 butternut squash weighing at least 1½ pounds
2 tablespoons olive oil
Salt
Pepper
1 clove garlic, chopped
4 to 5 sage leaves, chopped
About ½ cup dry jack or Romano cheese, grated
1 tablespoon parsley, chopped
1½ cups light cream
4 tablespoons clarified butter (page 325)
Few drops balsamic vinegar
¼ cup walnuts or hazelnuts, shelled

Prepare the pasta dough and set it aside to rest.

Preheat the oven to 375°F. Cut the squash in half lengthwise, scoop out the seeds, and brush the surface with some of the olive oil. Season it with salt and pepper and bake, cut side down, until it is completely soft. Scoop out the meat, and pass it through a food mill. Cook briefly to dry it out: Warm the rest of the oil in a skillet with the garlic and the sage leaves until they are aromatic, taking care not to brown the garlic. Add the squash and cook, stirring frequently, until it is fairly dry, 5 to 10 minutes, depending on the type of squash used. Remove it from the heat and season it with several tablespoons of the cheese, salt and pepper, and half the parsley. Make sure the filling is cool or at room temperature before forming the ravioli.

When the dough has rested and you are ready to make the ravioli, have at hand a spray bottle of water, or a bowl of water and a pastry brush, as well as a ravioli cutter. Roll the pasta to the thinnest setting on your machine and cut the final pieces into lengths that are easy to handle, about 12 to 18 inches long.

Lightly dust each strip of pasta with flour, and set the strips on top of one another. Work with one strip at a time, and cover the others with a kitchen towel. Lay the pasta on a lightly floured surface, fold to make a line, then open it up. Using the line as a guide, place rounded tablespoons of the squash filling just below the line, leaving at least 2 inches between each spoonful. Spray a fine mist over the pasta or paint a strip of water around the edges and between each spoonful of filling. Roll the top half of the pasta over the filling. Press between each ravioli to form a seal, forcing out the air as you do so; then press around the bottom and sides of the strip. Use a ravioli cutter to finally seal and separate each ravioli; then set the finished squares onto a floured baking sheet. If they are not to be cooked right away, cover them with plastic wrap and refrigerate until needed. If the filling is not too wet, they should keep well this way for several hours.

Roast the nuts in a 350°F oven for 5 to 8 minutes, and then chop them finely.

When you are ready to cook the ravioli, bring a large pot of water to a boil, and while it is heating, make the sauce. Combine the cream and the clarified butter in a wide skillet, bring to a boil, and reduce until slightly thickened. Stir in the remaining parsley, season with salt and freshly ground black pepper, and add a few drops of vinegar. Salt the pasta water and add the ravioli. Cook them at a gentle boil until they are done, about 2 to 4 minutes (sample a corner of one); then scoop them out and add them to the pan with the cream. Slide the pan back and forth a few times to coat them with the sauce. Serve garnished with additional cheese, freshly milled pepper, and the roasted nuts. For wine, consider a medium-bodied zinfandel or a Côtes-du-Rhône.

MAKES ABOUT 30 RAVIOLI; SERVES FOUR TO SIX

Spaghetti Tossed with Eggs, Smoked Cheese, and Fried Bread Crumbs

This spaghetti dish makes a perfectly satisfying late night meal, as well as a simple nourishing supper after a long, tiring day.

4 tablespoons virgin olive oil
1 large yellow onion, diced into ½-inch squares
½ teaspoon red chili flakes
Salt
2 cloves garlic, finely chopped
12 green olives, chopped into small pieces
2 tablespoons parsley, chopped
2 eggs
4 tablespoons Parmesan, grated
¾ cup tiny croutons or coarse bread crumbs
3 tablespoons butter
8 ounces dried spaghetti
3 ounces smoked cheese, grated
Pepper

Bring a pot of water to a boil for the spaghetti. Heat the oil in a frying pan, add the onions and the chili flakes, and cook over medium-high heat, stirring frequently until the onion is nicely browned. Season with salt, turn off the heat, add the garlic, and stir for 20 seconds or so; then scrape the contents into a large bowl and add the olives and the parsley.

Beat the eggs in a small bowl with the Parmesan. Fry the croutons or bread crumbs in the butter until they are crisp and golden.

When you are ready to cook the spaghetti, add salt to the water, then the pasta, and cook until it is *al dente*. Pour it directly into a colander, and shake off the excess water; then add the spaghetti to the bowl with the onion. Pour in the eggs and toss well to coat the noodles and cook the eggs. If the eggs don't cook as much as you would like, put everything in a non-stick pan and warm it gently while stirring, until the eggs are properly done; then stir in the cheese and season with plenty of coarsely ground pepper. Toss one more time with the croutons or bread crumbs.

SERVES TWO TO FOUR

Linguine with Fresh and Dry Shiitake Mushrooms

Dry shiitake mushrooms have a concentrated flavor; the fresh ones have a firm, meaty texture. If fresh shiitake aren't available, use cultivated field mushrooms. Egg, Spinach, and Buckwheat Pasta all go well with mushrooms.

1 recipe Spinach Pasta (page 156), Egg Pasta (page 155), or Buckwheat Pasta (page 156)
1 ounce dried shiitake mushrooms
8 ounces fresh shiitake mushrooms
1½ cups light or heavy cream
½ small onion, chopped
Several thyme branches
1 bay leaf
2 tablespoons olive oil
2 tablespoons butter
Salt and pepper
2 cloves garlic, finely chopped
2 teaspoons parsley, chopped
2 teaspoons marjoram, chopped

Prepare the pasta and set it aside to rest. Roll it out and cut it into strips ⅛ inch wide. Bring a large pot of water to a boil.

Cover the dried mushrooms with 1½ cups boiling water and let them stand until they have softened, about 20 minutes. Run your fingers over the underside of the caps and around the stems to loosen any sand and grit; then squeeze them dry, saving the soaking liquid. Cut off the stems, set them aside, and slice the caps into thin strips. Strain the soaking liquid through a strainer lined with a paper towel or a coffee filter, and set it aside. Wipe or brush the fresh mushrooms if they are dirty, and remove the stems that are tough and rubbery. Thinly slice the caps.

Slowly heat the cream in a small saucepan with the stems from both the dried and fresh mushrooms, the onion, thyme, and bay leaf. Bring the cream to a boil; then turn off the heat, cover, and set aside to steep for 20 minutes.

After the cream has steeped, heat the oil and the butter in a sauté pan. Add all the mushrooms, and sauté over high heat for 3 to 4 minutes. Lower the heat, season with salt and freshly ground black pepper, add the garlic, and cook another 1 or 2 minutes, stirring constantly. Add the mushroom soaking water and let it cook with the mushrooms until it is reduced by half. Then pour the cream through a strainer into the pan, bring to a boil, and reduce for 30 seconds.

Salt the boiling water and cook the pasta, scoop it out, and add it to the pan along with the fresh herbs. Turn the pasta over in the sauce several times to coat it well; then serve it garnished with additional milled pepper. A medium-bodied zinfandel would go well with this pasta, as would a Côtes-du-Rhône.

SERVES TWO TO FOUR

Buckwheat Linguine with French Lentils, Carrots, and Chard

Made with fresh narrow noodles and tiny French lentils, this dish is not as heavy as one might guess, but light and earthy with beautiful tones of brown, green, and orange. It is a perfect dish for fall or winter.

1 recipe Buckwheat Pasta (page 156) or 8 ounces soba *(Japanese buckwheat noodles)*
½ cup French lentils
1 bay leaf
¼ teaspoon salt
Few spoonfuls virgin olive oil
Pepper
1 bunch red or green chard
6 tablespoons extra virgin olive oil
2 cloves garlic, finely chopped
2 medium carrots, cut into ¼-inch squares
1 celery stalk, cut into ¼-inch squares
1 or 2 leeks (about 5 ounces), white parts only, finely chopped
Water or vegetable stock
1 tablespoon parsley, chopped
Parmesan

Prepare the pasta dough and set it aside to rest. Then roll it out and cut it into strips ⅛ inch wide. Bring a large pot of water to a boil.

Sort and rinse the lentils well; then cover them generously with water and bring them to a boil with the bay leaf and the salt. Cook at a slow boil until they are tender, 15 to 20 minutes. Be careful not to overcook them or they will lose their shape and texture. Drain them and save the liquid for soup stock. Toss the lentils with a little olive oil. Season with salt and freshly ground black pepper, and set them aside.

Cut the chard leaves away from the stems, wash them well, and slice the leaves into strips about 1 inch wide. Save the stems to cook by themselves or to use in stock.

Slowly warm 4 tablespoons of the olive oil in a skillet or sauté pan with the garlic and cook for about 1 minute, taking care that the garlic doesn't color. Add the lentils, carrots, celery, and leeks, and stir to coat them with oil. Cook for 1 minute over medium heat with a sprinkling of salt; then pour in ¾ cup water or stock and add the chard. Stew until the vegetables are tender. If the liquid evaporates, add more so that there will be a little sauce at the end.

When the vegetables are done, salt the boiling water and cook the noodles; then scoop them out and add them to the vegetables. Toss everything together, add the parsley, and season with freshly ground pepper. Serve the noodles and spoon the remaining olive oil over the top. Finish with a handful of grated Parmesan cheese. For a wine, you could serve a light pinot noir or Côtes-du-Rhône.

Variation
BUCKWHEAT PASTA WITH FRENCH LENTILS AND GOAT CHEESE
Goat cheese goes very well both with chard and buckwheat. Crumble 5 ounces goat cheese into the pasta and vegetables, and toss just enough to incorporate it; then finish with olive oil and Parmesan.

SERVES TWO TO FOUR

Baked Buckwheat Noodles with Brown Butter and Savoy Cabbage

The idea for this pasta came from a one-line description in Waverley Root's *Foods of Italy*. Buckwheat noodles are layered and baked with potatoes, leeks, and savoy cabbage, and seasoned with pepper, sage, and a soft, creamy Taleggio cheese. The potatoes are not a redundant starch but provide a textural contrast to the noodles. There is an imported buckwheat pasta from Italy, *pizzocher*, but since it is difficult to find, we usually use the Japanese dried buckwheat noodles, *soba*, which have a good chewy texture and strong buckwheat flavor. You can also make your own buckwheat pasta and cut it into wide strips. This is hearty cold-weather fare.

1 stick sweet butter, cut into pieces
8 to 10 large fresh sage leaves or 1 teaspoon dried sage
1 large clove garlic, sliced
Salt
8 ounces potatoes, peeled and cut into ½-inch cubes
2 to 3 large leeks (about 3 cups), white parts only, quartered and sliced ⅜ inch thick
2 cloves garlic, minced
1 small dry red chili, broken into pieces, seeds removed
1 to 1½ pounds savoy cabbage, quartered and shredded into ½-inch slices
½ cup Parmesan, freshly grated
Pepper
1 pound buckwheat noodles
½ pound soft cheese, such as Taleggio or Bel Paese, or fresh mozzarella, sliced

Slowly melt the butter in a heavy pan over low heat with 4 of the sage leaves, or half the dried sage, and the sliced garlic. When the garlic is browned, remove it, but continue to cook the butter until it is light brown and has a distinctly nutty aroma. Pour it through a strainer lined with a layer of cheesecloth to remove the sediment.

While the butter is browning, bring 4 quarts of water to a boil, add 1 tablespoon of salt, and the potatoes. Cook until they are fairly tender (5 to 8 minutes), but just short of being completely done—they will bake further in the oven. Scoop them out, rinse them immediately with cool water, and set them in a colander to drain. Save the cooking water for the pasta.

Chop the remaining sage leaves. Heat half the strained butter in a wide sauté pan, add the leeks, the sage, half the minced garlic, and the chili. Cook over medium-low heat until the leeks are soft; then add the cabbage, 1 teaspoon of salt, and a little water. If necessary, add the cabbage in stages, letting some of it cook down before adding the rest. Cover the pan with a lid, and stew the vegetables slowly until the cabbage is cooked. Add the Parmesan and season with plenty of freshly ground black pepper and more salt, if needed, to make the flavors bright and strong.

Return the water to a boil, add the pasta, and partially cook it, leaving it a little chewier than you would want to eat. Drain it in a colander; then return it to the empty pot and toss it with the rest of the butter, the remaining garlic, and the potatoes. Season to taste with pepper, and salt if needed.

Butter an earthenware casserole. Lay down half the noodles, half the vegetables, and most of the sliced cheese. With your fingers or a fork, wiggle the three layers so that the vegetables and cheese can slip in among the noodles. Add the rest of the pasta and the cheese and end with a layer of vegetables. At this point the casserole can be refrigerated until you are ready to prepare dinner.

Preheat the oven to 425°F. Put the casserole in the oven and bake until it is hot throughout and the cheese is melted, about 15 to 20 minutes. If the casserole is cold when put in the oven, cover it for the first 15 minutes; then remove the cover and continue baking until it is heated. Serve this hearty, full-flavored dish with a full-bodied Chianti or a light to medium cabernet sauvignon.

SERVES FOUR TO SIX

Rosemary Linguine with Caramelized Onions and Walnuts

Rosemary has a singularly strong flavor that goes well with sweet caramelized onions and roasted walnuts. Greens such as turnip greens, mustard greens, and broccoli rabe, go well served alongside.

1 recipe Rosemary Pasta (page 156)
½ cup walnuts, freshly cracked
4 large red onions
2 tablespoons butter
2 tablespoons virgin olive oil
2 bay leaves
½ teaspoon rosemary, chopped
1 teaspoon dried sage or 2 teaspoons fresh sage leaves, roughly chopped,
    or 4 thyme branches or ¼ tablespoon dried thyme
1 teaspoon salt
1 clove garlic, finely chopped or mashed in a mortar
½ cup dry white wine
1 cup water
1 tablespoon walnut oil
Pepper
¾ cup Gruyère cheese, grated
Parmesan (optional)

Prepare the pasta and set it aside to rest. Then roll it out and cut it into strips ⅛ inch wide. Bring a large pot of water to a boil.

Preheat the oven to 350°F. Roast the walnuts for 5 to 7 minutes, until they smell toasted. Chop them into small pieces.

Quarter the onions and slice them crosswise as thinly and as close to the same size as possible so that they will cook evenly. Warm the butter and the olive oil slowly in a wide skillet with the bay leaves, rosemary, and sage or thyme to bring out the flavor of the herbs.

When the butter and oil are hot and the herbs are fragrant, add the onions and the salt. Stir well to coat the onions thoroughly with the butter and oil; then cook slowly over low heat, stirring occasionally for 15 to 20 minutes, then frequently until they are a deep golden-brown. While cooking the onions, be sure that none are left stuck to the upper sides of the pan, where they will dry out and burn.

Once the onions are caramelized, add the garlic and the wine. Raise the heat slightly and cook until the wine is reduced to a syrupy consistency; then add the water and the walnut oil. Stir well, and cook slowly until it is reduced by about one-third, leaving enough liquid to form a little sauce. Add more water if necessary, and season to taste with salt and freshly ground black pepper.

Salt the boiling water and cook the pasta; then scoop it out. Add it to the onions along with half the walnuts and the Gruyère cheese. Toss well to mix everything; then serve on heated plates with the rest of the walnuts on top. Pass the Parmesan for those who wish it. This is a pasta with strong, rich tastes. For wine, consider a California cabernet or a Chianti.

SERVES TWO TO FOUR

Mushroom Lasagne

The effort to make your own pasta dough is well repaid by the lightness and tenderness of this lasagne. Dried wild mushrooms give a pervasive woodsy flavor to the cultivated mushrooms, and both egg and spinach pasta are excellent choices. Additional cheese can be included if desired, perhaps a mild fresh mozzarella, thinly sliced, and layered with the mushrooms.

There are three parts to this recipe: first, make the pasta dough; second, cook the mushrooms; third, prepare the béchamel; then assemble the lasagne.

2 recipes Egg Pasta (page 155) or Spinach Pasta (page 156), or one recipe each
1 cup Parmesan, Asiago, or dry jack cheese
½ ounce dried porcini mushrooms
4 tablespoons butter
2 tablespoons olive oil
2 bay leaves
1 small onion, finely diced
2 medium carrots, peeled and finely diced into small squares
2 celery stalks, diced into small squares
½ teaspoon dried thyme
1 tablespoon marjoram, chopped, or 1 teaspoon dried marjoram
1 tablespoon parsley, chopped
1½ pounds mushrooms, wiped clean and thinly sliced
3 cloves garlic, finely chopped
Salt and pepper
4 tablespoons tomato purée

Prepare the pasta dough and set it aside to rest. Grate the cheese and set it aside.

Cover the dried mushrooms with 1 cup boiling water and let them sit for 20 minutes. Squeeze them dry, saving the soaking liquid, and roughly chop them into small pieces. Pour the soaking liquid through a strainer lined with a paper towel.

A 12-inch cast iron skillet or fireproof casserole is ideal for cooking the fresh mushrooms because it can comfortably contain all of them at once. If you don't have a large enough pan, cook some of the mushrooms separately in a few tablespoons olive oil; you can add them back to the other vegetables later.

Gradually warm the butter and the olive oil with the bay leaves over medium heat; then add the onion, carrots, celery, and herbs. Raise the heat, and cook briskly, stirring frequently, for 3 or 4 minutes; then add the sliced mushrooms, the garlic, and the dried mushrooms. Season with salt and cook 3 minutes; then add the soaking water from the mushrooms and the tomato purée. Continue to cook until the mushrooms are tender and a syrupy juice remains on the bottom of the pan. Season with freshly ground black pepper, and more salt if needed.

THE BÉCHAMEL
3 tablespoons butter
1 tablespoon shallot or onion, minced
3 tablespoons flour
2½ cups milk
½ cup light or heavy cream
Nutmeg
Salt and pepper

Melt the butter, add the shallot or onion, and cook slowly until it is soft. Stir in the flour to make a roux, and cook it gently over a low heat for 3 to 4 minutes; then set it aside to cool. Combine the milk and the cream, and heat nearly to the boiling point; then whisk into the cooled roux. Return the pot to the heat and cook 15 to 20 minutes, stirring frequently. Season with a few scrapings of nutmeg, and salt and pepper to taste.

To assemble the lasagne, roll the pasta dough to the thinnest setting, and cut the final strip of dough into pieces that fit your baking pan (although they needn't fit exactly). Bring a pot of water to a boil, and have ready a large bowl of cold water. When the water is boiling, add salt, and drop the pieces of dough, several at a time, into the water. They will sink. When they rise to the surface, pull them out and put them into the cold water to cool. Then spread them out on a clean kitchen towel.

Preheat the oven to 375°F. Butter a 9-by-13-inch baking pan, and spoon a scant ½ cup of the béchamel over the bottom. Lay down enough pieces of pasta so that they cover the bottom and hang over the edges of the pan. Later the flaps will be folded over the top to seal in the filling. Spread another ½ cup of béchamel on this first layer of pasta, a quarter of the mushrooms, and some grated cheese. Cover with another layer of pasta; then add more béchamel, mushrooms, and grated cheese. Continue in this fashion, making four layers in all. Finish by laying one or two pieces of pasta down the middle and folding the overlapping pasta over it to seal in the filling. Spread the remaining béchamel over the top, followed by the rest of the cheese.

Cover the lasagne loosely with foil and bake for 15 minutes. Then remove the foil and continue baking until the top is puffed and browned, about 25 minutes. Let the lasagne rest a few minutes; then cut it into pieces and serve. For a wine, serve any number of reds—zinfandel, a California barbera, or a French Côtes-du-Rhône.

Note: Lasagne can also be made using commercial fresh pasta sheets, which will be thicker than those you make at home. These commercial pasta sheets often come in pieces about 9 by 13 inches, each weighing about 4 ounces; 1¼ pounds should be about right. Use 4 or 5 sheets and do not try to overlap the bottom layer as in the basic recipe. Though pasta makers often say fresh lasagne sheets need not be precooked, the lasagne will be lighter and moister if they are.

SERVES SIX

GRATINS

STEWS *and*

CASSEROLES

This group of dishes has enormous diversity ranging from simple, homey fare to complex layerings of ingredients, from delicate vegetable mixtures to spicy Mexican casseroles. What they have in common is their eminent suitability as main course dishes, whether the meal is an informal weekday supper or a Sunday dinner.

Although gratins, stews, and casseroles are somewhat overlapping categories, some general distinctions can be drawn. The gratins are made with vegetables layered with cheese or a starch, such as polenta. Cream or liquid from the vegetables provides a sauce, and when they are baked in shallow earthenware dishes, a handsome crust forms on top. They are served from the dishes in which they are baked. Stews are usually cooked on top of the stove, although they can be finished in the oven, baked under a pastry crust or a blanket of potatoes. Moist and succulent, stews go well with starchy accompaniments such as polenta, potato gordas, rice pilafs, or corn bread. Casseroles, the least formal of this group, are baked, and combine vegetables and starchier foods with a suitable stock or sauce.

The tone of these foods, whether they appear to be plain, down-to-earth cooking or something more fancy, is frequently affected by the type of dish in which they are baked. The use of individual crocks, casseroles, and gratin dishes give an otherwise simple, even homey, dish a very special feeling. This is particularly true when the contents have a more homogenous texture, such as chilaquiles and budín, or consist of rather ordinary ingredients, such as pasticcio.

Some of the gratins are frankly and unabashedly rich with cream. They are delicious this way, and can be regarded as dishes to serve for a special occasion, rather than as everyday fare. Some recipes call for cheese, partially to make the dishes more amenable as entrées, but the amount can always be lessened or even omitted if you wish. And many of the recipes contain no dairy products at all.

The preparation of gratins, stews, and casseroles varies from simple to elaborate. Acquainting yourself with a recipe before you begin is a helpful practice. Those recipes that are more complicated and time consuming can be accomplished with relative ease if some of the parts are prepared ahead of time.

Spring Vegetable Ragout

The simple, clean taste of this stew reflects the delicacy of spring vegetables. There are many to choose from—English peas and edible pod peas, asparagus, tiny artichokes, fava beans, new carrots and turnips, the tender leaves of spinach, chard, and sorrel, spring onions, and so forth. Select five or six, considering not only the flavors, but their colors and textures.

1 pound fava beans
1 bunch asparagus
4 ounces snow peas or sugar snap peas
8 small tender chard leaves or a handful of sorrel or young spinach
4 ounces leeks or scallions
4 ounces oyster mushrooms or other variety
6 tablespoons unsalted butter, cut into pieces
1 tablespoon virgin olive oil
Twelve 3-inch carrots, peeled and halved lengthwise
1 clove garlic, finely chopped
Small handful fresh herbs: chervil, savory, basil, chives, parsley
Salt
Juice of 1 lemon
Pepper

Slit open the long pods of the fava beans with your fingers and take out the beans. Drop them in a pan of boiling water and leave them for 30 seconds; then scoop them out, and put them into a bowl of cold water to stop the cooking. Pop off the outer skins, and set the peeled beans aside.

Snap off the tough ends of the asparagus; then cut off the tips, leaving them 2 to 3 inches long. If you wish to use more asparagus in the stew, use the middle stems and cut them into small rounds or long diagonal pieces. Trim the peas on both ends and pull off the strings. If young chard is used, cut the stems into pieces about ½ inch wide, and separately shred the leaves into ribbons also ½ inch wide. If using sorrel or spinach, cut into ½-inch pieces. Slice the leeks or scallions in half, lengthwise, then into pieces about 2 inches long. Separate the oyster mushrooms from one another.

To make the ragout use a wide sauté pan or a skillet with straight 2-inch sides. Heat 2 tablespoons of the butter with the oil. Add the leeks or scallions and sauté briskly for about ½ minute. Next add the mushrooms, carrots, chard stems, garlic, a few large pinches of herbs, and some salt. Squeeze about a tablespoon of lemon juice over all and add a cup of hot water. Give the pan a shake, and cover; then lower the heat and cook for about 2 minutes, or until the carrots have begun to soften but are not yet fully cooked. Add the asparagus, peas, greens, and fava beans, cover again, and cook another 1 or 2 minutes.

Remove the lid and add the rest of the butter and the remaining herbs. Cook until the butter has melted into the liquid, forming a sauce, and the vegetables are as done as you like them. Taste, and season with more salt, if necessary, and freshly ground black pepper. Serve the ragout on warmed plates with old-fashioned toast points or croutons to draw up the juices. For wine, try a California chardonnay.

SERVES FOUR TO SIX

Artichoke and Fennel Stew Covered with Pastry

This vegetable stew is covered with a cream cheese pastry crust and baked in individual ramekins. It can also be baked as a large covered pie or made without the crust and served with the wild rice pilaf or squares of puff pastry. As in the Winter Vegetable Stew, Wild Mushroom Stock is used to prepare the sauce, giving it a deep background flavor. As spring produce begins to come in, include fava beans or peas and add them to the stew before it goes into the oven. Both go well with artichokes and fennel.

THE SAUCE
2 tablespoons butter
1 tablespoon olive oil
1 medium yellow onion, diced into small squares
¼ teaspoon dried thyme
½ teaspoon dried savory or about 1 teaspoon fresh winter savory, chopped
½ teaspoon fennel seed, lightly crushed in a mortar
1 bay leaf
½ teaspoon salt
½ cup white wine
3 tablespoons flour
3 cups Wild Mushroom Stock (page 66), heated
2 tablespoons parsley leaves, finely chopped
Pepper

Heat the butter and the oil in a wide soup pot with a heavy bottom; then add the onion, thyme, savory, fennel seeds, bay leaf, and salt. Cook the onion, stirring occasionally, over medium-high heat until it is a light golden brown, but not heavily caramelized, about 10 to 12 minutes. Pour in the wine, and scrape the sides and bottom of the pot; then let the wine reduce until it is thick and syrupy, about 3 minutes. Stir in the flour, cook it for 1 minute, then whisk in the mushroom stock. Add the parsley, bring to a boil, and simmer slowly, partially covered, for 15 minutes. Taste for salt, and season with freshly ground black pepper. Set aside.

THE STEW

Cream Cheese Pastry (see below)
3 large or 6 small leeks, white parts only
8 tablespoons lemon juice
3 large artichokes
2 small or 1 large fennel bulb, about 12 ounces trimmed
4½ tablespoons butter
½ teaspoon salt
½ to ¾ cup Wild Mushroom Stock (page 66), Winter Vegetable Stock (page 65), or water
Parchment paper
8 ounces large white mushrooms or Italian field mushrooms, roughly sliced
1 clove garlic, finely chopped
Pepper
Small handful fresh herbs: Italian parsley, fennel greens, winter savory, chervil, a small amount of thyme, or parsley alone, finely chopped
1 beaten egg, for egg wash

Prepare the cream cheese pastry, wrap it in plastic, and set it aside to rest in the refrigerator while you prepare the vegetables.

Halve the leeks lengthwise, cut them into pieces about 1½ inches long, then lengthwise into narrow strips. Wash them well; then set them aside.

Have ready a bowl of water containing the juice of 1 lemon (about 4 tablespoons). Cut two thirds off the top of each artichoke, and break off the tough outer leaves. Trim the base and stem, cutting away any dark green parts, rubbing the cut surfaces with lemon as you work. Quarter the artichokes, cut out the choke with a paring knife, and slice each quarter into halves or thirds. Put the pieces into the acidulated water as you go.

Trim the fennel. Take a slice off the root end, and pull off the thick outer leaves if they look tough or bruised. If the bulbs are very small and tender, cut each into quarters or sixths, leaving the inner core, so that the sections are held together at the base. If the bulb is large, quarter it, take out the core, and slice it crosswise into pieces about ½ inch wide.

Melt 3 tablespoons of the butter in a wide skillet. Drain the artichokes and add them to the pan with 2 tablespoons of lemon juice. Stir to coat them well with butter; then add the leeks, the salt, and the stock or water. Rub some butter over the parchment paper; then press it onto the vegetables. Stew slowly over fairly low heat for about 15 minutes—the artichokes should be tender around the edges but still only partially cooked at the center.

While the artichokes are cooking, heat the remaining butter in a sauté pan, and add the mushrooms. Sauté briefly; then add the garlic, 2 tablespoons lemon juice, and some salt and freshly ground black pepper. Cook until the mushrooms just begin to give up their juices, without letting them brown.

Remove the parchment paper; then add the mushrooms and the fennel to the artichokes, and fold in the sauce. Return the parchment to the top, and cook the stew over medium heat for another 5 minutes or so. The vegetables should still be a little underdone, as they will continue to bake in the oven. Add the fresh herbs, and season to taste with salt and milled pepper.

Preheat the oven to 375°F. Ladle the vegetables into 6 ramekins or individual baking dishes. Divide the pastry, roll out each piece into a circle, and lay it over the vegetables. Tuck in the edges, crimp them nicely, and cut a simple design in the top. Brush the surfaces with beaten egg, and bake until the crust is browned, 30 minutes or so. Let the stew settle several minutes before serving. The ramekins will hold their heat for a while, so there is no need to rush them to the table. This stew could be served with a dry chenin blanc or pinot blanc, or if red is preferred, a zinfandel.

CREAM CHEESE PASTRY
1 cup all-purpose flour
¼ teaspoon salt
3 tablespoons unsalted butter, cut into small pieces
5 tablespoons cream cheese

Combine the flour and the salt in a bowl, and work in the butter, using your fingertips or two knives. When it is well blended, add the cream cheese and lightly work it in with your fingers until the dough comes together. Wrap it in plastic, press it into a disk, and refrigerate for 10 to 15 minutes, or until needed. If it has been refrigerated more than 1 hour before using, let it rest at room temperature for 15 minutes before rolling it out.

This is an easy, malleable dough to handle, one that looks very pretty when baked. Leftover pieces can be rolled, cut into decorative shapes, and fastened to the crust with an egg wash.

SERVES SIX

Baked Polenta Layered with Tomato, Fontina, and Gorgonzola

This polenta gratin looks inviting baked in a large earthenware dish—bring it to the table bubbling and fragrant and serve it family style. For more formal occasions, it is very attractive baked in individual dishes. Both the polenta and the tomato sauce can be made well in advance. Putting the casserole together takes only a short time.

1½ to 2 pounds meaty tomatoes or canned whole tomatoes, roughly chopped
1 tablespoon olive oil
1 bay leaf
2 basil leaves or a good pinch dried basil
2 branches parsley
½ small yellow onion, finely diced
1 clove garlic, finely chopped
Sugar, if necessary
Salt and pepper
1½ cups coarse cornmeal
8 ounces Fontina cheese, thinly sliced
5 ounces Gorgonzola cheese
Fresh herbs: oregano or marjoram, basil, chopped, for garnish

Make a simple tomato sauce. Warm the olive oil with the bay leaf, basil, parsley, onion, and garlic, and cook slowly for 3 to 4 minutes. Add the tomatoes, raise the heat to medium high, and cook until they are quite soft and broken apart, about 15 minutes. Pass them through a food mill; then return the sauce to the pan, and simmer until quite thick. If needed, add a pinch or two of sugar to balance the acidity, and season with salt and freshly ground black pepper. This should make 1½ cups.

While the sauce is cooking, bring 4½ cups water to a boil and add 1½ teaspoons salt. Whisk in the cornmeal in a stream so that lumps don't form, and when it has all been added, switch to a wooden spoon, lower the heat, and stir for 15 minutes. Pour it into a loaf pan or a 9-by-12-inch baking dish, and set it aside to cool. When it is thoroughly cool and firm, turn it out and slice it into pieces about ½ inch thick and about 3 inches long. If a loaf pan was used, cut the pieces again, diagonally.

Preheat the oven to 400°F. Lightly butter a gratin dish, and spread about 1 cup of the tomato sauce over the bottom. Arrange the polenta and the slices of Fontina in overlapping layers. Carefully spoon the remaining tomato sauce over the layers in a decorative way, leaving bands of red sauce between the yellow polenta and cheese. Crumble Gorgonzola over the top, pepper generously, and bake the gratin, uncovered, for 25 to 35 minutes. The cheese will melt into the tomato, making a sauce to spoon over the polenta. Garnish with the fresh herbs.

SERVES FOUR TO SIX

Provençal Potato Gratin with Olives and Lemon Thyme

Based on a recipe from the Salvador Dalí cookbook, *Les Dîners de Galla,* this gratin can be eaten either hot or at room temperature, which makes it a fine dish for a summer meal outside. Though made with potatoes, it is neither heavy nor rich, giving it a place in a menu where other dishes include cream, eggs, or cheese. The lemon thyme is bright and refreshing, and if the gratin is to be eaten cold, a garnish of fresh lovage leaves would also be good.

Salt
1½ pounds Yellow Finnish or russet potatoes
3 to 4 large ripe tomatoes
4 to 6 tablespoons virgin olive oil
2 medium red onions, sliced ¼ inch thick
¼ teaspoon dried thyme
¼ teaspoon fennel seeds, lightly crushed
Pepper
3 cloves garlic, thinly sliced
½ cup green or black Niçoise olives, pitted and roughly chopped
12 branches lemon thyme or 8 branches thyme, the leaves plucked from the stems
1 tablespoon small capers (optional)

Bring 3 to 4 quarts of water to a boil and add 1 tablespoon salt. Peel the potatoes, slice them ¼ to ⅜ inch thick, add them to the water, and boil for 3 minutes. Scoop them out with a strainer, and set them aside in a colander to drain.

Using the same water, drop in the tomatoes, count 10 seconds, then plunge them into cold water. Remove the cores, peel, and halve the tomatoes crosswise. Gently squeeze out the juice and seeds. Roughly chop half of one tomato and set aside, and cut the rest into slices about ¼ inch thick.

Heat 2 tablespoons of the olive oil in a large skillet, and when it is hot, add the onions with the dried thyme, the fennel seeds, and a grinding of black pepper. Sauté briskly over a medium-high flame, stirring frequently until the onions brown slightly and soften, about 3 minutes. Season with salt and set aside.

Preheat the oven to 400°F. Assemble the gratin in a shallow 8-cup baking dish, preferably earthenware. Cover the bottom with a thin film of olive oil; then add half the onions and garlic, the chopped tomato, the olives, and half the thyme leaves. Layer the potatoes and the tomatoes over the onions, tuck the remaining slivers of garlic in among them, and season with salt and freshly ground pepper. (If you are planning to serve the gratin at room temperature, add the capers.) Cover the potatoes with the rest of the onions and spoon olive oil over the top. Bake the gratin for 20 minutes loosely covered with foil; then bake uncovered another 15 minutes, or until the potatoes are done. Scatter the remaining thyme leaves over the gratin when it comes out of the oven. A California vin gris (or a Provençal rosé) would go well with these Provençal flavors.

Variation: Layer the potatoes and the tomatoes with cheese: smoked or fresh mozzarella, Gouda, or Fontina, or dot with pieces of goat cheese. Bake at 375°F, covered with foil the first 20 minutes, then uncovered for another 20 to 25 minutes, or until the potatoes are done. Serve warm.

SERVES FOUR TO SIX

Eggplant Gratin with Saffron Custard

With its handsome dome of saffron custard, this richly aromatic gratin is a wonderful dish to make in late summer when there is an abundance of good garden tomatoes as well as eggplant and basil. Serve it with tender egg noodles or white rice, seasoned with lemon—both are neutral dishes that will absorb the flavorful juices.

2 pounds Japanese eggplants or small globe eggplants
Light olive oil or vegetable oil for frying
2 tablespoons virgin olive oil
1 small red onion, finely chopped
1 clove garlic, finely chopped
½ teaspoon Herbes de Provence or ¼ teaspoon each dried thyme and savory
2½ pounds ripe tomatoes, peeled, seeded, and chopped
Salt
Pepper
Sugar, if necessary
2 eggs
1 cup ricotta
¾ cup milk or cream
⅛ teaspoon saffron threads, crumbled and soaked in 3 tablespoons hot water
½ cup Parmesan, freshly grated
10 large basil leaves, cut or torn into small pieces
3 ounces Gruyère cheese, grated or sliced

Slice the Japanese eggplants diagonally into pieces about ½ inch thick. Discard the end pieces that are entirely skin on one side. If using globe eggplants, halve them lengthwise, and then cut them in halves or quarter rounds, also about ½ inch thick. Pour enough oil into a skillet to cover the bottom generously; when it is hot, add the eggplant in a single layer and fry until it is well colored on both sides and the flesh is tender. Remove the finished pieces to paper toweling to drain. Add more oil as needed, and finish frying the rest of the eggplant, making sure the oil is hot each time more eggplant is added.

THE SAUCE

Warm the virgin olive oil in a skillet and add the onion, garlic, and dried herbs, crushed first between the fingers. Stir to coat the onion with the oil; then cook slowly until it is soft, 10 to 15 minutes. Add the chopped tomatoes, raise the heat, and cook until the sauce is thickened, about 15 minutes. Taste and season with salt and freshly ground black pepper. If the tomatoes are unusually tart, add enough sugar to correct the balance.

THE CUSTARD

To make the custard, beat the eggs, and stir in the ricotta, milk or cream, saffron, and Parmesan cheese. Season with salt and pepper.

Preheat the oven to 350°F. Assemble the gratin in an attractive baking dish, preferably earthenware, with 2-inch sides. Spread a little tomato sauce over the bottom; then lay down an overlapping layer of eggplant. Salt and pepper the eggplant, and scatter half the basil over the surface, followed by the grated or sliced Gruyère. Make another layer of eggplant and basil, and cover with the rest of the tomato sauce. Pour the ricotta custard over the top and bake the gratin until the custard has gently swelled and is lightly browned, about 40 minutes. Remove it from the oven and let it rest a few minutes before serving. For wine, choose a zinfandel or Beaujolais.

This gratin was inspired by a Provençal recipe from Richard Olney's *Simple French Food*. We have included the cheese to make it more substantial as a main course dish.

SERVES FOUR TO SIX

Eggplant and Mushroom Pasticcio

There are several parts to this dish—the tomato sauce, the vegetables, and the custard. Begin by making the tomato sauce, then continue with the other parts. For the pasta, use a dry tubular pasta such as mostaccioli or penne, which will catch and hold the sauce.

THE TOMATO SAUCE
2 pounds tomatoes, fresh or canned
3 to 4 sun-dried tomatoes (optional)
2 tablespoons virgin olive oil
1 small yellow onion, finely diced
2 cloves garlic, finely chopped
2 tablespoons parsley, chopped
Several basil leaves or ½ teaspoon dried basil
1 teaspoon fresh thyme leaves or ¼ teaspoon dried thyme
1 teaspoon marjoram, chopped, or ½ teaspoon dried marjoram
Salt
½ cup red wine
Sugar, if necessary

Plunge the tomatoes in boiling water for 10 seconds; then peel, seed, and chop them into small pieces. If you are using canned tomatoes, drain them and reserve the juice. Halve them, squeeze out the seeds, and chop them finely. If the juice is very thick, combine it with the tomatoes. If it is watery, blend 3 or 4 sun-dried tomatoes with some of the juice to make a purée, and set it aside.

Warm the oil in a skillet, add the onion, and stir to coat it with the oil. Add the garlic and the herbs, season with salt, and cook over low heat until the onion has softened, stirring occasionally. Add the tomatoes, sun-dried tomato purée, if using, and wine, and simmer for 20 to 30 minutes, or until the sauce has thickened and reduced to about 3 cups. Taste for salt. If the tomatoes are excessively tart, add one or two pinches of sugar to correct the acidity.

THE EGGPLANT AND MUSHROOMS
4 tablespoons virgin olive oil
1 globe eggplant (about 1½ pounds), cut into ½-inch cubes
Salt
1 yellow onion, thinly sliced
3 cloves garlic, finely chopped
2 teaspoons basil, chopped
2 teaspoons marjoram, chopped
4 ounces mushrooms, wiped clean and sliced
Pepper

Heat 2 tablespoons of the olive oil in a wide skillet, add the eggplant, and season with salt. Toss it with the oil; then cook for 8 to 10 minutes, or until it is nicely browned and soft. Remove it to a bowl.

Heat the remaining oil in the same skillet, add the onion, stir to coat it with oil, then stew over medium heat with the garlic and the herbs. Season with salt, and cook until the onion has softened, 4 to 5 minutes. Add the mushrooms, raise the heat, and cook until they have browned and released their juices. Add these to the eggplant and season with salt and freshly ground black pepper.

THE PASTA AND THE CUSTARD
4 ounces dried pasta (mostaccioli or penne)
1 cup ricotta
2 eggs, beaten
¾ cup half-and-half or light cream
3 to 4 ounces Parmesan, freshly grated, or a mixture of Parmesan and Romano cheese
Salt and pepper
Nutmeg

Bring a pot of water to a boil, add salt, and cook the pasta, leaving it a little short of *al dente*. Drain it in a colander, rinse it with cold water to stop the cooking, and return it to the pot or a bowl.

Combine the ricotta, eggs, and half-and-half or light cream in a small bowl; add a quarter of the cheese and season with salt, freshly ground black pepper, and a few scrapings of nutmeg.

Before assembling the pasticcio, check the seasonings of the various parts to make sure they are all lively and strong. Use a 2-quart casserole or six individual casseroles that hold 1½ cups each. Preheat the oven to 350°F. Butter or oil the baking dishes, and spoon a small amount of tomato sauce on the bottom; then mix the remaining sauce with the pasta. Layer the noodles over the sauce, cover them with the eggplant and mushrooms, and dust with the remaining cheese. Pour the ricotta custard over the top, and bake for 25 to 35 minutes, or until the custard has set and turned a golden brown. Remove from the oven and let the pasticcio settle for several minutes before serving. If serving with wine, try a California pinot noir.

Variations: This is a versatile dish that can be made with many different vegetables. We often make it in the summer with green beans, or in the spring with artichokes. Mixtures of both summer and winter vegetables can be used, and the custard itself can be flavored and colored with saffron if desired.

MAKES SIX 1½-CUP CASSEROLES

Indian Vegetable Stew with Yellow Dal

Summer vegetables are cooked in a spicy golden sauce, or dal, made from dried yellow peas. The flavors of the spices lean toward the hot and pungent rather than the sweet. Serve the dal with simply prepared rice, and the Coconut Crème Caramel for dessert.

THE DAL
¾ cup yellow split peas
1 tablespoon fresh ginger, peeled and minced
3 cloves garlic, finely chopped
½ teaspoon turmeric
2 serrano chilies or 2 jalapeño peppers, seeded and finely chopped

Sort through the peas, remove any chaff or small stones, and rinse them well; then cover them with water and leave them to soak at least 2 hours ahead of time so that the peas will not continue to absorb liquid and thicken the sauce once it is made. Pour off the soaking water, and add 3 cups fresh water and the remaining ingredients. Bring to a boil; then simmer until the peas are completely soft and have fallen apart, about 45 minutes. Cool slightly; then blend to make a smooth purée. Measure the amount of purée, and add water to bring it up to 3½ cups.

THE VEGETABLES AND SPICES
3 medium tomatoes
2 Japanese eggplants or ½ globe eggplant
2 medium zucchini
2 medium carrots
4 tablespoons clarified butter (page 325)
1 teaspoon brown mustard seeds
1 teaspoon cumin seeds
1 small yellow onion, thinly sliced
½ small cauliflower, broken into florets
1 teaspoon salt
Fresh cilantro leaves, roughly chopped, for garnish

While the peas are cooking, prepare the vegetables. Plunge the tomatoes into boiling water for a count of 10 seconds; then place them in a bowl of cold water. Remove the peels; then halve them and gently squeeze out the seeds. Cut them into large pieces. Cut the eggplant into 1-inch cubes, and cut the zucchini and the carrots into batons or sticks about 1½ inches long. Whatever shapes you make, keep them large enough so that after cooking they will have a clear, distinct appearance on the plate.

When you are ready to cook the stew, have the dried spices ready on the stove, and a lid handy, in case the mustard seeds splatter and pop. Heat the clarified butter in a large wide skillet, and when it is hot, add the mustard seeds. Cook a brief 5 seconds or so, until the mustard seeds turn grayish and begin to explode; then add the cumin seeds, and after another 5 seconds the onion. Sauté for one minute over high heat; then add the tomatoes and the eggplant. Cook 2 or 3 minutes before adding the cauliflower and the carrots. Stir everything together; then add the puréed yellow peas. Add the salt, stir, and cook over medium-low heat until the vegetables are tender, about 25 minutes. Add the zucchini during the last 10 minutes, so that it will stay bright and somewhat firm.

Taste again for salt, and add more if necessary. Serve the vegetables and dal garnished with the fresh cilantro.

The inspiration for this dish came from Julie Sahni's recipe for Gujrati Dal in her book *Classic Indian Cooking*. Her version, which is very delicious, uses fewer vegetables but has a more complex dal, one made with a variety of legumes.

SERVES FOUR TO SIX

Butter-Fried Potatoes with Curry Spices and Cream

This aromatic stew is made with new potatoes that are first fried in clarified butter, then cooked in a sauce of yogurt, cream, and curry spices. The potato pieces should be large enough to be visually dominant, but not so thick that they don't absorb the flavors of the sauce. This dish has a wonderful merging of flavors, and it looks lovely with a strong garnish of cilantro sprigs or whole small leaves of cinnamon basil.

2 pounds small new potatoes
1 pound carrots
1½ pounds tomatoes, fresh or canned
2½ teaspoons cumin seeds
3 teaspoons coriander seeds
1-inch piece of cinnamon stick
1 teaspoon cardamom seeds
8 cloves
¼ teaspoon black peppercorns
6 to 8 tablespoons clarified butter (see page 325)
1 large red onion, cut into ½-inch squares
1 clove garlic, finely chopped
1½ to 2 ounces ginger root, peeled and minced
¼ teaspoon grated nutmeg
½ teaspoon turmeric
¾ cup yogurt
½ to 1 cup cream
Salt
1 to 2 tablespoons cilantro, chopped
Branches of cilantro or cinnamon basil leaves, for garnish

Peel the potatoes by first cutting a slice off each end, then cutting down the sides in five or six strokes. Cut them into halves, thirds, or slices no more than ½ inch thick. Put them in a bowl of water while the rest of the vegetables and spices are prepared. Peel the carrots. If they are small carrots, leave them whole; otherwise, cut them into pieces about 2 inches long, halving them as necessary to make them approximately the same size.

Bring a small pan of water to a boil, submerge the tomatoes to a count of ten. Remove, peel, and seed them; then finely chop them. Assemble all the whole spices, and grind them into a powder in an electric spice mill.

Drain the potatoes and blot them dry. Using a wide skillet or a heavy-bottomed casserole, heat 4 tablespoons of the clarified butter; add the potatoes and cook them over medium heat. Shake the pan occasionally or stir the potatoes so that all the surfaces are exposed to the butter. Fry until they are golden but not yet fully cooked;

then pierce them with a knife in several places to make openings for the sauce. Remove them from the pan. Add another 2 tablespoons of the butter, and cook the carrots until they are half done. Put the potatoes back into the pan.

In a second pan, heat the remaining butter; add the onion and fry over medium heat, stirring until it is a deep brown. As it darkens, lower the heat and stir more frequently so that it doesn't burn. Stir in the garlic, ginger, ground spices, nutmeg, and turmeric. Next add the tomatoes and the yogurt, stir well, and transfer the sauce to the pan with the carrots and potatoes. Simmer until the vegetables have finished cooking; then add the cream and cook another few minutes, reducing the sauce until it is as thick as you want. Check the seasoning, and season with salt.

Stir in the chopped cilantro; then serve garnished with the branches of cilantro or basil leaves. This is a very fragrant and rich dish. Follow with something refreshing—sliced oranges or the Honeydew in Ginger-Lemon Syrup.

SERVES SIX

Curried Vegetable Stew

This is a warm, invigorating stew in tones of gold, yellow, and orange. The vegetables should be cut into large enough pieces to give a substantial look and feel to the dish. Other vegetables than those listed can be included, but it is best to limit them to six, plus the onion, to keep each taste clear.

We usually serve this over white or brown basmati rice with the Banana and Yogurt Raita and the Fresh Fruit and Mint Chutney. Flavors and fragrances range from the hot to the pungent and sweet.

6 tablespoons clarified butter (page 325)
3 cups dried coconut
4 or 5 medium carrots
2 large parsnips
4 ounces button mushrooms, wiped clean
½ small cauliflower
2 stalks broccoli
3 to 4 red potatoes (about 12 ounces)
1 ounce fresh ginger root, minced
3 large cloves garlic, roughly chopped
2 teaspoons coriander seeds
2 teaspoons cumin seeds
1 teaspoon mustard seeds
1 teaspoon cardamom seeds
10 whole cloves
1 stick cinnamon, about 3 inches long, broken
¼ teaspoon cayenne pepper
1 teaspoon turmeric
1 large yellow onion, sliced ⅜ inch thick
1 teaspoon salt
Juice of 1 lemon
Cilantro leaves, for garnish
About 1 cup cashew nuts, roasted, for garnish

If you do not have any clarified butter, prepare some according to the recipe on page 325. Its flavor is essential in this curry.

Bring 3 cups of water to a boil, pour it over the coconut, and set it aside to steep for ½ hour. Then blend it at a high speed for at least 3 minutes; and pour it through a strainer lined with several layers of cheesecloth or a dampened kitchen towel. Twist the ends of the towel firmly to squeeze out as much coconut milk as possible.

Prepare the vegetables. Peel the carrots and cut them into log-shaped pieces about 1½ inches long. Halve them if necessary so that all the pieces are roughly the same size. Peel and quarter the parsnips, remove the fibrous inner cores, and slice crosswise into thick pieces. Leave the mushrooms whole, and break the cauliflower and the broccoli into florets. Cut the potatoes into ½-inch cubes, peeled or not, and cover them with water until needed. Put the ginger and the garlic in a mortar, and pound them until they form a fairly smooth paste, or mince well together. Grind the whole spices to a powder in a spice mill, and add the cayenne and the turmeric.

Using a skillet that is at least 12 inches wide or a large wide casserole, warm the clarified butter and add the onion and the garlic-ginger paste. Cook over medium heat, stirring frequently, until the onion has turned an even golden brown, about 7 minutes. Then lower the heat, add the salt and the ground spices, and continue to cook a few more minutes, stirring constantly. Add the carrots, coconut milk, and lemon juice, and raise the heat to warm the milk; then cover the pan and simmer for about 10 minutes. Add the remaining vegetables, except for the broccoli, cover, and continue to cook slowly until they are tender. Add the broccoli during the last 7 to 8 minutes, so its color stays bright, or blanch it separately and add just before serving.

Taste, and check for salt. Serve the curry garnished with fresh cilantro leaves and roasted cashews. Beer or fragrant teas are usually preferred with curried dishes to wines, but if you want to enjoy a wine, try serving a fairly dry riesling or gewurztraminer.

SERVES FOUR TO SIX

Potatoes and Chanterelles Baked in Cream

The amount of mushrooms called for is generous—fine for when you feel extravagant or have found the chanterelles yourself—but half the amount will be enough for their special flavor to come through. This is an earthy, rich dish. Accompany it with a salad of bitter winter greens, or precede it with a light, mildly acidic soup such as the Red Onion and Red Wine Soup with Tomatoes and Thyme.

2 pounds new or russet potatoes
Salt
1 pound chanterelles
2 tablespoons butter
2 cloves garlic, finely chopped
1½ cups heavy cream
Pepper

Peel the potatoes and slice them into rounds ¼ inch thick. Bring a large pot of water to a boil, add 1 tablespoon salt, and the potatoes. Return the water to a boil and cook the potatoes for 2 minutes. Drain them and set them aside.

Clean the chanterelles, if they need it, with a soft mushroom brush or a damp cloth. Slice them into pieces about ¼ inch thick. Heat the butter in a wide pan; then add the mushrooms, the garlic, and a little salt, and cook over medium-high heat for about 5 minutes.

Preheat the oven to 375°F. Lightly butter a gratin dish. Layer half the potatoes and season them with salt and freshly ground black pepper. Add the mushrooms; then cover them with the remaining slices of potatoes. Overlap the top layer, if you like, to make them look pretty, and season again with salt and pepper.

Pour the cream over the top and bake for 40 minutes, or until the potatoes have absorbed most of the cream and are covered with a golden crust. For wine, consider serving a California pinot noir, a medium-weight red Burgundy, or a Côtes-du-Rhône.

SERVES FOUR TO SIX

White Bean and Eggplant Gratin

Bake this filling dish in a large casserole or individual crocks and serve it with a salad of winter greens.

³/₄ cup navy beans
1 teaspoon dried sage or 2 teaspoons fresh sage leaves, chopped
2 bay leaves
2 cloves garlic, peeled but left whole
7 tablespoons virgin olive oil
Salt and pepper
½ teaspoon dried thyme or 1½ teaspoons fresh thyme leaves, chopped
2 large yellow onions, sliced ¼ inch thick
3 cloves garlic, finely chopped
1 can Italian plum tomatoes (1 pound, 12 ounces), with their juice
1 large globe eggplant, cut into ³/₄-inch cubes
1 cup bread crumbs

Sort through the beans and remove any small stones and chaff. Cover them generously with water, and set them aside to soak for 6 hours, or overnight. (Alternatively, cover them with boiling water and let them soak for 1 hour.) After the beans have soaked, drain them; then cover them with 4 cups fresh water. Bring to a boil with half the sage, the bay leaves, the whole garlic cloves, and a tablespoon of the olive oil. Simmer for ½ hour, add ½ teaspoon salt, and continue to cook until the beans are tender but still hold their shape, 45 minutes or longer, as needed. Drain the liquid and set it aside to use in the gratin or in a soup.

Warm 4 tablespoons of the oil in a wide skillet with the rest of the sage and the thyme, then add the onions, the chopped garlic, and 1 teaspoon salt. Cover and cook slowly until the onions are completely soft. While they are cooking, seed and chop the tomatoes; then strain the juice to remove the seeds. Once the onions are soft, add the eggplant, stirring well to combine; then cover and cook over medium heat for 10 minutes. Add the tomatoes with their juice, and continue cooking until the eggplant is tender.

Transfer the vegetables to a bowl and add the cooked beans. Season with plenty of freshly ground black pepper, and more salt if necessary. If a stronger flavor of sage and thyme is desired, add more, rubbing the dried herbs first between your fingers. The mixture needs to be well seasoned.

Preheat the oven to 350°F. Lightly oil a gratin dish large enough to hold 8 cups. Pour in the beans and vegetables. There should be enough liquid to come halfway up the sides of the dish. If more is needed, add some of the broth from the beans. Mix the bread crumbs with the remaining oil and spread them over the top. Bake the gratin until it is hot and bubbling, and the crust is browned, about 30 minutes.

SERVES SIX

Wild Mushroom Ragout

Both wild mushrooms and unusual cultivars of mushrooms normally found in the wild have become more available recently. They can be used separately, mixed with one another, or combined with the more common cultivated mushrooms, which do not have such distinctive flavor but absorb the flavors of other varieties well. For wild mushrooms, various kinds of chanterelles, porcini, and morels are most easily found, while cultivars include shiitake, Italian field mushrooms, oyster mushrooms, and matsutake. The latter are especially well suited to long-cooking stews. Use the trimmings and odd pieces of mushrooms in the stock. Many accompaniments go well with this stew; it can be served between layers of puff pastry, with fresh wide egg or herb noodles, with croutons, or over grilled polenta.

THE STOCK
If you have some Wild Mushroom Stock, use it in the stew. Boil 5 cups of the stock with trimmings from the stew mushrooms until it has reduced in volume to 3 cups. Remove it from the heat and strain. If you do not have any stock already prepared, make one with the following ingredients:

2 tablespoons olive oil
1 large yellow onion, cut into ½-inch squares
6 cups cold water
2 cloves garlic, roughly chopped
½ ounce dried mushrooms
4 ounces fresh mushrooms, including trimmings from wild mushrooms
2 small bay leaves
Pinch dried sage
Pinch dried thyme
1 carrot, peeled and chopped
1 stalk celery, chopped
4 parsley stems
6 borage leaves (optional)
½ teaspoon salt

Heat the oil in a heavy-bottomed soup pot; add the onion and cook it over medium-high heat, stirring frequently, until it is well-browned, about 15 minutes. Add the water and the rest of the ingredients and bring to a boil. Cover and simmer over low heat for ½ hour. Remove the dried mushrooms and set them aside to use in the stew; then strain the stock through a double layer of cheesecloth. Press firmly to get out as much liquid as possible. Measure the stock, return it to the stove, reduce to 3 cups, and set it aside.

THE RAGOUT

1½ pounds mushrooms (including ½ pound or more wild mushrooms, such as porcini,
*   chanterelles, matsutake, Italian field mushrooms, shiitake, etc.)*
2 tablespoons olive oil
1 large yellow onion, diced into ¼-inch squares
1 medium carrot, peeled and cut into small squares
2 celery stalks, cut into small squares
½ teaspoon salt
1 cup dry white or red wine
4 tablespoons butter
Pepper
3 cloves garlic, finely chopped
Reserved dried mushrooms from The Stock, sliced
2 tablespoons flour
Stock
Fresh parsley, finely chopped
A few tarragon leaves, finely chopped

Clean the wild mushrooms with a soft mushroom brush or cloth. Slice them a good ¼ inch thick. Clean the cultivated mushrooms if they need it, and cut across the caps at an angle to make irregularly shaped pieces.

The process of making the ragout is similar to that of making the stock. Warm the olive oil in a casserole, and add the onion. Cook over medium heat for 10 minutes; then add the carrot and the celery. Continue to cook, stirring occasionally at first, then more frequently as the onion browns. When the onion is well colored, after about 20 minutes, add the salt and the wine, raise the heat, and reduce the liquid by half.

Cook the mushrooms in two batches. For each batch, heat 2 tablespoons butter in a wide skillet. Add half the mushrooms, and sauté over high heat for about 2 minutes. When they begin to lose their juices, season with salt and freshly ground black pepper and half the garlic. Cook another few minutes; then add them to the casserole with the onion. Repeat the procedure, this time sautéing the reserved dried mushrooms along with the fresh. Add the second batch of mushrooms to the casserole when they are done cooking, return the casserole to the heat and add the flour. Cook for 2 minutes; then add the stock. Stir gently and well; then cook over a low heat for 15 to 20 minutes, or until the ragout tastes cooked. Add the fresh herbs and season to taste with salt and pepper.

Serve the ragout with the accompaniment you have chosen. The stew can be made ahead of time, left a little undercooked, then reheated before serving. For a wine, choose a red such as a California barbera or a French Côtes-du-Rhône. Dry chenin blanc also combines well with mushrooms.

SERVES FOUR TO SIX

Winter Squash Gratin

A not-so-usual way of preparing squash; it is first sliced and browned in oil, then layered with cheese and herbs, making an appealing dish. Butternut squash, banana squash, and sugar pumpkins all work well because of their large size. If fresh tomatoes are available, they can be grilled before using to add a subtle smoky flavor.

2 tablespoons olive oil
½ small onion, finely chopped
1 clove garlic, minced
¼ teaspoon thyme or 4 to 6 thyme branches
1 bay leaf
Salt
½ cup dry white wine
¼ teaspoon cayenne pepper or ½ teaspoon paprika
1 pound tomatoes, fresh or canned, peeled, seeded, and finely chopped
Sugar, if necessary
Pepper
1 winter squash, weighing 2½ to 3 pounds
Oil for frying
4 ounces Fontina or Gruyère cheese, sliced
Fresh herbs: parsley or marjoram, thyme, finely chopped

Heat the olive oil and add the onion, garlic, thyme, bay leaf, and a little salt. Cook over medium heat, stirring frequently, until the onion is soft; then add the wine and let it reduce by half. Add the cayenne or paprika and the tomatoes. Cook slowly for 25 minutes, stirring occasionally, until the sauce is thick. Taste, add a pinch of sugar if the tomatoes are tart, and season with salt and freshly ground black pepper.

While the tomatoes are cooking, prepare the squash. Cut it open, scoop out the seeds and strings, and then, with the flat cut surface resting on the counter, shave off the skin. (Butternut squash can be easily peeled with a vegetable peeler before it is cut in half.) Another method is to cut the squash into pieces and then remove the skin from each piece. This takes more time, but you may find it easier.

Slice the peeled squash into large pieces about 3 inches long and ¼ inch thick. Heat enough oil to generously coat the bottom of a large skillet, and fry the squash on both sides, so that it is browned and just tender. Remove it to some toweling to drain; then season with salt and freshly ground pepper.

Preheat the oven to 375°F. To form the gratin, put a few spoonfuls of the tomato sauce on the bottom of individual gratin dishes, or use it all to cover the bottom of one large dish. Lay the squash on top in overlapping layers with slices of the cheese interspersed between the layers. Bake until the cheese is melted and the gratin is hot, about 15 minutes, and serve with the fresh herbs scattered over the surface.

SERVES FOUR TO SIX

Zuñi Stew

Though the ingredients are ordinary, this bean and summer vegetable stew has an intricate balance of flavors. The inspiration for it came from a book on Pueblo Indian cookery. It goes well with the Potato Gordas, but if made a little on the dry side, it can be eaten in tortillas with Salsa Picante.

1¼ cups pinto beans, soaked overnight and drained
1 teaspoon salt
1 bay leaf
1 teaspoon dried oregano
1 pound tomatoes, fresh or canned, peeled, seeded, and chopped; juice reserved
2 ancho chilies
1 pound mixed summer squash
4 ears corn (about 2 cups kernels)
1 teaspoon cumin seeds
½ teaspoon coriander seeds
2 tablespoons corn or vegetable oil
2 yellow onions, cut into ¼-inch squares
2 cloves garlic, finely chopped
2 tablespoons red chili powder, or more, to taste
8 ounces green beans, cut into 1-inch lengths
4 ounces jack or muenster cheese, grated
½ bunch cilantro leaves, roughly chopped
Whole cilantro leaves, for garnish

Cook the pre-soaked beans for about 1½ to 2 hours in plenty of water with the salt, bay leaf, and oregano. Remove them from the heat when they are soft but not mushy, as they will continue to cook in the stew. Drain the beans, and save the broth.

Prepare the tomatoes, or use puréed charcoal-grilled tomatoes. Open the chili pods and remove the seeds and veins; then cut the chilies into narrow strips. Cut the squash into large pieces; shave the kernels from the corn. Grind the cumin and the coriander seeds into a powder in a spice mill or with a mortar and pestle.

Heat the oil in a large skillet, and sauté the onions over high heat for 1 to 2 minutes. Lower the heat, add the garlic, chili powder, cumin, and coriander, and stir everything together. Add a little bean broth, so that the chili doesn't scorch or burn. Cook until the onions have begun to soften, about 4 minutes, then add the tomatoes and stew for 5 minutes. Stir in the squash, corn, green beans, and chili strips along with the cooked beans and enough broth to make a fairly wet stew. Cook slowly until the vegetables are done, about 15 to 20 minutes.

Taste the stew and adjust the seasoning. Stir in the cheese and chopped cilantro, and garnish with whole leaves of cilantro.

SERVES SIX

Squash Stew with Chilies, Spices, and Ground Nuts (Legumbres en Pipian)

Roasted chilies, ground almonds, and sesame seeds give this stew a rich, earthy flavor. The vegetables used are primarily autumnal, but summer squash can be used instead of the winter squash. Serve the stew with the Potato Gordas or grilled Cheese Polenta.

1½ teaspoons cumin seeds
2 teaspoons dried oregano
3 tablespoons sesame seeds
1 ounce (about 24) whole almonds
2 pasilla chilies, for chili powder, or 3 to 4 tablespoons New Mexican chili powder
2 tablespoons corn oil or olive oil
2 yellow onions, cut into ½-inch squares
2 cloves garlic, finely chopped
3 cups winter squash, cut into ¾-inch chunks
6 to 8 ounces mushrooms, wiped clean and halved or quartered
Salt
3 to 4 cups water, juice from the tomatoes, or vegetable stock, heated
½ cauliflower, broken into florets
1 small can hominy, drained
2 pounds tomatoes, fresh or canned, peeled, seeded, and puréed
1 cup peas, fresh or frozen
2 tablespoons chopped cilantro leaves
Sour cream or crème fraîche
Sprigs of cilantro, for garnish

Toast the cumin seeds in a dry pan over medium heat for several minutes until they begin to brown and the aroma is strong. Shake the pan back and forth frequently so they won't burn. Add the oregano, toast for 5 seconds more, and remove to a bowl. Using the same pan, toast the sesame seeds until they are lightly browned and fragrant. Set them aside; then toast the almonds. When they are lightly browned, remove the almonds to a cutting board and roughly chop them. Grind the cumin and oregano to a powder in a spice mill; then grind the almonds and the sesame seeds to a fine meal.

Preheat the oven to 350°F. Roast the chilies until they puff up and are fragrant, about 4 to 5 minutes. Cool slightly; then cut them open, remove the stems, seeds, and veins, and tear them into pieces. Grind the chilies in a spice mill or small blender jar to make a coarse powder.

Heat the oil in a casserole, add the onions, and sauté over medium-high heat until they have begun to soften; then add the garlic, cumin, oregano, and 2 tablespoons of the chili powder, and cook another minute. Next add the squash, mushrooms, a sprinkling of salt, and 3 cups water, tomato juice, or stock. Bring to a boil; then lower the heat, cover, and cook slowly until the squash is tender, about 20 minutes. Check to see if the mixture dries out while cooking, and add more liquid if necessary.

Add the ground almonds and sesame seeds, cauliflower, hominy, and puréed tomato. Check for salt, and season with additional ground chili, to taste. Continue cooking until the cauliflower is nearly tender; add the peas and chopped cilantro, and let stew a few more minutes. Serve with the sour cream or crème fraîche and a garnish of cilantro sprigs. These spicy, peppery squash stews are good with a California vin gris or dry sauvignon blanc, or a light to medium zinfandel.

SERVES FOUR TO SIX

Corn, Bean, and Pumpkin Stew

A delicious and healthful combination of ingredients make up this homey autumnal stew. Make it hotter, if you like, with ground ancho chilies or chili powder.

1 cup pinto beans, soaked overnight and drained
Salt
1 pound tomatoes, fresh or canned, peeled, seeded, and chopped; juice reserved
3 ears corn (about 1½ cups kernels)
1 teaspoon cumin seeds
1 teaspoon oregano
1-inch piece cinnamon stick
3 cloves
4 tablespoons corn oil, light sesame oil, or light olive oil
1 large onion, cut into a medium dice
2 cloves garlic, finely chopped
1 tablespoon paprika
2 cups bean broth or Stock for Curried Soups and Dishes (page 67)
3 cups pumpkin or winter squash, peeled and cut into 1-inch cubes
2 serrano chilies, seeded and finely chopped
Cilantro or parsley, chopped, for garnish

If you have not pre-soaked the beans, clean them, rinse them well, cover them with boiling water, and let them soak for 1 hour. Drain them, cover them with fresh water, and bring to a boil. Add ½ teaspoon salt and cook about 1½ hours, or until the beans are tender. Drain the beans, and reserve the cooking liquid.

Warm a small heavy skillet and toast the cumin seeds until their fragrance emerges; then add the oregano, stir for 5 seconds, and quickly transfer the spices to a plate or bowl so they don't burn. Combine them with the cinnamon and the cloves, and grind to a powder in an electric spice mill.

Heat the oil in a wide skillet and sauté the onion briskly over high heat for 1 minute; then lower the heat to medium. Add the garlic, the spices, the paprika, and 1 teaspoon salt. Stir well to combine; then add ½ cup reserved bean broth or stock and cook, stirring occasionally, until the onion is soft. Next add the tomatoes and cook 5 minutes. Then add the pumpkin or winter squash along with another cup of bean broth or stock. After 20 to 30 minutes, or when the pumpkin is about half-cooked— soft but still too firm to eat—add the corn, the beans, and the fresh chilies. Thin with the reserved tomato juice, adding more broth or stock as necessary. Cook until the pumpkin is tender. Check the seasoning, and add more salt if necessary. Serve garnished with the chopped cilantro or parsley.

Even though there is corn in the stew, corn bread or tortillas make a good accompaniment.

SERVES FOUR TO SIX

Black Bean Enchiladas

A delicious enchilada can be prepared using the Black Bean Chili for the filling and the Tomatillo Sauce. Once these are made, it is a simple matter to assemble the enchiladas. The variations list some other ideas for enchilada fillings and sauces. This is hearty fare, so serve it with something light and crisp, such as the Jicama–Orange Salad.

3 cups Black Bean Chili (page 109)
Tomatillo Sauce (page 318)
½ cup peanut or light corn oil
12 corn or wheat tortillas
4 ounces Monterey Jack cheese, grated
Sprigs of cilantro, for garnish

Prepare the black bean chili and the tomatillo sauce, using the variation in which the onions are cooked.

Heat the oil in a large skillet until a tortilla will sizzle when it is put in. Lightly fry the tortillas on each side, about 20 to 30 seconds, not so long that they become crisp, and set them on paper toweling to drain.

Preheat the oven to 400°F. Oil a 9-by-13-inch baking pan, and spread ½ cup of sauce over the bottom. Put another ½ cup or so of sauce aside. Coat each tortilla on both sides with the sauce; then put ¼ cup of chili and a couple tablespoons of cheese in a strip down the middle of the tortilla, and roll the tortilla around the filling. Place them seam side down in the baking pan in a single layer. When they are all assembled, brush the tops with the remaining sauce.

Bake the enchiladas until heated through, 15 to 20 minutes. Garnish with sprigs of cilantro, and serve with the Salsa Picante, if desired.

Variations: In place of the Tomatillo Sauce, prepare a red sauce such as the Ancho Chili Sauce, or the red sauce in the Mushroom and Fennel Budín.

Replace the Black Bean Chili with a vegetable filling such as that used in Crepas con Queso y Verderas, or the corn-zucchini mixture used to make Corn and Zucchini Timbale.

A more strongly flavored cheese, a smoked cheese or sharp cheddar, for instance, can be used in place of the Monterey Jack.

MAKES 12 ENCHILADAS

Black Bean Chilaquiles

This version of chilaquiles layers tortillas with Black Bean Chili, cheese, and a pungent, earthy red sauce made with ground chilies and nuts. The dish is hearty and filling, and can be baked in a single large casserole or individual crocks. Although all the parts can be readied well in advance, the chilaquiles are best assembled just before baking, to retain the texture of the tortillas. Serve with the Tomatillo Sauce or the Salsa Picante and the Jicama-Orange Salad.

THE RED SAUCE

10 to 12 large cloves garlic, unpeeled
2 large or 3 small pasilla chilies, for chili powder, or 2 to 3 tablespoons ground chili
2 pounds tomatoes, fresh or canned
4 tablespoons almonds or walnuts
2 teaspoons dried oregano
1 small red onion, thinly sliced
1 tablespoon corn oil or vegetable oil
3/4 teaspoon cocoa powder
1/2 teaspoon ground cinnamon
Generous pinch of cloves
1 teaspoon chilpotle purée
Salt
Red wine vinegar to taste

Preheat the oven to 350°F. Roast the unpeeled cloves of garlic until they are fragrant and soft inside, about 20 minutes. Set them aside to cool; then remove the skins. Roast the chilies until they have puffed up and released their fragrance, about 4 minutes. Let them cool slightly; then remove the stems, seeds, and veins. Cut or tear them into pieces, and grind them to a powder in a spice mill or small blender jar.

Broil the tomatoes, if using fresh, turning them over, until they are soft and the skins are blistered but not charred. Purée in a blender; then pass them through a food mill or strainer. If you are using canned tomatoes, blend them together with their juice. Don't wash the blender, as it will be used again.

Roast the nuts in a dry skillet until they are lightly browned and somewhat crunchy. Chop them roughly; then grind them in a spice mill or small blender jar to make a coarse meal. Using the same pan, briefly toast the oregano just until it becomes fragrant; then immediately turn it out into a bowl so it doesn't scorch.

Sauté the onion in the oil for several minutes over medium heat. Add it with the roasted garlic to the tomato sauce, and blend until smooth. Stir in the ground nuts, oregano, cocoa, cinnamon, and cloves. Season to taste with the chili powder and chilpotle pepper or purée and add salt as needed. A small amount of red wine vinegar will bring up the flavors.

THE CHILAQUILES

10 to 12 corn tortillas, stale or fresh
½ cup peanut oil, for frying
3 cups Black Bean Chili (page 109)
4 ounces Monterey Jack or muenster cheese, grated
4 ounces cheddar cheese, grated
1 cup sour cream
Cilantro sprigs, for garnish
Salsa Picante (page 321) or Tomatillo Sauce (page 318)

Cut the tortillas into 1-inch strips or wedges, whatever shape will work best for lining the ramekins or casserole you are using. Heat the oil in a large skillet until it is hot enough to sizzle when a piece of tortilla is dropped in. Fry the tortillas, a single layer at a time, until they are lightly colored, but not crisp. Set them on paper toweling to drain.

Preheat the oven to 400°F. Assemble the ramekins or a large casserole beginning with a few spoonfuls of red sauce followed by a layer of tortillas, half the black bean chili, a third of the cheese, and a few more spoonfuls of red sauce. Repeat the layering of tortillas, chili, cheese, and red sauce. Make a final layer of tortillas, cover with the remaining red sauce and cheese, and the sour cream. Cover and bake until heated through. If all the ingredients are still warm, 10 minutes will suffice; if the ingredients have cooled, allow up to 30 minutes for individual casseroles, 40 minutes for a single large dish. The chilaquiles will remain quite hot for some time out of the oven. Serve garnished with sprigs of cilantro, and accompanied by a salsa picante or tomatillo sauce.

SERVES FOUR TO SIX

Individual Turnip Gratins with Toast Fingers

These gratins can be slid onto a plate and served with toast fingers to soak up the cream. The nutty flavor of the Gruyère and the savory thyme balance the sweetness of the turnips. The turnip greens, which are slightly peppery, would also be good stewed in butter and served with the gratins.

1½ pounds small to medium turnips
Salt
Pepper
1½ teaspoons thyme leaves, chopped
½ cup Gruyère cheese, grated
1½ cups heavy cream
2 to 3 slices Country French Bread, white bread, or whole wheat bread
Chervil or thyme leaves, for garnish

Peel the turnips, and slice them into thin rounds. Bring 3 to 4 quarts of water to a boil, add a tablespoon of salt, and cook the turnips for a minute to remove any bitterness. Pour them into a colander to drain.

Preheat the oven to 375°F. Butter shallow round gratin dishes that are about 5 to 6 inches across. Cover the bottom of each with an overlapping layer of turnips, and season with salt, freshly ground black pepper, and some of the thyme. Make a second layer of turnips and seasonings, ending with the cheese. Pour the cream over the top and bake. Check after 15 minutes and baste some of the cream over the top if it has not yet begun to boil. Remove the gratins when most of the cream has been absorbed and there is a golden crust over the top, about 30 minutes in all. Set them aside to cool for a few minutes.

Toast the bread and slice it into lengths about ½ inch wide. Slide a rubber spatula around the edge of each gratin, reaching across the bottom, then slide it out carefully onto a serving plate. Garnish with the fresh herbs and the toast fingers.

SERVES FOUR

White Winter Vegetables Baked in Cream

Winter vegetables, particularly the roots, are sweet and delicious when baked in cream and covered with a layer of crisp buttered bread crumbs. Other vegetables besides those listed can be used: kohlrabi, cauliflower, parsnips, and onions. Each has its own particular flavor to be considered. Plan on using about 1 cup of vegetables per person.

2 to 3 medium leeks, white parts only
1 fennel bulb
4 to 6 small red potatoes and/or turnips
1 celery root
1 clove garlic, crushed
Salt
White pepper
8 to 10 branches fresh lemon thyme or 6 branches thyme, the leaves removed from the stems
2 cups heavy cream or half milk and half cream
5 tablespoons butter
1 cup coarse bread crumbs

Slice the leeks into ¼-inch rounds or strips about 2 inches long, and wash them well. Quarter the fennel bulb, trim away most of the core, and slice it lengthwise into pieces about ¼ inch thick. Peel the potatoes or turnips, and slice them into rounds ⅛ inch thick. Cut away the gnarly surface of the celery root, cut it into quarters, and slice it thinly. If it is not to be used right away, cover it with water that has been acidulated with a few spoonfuls of lemon juice or vinegar.

Preheat the oven to 375°F. Butter the bottom and sides of a baking dish, and rub with the crushed garlic clove. Layer half of the vegetables in the dish, and season them with salt, freshly ground white pepper, and the lemon thyme or thyme leaves. Make a second layer with the rest of the vegetables, and season them as well. Add the cream, or milk and cream, and dot the surface with small pieces of butter, using about 2 tablespoons in all. Lay a piece of foil loosely over the top and bake.

Melt the rest of the butter, and toss it with the bread crumbs. Remove the gratin from the oven after ½ hour, take off the foil, and cover the surface with the bread crumbs. Return the gratin to the oven and continue baking until the vegetables are tender, about another ½ hour. Remove the gratin from the oven, and let it rest 5 to 10 minutes before serving.

This is a rich and creamy dish. Serve it with something clean and simple—spinach or chard, cold poached quince, or, if it is in season, asparagus with lemon juice.

SERVES FOUR TO SIX

Winter Vegetable Stew

A straightforward stew with robust and well-developed flavors, the vegetables are left whole or cut into good-size pieces so that they maintain their integrity and heartiness throughout the cooking. The sauce, the medium in which the various vegetables are cooked and brought together, uses the Wild Mushroom Stock for its liquid (the Winter Vegetable Stock, reduced by half, could also be used). The stock adds greatly to the overall depth and flavor of the stew, and it can be made in advance.

This stew can be served in different ways. It can be cooked entirely on the stove and served with biscuits or grilled polenta, or it can finish cooking in the oven as a shepherd's pie, or under a buttery crust of puff pastry or cream cheese pastry to make a more special presentation. It is also good reheated the next day.

THE SAUCE

2 tablespoons butter
1 tablespoon olive oil
1 medium yellow onion, cut into ½-inch squares
½ teaspoon dried thyme
½ teaspoon dried tarragon
1 bay leaf
½ teaspoon salt
3 cloves garlic, finely chopped
½ cup red wine
3 tablespoons flour
3 cups Wild Mushroom Stock (page 66), heated
2 tablespoons parsley, finely chopped

Heat the butter and the oil in a wide soup pot with a heavy bottom. Add the onion, dried herbs, bay leaf, and salt, and cook over medium heat, stirring frequently, until the onion is nicely browned all over, about 15 minutes. Stir in the garlic and the wine, and reduce by half. Add the flour and cook for 2 minutes; then whisk in the stock. Bring to a boil; then simmer slowly, partially covered, for 25 minutes. Add the parsley and check the seasoning. There will be about 2⅔ cups.

THE STEW

4 to 6 dried shiitake mushrooms
10 ounces boiling onions
4 medium carrots (about 10 ounces)
1 celery root
3 to 4 parsnips (about 10 ounces)
6 ounces mushrooms, wiped clean
1 small cauliflower, broken into large florets
5 ounces brussels sprouts
3 tablespoons butter
2 tablespoons olive oil
Salt
2 cloves garlic, finely chopped
Fresh herbs: parsley, thyme, tarragon, finely chopped
Pepper

Cover the dried mushrooms with a cup of hot water, and set them aside to soak for 20 minutes. Run your fingers over them to loosen any dirt or sand; then remove the caps and cut them into quarters. Strain the soaking water and set aside to use in the stew.

Peel the boiling onions. Leave them whole if they are small, and halve the larger ones, keeping the root end intact. Peel the carrots; then cut them into pieces about 1½ inches long; halve or quarter the thicker ones so that all the pieces are a similar size.

Cut away the gnarly skin of the celery root, cut it into large cubes, and put it in a bowl of water with a little lemon juice until needed. Peel and quarter the parsnips, cut out the cores, and slice them into wide sections. If the mushrooms are small, leave them whole; otherwise cut them into wide, uneven pieces.

Bring a pot of water to a boil, add salt, blanch the cauliflower for 30 seconds, and remove. Parboil the brussels sprouts for 1 minute and remove. Rinse both vegetables with cold water to stop their cooking.

Melt half the butter and a tablespoon of the olive oil in a large skillet or casserole. Add the onions and carrots, and cook over a medium heat about 3 or 4 minutes, until they begin to get a little color. Then add ½ teaspoon salt and ½ cup of the mushroom soaking water, Wild Mushroom Stock, or water. Lower the heat, cover the pan, and cook for 4 to 5 minutes.

In a second pan, heat the remaining butter and oil and add the fresh mushrooms. Cook them briskly over high heat until they begin to brown; then add a little salt, a few tablespoons of soaking water or mushroom stock, and the garlic. Cook another 2 minutes; then add them to the casserole along with the dried mushrooms, celery root, and parsnips. Cook over low heat, covered, for another 3 minutes; then add the sauce, cauliflower, brussels sprouts, and fresh herbs. Season with salt and freshly ground black pepper.

If the stew is to be baked further in the oven, as a shepherd's pie or under a pastry crust, remove it from the heat, transfer it to a suitable casserole, cover it as desired, and bake for 40 minutes at 375°F. Otherwise, continue cooking the stew on top of the stove, slowly, until all the vegetables are tender, 10 to 20 minutes; then serve, garnished with additional fresh herbs. This is a hearty, full-flavored dish that could be served with a zinfandel or a California pinot noir.

SERVES SIX

Shepherd's Pie

Shepherd's pie is traditionally an old-fashioned English lamb stew that is baked under a blanket of mashed potatoes. Here the potatoes cover a stew of winter vegetables.

1 recipe Winter Vegetable Stew (page 224)
4 medium potatoes (about 12 ounces), red or white
3 tablespoons butter
½ cup light cream
Salt
Pepper

Cut the potatoes into large chunks and boil or steam them. Pass them through a food mill or lightly mash them with a fork; then mix in the butter and the cream and season to taste with salt and freshly ground black pepper.

Preheat the oven to 375°F. Ladle the stew into a baking dish or individual ramekins, and cover with a blanket of the potatoes, either piped through a pastry bag or spread by hand. Make a design on the surface, if you like, with the tip of a knife or the tines of a fork. Bake until the potatoes brown slightly and the sauce bubbles to the surface, about 40 minutes.

SERVES FOUR

Cheese and Nut Loaf

This rich terrine, while not intended to imitate meat, is the closest we come to meat loaf. Soft, dense, and chewy, it makes a satisfying main course as well as an excellent filling for stuffed peppers, cabbages, and other vegetables. It is worth making extra to have enough left over for sandwiches.

1½ cups cooked brown rice (see page 284)
1½ cups walnuts
½ cup cashews
1 medium yellow onion, finely chopped
2 tablespoons butter
Salt
2 cloves garlic, finely chopped
½ cup mushrooms, wiped clean and chopped
½ to 1 ounce dried shiitake or porcini mushrooms, soaked for 20 minutes in hot water and chopped
2 tablespoons parsley, chopped
2 teaspoons thyme leaves, chopped, or ½ teaspoon dried thyme
1 tablespoon marjoram, chopped, or 1 teaspoon dried marjoram
1 teaspoon sage, chopped, or ½ teaspoon dried sage
4 eggs, beaten
1 cup cottage cheese
9 to 12 ounces cheese, grated (use a variety of cheeses, depending on what you have on hand and which tastes go well together, i.e., Gruyère, cheddars, muenster, Fontina, jack)
Pepper

Preheat the oven to 350°F. Begin by cooking the rice, unless you already have some cooked. Roast the nuts in the oven for 5 to 7 minutes; then chop them finely.

Cook the onion in the butter over moderate heat until it is translucent; then season with salt and add the garlic, chopped mushrooms, dried mushrooms, and herbs. Cook until the liquid released by the mushrooms has been reduced. Combine this mixture with the rice, nuts, eggs, cottage cheese, and grated cheese. Season to taste with freshly ground black pepper and additional salt, if needed.

Lightly butter a loaf pan; then line it with buttered waxed paper or parchment paper. Fill the pan and bake the loaf at 375°F until the top is golden and rounded, about 1 to 1¼ hours. The loaf should be firm when you give the pan a shake.

Let the loaf sit 10 minutes before turning it out onto a serving plate; then take off the paper. Serve with the Wild Mushroom Sauce or the Herb Béchamel Sauce.

This is a richly flavored, filling dish, so it can be served with light foods—with vegetables that are simply steamed or sautéed, and a brothy soup such as the Leek and Chervil Soup or the Red Onion and Red Wine Soup to begin with, and a salad to finish. For a complementary wine, choose a California cabernet sauvignon.

MAKES 1 LOAF

Brown Rice Casserole

This casserole makes use of leftover brown rice and accumulated ends of various good cheeses, tofu, and vegetables. It makes an unpretentious meal that is wholesome and good. Use vegetables other than those listed—winter squash and yams, celery root, green beans, tomatoes, fennel, eggplant—whatever is appealing.

4 cups cooked brown rice (1⅓ cups raw)
Half block of tofu (8 to 9 ounces)
1 large onion
2 medium carrots
2 stalks celery
1 green pepper
2 medium zucchini or other summer squash
6 ounces mushrooms, wiped clean
1 tablespoon olive oil
1 tablespoon butter
3 cloves garlic, finely chopped
1 teaspoon nutritional yeast (optional)
1 teaspoon ground cumin seeds
1 teaspoon salt
1 cup mushroom broth, vegetable stock, or water
6 ounces grated cheese (jack, muenster, cheddar, Gouda, etc.)
Pepper
Fresh herbs: parsley or cilantro, thyme, marjoram, for garnish

If you don't have any leftover cooked rice, begin by cooking 1⅓ cups of brown rice according to the recipe on page 284. Set the tofu on a slanted board or pan to drain, and prepare the vegetables. Chop the onion, carrots, celery, pepper, and zucchini into pieces that are roughly ½-inch square. Quarter the mushrooms if they are small, and cut them into sixths or eighths if they are large. Return to the tofu, and cut it into ½-inch cubes.

Heat the olive oil and the butter, and fry the onion over medium heat until it is lightly browned, about 5 minutes. Add the garlic, nutritional yeast, if using, cumin, and salt. Stir until blended and cook for 1 minute; then add the carrots, celery, and green pepper. Add ½ cup of the liquid, cover the pan, and braise the vegetables until they have begun to soften, about 5 minutes. Then add the zucchini and the mushrooms and cook another 7 to 10 minutes. The vegetables should be nearly, but not completely, cooked. If the pan gets dry while they are cooking, add a little more liquid.

Preheat the oven to 350°F. Combine the vegetables with the rice and the cheese. Season with salt and plenty of freshly ground black pepper. Gently mix in the tofu, and put the whole mixture into a casserole that has been lightly oiled or buttered, and add a little more liquid to moisten. Cover the casserole with foil and bake for ½ hour. Remove the foil and bake another 15 minutes. Serve garnished with the fresh herbs. This dish, while not an elegant one, would be nicely set off with any number of white wines: a sauvignon blanc, a lesser chardonnay, a dry chenin blanc, or a French colombard.

SERVES FOUR TO SIX

Savory Bread Pudding

At the restaurant we tend to accumulate odds and ends of good cheeses and extra loaves of bread that have gone slightly stale. This pudding is one way to use such leftovers and make a gratifying, though perhaps homely, meal for family and close friends.

Made with white bread, such as the Cottage Cheese-Dill, the pudding is soft and light, and will swell in the oven like a soufflé. If a denser whole grain bread is used, the pudding will be more firm, with a nutty taste. A portion of smoked cheese will enhance the flavor as well.

1 tablespoon butter
1 medium yellow onion, diced
½ teaspoon dried oregano
½ teaspoon dried thyme
¼ cup white wine or water
1 tablespoon olive oil
8 ounces mushrooms, wiped clean and sliced irregularly
Salt
Pepper
2 cups milk
3 eggs, beaten
2 tablespoons chives or green onions, chopped
6 to 8 slices bread
2 cups mixed grated cheeses: Provolone, Parmesan, smoked, jack, Swiss, etc.

Warm the butter in a large skillet over medium heat and begin cooking the onion. Crumble the dried herbs between your fingers onto the onion, and cook until the onion is soft, about 10 to 15 minutes, stirring occasionally. Add a little white wine or water when the pan gets dry.

Add the olive oil, raise the heat, and add the mushrooms; stir until they are coated with oil. Cook them for 3 to 4 minutes, stirring frequently. Remove them from the heat and season with salt and freshly ground black pepper.

Whisk the milk into the beaten eggs and season with ½ teaspoon salt and the chives or green onions.

Trim the crusts from the bread and slice the pieces in half. Butter an oblong baking dish, deep-dish pie plate, or individual ramekins, and arrange half the bread over the bottom, trimming the bread to fit the empty spaces. Spoon the mushroom mixture over the bread, then half the cheese. Follow this with the rest of the bread and the remaining cheese.

Preheat the oven to 375°F. Pour the custard over the top. Cover and bake for 20 minutes. Then remove the cover and continue baking until the custard is set, about another 10 to 15 minutes. The pieces of bread not covered by the custard will get brown and crusty, contrasting with the soft pudding underneath.

Serve with the Late Summer Tomatoes with Fresh Herbs, or another salad that is moist and fresh tasting. This also goes well with a lively tasting accompaniment such as Cherry Tomatoes Sautéed with Shallots and Herbs, or two or three simple vegetable salads.

SERVES FOUR TO SIX

Cheese and Onion Pudding

This pudding is simple to put together for a light lunch or supper. Onions are stewed in butter with thyme, baked in a batter, and cut into wedges like a pie. Serve it with something fresh and firm to play against the tender onions and the richness of the dish. Carrots, asparagus, broccoli, or beets stewed and seasoned with lemon juice would all be fine accompaniments, or a crisp romaine salad and dark, chewy bread.

1½ pounds yellow onions
4 tablespoons butter
1 teaspoon fresh thyme leaves, chopped, or ¼ teaspoon dried thyme
Salt
2 eggs
1 cup milk or light cream
4 tablespoons flour
Pepper
Nutmeg
3 ounces Emmentaler or Gruyère cheese, grated

Peel and halve the onions, and slice them crosswise into pieces ¼ inch thick. Melt 3 tablespoons of the butter in a wide skillet, letting it brown; then add the onions, the thyme, and ½ teaspoon salt. Stir to coat the onions with butter; then turn the heat very low and cook, stirring occasionally, until they are melted and soft, about 30 minutes. Although they will color some, they shouldn't caramelize or brown.

In a large bowl, beat the eggs well with a fork; then mix in the milk, or cream, and the flour. Add ¼ teaspoon salt, and season with freshly ground black pepper and a few scrapings of nutmeg. Strain the batter to remove any lumps.

Preheat the oven to 400°F. Add the onions and most of the cheese to the batter. Butter a 9-inch pie plate or individual gratin dishes. Pour in the onion mixture and cover the top with the remaining cheese. Bake until the surface is firm and browned, about 25 minutes. Let it cool a few minutes; then loosen the edges, cut the pudding into wedges, and serve.

Variation: Use ½ teaspoon ground cumin seeds in place of the thyme.

SERVES FOUR

TARTS *and*

TIMBALES

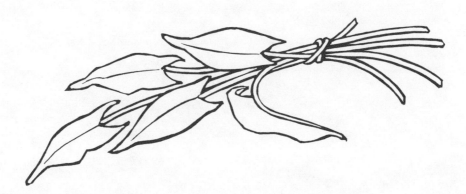

Tarts and timbales are soft, creamy-textured custards containing herbs, often cheese, and vegetables that have been cut very finely or puréed. A tart contains the custard in a pastry shell, while a timbale is baked in ramekins lined with bread crumbs. The fillings for tarts can be baked as timbales, and the reverse is true as well.

Tarts are visually very appealing. Baked in large low pans, the fillings swell and color beautifully, and are framed with a golden crust. Timbales are charming baked in small individual molds, turned out, set on a plate, and ringed with sauce. They can also be baked in a large mold or loaf pan, unmolded, and then sliced. They require long, slow baking in a water bath so that the texture will be smooth, but the initial preparations take very little time. Once finished, timbales in ramekins hold their heat well. The tarts bake at a higher heat in less time, but being broad and flat, they quickly cool.

Many of these recipes call for cream, which gives a silky, smooth texture to the fillings, but because it is rich, cream may best be used when the dishes are to be served as appetizers or in small portions. Milk, or a mixture of milk and cream, can be used in place of the cream.

Tarts and timbales can be offered confidently as a main course at a lunch or dinner, accompanied with simply prepared vegetables of contrasting color and feel. Serve a sauce with the timbales, and a salad with either.

Tart Dough

This buttery crust can be used for sweet or savory dishes, baked in either a pie pan or a fluted French tart pan with a removable bottom. This recipe will make a crust for a 9-inch pie or tart.

1 cup unbleached white flour
⅜ teaspoon salt
4 tablespoons cold unsalted butter, cut into small cubes
1½ tablespoons solid vegetable shortening
2½ to 3 tablespoons ice water

Combine the flour and salt in a bowl; then add the butter and shortening. With your hands, work the fat and flour together, sliding and flattening the mixture between your palms, or thumb and fingertips, until the butter and shortening are evenly distributed. Add 2½ tablespoons cold water, and lightly work it into the flour, using your fingers, slightly cupped together, or a fork. Gather the dough into a ball, sprinkle a few drops of water over any remaining dry ingredients, and gather them together. Cover the dough with waxed paper or plastic wrap, flatten it into a disk, and let it rest at least 30 minutes in the refrigerator before using. The dough can also be frozen at this point for future use.

When you are ready to roll the dough, lightly flour the work surface and the top of the dough. If it is stiff from the cold, let it sit for 20 minutes before you roll it out. Roll it out with firm, even strokes into a circle about ⅛ inch thick. Pick it up on the rolling pin and slide it onto the pie dish or tart mold. Or, alternatively, fold it into quarters, lay it with the point in the center of the pan, then unfold. Trim the edges, leaving an overhang of an inch or so; then fold the overhang under and crimp the edge.

To partially prebake the crust, first freeze the empty shell until it is quite firm. If you intend to freeze the crust for an extended period of time, wrap it in foil. When ready to use, preheat the oven to 425°F. Set the frozen tart shell directly into the oven, and bake until the crust has a "set" appearance and is just beginning to color, about 8 to 10 minutes. While the crust is baking, check to see that the bottom is not swelling with steam and air. If it does, prick it lightly with a paring knife.

More traditionally, the crust may be prebaked unfrozen, first lining it with buttered foil, filling the foil with pie weights or dry beans, then baking, as above, until the edges are set and slightly browned.

DOUGH FOR ONE 9-INCH TART

Yeasted Tart Dough

This is tender dough, very quick to assemble, that makes a tart shell with a buttery, yeasty flavor and a light, bready crust. It uses less butter than most tart pastry doughs and is particularly good filled with cheeses and custards.

1 teaspoon active dry yeast (½ package)
Pinch sugar
¼ cup warm water
1 large egg, room temperature
About 1¼ cups unbleached white flour
½ teaspoon salt
½ teaspoon grated lemon peel (optional)
3 tablespoons crème fraîche or soft unsalted butter

Dissolve the yeast and sugar in the water, and set it in a warm place. Meanwhile, if the egg is cold from the refrigerator, cover it with hot water, let it sit a few minutes to bring it up to room temperature. Combine 1 cup of the flour, the salt, and the grated lemon peel, if using, in a bowl and make a well. Break the egg into the middle of it; add the crème fraîche or butter and pour in the yeast mixture, which should be foamy with bubbles. Mix everything together with a wooden spoon to form a smooth, soft dough. Dust it with flour, gather it into a ball, and set it in a clean bowl and cover. Let the dough rise in a warm place until it is doubled in bulk, 45 minutes to an hour. If you are not ready to shape the dough at this time, punch it down, and let it rise again.

Use a 10-inch tart pan with a removable bottom. Flatten the dough, place it in the center of the pan, and press it out to the edge using either your knuckles or the heel of your hand. Add only enough flour to keep the dough from sticking. If the dough shrinks back while you are shaping it, cover it with a towel, let it relax for 20 minutes, then finish pressing it out. It should be thin on the bottom and thicker at the sides, about ¼ inch higher than the rim of the pan. It can be filled immediately or refrigerated until needed. Once the tart is filled, bake in the middle of a 375°F oven for 35 to 45 minutes.

DOUGH FOR ONE 10-INCH TART

Artichoke Tart

This large handsome tart is made with small artichokes that are baked in a custard infused with garlic and herbs. Although 2 pounds of artichokes may look overwhelming, they can be easily trimmed and quartered in about 15 minutes.

1 recipe Yeasted Tart Dough (page 237)
4 whole cloves garlic, unpeeled
2 lemons
2 pounds small artichokes, about 2 inches long
3 tablespoons virgin olive oil
1 large onion, chopped into ¼-inch squares
1½ tablespoons parsley, finely chopped
1 tablespoon fresh thyme leaves, finely chopped, or ½ teaspoon dried thyme
½ teaspoon salt
½ cup white wine
3 cloves garlic, finely chopped
¼ cup water
Pepper
1½ cups heavy or light cream, or half-and-half
1 bay leaf
4 eggs
2 ounces Provolone cheese, grated

Prepare the yeasted tart dough, and set it aside to rise in a warm place while you prepare the filling.

Put the whole cloves of garlic in a small saucepan, cover them with water, bring to a boil, then lower the heat and simmer, covered, until the insides are soft, about 20 minutes. Drain, and set them aside until needed.

Squeeze the lemons into a bowl of water. Take each artichoke, cut off the stem at the base, and remove the dark green outer leaves, snapping them backward until they break. Stop when you reach the pale tender leaves; then slice off the top third of each artichoke. Trim the base so it is smooth. Halve the smallest artichokes and quarter the larger ones. If there are any signs of choke, cut it out. As soon as you finish trimming the pieces, put them in the acidulated water to prevent their discoloring.

Heat 2 tablespoons of the olive oil, add the onion, a tablespoon of the parsley, a teaspoon of the thyme, and the salt. Cook for several minutes over medium-high heat; then add the wine and reduce it to a syrupy consistency. Add the last tablespoon of oil, the chopped garlic, and the artichokes. Toss everything together to coat with the oil and cook for several minutes; then add the quarter cup of water, lower the heat, and cover. Cook until the artichokes are tender, about 15 minutes; then season with salt and freshly ground black pepper.

While the artichokes are cooking, combine the cream with the remaining fresh herbs and bay leaf in a small saucepan. Take the cooked garlic cloves, squeeze out the soft insides, then smooth them out by pressing on them with the flat side of a knife. Stir this garlic purée into the cream; then heat until little bubbles have formed around the edge. Turn off the heat and let stand, covered, until needed. When you are ready to make the custard, beat the eggs, remove the bay leaf from the cream, then slowly whisk the cream into the eggs. Season with salt and milled pepper.

Fit the yeasted pastry into the tart pan, pressing it out evenly to the edges. Wait 10 minutes, and then press it up the sides so that it is thin on the bottom and thicker on the sides. Preheat the oven to 350°F. Reserve eight or more artichoke pieces for a decorative garnish, and purée the remainder in a food processor, leaving some texture, if you wish. Cover the tart dough with the artichoke purée, then the grated cheese, and carefully pour the custard over all. Set the reserved pieces of artichoke in the custard. The artichoke purée and custard will form two distinct layers as they bake.

Bake the tart until the custard is set and the top is golden, 40 to 50 minutes. Remove it from the oven, brush a little olive oil over the crust, and let it rest 5 minutes or so before serving. Artichokes have a unique flavor that needs a wine with moderate flavor, such as a dry chenin blanc or a vin gris.

MAKES ONE 10-INCH TART

Eggplant-Tomato Tart

Slender, oval Roma or plum tomatoes are ideal to use in this tart: They have a firm flesh, little juice, and are not too large. For a variation in flavor, especially when good ripe tomatoes aren't available, use three or four sun-dried tomatoes, puréed or cut into narrow strips, and add them to the eggplant and fresh tomatoes.

1 recipe Tart Dough (page 236)
3 to 4 Japanese eggplants (about 12 ounces)
About ⅓ cup olive oil
Salt
Pepper
3 tomatoes (about 8 ounces)
2 whole eggs
1 egg yolk
1½ cups light cream or half-and-half
Nutmeg
½ cup basil leaves, loosely packed and thinly sliced
½ cup Gruyère or Provolone cheese, grated

Prepare the tart dough. Partially prebake it, and set it aside.

Preheat the oven to 450°F. Slice the eggplants into rounds or diagonal pieces about ⅜ inch thick. Coat a baking sheet with a film of oil; then lay down the eggplant slices. Brush the surfaces generously with plenty of oil so that the eggplant will not dry out; excess oil can always be blotted up later with paper towels. Season with salt and pepper and bake in a 450°F to 500°F oven until the eggplant slices are lightly browned and tender, but not completely soft, about 10 minutes on each side—they will bake further in the tart.

Bring a pan of water to a boil, plunge in the tomatoes to a count of ten, and immediately remove them to a bowl of cold water to stop the cooking. When they have cooled, peel them, then slice off one end, pull out the juice and seeds with your fingers, then slice them into rounds as thick as the eggplant. (If the tomatoes are large, cut the slices in half.)

Set the oven heat at 375°F. Beat the eggs and egg yolk together; then whisk in the light cream. Add ½ teaspoon salt, several grindings of black pepper, a few scrapings of nutmeg, and the basil. Scatter the cheese over the surface of the partially baked crust. Loosely layer the eggplant and tomatoes over the cheese; then pour the custard over all. Bake the tart until the custard is set and the surface is golden—about 35 to 40 minutes. Let it cool at least 10 minutes before serving. This tart would go nicely with a California pinot noir.

MAKES ONE 9-INCH TART

Red and Yellow Pepper Tart

This hot weather tart is colorful, sweet, and flavorful with basil. Thinly sliced peppers are baked in a custard laced with cheese. Serve with Grilled Zucchini with Herb Butter, or a trio of summer vegetable salads, and Peach Ice Cream for dessert.

1 recipe Yeasted Tart Dough (page 237) or Tart Dough (page 236)
3 medium or 2 large bell peppers, mixed colors, but preferably red and yellow
4 tablespoons olive oil
1 small red onion, quartered, sliced thinly crosswise
2 cloves garlic, finely chopped
Salt
¼ cup water or white wine
Pepper
1 cup basil leaves, loosely packed and roughly chopped
2 tablespoons Parmesan or Romano cheese, grated
2 whole eggs plus 2 egg yolks
1½ cups light cream
1 cup Provolone cheese, grated
20 black Niçoise olives, pitted

Prepare the tart dough. If you are using the unyeasted crust, partially prebake it.

Halve the peppers lengthwise, remove the seeds and veins, then halve them crosswise and slice very thinly. Warm 2 tablespoons of the olive oil in a wide pan, add the peppers, onion, half the garlic, and ¼ teaspoon salt. Sauté over medium–high heat for several minutes; then lower the heat, add the water or white wine, cover, and stew until the peppers and onion are very soft and sweet. If the peppers and onion threaten to stick as the sugars are released, add additional small amounts of water or wine. Taste for salt, and season with freshly ground black pepper when the peppers and onion are finished cooking.

Put 2 tablespoons of the olive oil in a blender jar with the remaining garlic and a few of the basil leaves, and purée. Gradually add the rest of the basil leaves, using more oil if necessary. Scrape the purée out of the jar, stir in the Parmesan or Romano cheese, and season with salt.

If using the yeasted tart dough, prepare the shell; then make the custard. Beat the eggs and yolks together; then add the cream, ½ teaspoon salt, and pepper.

Preheat the oven to 400°F. Paint the crust with the basil purée; then lay half the grated Provolone cheese on top, followed by the peppers and onion, and the olives. Add the remaining cheese, then the custard. Bake the tart in the center of the oven until it is golden brown and set, 35 to 40 minutes. Let the tart rest 5 or 10 minutes before serving. For wine, serve this tart with a red or white zinfandel, a French Côtes-du-Rhône, or perhaps a California cabernet.

MAKES ONE 9-INCH TART

Spinach and Goat Cheese Pie

In this country pie the spinach leaves are left in large pieces and the cheese is coarsely crumbled, giving it a marbled appearance. Use a creamy French goat cheese such as Boucheron or Lezay, or a feta. If you do use feta cheese, be prepared to reduce the amount of salt in the custard.

1 recipe Tart Dough (page 236)
1 bunch (1 pound) spinach
2 bunches scallions
3 tablespoons butter
1 to 2 cloves garlic, finely chopped
1 tablespoon fresh marjoram leaves or ½ teaspoon dried marjoram
1 tablespoon parsley, chopped
Salt
Pepper
2 whole eggs
2 egg yolks
5 ounces goat cheese (Boucheron, Montrachet, Lezay, etc.)
1 cup milk
1 cup heavy cream
Nutmeg

Prepare the tart dough, and partially prebake it. Set it aside until needed.

Remove the stems from the spinach and cut the leaves into large pieces. Wash them thoroughly in a large bowl of water, using 2 changes of water if it is particularly sandy.

Trim the roots and most of the greens off the scallions, and thinly slice them. Melt the butter in a wide skillet, add the scallions, garlic, marjoram, and parsley, and cook over medium heat for about 1 minute. Gradually begin to add the spinach, handfuls at a time, as much as the pan will comfortably take. Let each batch of spinach begin to soften and wilt before adding the next. Season with salt and freshly ground black pepper, and set aside.

Beat the eggs and egg yolks with half the cheese until they are fairly smooth; then add the milk and cream, a scraping of nutmeg, ½ teaspoon salt, and some milled black pepper.

Preheat the oven to 375°F. Lay the spinach over the bottom of the partially baked crust and crumble the remaining cheese on top. Add the custard; then bake the pie until it is set and lightly browned, about 35 to 45 minutes. Let it rest 5 minutes before serving.

MAKES ONE 9-INCH PIE

Chard and Saffron Tart

The combination of saffron and chard is unusual and interesting. The pine nuts turn golden as they bake and look pretty scattered over the surface. Serve with a salad of butter lettuces with oranges, or fennel, either sautéed in olive oil or baked in the oven with a little Parmesan.

1 recipe Yeasted Tart Dough (page 237)
1 large bunch of chard, enough to make 6 to 8 cups leaves, roughly chopped
1 tablespoon butter
1 tablespoon olive oil
1 large yellow onion, cut into ¼-inch squares
2 cloves garlic, finely chopped
¾ teaspoon salt
3 eggs
1½ cups milk or cream
Large pinch saffron threads, soaked in 1 tablespoon hot water
½ teaspoon lemon peel or ¼ teaspoon orange peel, grated
3 tablespoons Parmesan, freshly grated
Nutmeg
1 tablespoon parsley, chopped
Pepper
3 tablespoons pine nuts

Prepare the yeasted tart dough, and set it aside to rise in a warm place.

Cut the chard leaves away from the stems, and save the stems for another purpose. Chop the leaves into pieces roughly an inch square, wash them in a large bowl of water, and set them aside in a colander.

Heat the butter and oil in a wide skillet; add the onion and cook it over medium heat until it is translucent and soft. Add the garlic, the chard leaves, by handfuls, if necessary, until they all fit, and the salt. Turn the leaves over repeatedly with a pair of tongs so that they are all exposed to the heat of the pan, and cook until they are tender, 5 minutes or more.

Prepare the tart shell; then make the custard. Beat the eggs; then stir in the milk or cream, infused saffron, lemon or orange peel, grated Parmesan, a few scrapings of nutmeg, and the parsley. Stir in the chard and onion mixture; taste, and season with more salt, if needed, and freshly ground black pepper.

Preheat the oven to 375°F. Toast the pine nuts in a small pan until they are lightly colored. Pour the filling into the tart shell and scatter the pine nuts over the surface. Bake until the top is golden and firm, about 40 minutes. For wine, consider a light zinfandel, or a vin gris.

SERVES FOUR TO SIX

Sorrel-Onion Tart

The almost lemony, tart taste of sorrel is very pleasing with the sweet stewed onions. Even a small amount of sorrel will transform the character of what would otherwise be a more predictable onion pie. Though expensive to buy, sorrel is easy to grow. Plants can be bought in nurseries, put in the ground, and harvested leaf-by-leaf for several years. It would be worth having a few plants to be able to make this tart on a regular basis.

1 recipe Tart Dough (page 236)
4 tablespoons butter, in all
1 large red onion, thinly sliced
½ teaspoon salt
4 to 8 ounces sorrel leaves
2 large eggs
1 cup heavy cream
2 ounces Gruyère cheese, grated
Pepper

Prepare the tart dough, partially prebake it, and set it aside.

Melt 3 tablespoons of the butter in a wide pan, add the onion and the salt. Cover the pan, and stew slowly until the onion is completely soft, about 10 minutes. Check it occasionally and give it a stir.

While the onion is cooking, cut off the stems of the sorrel leaves and roughly slice the leaves. Melt the remaining tablespoon of butter in a pan, and add the sorrel by large handfuls. Although the amount of leaves will seem voluminous, they will quickly cook down to almost nothing. Cook over a low heat until they have wilted and turned a grayish-green color, 3 to 4 minutes.

Whisk the eggs with the cream; then stir in the onion, sorrel, and half of the cheese. Taste for salt, and season with freshly ground black pepper.

Preheat the oven to 375°F. Distribute the remaining cheese over the crust; then pour the filling on top. Bake in the center of the oven until the custard is set and well colored, about 35 to 40 minutes. Serve the tart while it is hot. For wine, consider serving a chardonnay or French white Burgundy.

This tart is based on a recipe from Richard Olney's *Simple French Food*.

MAKES ONE 9-INCH TART

Leek and Mustard Pie

The mustard gives a little bite to the natural sweetness of the leeks in this pie. Different kinds of cheese go well with leeks, particularly a sharp natural cheddar or Cantal. Swiss, Gruyère, and creamy goat cheese are also good.

1 recipe Tart Dough (page 236)
4 to 5 cups leeks (about 1 pound, trimmed), cut into ¼-inch rings
3 tablespoons butter
½ cup white wine or water
½ teaspoon salt
Pepper
2 eggs
1 cup cream or crème fraîche
2 to 3 tablespoons good quality smooth or coarse mustard
3 ounces grated cheese, or 4 ounces goat cheese
2 tablespoons chives, sliced into narrow rounds

Prepare the tart dough, and partially prebake it.

Wash the leeks well and set them aside. Melt the butter in a wide skillet, add the leeks along with the water that still clings to them, and cook 2 to 3 minutes, stirring frequently.

Add the wine or water and the salt, cover, reduce the heat, and cook slowly until the leeks are tender, about 10 to 15 minutes. Check the pan after 7 minutes, and add more wine or water, if necessary. When done, season with freshly ground black pepper.

Beat the eggs and stir in the cream, crème fraîche, mustard, leeks, and grated cheese. If you are using goat cheese, work half of it into the custard and crumble the other half over the top just before baking.

Preheat the oven to 375°F. Pour the custard into the prebaked shell, smooth down the top, and scatter the chives over the entire surface. Bake the pie until the top is firm and golden brown. Let it sit for 5 minutes before serving.

MAKES ONE 9-INCH PIE

Winter Squash Tart

Delicate and naturally sweet from the squash and the leeks, this tart has a mild flavor. Accompany it with strong foods such as the Wild Rice Pilaf with Dried Mushrooms, Butter-Fried Onions with Vinegar and Thyme, or an endive salad with Gorgonzola cheese. Perfection, butternut, and acorn squash are all excellent choices. The buttery flavor and crispness of the short crust make a good contrast to the smoothness of the filling.

1 winter squash or pumpkin (about 1½ pounds)
Olive oil
Salt
Pepper
1 recipe Tart Dough (page 236)
2 medium leeks (about 4 to 5 ounces), white parts with a little green
2 tablespoons butter
2 eggs
⅓ cup crème fraîche or heavy cream
½ cup milk
3 ounces Gruyère cheese, grated
½ teaspoon thyme leaves, finely chopped
1 teaspoon parsley, finely chopped
Nutmeg

Preheat the oven to 400°F. Cut the squash in half, remove the seeds and pulp, brush the surface with oil, and season with salt and pepper. Place it cut side down on a baking sheet, and bake until the skin is puckered and the squash is soft, about an hour. Remove it from the oven, let it cool enough to handle easily, then scoop out the flesh. Pass it through a food mill or chinoise to smooth out the texture. There should be about 1½ cups.

While the squash is baking, prepare the tart dough. Partially bake it and set it aside.

Trim the leeks, quarter them lengthwise, slice them into ¼-inch squares, and wash them well. Melt the butter in a skillet, add the leeks, and cook over medium-high heat until they are tender, 7 to 10 minutes. Add a little water after the first 3 or 4 minutes to help the cooking and keep them from burning. Season with salt.

Beat the eggs in a bowl with the crème fraîche or cream, milk, and squash. Stir in the leeks, grated cheese, and herbs; then season to taste with salt, pepper, and a few scrapings of nutmeg.

Set the oven heat at 375°F. Pour the batter into the tart shell and bake in the center of the oven until it is firm and flecked with spots of brown from the melted cheese, about 45 to 50 minutes. Remove the tart from the oven, let it rest for 5 to 10 minutes, and serve it on a platter.

MAKES ONE 9- OR 10-INCH TART

Roquefort Tart

This large fragrant tart is especially well suited to the yeasted crust. Rich and strongly flavored, it can be served as an appetizer as well as an entrée, and it is especially good eaten in the fall and winter months. Because Roquefort is often salty, no additional salt is called for in this recipe. Other blue cheeses could also be used, but avoid those with heavy blue veining or the tart will have a green-gray cast to it.

1 recipe Yeasted Tart Dough (page 237)
6 ounces Roquefort cheese
3 ounces cream cheese
3/4 cup heavy cream
4 eggs, 1 tablespoon egg white set aside
Pepper
Nutmeg
1/2 cup bread crumbs

Prepare the dough for the yeasted tart, and set it aside to rise. Then press it into a 10-inch tart pan.

For the filling, work the cheeses and cream together to make a fairly smooth paste. Any lumps of cheese will melt as they bake. Set aside a tablespoon of egg white; then beat in the eggs one at a time. Season with freshly ground black pepper and a few scrapings of nutmeg.

Preheat the oven to 375°F. Toast the bread crumbs until they are dry and browned. Brush the tart shell with the reserved egg white, and press the bread crumbs over the bottom of the tart.

Add the filling and bake the tart in the center of the oven until the surface is golden and firm, 45 to 50 minutes. Remove the rim from the pan, set the tart on a platter, and serve while hot.

A salad of mixed greens including chicories with small branches of chervil, parsley, and other herbs would nicely complement this rich, creamy tart.

MAKES ONE 10-INCH TART

Creamy Asparagus Timbale

Made with a purée of asparagus, the texture of this timbale is completely soft and smooth. The tips are cooked separately and served on the side to provide a contrasting texture. This creamy type of timbale works best baked in small ramekins, and served as a first course, or as a small entrée in a meal with many courses. In this recipe, stock is used rather than cream, to make a lighter, less rich timbale, but cream can be used if you prefer.

2 pounds asparagus
½ yellow onion, roughly chopped
5 sprigs parsley
Few branches fresh thyme or a pinch dried thyme
1 bay leaf
Salt
3½ cups water
2 bunches scallions
2 tablespoons butter
1 tablespoon parsley, finely chopped
5 eggs
Pepper
Nutmeg
¼ cup Parmesan, finely grated (optional)
About ½ cup toasted bread crumbs

Wash the asparagus, cut off the tips, and set them aside. Snap off the tough ends; then break or cut them into large pieces and make a stock: Combine the asparagus ends with the onion, parsley sprigs, thyme, bay leaf, and ½ teaspoon salt in a saucepan; cover with the water, bring to a boil, then lower the heat and simmer 30 minutes; then strain.

Chop the remaining stalks of asparagus into small pieces. Remove the roots and all but an inch of the greens from the scallions, and chop them into large pieces. Melt the butter, add the chopped asparagus, scallions, chopped parsley, and ½ teaspoon salt. Cook for about 1 minute, stirring frequently; then add a cup of the stock. Cover the pan, simmer over medium-low heat until the asparagus is tender, about 4 to 5 minutes, and drain. Blend or work in a food processor to make a smooth purée without any fibrous matter in it; if necessary, pass it through a fine sieve or chinoise. Measure the purée and add enough stock to make 2 cups.

Beat the eggs well; then stir in the asparagus purée. Season with salt, freshly ground black pepper, and a modest grating of nutmeg. Add the grated Parmesan, if using.

Preheat the oven to 325°F. Use ramekins with a 1-cup capacity; butter them well, and line them generously with the bread crumbs. Fill them ¾ full, set them in a deep baking pan, and add enough hot water to come halfway up their sides. Bake until they are well set and slightly puffed, about 1 hour or so. Remove them from the oven, let them sit a few minutes, then turn them out onto serving plates, top side up, and serve with the asparagus tips.

To cook the asparagus tips, melt 2 tablespoons of butter in a sauté pan with ½ cup or more of the remaining stock, add the asparagus, and season with salt. Cook over medium-high heat about 3 to 4 minutes until the tips are done; then serve them around the timbales.

In addition to, or instead of, serving the timbale with an accompaniment of asparagus tips, serve it with the Béchamel with Lemon and Lemon Thyme, with the tops of the timbales garnished with bread crumbs that have been fried in butter until they are crisp and crunchy. For a wine, choose a young, fresh Beaujolais or a vin gris.

SERVES FOUR TO SIX

Asparagus and Green Onion Timbale

In early spring, asparagus is always tempting even though it's expensive. Here is a way to enjoy it as a main course.

2 bunches green onions (scallions)
1 pound thin asparagus
2 tablespoons butter
1 small clove garlic, finely chopped
½ teaspoon salt
White pepper
4 tablespoons white wine or water
4 to 5 eggs
2 cups milk or cream, heated
3 ounces Gruyère cheese, grated
1 to 2 ounces Parmesan, finely grated
Nutmeg
About ½ cup toasted bread crumbs
Herb Béchamel (page 310) or Béchamel with Lemon and Lemon Thyme (page 310)

Cut off the root ends of the scallions, and all but an inch of the greens, and rinse them well. Slice them lengthwise; then chop them finely. Snap off the tough ends of the asparagus and discard, or save them to use in a soup stock. Cut off the tips and slice the remaining stalks into narrow rounds. In all there should be 2½ to 3 cups.

Melt the butter in a skillet; add the scallions, asparagus, and garlic. Stir to coat everything with the butter, and season with the salt and freshly ground white pepper. Cook over medium heat for a minute, stirring frequently, add the wine or water, and continue to cook until the asparagus is nearly done and the liquid is reduced, about 3 minutes. Set aside.

Beat the eggs well, gradually whisk in the warmed milk, then stir in the cheeses and the asparagus and scallions. Season with just a few scrapings of nutmeg, and taste for salt and pepper.

Preheat the oven to 325°F. Generously butter 1-cup-capacity ramekins and line them with the bread crumbs. Put any extra bread crumbs into the timbale mixture. Divide the custard among the ramekins, place them in a deep baking pan, and fill it with enough hot water to come halfway up the ramekins' sides. Bake until the tops are well-colored and firm, about 1 hour. Make the sauce while the timbales are cooking. When they are done remove them from the oven and let them rest for a few minutes before unmolding. Slide a knife around the edge, turn them out onto your hand, and then place them, top side up, on each serving plate. Serve with the sauce spooned attractively around or over it. A California pinot blanc or pinot bianco would be a good wine to serve with this timbale.

SERVES FOUR TO SIX

Corn Pudding with Dill and Parsley

When made with really fresh, sweet corn, this pudding can be quite delicate. If the corn is not so fresh and its sugars have turned to starch, the pudding will have a little more heft, but either way, the corn flavor pervades the entire dish. Bake it in one large dish or individual ramekins, and serve it with something cool and fresh—the Sweet Pepper Relish or thick slices of ripe summer tomatoes—and a side of Black Bean Chili. This is quick to assemble and makes a filling family supper.

6 ears white or yellow sweet corn
½ cup milk
4 or 5 eggs
¾ cup cream, warmed
3 ounces jack or muenster cheese, grated
1 tablespoon each dill and parsley, finely chopped
½ teaspoon salt
White or black pepper
About ½ cup toasted bread crumbs

Shave the kernels from the corn with a knife. Set aside 1 cup of kernels, and put the rest in a blender with the milk and make a fairly smooth purée. This will take from 2 to 3 minutes, which may seem like a long time for the blender to be running.

Beat the eggs well with a whisk; then stir in the corn purée, corn kernels, cream, cheese, dill, and parsley. Season with the salt and several grindings of pepper.

Preheat the oven to 325°F. Thoroughly coat a large baking dish, or 1-cup-capacity ramekins, with butter, and line them liberally with bread crumbs. Add the custard, set the baking dish in a deep pan, and add hot water to come halfway up the sides. Bake the pudding for about 1 hour and 10 minutes if it is in a single dish, 50 to 55 minutes if divided among smaller ramekins. When the top is firm and lightly browned, remove the pudding from the oven and let it rest a few minutes before serving. Serve the pudding in its baking dish, or unmold it and serve it top side up. With its herbal seasoning, this corn pudding could be complemented with either a cabernet sauvignon or a sauvignon blanc.

SERVES FOUR TO SIX

Corn and Zucchini Timbale with Ancho Chili Sauce

This is one of our favorite dishes to make in the summer when the local corn and tomatoes come in. The timbale is seasoned with cilantro, and the tomato sauce with roasted garlic and chilies, making a colorful and highly flavorful meal.

4 to 5 medium zucchini (1 pound)
Salt
2 tablespoons butter
4 tablespoons yellow onion, diced into ¼-inch squares
2 cups fresh yellow corn kernels (about 4 ears)
4 tablespoons parsley, finely chopped
3 tablespoons cilantro, finely chopped
¼ cup white wine
5 eggs
⅔ cup heavy cream, warmed
3 ounces or 1 cup sharp cheddar cheese, grated
¼ teaspoon cayenne pepper
Tabasco sauce to taste (optional)
¾ cup bread crumbs
Ancho Chili Sauce (page 317)

Grate the zucchini by hand using the large holes on a grater, or process it in a food processor. Toss it with salt, let it sit for a half hour, then drain and squeeze out the water, either using your hands or putting the mass in a clean kitchen towel and twisting hard several times.

Melt the butter, add the onion, followed a minute later with the corn, parsley, and cilantro. Stir together and cook over medium heat for a minute; then add the zucchini and wine, lower the heat, and cook covered for about 3 minutes. Remove the lid, and cook off any remaining liquid. Taste, and season with salt, if needed.

Beat the eggs, whisk in the cream, then add the vegetables and cheese. Season with the cayenne and Tabasco sauce to taste, if using, and taste again for salt.

Preheat the oven to 325°F. Generously butter 1-cup-capacity ramekins, or a large mold, and coat them with the bread crumbs. Mix any extra bread crumbs into the custard; then ladle it into the ramekins, making sure there is an even distribution of vegetables. Set the ramekins in a deep pan and add enough hot water to come halfway up their sides. Bake until the tops puff up and are browned, about 1 hour. Prepare the Ancho Chili Sauce while the custards are baking. Take the custards out of the oven and let them sit for a few minutes, then unmold them. Serve them top side up on a plate with the sauce spooned around or over them. This timbale is also good with the Grilled Tomato Sauce or the Fresh Tomato Sauce.

SERVES FOUR TO SIX

Mushroom Timbale with Sorrel Sauce

There is a pure mushroom flavor in this timbale that comes through whether it is made with wild or cultivated mushrooms. The texture is smooth and uniform. Serve this with the Sorrel Sauce, which is slightly tart, making a pleasing contrast to the richness of the timbales.

14 ounces mushrooms
2 tablespoons butter
¼ small yellow onion, very finely chopped
1 clove garlic, finely chopped
2 teaspoons parsley, finely chopped
1 teaspoon thyme leaves and blossoms, finely chopped, or ¼ teaspoon dried thyme
Salt
Pepper
5 eggs
2 cups light cream or milk, warmed
Nutmeg
About ½ cup toasted bread crumbs
Sorrel Sauce (page 312)

Clean the mushrooms and chop them finely, either by hand or in a food processor. Heat the butter in a skillet; add the onion and cook for a minute or two until it has softened and colored a little. Add the mushrooms, garlic, parsley, and thyme, raise the heat, and cook briskly until all the moisture has been reabsorbed, about 3 to 4 minutes. Turn off the heat and season with salt and freshly ground black pepper.

Beat the eggs well; then stir in the cream or milk, and add the mushrooms. Season with a few scrapings of nutmeg, and salt and black pepper to taste. Put the filling in a food processor or blender and process until the custard is fairly smooth but still retains some flecks of mushroom.

Preheat the oven to 325°F. Butter 1-cup-capacity ramekins well, and coat them liberally with the bread crumbs. Fill them; then set them in a deep pan and add enough hot water to come halfway up their sides. Bake until they are firm to the touch, about 1 hour. Prepare the sorrel sauce while the timbales are cooking. When they are done let them cool briefly; then unmold them onto your hand and set them on serving plates, top side up, with the sauce spooned around or over them.

This could also be served with the Herb Béchamel Sauce or the Béchamel Sauce with Lemon and Lemon Thyme. For a wine, try a California barbera, a Chianti, or a French Côtes-du-Rhône.

SERVES FOUR TO SIX

Eggplant and Zucchini Timbale with Sweet Pepper Relish

When the distinct flavors of the zucchini and eggplant merge, they become surprisingly evocative of corn and mushrooms. It is very good served with the Sweet Pepper Relish, which makes an interesting change from the more usual creamy kind of sauce.

Sweet Pepper Relish (page 319)
4 to 5 medium zucchini (1 pound)
1 medium eggplant (1 pound)
Salt
2 tablespoons virgin olive oil
2 medium yellow onions, cut into a small dice
3 cloves garlic, finely chopped
¼ cup parsley, chopped
2 teaspoons fresh oregano or marjoram, chopped
1½ teaspoons fresh thyme, chopped
½ cup white wine
5 eggs, beaten
⅔ cup cream or half-and-half, warmed
3 ounces Provolone cheese, grated
1 ounce Parmesan or Asiago cheese, grated
Pepper
½ cup bread crumbs

Prepare the sweet pepper relish and set it aside to marinate.

Grate the zucchini and the eggplant on the large holes of a four-sided grater, or in a food processor. If it is difficult to grate the eggplant, chop it finely by hand. Toss the zucchini with ½ teaspoon of salt, and the eggplant with 1 teaspoon of salt, and set them aside for ½ hour to drain. Press out the liquid by squeezing the vegetables firmly in your hands or wrapping them in a corner of a clean kitchen towel and twisting hard several times.

Heat the oil in a skillet; add the onions and sauté over medium–high heat. After a few minutes add the zucchini, eggplant, garlic, and fresh herbs, lower the heat to medium, and cook for about 3 minutes. Add the wine, cover the pan, and stew over a low heat for 15 to 20 minutes, until the eggplant is well cooked.

Beat the eggs; then stir in the cream, or half-and-half, the cheeses, and the cooked vegetables. Season with freshly ground black pepper, and taste for salt.

Preheat the oven to 325°F. Coat 1-cup-capacity ramekins generously with butter, then with bread crumbs. Ladle in the custard, and set the dishes in a deep pan and add enough hot water to come halfway up their sides. Bake in the middle of the oven until they are set, swollen, and lightly browned on top, about 1 hour.

When the timbales are done, remove them from the oven, let them rest for 5 minutes, then slide a knife around the edges and unmold. Serve them top side up with the sweet pepper relish and a garnish of something fresh and green, such as watercress.

SERVES FOUR TO SIX

Mosaic Timbale

Making this custard is a way to use whatever vegetables you have on hand. This version is made with summer vegetables, but others can be used as well—asparagus and peas in the spring; broccoli, carrots, and cauliflower in the fall; and various root vegetables in the winter. Regardless of the season, finely cut leeks and onions, stewed in butter, as well as fresh herbs, always lend good flavor to timbales.

1 to 2 leeks, white parts only (about 3 ounces)
1 tablespoon butter
1 medium carrot, diced into ¼-inch squares
2 cloves garlic, finely chopped
2 teaspoons parsley, finely chopped
1 teaspoon thyme or marjoram, finely chopped, or ¼ teaspoon dried thyme and
*   ½ teaspoon marjoram*
Salt
Pepper
1 cup each yellow and red pepper, diced into small squares
1 cup small green beans, cut into ¼-inch rounds
2 to 2½ cups spinach or chard leaves, washed and roughly cut into 1-inch squares
5 eggs
¾ cup light cream or milk, warmed
1½ ounces smoked cheese, grated , (Brüder Basil, smoked Gruyère)
1½ ounces Gruyère cheese, grated
½ cup bread crumbs
Fresh Tomato Sauce (page 314) or Herb Béchamel (page 310)

Quarter the leeks, cut them into small squares, and wash them well. Melt the butter in a pan large enough to hold all the vegetables; add the leeks and cook over a high flame, stirring frequently, for about 1 minute. Then lower the heat and cook for 3 or 4 minutes. Add the carrot, garlic, herbs, and salt and freshly ground black pepper. Cook for 1 minute; then add the peppers and beans. Stir well, cover the pan, and cook another 2 minutes. Add the spinach or chard, and continue to cook until it is just wilted; then remove from the heat.

Beat the eggs in a large bowl and whisk in the cream or milk; then stir in the vegetables and the cheeses. Check the seasonings one more time.

Preheat the oven to 325°F. Generously butter 1-cup-capacity ramekins and coat them with bread crumbs, adding any extra bread crumbs to the timbale mixture. Ladle the custard into the molds, set them in a deep pan and add enough hot water to come halfway up their sides and bake until they are set and nicely colored, about 1 hour. Let them sit for a few minutes; then run a knife around the edge and unmold onto a plate. Serve top side up, with the sauce spooned around or over them.

SERVES FOUR TO SIX

FILO PASTRIES

FRITTATAS

CREPES *and*

ROULADES

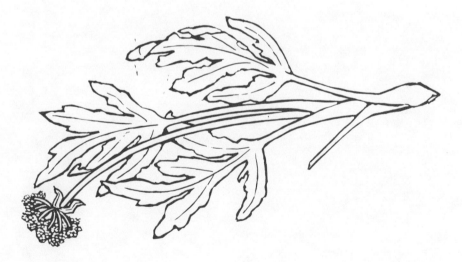

Savory filo pastries have many layers of thin, flaky pastry with a vegetable filling tucked in the middle. Their festive appearance suggests a complicated construction, but they are, in fact, simple to make and a useful dish to know—they can be put together well ahead of baking, are especially suitable to make for a crowd, and can be served either hot or warm. The filo dough, prepared commercially and sold frozen, can be found in Greek and Middle Eastern delicatessens as well as in many supermarkets. A single package contains enough dough to make two 9-by-13-inch pans of pastry. The unused sheets can be tightly wrapped and refrozen, or refrigerated for several days. Accompany filo pastries with something clean tasting and a little sharp—cooked greens, such as mustard or beet greens, sautéed cherry tomatoes, or a fresh salad mixed with herbs and wild greens.

Frittatas are familiar large flat omelets that can be made with all sorts of vegetables and served hot, warm, or at room temperature. They are a versatile food, good to eat at any meal and durable enough to carry on a picnic. Serve frittatas cut into wedges or small squares as the main dish in an informal meal, as appetizers, or as an element on a composed salad plate. Since frittatas are soft and creamy textured, accompany them with a fresh or crisp vegetable, such as sliced tomatoes, Bush Beans with Tarragon, or Butter-Fried Onions with Vinegar and Thyme.

Crepes are tender and versatile, and their flavor can be varied with the type of flour used. Crepe batter can be prepared and the crepes themselves cooked hours in advance, as can many of the fillings, making the final assembly relatively straightforward. Wrapped, folded, or layered with fillings, their contained, attractive appearance provides a strong visual focus for a meal, which makes them particularly effective as an entrée. We often accompany crepes with a sauce and a simply prepared vegetable, such as grilled vegetables, Summer Leeks and Yellow Peppers, or fresh corn with dill.

A roulade is a soufflé that has been baked flat, covered with a filling, and rolled. When the roulade is sliced, a pretty spiraled pattern is revealed. The soufflé can be baked and the roulade formed one or two hours in advance of serving, leaving the cook free to tend to other things. Depending on the filling, it can be served hot or cold. Warm roulades, served with a sauce, make a handsome entrée for a special dinner, while cold roulades can be used in a composed salad plate as well as at the center of a light, summery meal. Many of the fillings used in this book, such as the fillings for crepes and filo pastries, will adapt very nicely as fillings for roulades.

Zucchini and Basil Filo with Pine Nuts

This is best when made in the summertime. Serve it with sliced ripe tomatoes or a crisp lettuce salad.

½ package frozen filo pastry
5 to 6 medium zucchini (1½ pounds)
½ teaspoon salt
¾ cup (3 to 4 ounces) pine nuts
2 tablespoons virgin olive oil
1 small red onion, diced into ¼-inch pieces
Pepper
2 cloves garlic, finely chopped
½ cup chopped basil, loosely packed
3 tablespoons parsley, minced
¼ cup white wine or water
2 eggs
⅔ cup (about 2 ounces) Parmesan, grated
3 ounces feta cheese, crumbled
8 tablespoons melted unsalted butter or a mixture of butter and olive oil

Remove the filo pastry from the freezer and let it come to room temperature while you prepare the filling. Unfold the dough, and cut the stack of sheets in two. If you are making just one recipe, refold half the dough, and wrap it in plastic. It can either be refrozen or kept for a few days in the refrigerator. Cover the sheets to be used with a sheet of waxed paper covered in turn with a damp kitchen towel, to keep them from becoming dry and brittle.

Grate the zucchini on the large holes of a hand grater or in a food processor. Toss with the salt and set aside for 30 minutes. Then drain and squeeze dry in a clean kitchen towel. Preheat the oven to 350°F. Roast the pine nuts for 5 to 8 minutes, chop them finely, and set them aside.

Heat the olive oil in a large skillet and sauté the onion until it begins to soften, about 2 minutes. Add the zucchini, season with freshly ground black pepper, and cook another 4 minutes; then add the garlic, basil, parsley, and white wine or water. Cook covered for 3 to 4 minutes, and then remove from the heat. Beat the eggs, stir in the cheeses, then the cooked vegetables. Check the seasoning.

Brush a 9-by-13-by-2-inch pan with the melted butter and lay down a sheet of the filo pastry. Brush the pastry with butter, or a mixture of butter and olive oil, and continue buttering and layering, until you have used half the sheets. Scatter half of the chopped pine nuts between several of the layers. Brush the top sheet with butter, and spread the filling over it. Continue layering the rest of the pastry sheets, buttering each sheet, and again distributing pine nuts between several of the sheets. If the butter begins to congeal, reheat it so it will spread easily.

Cut the assembled pastry into 3-inch squares, then diagonally into diamonds, making sure you cut through all the layers; refrigerate the pastry if you will not be baking it right away. Bake in a preheated 400°F oven for 40 to 50 minutes, or until browned. Serve the pastries warm from the oven, slightly cooled, or at room temperature.

MAKES ONE 9-BY-13-INCH FILO PASTRY; SERVES SIX

Artichoke, Hazelnut, and Mushroom Filo

Hazelnuts, layered between the sheets of filo in this unusual pastry, enhance the flavor of the artichokes. A wintery dish, serve it with the White Beans with Shallots, Chervil, and Cream, or the Green Chard with Slivered Carrots.

½ package frozen filo pastry
¾ cup hazelnuts
18 to 20 baby artichokes or 6 large ones
Juice of two lemons
3 tablespoons virgin olive oil
1 yellow onion, diced into ¼-inch squares
¼ teaspoon fennel seeds, lightly crushed
Pinch of dried thyme
3 cloves garlic, finely chopped
Salt
Pepper
½ cup water or white wine
2 tablespoons butter
8 ounces mushrooms, sliced
1 cup ricotta
2 eggs, beaten
2 tablespoons parsley, chopped
1 teaspoon tarragon, chopped
8 tablespoons melted unsalted butter or a mixture of butter and olive oil

Remove the filo pastry from the freezer and let it come to room temperature while you prepare the filling. Unfold the dough, and cut the stack of sheets in two. If you are making just one recipe, refold half the dough, and wrap it in plastic. It can either be refrozen or kept for a few days in the refrigerator. Cover the sheets to be used with a sheet of waxed paper covered in turn with a damp kitchen towel, to keep them from becoming dry and brittle.

Preheat the oven to 350°F. Roast the hazelnuts for 7 to 10 minutes, or until they smell toasty. Let them cool slightly; then rub them in a kitchen towel to remove the loose papery skins. Leave on any flecks of skins that won't come off easily. Chop the nuts finely, and set them aside.

To prepare the artichokes, cut off the stems and the upper third of the leaves. Break off the dark green outer leaves until you reach the pale inner leaves, and trim the broken bases with a paring knife. If you are using baby artichokes, cut them into quarters or sixths and immediately put them in a bowl of water that has been acidulated with the lemon juice. If using large artichokes, trim off all the outer leaves, cut the hearts into quarters, remove the choke with a paring knife, then thinly slice the quarters and put them into the acidulated water.

Heat the olive oil and sauté the onion with the fennel and thyme for 2 to 3 minutes, until it softens; then lower the heat, and add the artichokes and two thirds of the garlic. Stir to coat them with the oil, season with salt and pepper, then add the water or wine. Cover the pan, and cook until the artichokes are tender, about 15 to 20 minutes. If there is liquid left in the pan when the artichokes are done, remove the lid and continue cooking until the liquid is reduced to a thick syrup.

While the artichokes are cooking, heat the 2 tablespoons butter in another large pan, and when it is hot and foamy, add the mushrooms and sauté for 3 to 5 minutes. Season with salt and freshly ground black pepper, add the remaining garlic, and cook until the juices are reabsorbed and the pan is dry.

Combine the artichokes and mushrooms in a bowl with the ricotta, eggs, parsley, and tarragon. Taste, and season with salt and milled pepper.

Brush a 9-by-13-by-2-inch pan with the melted butter, and lay down a sheet of the filo pastry. Brush the pastry with butter, or a mixture of butter and olive oil, and continue buttering and layering until you have used half the sheets, scattering half of the chopped hazelnuts between several of the pastry sheets. Brush the top sheet with butter, and spread the filling over it. Continue layering the rest of the pastry sheets, buttering each sheet, and again distributing the nuts between several of the sheets.

Cut the pastry into 3-inch squares, then diagonally into diamonds, making sure you cut through all the layers; refrigerate the pastry if you will not be baking it right away. Bake in a preheated 400°F oven for 40 to 50 minutes, or until browned. Serve the pastries warm from the oven, slightly cooled, or at room temperature.

MAKES ONE 9-BY-13-INCH FILO PASTRY; SERVES SIX

Filo Pastry with Goat Cheese and Spinach

The filling in this filo pastry is moist, creamy, and seasoned with herbs. Finely chopped roasted walnuts scattered between the sheets of pastry round out the flavors of the dish.

½ package frozen filo pastry
1 cup walnuts, freshly cracked, if possible
2 to 3 leeks, white parts only, thinly sliced
2 tablespoons butter
2 cloves garlic, finely chopped
Salt
Pepper
1 teaspoon thyme leaves, finely chopped, or ¼ teaspoon dried thyme
½ teaspoon rosemary, finely chopped
2 teaspoons marjoram, finely chopped
¼ cup white wine or water
1 large bunch spinach or chard, washed and finely shredded
8 ounces creamy goat cheese (Montrachet, Boucheron, Lezay)
⅔ cup ricotta
2 eggs, beaten
8 tablespoons unsalted butter, melted

Remove the filo pastry from the freezer and let it come to room temperature while you prepare the filling. Unfold the dough, and cut the stack of sheets in two. If you are making just one recipe, refold half the dough, and wrap it in plastic. It can either be refrozen or kept for a few days in the refrigerator. Cover the sheets to be used with a sheet of waxed paper covered in turn with a damp kitchen towel, to keep them from becoming dry and brittle.

Preheat the oven to 350°F. Roast the walnuts for 5 to 8 minutes until they are fragrant; chop them finely, and set them aside. Rinse the leeks, and shake off the excess water. Heat the butter in a large skillet, and sauté the leeks for 2 to 3 minutes before adding the garlic, some salt and freshly ground black pepper, and the herbs. Stir to combine, add the wine or water, and cook slowly, covered, until the leeks are soft. Add the spinach, toss with the leeks, then re-cover and cook until the spinach is wilted.

Remove the vegetables to a bowl, and combine them with the goat cheese, ricotta, and eggs. Season with more salt and pepper, if needed.

Brush a 9-by-13-by-2-inch pan with the melted butter and lay down a sheet of the filo pastry. Brush the pastry with butter and continue layering and buttering until you have used half the sheets, scattering half of the chopped walnuts between several of the pastry sheets. Brush the top sheet with butter, and spread the filling over it. Continue layering the rest of the pastry sheets, buttering each sheet, and again distributing nuts between several of the sheets.

Cut the pastry into 3-inch squares, then diagonally into diamonds, making sure you cut through all the layers; refrigerate the pastry if you will not be baking it right away. Bake in a preheated 400°F oven for 40 to 50 minutes, or until browned. Serve the pastries warm from the oven, slightly cooled, or at room temperature. For a wine, serve a dry sauvignon blanc.

SERVES SIX

Summer Squash Frittata with Green Sauce

Made with green or golden zucchini and a sauce of fresh green herbs, this is an aromatic, summery dish. Although frittatas are fine eaten at room temperature, the aromas and flavors of the melted Provolone, the olive oil, and the herbs are much more pronounced when the frittata is warm. Slices of this frittata might be included on a composed salad plate, or it could be the mainstay of a summer lunch or dinner.

4 to 5 medium green or golden zucchini, or a mixture of the two (about 1 pound)
Salt
Green Sauce (page 320)
2 tablespoons virgin olive oil
½ bunch scallions, finely chopped
Pepper
6 large eggs
2 ounces Provolone cheese, grated
2 to 3 tablespoons Parmesan, freshly grated
1 tablespoon butter

Slice the zucchini diagonally into slices about ¹⁄₁₆ inch thick, then into long, narrow matchsticks. Toss with ½ teaspoon salt, and set aside in a strainer for at least a half hour, to draw out the juices. Then squeeze out the liquid with your hands, or wrap the zucchini in a clean kitchen towel and twist hard. While the zucchini are draining, prepare the green sauce, but don't add the vinegar or lemon juice.

Heat the olive oil and add the scallions. Toss to cover them in the oil; then add the zucchini. Cook over a medium-high flame, stirring frequently, until the zucchini is dry and starting to color a little, about 4 minutes. Remove from the heat and set aside. Season with salt and freshly ground black pepper if needed.

Beat the eggs well and add the cheeses, 2 tablespoons of the green sauce (without the vinegar), ¼ teaspoon salt, and some pepper. Then stir in the zucchini mixture.

Melt the butter in a 10-inch skillet, and when it foams, quickly pour in the eggs and lower the heat as much as possible. Loosely cover the pan, and cook very slowly until the eggs are mostly set, but still a little loose in the center. Slide the frittata out onto a plate, and invert it back into the pan, or finish cooking the top side under a broiler until it is firm. Slide the finished frittata onto a serving plate. Season the green sauce with salt and vinegar; then brush or spoon the sauce over the frittata. Serve sliced into wedges.

In place of the green sauce, this can be served with the Sweet Pepper Relish. For wine, try a light zinfandel or California barbera, or a vin gris.

SERVES FOUR TO SIX

Potato and Lovage Frittata

The bright celerylike flavor of the lovage goes very well with potatoes. Yellow Finnish and Rose Fir potatoes are ideal—they are dense and creamy with good flavor. Roasted or steamed first (leftover potatoes can be used) and sliced thinly, they will absorb the flavors of the butter and lovage. Use a large pan to keep the potatoes in a single layer. If lovage isn't available to you, use celery leaves in its place.

10 small or 4 medium potatoes (about 1 pound)
1 tablespoon olive oil
3 tablespoons butter
1 medium yellow onion, sliced crosswise into ¼-inch slices
Salt
Pepper
8 eggs
2 to 3 teaspoons lovage leaves, chopped, or ¼ cup pale inner celery leaves
Whole lovage or celery leaves, for garnish

Wash the potatoes, but leave the skins on. Steam them for 25 to 35 minutes or roast them in a preheated 400°F oven with a little oil and water until they are done, about 30 to 35 minutes. When they are cool enough to handle, slice them thinly.

Heat the olive oil and half the butter in a 10- or 12-inch pan with a non-stick surface. Add the onion and cook it over medium heat, stirring frequently, until it is soft and lightly colored. Next add the potatoes and cook them until they are lightly colored, turning them gently from time to time. Season with salt and freshly ground black pepper. While the potatoes are cooking, beat the eggs well with a fork, and add ½ teaspoon salt, some black pepper, and the lovage.

Add the rest of the butter to the pan, let it foam, then quickly pour in the eggs. Cook over medium-low heat, covered, until the eggs are mostly set and golden brown on the bottom.

Slide the frittata onto a large plate, cover it with the pan, then holding both together, invert the frittata back into the pan. Return to the heat to brown the second side. Or, you can finish the frittata by browning the top under the broiler for 2 or 3 minutes. Turn the frittata onto a serving plate, garnish with whole lovage or celery leaves, cut into wedges, and serve. For a wine, choose a crisp vin gris or dry sauvignon blanc.

SERVES FOUR TO SIX

Escarole Frittata

Cooked escarole has a warm, almost nutty, flavor. It is delightful when mixed with eggs.

1 large head of escarole
3 tablespoons virgin olive oil
1 yellow onion, diced into 3/8-inch squares
2 cloves garlic, finely chopped
Salt
Pepper
Champagne vinegar or red wine vinegar to taste
8 eggs
2/3 cup (about 2 ounces) Fontina cheese, grated

Separate the leaves of the escarole, and discard any that are bruised. Cut them into pieces roughly 2 inches square, and wash them in a large bowl of water, giving special attention to the stems.

Heat 2 tablespoons of the olive oil in a wide skillet, and cook the onion briskly over high heat, stirring continually, for about 2 minutes. Add the garlic, escarole, and a sprinkling of salt. Lower the heat and cook until the greens are wilted and the stems are fairly tender, about 5 minutes. Season to taste with freshly ground black pepper, additional salt, if needed, and a little vinegar to sharpen the flavors.

Beat the eggs in a bowl, then stir in the cheese and the cooked escarole.

Heat the remaining tablespoon of oil in a 10-inch skillet, tip the pan to coat the surface, and quickly pour in the egg mixture. Loosely cover the pan, and cook the eggs over medium heat until they are nearly set. Remove the lid and finish cooking the frittata under the broiler until it is browned, about 2 or 3 minutes, or turn the frittata out onto a plate and invert it back into the pan to finish the top.

Gently loosen the eggs around the sides of the pan to make sure they are not stuck to the bottom. Turn the frittata out onto a platter, the golden brown side facing up. Serve hot, warm, or at room temperature. This frittata goes well with a California cabernet, or for something lighter, a Beaujolais.

SERVES FOUR TO SIX

Crepe Batter

This is a basic, versatile batter that can be used both for savory and sweet crepe dishes. If the crepes are intended for a dessert, use butter rather than olive oil. A portion of the flour can be replaced with whole wheat pastry flour, if you wish.

3 medium or 2 large eggs
1 cup milk
½ cup water
½ teaspoon salt
1 cup flour
2 to 3 tablespoons olive oil or melted butter

Put all the ingredients into a blender jar in the order given, and blend briefly at medium speed. Stop and scrape down the sides of the jar; then blend for another 10 seconds or so. Pour the batter into a bowl, cover, and let it rest at least 1 hour before using.

To make the batter by hand, beat the eggs lightly, add the milk, water, salt, and oil, and then gently whisk in the flour. Stir just enough to combine the ingredients well, and then pour the batter through a strainer to remove any lumps. Let the batter rest ½ hour before using.

To cook the crepes, heat a crepe pan with just a little butter. When it is hot, pour in just enough batter to lightly coat the pan. Rotate the pan to distribute the batter. Cook the crepe a few minutes, until it is golden brown on the bottom and the top surface is beginning to dry. Turn it over, pulling it up with the tip of a knife or a fork, and cook the second side until it is lightly browned, about a minute. The first crepe is often not usable, as the pan is not properly seasoned; but the following crepes should be fine. If the batter seems too thick, thin it with additional water or milk. It shouldn't be necessary to add any more butter to the pan after the first crepe. If the pan heats up too much in the course of cooking the crepes, take it off the heat and swing it back and forth a few times to cool it.

Stack the finished crepes on top of one another. If they are not to be used right away, wrap them in plastic.

Variation
CORN CREPE BATTER
To make corn crepes, substitute ¼ cup corn flour for ¼ cup flour in the basic recipe. Corn flour, which is much finer than cornmeal, can be found in natural food stores. Masa harina, a flour made from corn that has been treated with lime, can also be used, although it has a distinctly different—but good—flavor.

MAKES TWELVE 8-INCH CREPES OR SIXTEEN 6-INCH CREPES

Buckwheat Crepe Batter

Earthy-flavored buckwheat colors the batter with flecks of brown and gray. Light and delicate, buckwheat crepes go well with mushrooms, chard, and other earthy, wintery things. They also make good dessert crepes when filled with poached dried fruits or stewed quinces and pears.

1 cup water
1 cup milk
3 eggs
½ cup buckwheat flour
⅔ cup white flour
½ teaspoon salt
3 tablespoons melted butter

To make the batter in a blender, put all the ingredients into a blender jar in the order given, and blend briefly at medium speed. Stop and scrape down the sides of the blender jar; then blend for another 5 seconds or so. Pour the batter into a bowl, cover, and let it rest for 1 hour before using.

To make the batter by hand, beat the eggs lightly, add the milk, water, salt, and melted butter, and then gently whisk in the flours. Pour the batter through a strainer and let it sit ½ hour before using.

To cook the crepes, melt a little butter in a crepe pan and cook according to the instructions on page 269. As buckwheat has an enormous capacity to absorb liquid, you might find it necessary to thin the batter with more milk or water.

MAKES FIFTEEN 8-INCH CREPES OR TWENTY 6-INCH CREPES

Asparagus Crepes with Fontina Cheese

Part of the appeal of these crepes is that they are straightforward and uncomplicated. The thin asparagus work well because the stalks are long and tender and can be used whole. Two pounds will provide an ample bundle for each crepe. For a variation, the crepes might be colored and seasoned with saffron.

1 recipe Crepe Batter (page 269)
Pinch saffron (optional)
Herb Béchamel (page 310)
2 pounds pencil-thin asparagus
5 ounces Taleggio or Fontina cheese, grated
Handful of chervil or Italian parsley, chopped

Prepare the crepe batter, let it rest, then cook twelve 8-inch crepes. If you wish to use saffron in the batter, dissolve a pinch of threads or powder in a few spoonfuls of hot water, and then add it to the batter.

Prepare the béchamel, but wait to add the chervil or parsley until you are ready to serve the crepes. Line up the asparagus, tips together, and cut the spears into 7-inch lengths. Bring a large pot of water to a boil, add salt, and the asparagus, and cook until the asparagus is as tender as you like. As soon as it is done, spread the spears on a clean kitchen towel to drain and cool.

To assemble the crepes, place them so that the prettiest side, the first side cooked, is facing down. Distribute about 2 tablespoons of cheese over half the crepe, set a bundle of asparagus at one edge, and gently roll the crepe around it. Repeat until all the crepes, asparagus, and cheese have been used.

Preheat the oven to 400°F. Butter a baking sheet or dish, put in the crepes in a single layer, seam side down, and brush a little sauce over the tops. Bake them until the cheese is melted and the crepes are hot in the middle, about 8 to 10 minutes. Heat the sauce, stir in the fresh herbs, and serve the crepes, the sauce ladled first onto warm plates or passed separately. This distinctive entrée could be complemented with a dry sauvignon blanc or contrasted with a lighter pinot noir.

MAKES TWELVE 8-INCH CREPES

Many-Layered Crepe Cake

This is an impressive cake, and a particularly nice dish to bring whole to the table. When it is cut, the layers of red, green, and black fillings are revealed. The flavors are summery, the texture moist and tender. Because it is a complex dish, it should be served with something simple, such as generous slabs of sweet summer onions that have been charcoal grilled and removed from the coals when still a little crisp. Although there are several parts to this dish, all can be prepared well in advance, and the actual assembly is straightforward and quickly done.

1 recipe Crepe Batter (page 269)
1 pound ripe tomatoes, such as Roma
4 tablespoons virgin olive oil
½ medium onion, finely chopped
1 teaspoon basil leaves, finely chopped
Salt
Pepper
Sugar, if necessary
1 pound zucchini, green or golden
½ teaspoon Herbes de Provence or 2 teaspoons fresh marjoram, thyme, savory, mixed
1 cup Niçoise or Gaeta olives, or ½ cup olive paste
4 tablespoons Parmesan, freshly grated
8 ounces plain or peppered Gouda or Basque pepper cheese, thinly sliced

THE CREPES

Prepare the crepe batter and let it rest. Cook nine 8-inch crepes, and set them aside until needed. If they are made much ahead of time, wrap them in plastic to keep them from drying out.

THE TOMATO SAUCE

Submerge the tomatoes in boiling water to a count of ten. Remove them from the water; then peel, seed, and chop them finely. Warm 2½ tablespoons of the olive oil and add 2 tablespoons of the onion. Cook the onion until it has begun to soften, about 2 to 3 minutes; then add the tomatoes and basil. Cook over medium heat until the tomato has broken down and the liquid is completely reduced, about 10 to 15 minutes. The sauce should be thick and fairly dry so that it will moisten the crepes without making them soggy. If necessary, pass the sauce through a food mill to make it smooth. Season to taste with salt and pepper, and add a pinch or two of sugar to correct any excessive tartness.

THE ZUCCHINI

Grate the zucchini on the large hole of a hand grater or in a food processor. Toss it with ½ teaspoon salt, and set it aside for ½ hour to draw out the juices; then squeeze out the excess liquid with your hands, or wrap the zucchini in the corner of a clean kitchen towel and firmly twist the ends. Heat a tablespoon of oil and add the rest of the onion and the Herbes de Provence or mixed herbs. Cook until the onion is soft; then add the zucchini. Stir frequently, and cook until all the moisture is gone and the pan is dry, 6 to 7 minutes. Season with salt, if needed, and freshly ground black pepper, and set aside.

THE OLIVES

If you are using whole olives, press on them with the heel of your palm to split them, and then pull out the pits. Chop them finely and moisten them with a little olive oil.

Preheat the oven to 400°F. To assemble the cake, first lightly oil or butter the baking dish. Plan to bake the cake in the dish it will be served in or on the flat bottom of a tart pan, which can later be transferred, as a whole, to a platter. As you work, make sure that each filling is spread to the edge of the crepe, or the cake will droop and become difficult to layer. Lay down the first crepe, brush it with a tablespoon of the tomato sauce, cover it with a third of the zucchini mixture, and dust it with a tablespoon of Parmesan. Add the second crepe; spread it with tomato sauce and a third of the olives. Add the third crepe; spread it with tomato sauce, and cover it with approximately half the Gouda. Repeat the first three layers; next add a crepe with tomato sauce and zucchini and another with tomato sauce and olives. Cover the cake with the last crepe; brush it with tomato sauce and sprinkle on the remaining Parmesan. Cover the completed cake loosely with foil, and bake for 15 minutes. Remove the foil and bake another 10 minutes until the cake is hot in the center.

SERVES SIX

Crepas con Queso y Verduras
(Crepes with Cheese and Tiny Diced Vegetables)

The tiny cubes of diced vegetables in these crepes are festive and bright. They are accompanied with a tomato sauce seasoned with roasted garlic and chilies. Aside from the onions, use about 5 cups of vegetables. This vegetable filling and sauce could also be used to make a good roulade.

1 recipe Corn Crepe Batter (page 269)
Ancho Chili Sauce (page 317)
1 teaspoon whole cumin seeds
2 tablespoons peanut or corn oil
1 medium red onion, finely diced
1 carrot, diced into ¼-inch cubes
1 red potato, diced into ¼-inch cubes
2 zucchini, diced into ¼-inch cubes
1 yellow squash, diced into ¼-inch cubes
1 red or yellow bell pepper, diced into ¼-inch squares
Salt
Pepper
6 ounces Monterey Jack cheese, grated
1 cup ricotta
About ⅓ cup heavy cream
1 cup crème fraîche or sour cream, for garnish
Sprigs of cilantro, for garnish

Prepare the corn crepe batter and set it aside to rest. Then make the ancho chili sauce.

Roast the cumin seeds in a dry skillet over moderate heat until they are fragrant and lightly browned. Grind them in a mortar or an electric spice mill.

Heat the oil in a large skillet, and sauté the onion. After a few minutes add the carrot and potato; stir briefly and cover the pan. Lower the heat and cook for about 8 minutes, until the carrot and potato have begun to soften. Add the zucchini, yellow squash, and bell pepper, and continue cooking, covered, until the vegetables are just tender. Remove to a bowl and season with salt, freshly ground black pepper, and the ground cumin.

In another bowl, combine the Monterey Jack cheese with the ricotta, and season with salt and milled pepper. Cook the crepes according to the directions on page 269.

Preheat the oven to 400°F. To fill the crepes, place each crepe with its more attractive side down. Spread about 2 tablespoons of the cheese mixture on the crepe in a strip down the middle, stopping about an inch from either edge. Mount ¼ cup or so of the diced vegetables on top of the cheese. Fold the near side of the crepe over the vegetables, tuck in the ends, and then roll up the crepe. Place the crepes in a single layer on a buttered baking sheet or pan.

Brush the crepes with the cream and bake. If the filling is still warm, this should take about 5 to 8 minutes. Otherwise the crepes will need 12 to 15 minutes to heat.

Make sure the sauce is hot and check the seasoning. Lightly stir the crème fraîche with a fork to make it soft and creamy. Ladle some of the sauce onto a serving platter or individual plates. Arrange the crepes on top. Garnish with the crème fraîche or sour cream and sprigs of cilantro. This peppery dish needs a good crisp wine to accompany it, either a sauvignon blanc, a vin gris, or perhaps a zinfandel.

MAKES TWELVE 8-INCH CREPES

Buckwheat Crepes with Mushrooms

These filling crepes are good in colder months. They have a full mushroom flavor and can be served with the Herb Béchamel or the Sorrel Sauce.

1 recipe Buckwheat Crepes (page 270)
Herb Béchamel (page 310) or Sorrel Sauce (page 312)
½ ounce dried porcini mushrooms
4 tablespoons butter or olive oil
1 small yellow onion, finely diced
2 pinches dried thyme
1 tablespoon parsley or chervil, finely chopped
1 small piece lemon peel, minced
1½ pounds mushrooms, wiped clean and thinly sliced
2 cloves garlic, finely chopped
½ teaspoon salt
½ cup white wine or water
Pepper
Lemon juice to taste
2 tablespoons chives for the sauce, cut into narrow rounds (optional)

Prepare the buckwheat crepes. Prepare the sauce and set it aside. Cover the dried mushrooms with a cup of hot water and set them aside to soften for 20 minutes or so. Run your fingers over the mushrooms, rubbing them back and forth to loosen any grit and sand; then squeeze them dry and chop them fairly fine. Pour the soaking water through a strainer lined with a paper towel or a coffee filter, and set it aside to use later.

Heat half the butter or olive oil in a wide skillet, and add the dried mushrooms, onion, thyme, parsley or chervil, and lemon peel. Cook over medium-high heat, stirring frequently until the onion has softened, about 3 minutes. Pour in ¼ cup of the reserved mushroom liquid, let it reduce by half, and add the rest of the butter to the pan. When it has melted, add the sliced fresh mushrooms, garlic, and salt. Stir to coat the mushrooms with butter and cook on high heat for 3 to 4 minutes. Add the wine or water and another ½ cup of the mushroom liquid. Cook until the liquid is reduced to a syrupy sauce; then remove from the heat and season to taste with salt, freshly ground black pepper, and lemon juice.

Place each crepe with its more attractive side facing down. Cover half the crepe with mushrooms and fold over the other half; then cover half of this surface with more mushrooms, and fold again to make a fat, wedge-shaped crepe. If you are using the smaller crepes, put a strip of mushrooms down the middle and loosely roll the crepe around it.

Preheat the oven to 400°F. Set the crepes in a single layer on a buttered baking dish or baking sheet (seam side down for the rolled ones) and brush them with the sauce or some cream. Just before serving, bake them for 8 to 10 minutes, or until they are heated through. If you are using the Herb Béchamel, stir in the chives just before serving. Ladle some sauce onto each plate and serve the crepes. Pass additional sauce for those who wish. For wine, try a Côtes-du-Rhône or a lighter California cabernet to match the earthy flavor of the mushrooms.

MAKES SIX 8-INCH CREPES OR TWELVE 6-INCH CREPES

Soufflé Base for Roulades

This recipe makes enough to cover a 10-by-15-inch baking sheet. The soufflé may puff and swell dramatically while it is baking, but like all soufflés, it will collapse as soon as it cools, leaving a single flat sheet which is ready to be filled and rolled.

5 eggs
1½ cups milk
4 tablespoons butter
5 tablespoons flour
Salt
Pinch cayenne pepper
½ cup Parmesan, freshly grated

Preheat the oven to 400°F. Line a 10-by-15-inch baking sheet with parchment or waxed paper. Put a few dabs of butter on the pan to help anchor the paper; then lightly butter and flour the paper, knocking off any excess flour.

Separate the yolks and the whites; lightly beat the yolks and set them aside. Heat the milk and make the roux: Melt the butter, add the flour, and, stirring constantly, cook for 1 to 2 minutes over medium heat until the roux is lightly colored. Whisk in the heated milk, and cook for another 3 minutes, stirring constantly; then remove from the heat and season with ½ teaspoon salt and the cayenne. Gradually whisk some of the hot mixture into the yolks to warm them; then return to the pan to finish combining.

In a large bowl, whisk or beat the egg whites with a pinch of salt until they form smooth, firm peaks. Stir about a quarter of the whites and half the grated cheese into the milk-egg yolk mixture; then gently fold in the rest of the whites. Pour the soufflé mixture onto the baking sheet, spread it to fill all the corners, and sprinkle the rest of the cheese over the surface. Bake until the top is nicely browned and puffed, about 15 minutes.

Remove the soufflé from the oven and let it cool. Carefully turn it out onto a counter by turning over the pan, and remove the paper. It is now ready to be filled and rolled.

MAKES ONE 10-BY-15-INCH SOUFFLÉ BASE

Summer Roulade with Tomatoes, Cream Cheese, and Herbs

This rolled soufflé makes a cool and refreshing lunch or supper on a hot summer day. It can be made hours in advance, as long as it is wrapped tightly in plastic and refrigerated. The wrapping helps it form and hold its shape, as well as making it secure enough to carry in a picnic basket. Serve the roulade as a main course, preceded by a light summery soup, or as part of a composed salad plate.

1 recipe Soufflé Base for Roulades (page 278)
2 pounds ripe, flavorful tomatoes
3 tablespoons virgin olive oil
Sugar, if necessary
Salt
Pepper
Balsamic vinegar to taste
8 ounces cream cheese
2 to 4 tablespoons milk
1 bunch scallions, white parts only, finely chopped
½ cup mixed herbs: parsley, chervil, basil or tarragon, dill, oregano, finely chopped

Prepare the soufflé base and set it aside. Drop the tomatoes into boiling water for a count of ten; then peel, seed, and chop the tomatoes into pieces no larger than ½-inch square. Heat the oil in a wide pan, add the tomatoes, and cook them briskly over high heat to evaporate the juices, stirring frequently for about 5 minutes. If the tomatoes are especially tart, add a pinch or two of sugar while they are cooking. Remove them from the heat and season to taste with salt, freshly ground black pepper, and balsamic vinegar. Set aside to cool.

To construct the roulade, first thin the cream cheese with enough milk to make it soft and pliable. Then carefully spread it over the entire surface of the soufflé. Cover with the scallions and chopped herbs and lastly the cooked tomatoes. Roll the soufflé tightly, starting at a short end. If it is not to be served right away, wrap it well in plastic wrap and refrigerate until needed. Remove 20 minutes before serving to take off the chill and bring it to room temperature. Slice thinly and serve. Leftovers will keep, wrapped, in the refrigerator for one or two days. For wine, serve a light crisp vin gris or a chilled Beaujolais.

SERVES SIX

Spinach and Ricotta Roulade

Once it is filled, this roulade is baked and served warm. A number of sauces would make good accompaniments—the Sorrel Sauce, the Wild Mushroom Sauce, or any of the tomato sauces, whatever is appropriate for the season.

1 recipe Soufflé Base for Roulades (page 278)
Sorrel Sauce (page 312), Wild Mushroom Sauce (page 311), or any of the tomato sauces
2 pounds spinach
Salt
4 tablespoons butter
½ small yellow onion, finely diced
8 ounces ricotta
About ¼ cup light cream or milk
Nutmeg
Pepper
Cream, for baking

Prepare the soufflé base and set it aside.

Cut the stems off the spinach, and wash the leaves in a large bowl of water, using two changes of water, if necessary, to remove all the sand and dirt. Cook the spinach in a large pan with the water that clings to the leaves, and season with a little salt. When it is wilted, after a few minutes, remove it to a colander to drain. Melt the butter in the same skillet, and slowly cook the onion until it is soft, about 6 to 8 minutes. While it is cooking, squeeze the water out of the spinach, and chop it fairly fine. Add it to the cooking onion, and cook another few minutes, until the butter is absorbed.

Thin the ricotta with enough cream or milk to make it soft and pliable; then season to taste with a few scrapings of nutmeg, salt, and freshly ground black pepper.

Preheat the oven to 400°F. Spread the ricotta over the soufflé; then cover it with the spinach. Roll the soufflé tightly, starting with a short end; then transfer it carefully to a lightly buttered baking sheet. (If it is not to be baked for several hours, wrap the roulade tightly in plastic and refrigerate.) Just before baking, brush the surface of the roulade with cream; then bake, lightly covered, until it is heated through, about 25 minutes.

To serve, ladle sauce onto each plate, slice the roulade into ½- or 1-inch pieces, and carefully set them on the sauce. The spiral pattern of the slices is set off by the sauce.

SERVES SIX

COMPANION

DISHES

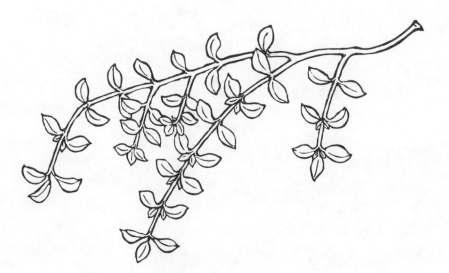

This chapter is a diverse collection of dishes that can be served alongside an entrée or as a course in themselves. Some of them, such as the fritters, brochettes, stuffed peppers, and white beans, could even be made the center of a light meal. With few exceptions, these are easy-to-prepare recipes that can be made fairly quickly, and some of the techniques used, such as baking in parchment, grilling, or making vegetable fritters, can be used with vegetables other than those specified.

Brown Rice

We always have on hand a pot of short-grained brown rice, which we serve with Herb Butter alongside the grilled Vegetable Brochettes, and as an extra side dish for those who request it.

1 cup brown rice, short- or long-grained
2 cups water
½ teaspoon salt
1 tablespoon butter or olive oil

Rinse the rice well and drain it. Put it in a heavy saucepan with the water, salt, and butter or olive oil. Bring to a boil; then cover the pot with a tight-fitting lid and reduce the heat to low. Cook the rice for 45 minutes, without disturbing it; if the lid is removed, the steam, which cooks the rice, will be lost. If you have lost track of the time and aren't sure if the rice is done, put your ear to the pot and listen. If there is no sound of water bubbling, the rice should be done. Just before serving, fluff the grains gently with a fork.

MAKES 3 CUPS

Wild Rice and Brown Rice Pilaf

This pilaf has a nutty flavor and a texture that is satisfying and chewy. It is good with winter vegetable stews and can be used as a filling for stuffed vegetables. Leftovers would be delicious in the Cheese and Nut Loaf. As the two kinds of rice require different cooking times, the wild rice is cooked separately and added in at the end.

½ cup wild rice
Salt
3 tablespoons butter or olive oil
1 medium carrot, diced into ¼-inch squares
½ small onion, cut into a fine dice
1 bay leaf
1 cup short-grained brown rice
2 cups water or Winter Vegetable Stock (page 65), brought to a boil

Rinse the wild rice. Bring 3 cups of water to a boil; add ¼ teaspoon salt and the rice. Cook slowly, uncovered, until the rice is done but still a little chewy, about ½ hour. Pour it into a colander and set it aside to drain. Any extra liquid can be used with the water or stock to cook the brown rice.

Melt the butter or olive oil in a wide-bottomed soup pot. Add the carrot, onion, and bay leaf, and cook over medium heat, stirring occasionally, for 3 to 4 minutes. Add the brown rice and ½ teaspoon salt, and cook another 5 minutes. Add the boiling water or stock, lower the heat, cover the pan, and cook until the water has been absorbed, about 45 minutes. Taste the rice. If it is not sufficiently cooked, add a small amount of liquid and continue cooking until it is done. Using a fork, lightly stir in the wild rice and let it steam a few minutes to reheat.

Variation
WILD RICE PILAF WITH DRIED MUSHROOMS
Soak ½ to 1 ounce dried mushrooms (shiitake, porcini, morels) in 2 cups very hot water for ½ hour. Before draining, run your fingers over the mushrooms to loosen any sand and soil. Pour the soaking liquid through a coffee filter, or a strainer lined with a paper towel. Set it aside and squeeze the extra moisture out of the mushrooms. Remove and discard any tough, wiry stems. Chop or slice the mushrooms. Follow the recipe for the wild rice pilaf—add the mushrooms to the butter along with the carrot and onion and use the mushroom liquid in place of the water or stock.

SERVES FOUR

Corn Bread

Corn bread is quick to prepare, and a good accompaniment to stews, especially those with chili, such as the Zuñi Stew, the Winter Vegetable Stew, and the Corn, Bean, and Pumpkin Stew. It is best eaten warm, as corn bread soon dries out.

1 cup white flour
1 cup corn flour or fine cornmeal
2 tablespoons sugar
2½ teaspoons baking powder
½ teaspoon salt
2 eggs
1 cup milk
2 tablespoons melted butter

Preheat the oven to 400°F. Combine the white flour, corn flour or cornmeal, sugar, baking powder, and salt. In a separate bowl, beat the eggs; then stir in the milk and butter. Pour the wet ingredients into the dry ones, and stir just enough to combine, in about 15 or 16 strokes. Overmixing causes the corn bread to be tough. Pour into a buttered baking pan and bake until the corn bread is firm and a toothpick comes out clean, about 30 minutes.

MAKES ONE 8-BY-8-INCH LOAF

Polenta

Extremely·versatile and very economical, polenta is easy to make, taking little time except for cooking. It can be eaten soft, or allowed to harden and then sliced and served grilled or fried. Serve it alongside another dish, such as a stew of wild mushrooms, or use it in a gratin, as in the Baked Polenta Layered with Tomato, Fontina, and Gorgonzola. Coarse cornmeal is best for making polenta. It is generally available in Italian delicatessens and natural food stores, sold in five-pound bags or in bulk.

5 cups water
1 teaspoon salt
1½ cups polenta (coarse cornmeal)

Bring the water to a boil, add the salt, then whisk in the polenta, pouring it in a slow, steady stream so that lumps don't form. Lower the heat, and cook about 30 minutes, while stirring. Or cook the polenta in a double boiler for 45 minutes, giving it a stir every 15 minutes or so.

If you wish to serve the polenta soft, keep it over the heat in a double boiler until needed. To make firm polenta, pour it into a pan, and set it aside; after a while it will cool and firm up. Turn it out of its pan, and cut it into ½-inch slices.

To broil or grill the polenta, brush both sides of each slice with olive oil and cook until lightly browned. The slices can also be fried in butter or olive oil, either until lightly colored or until crisp, and they can be used as layers in a casserole.

Variation

CHEESE POLENTA

Prepare the polenta according to the recipe. At the end of the cooking, add a few tablespoons of butter and 4 ounces of grated cheese, such as Fontina, smoked cheese, or a portion of grated Parmesan, and stir until the butter and cheese have melted. Serve either as a soft or firm polenta. This is a good way to use up odds and ends of cheese that are too small or too dry to be served.

MAKES ONE 5-BY-9-INCH LOAF; SERVES FOUR TO SIX

Potato Gordas

These fritters combine the flavors of potato with corn, chilies, and cheese. They go well with the Zuñi Stew and the Squash Stew with Chilies, Spices, and Ground Nuts (Legumbres en Pipian). Masa harina, a fine flour made from corn that has been treated with lime, is available in Mexican markets. In the West, it is commonly found in supermarkets.

1 pound russet potatoes
4 ounces fresh Anaheim chilies or canned green chilies
8 ounces cheddar cheese, grated
2 cups masa harina
1 teaspoon baking powder
½ teaspoon salt
Water
Oil for frying
Sprigs of cilantro, for garnish

Scrub the potatoes and peel them or not, as desired. Cut them into chunks that are roughly the same size, and steam or boil them until tender. Pass them through a food mill or lightly break them up with a fork.

If you are using fresh chilies, roast them over a flame until they are evenly charred all over; then put them in a covered bowl to steam for 5 to 10 minutes. Scrape off the skins, remove the seeds and veins, and chop them into small squares. If using canned chilies, rinse them well, then chop. Stir the chilies and the cheese into the potatoes; then add the masa harina, baking powder, and salt. Add water slowly, up to a cup, until the mixture comes together.

Shape the dough into patties and fry them on both sides in a generous amount of hot oil on a griddle or in a skillet until they are nicely browned. Drain on paper toweling, and serve garnished with sprigs of cilantro.

SERVES FOUR TO SIX

Potato Fritters Two Ways

These fritters are versatile and quick. Don't wait for an accumulation of leftover mashed potatoes—potatoes take only minutes to steam and are more tender and flavorful when freshly cooked. If the skins are firm and clean, leave them on, both for their flavor and texture. A coating of bread crumbs helps keep the fritters from sticking, which can be a problem if they contain cheese. A coating of sesame seeds will serve the same purpose and make a beautiful golden, crunchy surface.

THE FIRST WAY

1½ pounds White Rose or russet potatoes
2 egg yolks
4 tablespoons cilantro leaves, roughly chopped
1 bunch scallions, sliced, white parts with some greens
1 jalapeño pepper, seeded and chopped, or 3 tablespoons bell pepper, finely diced
1 cup grated muenster, cheddar, or jack cheese (optional, but good)
Salt
1 cup bread crumbs or toasted sesame seeds
4 tablespoons clarified butter (see page 325) or oil

Cut the potatoes into pieces roughly an inch square. Set them in a steamer over a pan of boiling water, and steam until they are tender, about 20 minutes. Transfer them to a bowl, and gently break them up, using the side of a fork so as not to overwork them. They need not be smooth; the irregular texture makes them more interesting. Incorporate the egg yolks; then add the cilantro, scallions, jalapeño pepper, and cheese, if using, and combine. Season to taste with salt. Shape the potato mixture into patties of any shape or size, and press each one into the bread crumbs or sesame seeds so that both sides are covered. Heat the butter or oil in a heavy skillet—a cast iron or non-stick frying pan works well—and fry the potato cakes until they are browned on both sides. Serve them with something cool and refreshing: Fresh Fruit and Mint Chutney (page 323), Sweet Pepper Relish (page 319), sour cream, or a salad.

THE SECOND WAY

Replace the cilantro, green onions, and jalapeño pepper with the following ingredients:
1 small onion, finely diced
1 additional tablespoon butter, or oil
Handful of herbs: parsley, thyme, lovage, or basil, chopped, or rocket leaves, chopped

Cook the onion in the butter until it is soft; then add it to the potatoes with the rest of the ingredients after the eggs have been incorporated, and proceed according to the recipe.

MAKES EIGHT 4-INCH FRITTERS

Zucchini Fritters

Zucchini lends itself well to various seasonings. Here the fritters are seasoned with mint, dill, and feta cheese, but some other choices might include parsley mixed with a strong herb like lovage or hyssop; or a mixture of parsley and thyme with marjoram, basil, or rosemary, or cilantro and minced jalapeños. Other cheeses can replace the feta. Cook the zucchini as briefly as possible, so that the fritters will have texture.

4 to 5 medium green or green and yellow zucchini (1 pound)
1 tablespoon olive oil
6 to 8 scallions, white parts with some greens, thinly sliced
½ to 1 cup feta cheese, crumbled
1 teaspoon dill, finely chopped
½ teaspoon mint leaves, finely chopped
½ teaspoon grated lemon peel
Pepper
4 eggs, separated
¼ cup flour
Oil for frying
Salt

Cut the zucchini into ¼-inch cubes. Heat the olive oil in a wide skillet, add the scallions and zucchini, and cook them over medium-high heat, stirring frequently, for several minutes, until the zucchini are just starting to color and taste cooked, but are still somewhat firm. Add a little water if they stick at all. Remove the zucchini to a bowl, add the feta, and season to taste with the herbs, lemon peel, and freshly ground black pepper. (Because feta is usually salty, it probably won't be necessary to add salt.) Make sure the flavors are bright and strong because they will be diluted when the eggs are added.

Stir the egg yolks into the zucchini mixture, and add the flour. Beat the whites with a pinch of salt until stiff peaks are formed. Stir about a quarter of them into the zucchini mixture to loosen it; then gently fold in the remaining whites with a rubber spatula.

Cook the fritters on a griddle or in a wide cast iron frying pan or non-stick skillet. Heat a tablespoon or so of oil. When it is hot enough to sizzle a drop of water, lower the heat to medium, and add the batter. Quarter cupfuls will make a fritter about 3 inches across. Turn the fritters over when they are nicely browned, frying once on each side. They will be soft and a little moist in the middle. Serve them hot with the Grilled Tomato Sauce, the Herb Butter, made with dill and mint as well as parsley or the Sweet Pepper Relish. If you have used cilantro and chilies in the fritters, serve the fritters with the Chili Butter or Ancho Chili Sauce.

MAKES TWELVE 3-INCH FRITTERS

Sweet Corn Fritters

Serve these golden fritters as part of a lunch or supper with a spicy accompaniment, or serve them for breakfast with maple syrup. It is not necessary to precook the tender kernels of fresh sweet corn—they will emerge in their light batter coating still sweet and just a little crunchy.

1 cup flour
½ teaspoon salt
2 large or 3 medium eggs, separated
2 tablespoons light olive oil, corn oil, or melted butter
1 cup milk
2 cups corn kernels (about 4 to 6 ears)
Light olive or vegetable oil for frying
Clarified butter for frying (page 325) (optional)

Put the flour and salt in a bowl and make a well in the center. Add the egg yolks, oil or butter, and milk; then whisk everything together just enough to make a smooth batter. Set it in the refrigerator, covered, to rest for about 1 hour.

While the batter is resting, shave the kernels from the corn with a sharp knife; then toss them with your fingers to break apart any that are stuck together. After the batter has rested, gently stir in the corn. Beat the egg whites until soft peaks hold their shape; then gently fold them into the batter.

Pour enough oil in a skillet to come ⅜ to ½ inch up the side. (This can be mixed with clarified butter for its flavor, if desired.) Heat it until a drop of water sizzles when dropped into the pan. Drop the fritter batter by large spoonfuls and fry, once on each side, until they are colored a deep golden brown. Remove them from the oil and drain on paper toweling. Keep them in a warm oven until all are made; then serve on heated plates. Serve with Chili Butter, Sweet Pepper Relish, or Grilled Tomato Sauce, with a spoonful of sour cream on the side.

Variations
Include fresh herbs—dill, marjoram, parsley, cilantro, basil, and chives are all good with corn—finely chopped, and added to the batter just before frying.

SWEET CORN FRITTERS WITH CHEESE
Cut 2 or 3 ounces of Monterey Jack or muenster cheese into ¼-inch cubes. Drop the fritter batter into the skillet and when the bottom has set, after 30 seconds or so, drop several cubes of the cheese onto the uncooked side. Turn the fritter over and finish cooking.

MAKES TWELVE TO SIXTEEN FRITTERS

Pepper Fritters

Use peppers of any color, or a mix of colors. The red and yellow ones will be sweeter. Serve the fritters with a tomato sauce or a flavored butter, a salad or a soup, and Country French Bread to make a light late summer lunch or dinner.

1 pound bell peppers, red, yellow, green, or mixed
½ medium yellow onion
2 tablespoons virgin olive oil
1 to 2 cloves garlic, finely chopped
1 teaspoon thyme leaves and blossoms, finely chopped
1 teaspoon oregano or marjoram, finely chopped
2 teaspoons basil leaves and blossoms, finely chopped
¼ cup water or red wine
Salt
Pepper
Cayenne pepper to taste (optional)
Balsamic or red wine vinegar to taste
4 eggs, separated
¼ cup flour
½ to 1 cup grated dry cheese: Asiago, Parmesan, or dry jack
Oil for frying

Cut the peppers lengthwise into quarters, and remove the veins, seeds, and stems; then slice them crosswise into strips ¼ inch wide. (Leaving them this wide will give texture to the fritters.) Cut the onion again in half, and slice it crosswise, also into pieces ¼ inch wide.

Heat the 2 tablespoons olive oil in a skillet, add the onion, and sauté it for 1 minute over medium-high heat; then add the peppers and cook another 2 to 3 minutes. Stir in the garlic, herbs, and water or wine, and season with salt. Lower the heat, cover the pan, and stew for 3 to 5 minutes. The peppers should cook until they are tender but still retain a little of their firmness. Taste them, and season as needed with salt, freshly ground black pepper, cayenne, if desired, and a few drops of vinegar to bring up the flavors. At this point the peppers should be highly seasoned as the addition of the eggs will dilute the flavors.

Stir the peppers gradually into the egg yolks, then add the flour. Whisk the egg whites with a pinch of salt until they form firm peaks. Add a quarter of the egg whites to the peppers, and stir them in well to loosen the mixture; then stir in the cheese. Add the rest of the whites, and gently fold everything together using a wide rubber spatula.

Heat a tablespoon or so of oil in a wide cast iron frying pan or non-stick skillet until it will sputter a drop of water. Lower the heat to medium; then add the batter by spoonfuls (a quarter cup of batter will make a 3-inch fritter), and fry them once on each side until they are golden brown on the outside and tender and moist in the middle.

Serve the fritters hot from the pan or griddle with the Grilled Tomato Sauce, the Herb Butter, the Chili Butter, or the Green Sauce.

MAKES TWELVE 3-INCH FRITTERS

Cherry Tomatoes Sautéed with Shallots and Herbs

Quick to prepare, these sautéed tomatoes work well with creamy dishes, offering the contrasting taste of something mildly acid. Use a mixture of many herbs or a single pronounced one, such as tarragon or basil. The colors—red, yellow, and green—are bright and lively.

4 cups mixed cherry and yellow pear tomatoes
2 tablespoons butter or olive oil
3 shallots, finely diced
1 to 2 tablespoons mixed herbs, chopped, or 1 tablespoon tarragon or basil, chopped
Salt
Pepper

Slice the tomatoes into halves or quarters, depending on their size—a serrated knife works much better than a standard flat-edged knife.

Just before you want to serve the tomatoes, warm the butter or oil with the shallots, and cook gently for about 1 minute; then add the tomatoes and raise the heat. Sauté quickly until the tomatoes are just warm. Do not cook longer or the tomatoes will turn to stew and the skins will toughen. Add the herbs, season with salt and freshly ground black pepper, and serve.

SERVES FOUR TO SIX

Summer Leeks and Yellow Peppers

Made with tender summer leeks and yellow peppers, this ragout makes a good accompaniment to a filo pastry, a crepe, or a timbale.

6 leeks, about an inch across, white parts with some pale greens
4 yellow bell peppers
2 tablespoons butter
Salt
1 tablespoon virgin olive oil
Small handful fresh mixed herbs: Italian parsley, lemon or opal basil, marjoram, etc.
Additional butter (optional)
Pepper

Slice the leeks into thin rounds and wash them well. Halve the peppers lengthwise, remove the seeds, stems, and veins, and slice them thinly into strips. If they are very long, halve them crosswise first.

Melt the butter in a sauté pan with a few tablespoons of water, and begin cooking the leeks over medium heat with a little salt. Cover and stew until they are tender, about 6 to 8 minutes; then add the olive oil, and raise the heat. Add the peppers and sauté briskly for 2 minutes; then add a little more water, lower the heat, and cook another few minutes, until the peppers are soft. Add the herbs toward the end of the cooking, and, if you wish, another spoonful of butter. Season with salt and freshly ground black pepper. There should be a sweet yellow sauce in the bottom of the pan when the vegetables are done.

SERVES FOUR TO SIX

Whole Baked Eggplants

Use short purple eggplants, 3 to 4 inches long, and bake them whole. Two or three can be served as an appetizer or alongside a main course such as a crepe or a filo pastry. When allowed to sit, the flavors develop and strengthen. These eggplants can also be served at room temperature, as a cooked salad, with a wedge of lemon and a garnish of roasted pine nuts.

2 large ripe tomatoes
5 to 6 tablespoons virgin olive oil
1 pound red or yellow onions, cut into ¼-inch slices
¼ teaspoon fennel seeds, crushed with the back of a spoon
½ teaspoons Herbes de Provence, or a mixture of dried savory, marjoram, and thyme,
  crushed between your fingers
Salt
Pepper
2 cloves garlic, thinly sliced
2 small bay leaves
6 to 8 thyme branches
12 tiny eggplants
12 to 18 Niçoise olives
⅓ cup wine or water

Plunge the tomatoes into boiling water for a count of 10 seconds. Remove the cores and skins, halve them crosswise, and squeeze out the juice and the seeds. Cut the halves into slices about ½ inch wide.

Warm 3 tablespoons of the olive oil in a wide skillet, and add the onions along with the fennel seeds and the Herbes de Provence or mixed herbs. Cook the onions over low heat until they have begun to soften, about 3 minutes. Season them with salt and freshly ground black pepper. Lay most of them in the bottom of an earthenware gratin dish with the tomatoes, garlic, bay leaves, and half the thyme branches.

If the eggplants are small and there is room in the gratin dish, leave their flower caps and stems on. Otherwise trim the tops.

Preheat the oven to 400°F. In another dish toss the eggplants with a spoonful or two of olive oil and season them with salt. Nestle the eggplants among the onions, tuck the olives between and around them, and strew the remaining onions over the top, along with the rest of the thyme. Add the wine or water and a final drizzle of olive oil. Cover with foil and bake until the eggplants are very soft, about 35 to 45 minutes. Serve warm.

SERVES FOUR TO SIX

Fresh Sweet Corn and Chives

It is not often remembered that fresh sweet corn, white or yellow, can be just as good cooked off the cob as on. Chili Butter, Herb Butter, cilantro, parsley, or basil butter all could go well with the corn in place of the chives.

8 to 10 ears corn
4 tablespoons butter
1 small yellow onion, finely diced
Salt
Pepper
1 tablespoon chives, sliced into narrow rounds

Using a sharp knife, shave the kernels from the corn with a sawing motion. Break up the kernels that are stuck together.

Melt 1 tablespoon of the butter with a few tablespoons of water and cook the onion until it begins to soften, just a few minutes. Add the corn and ½ cup water. Raise the heat, bring to a boil, and cook until the water is almost boiled off. Toward the end, add the remaining butter and let it melt into the juices. Season the corn with salt and freshly ground black pepper, and toss it with the chives.

Variation
FRESH CORN SALAD

To make a corn salad, cook the corn in water according to the recipe, but omit the onions and butter. Toss with the Sweet Pepper Relish (page 319) and parsley or cilantro.

MAKES ABOUT 4 CUPS

Green Chard and Slivered Carrots

The leaves and the stems of chard are almost two different vegetables in terms of texture and taste. Here they are served together with narrow slivers of carrots, dressed with oil, and seasoned with garlic and chilies. This is a clean dish, and goes well with more complicated and creamy dishes. It can also be served at room temperature, as a salad with a splash of vinegar or lemon juice added for tartness.

3 tablespoons virgin olive oil
1 clove garlic, sliced
2 to 4 small dried red chili peppers
1 bunch Swiss chard (about 1½ pounds)
3 medium carrots
Salt
Pepper
Vinegar or sliced lemon wedges

Warm the olive oil in a pan with the garlic and chili peppers. Once the garlic slices are brown, remove them and set the oil and peppers aside.

Separate the chard stems from the leaves. Cut the leaves into large pieces and wash them. Trim the uneven ends off the stems. Then, to make the stems as tender as possible, peel off the thin, transparent outer skin from each stem. Catch the edge of a knife under the top layer of skin, and pull it down the length of the stem. It sometimes helps, especially if the stem is curved, to first cut the stem in half lengthwise. Peel both sides of the stems, cut them into 2-inch lengths, then lengthwise into narrow strips.

Peel the carrots, slice them into long, ¼-inch, diagonals, then into narrow strips.

Bring 4 to 5 quarts of water to a boil, and add 4 teaspoons of salt. Briefly cook the chard stems and the carrots separately until each is tender—about a minute for the carrots, two to three minutes for the chard. Remove them from the water and set them aside. Plunge the chard leaves into the water and cook until they are tender, 3 to 5 minutes, depending on the quality of the chard. When they are done, remove them to a colander. Press against the leaves with the back of a wooden spoon to get rid of the water; then put them in a bowl with the stems and the carrots, and toss them with the olive oil. Season with salt and serve with vinegar or slices of lemon.

SERVES FOUR

Butter-Fried Onions with Vinegar and Thyme

This is another quick dish to prepare when you want a vegetable that is uncomplicated and lively. There is a fragrant explosion when the vinegar is added to the pan of sizzling onions. A grinding of black pepper and the fresh thyme leaves tie the sweet and sharp tastes together. This goes especially well with frittatas and dishes made with winter squash.

4 medium red onions
4 tablespoons butter
2 to 3 tablespoons sherry vinegar, balsamic vinegar, or red wine vinegar
Salt
Pepper
Several branches of thyme leaves, roughly chopped

Halve the onions and cut them crosswise into slices about ⅜ inch thick. Melt the butter in a wide sauté pan or skillet. When it foams, add the onions, and sauté briskly over high heat, flipping or stirring them frequently. After 4 or 5 minutes they will be lightly browned, sweet, and still a little crunchy. If you prefer them softer, continue to cook until they are sufficiently done for you; then add the vinegar. Stir quickly as the vinegar cooks off, and season the onions to taste with salt, a generous grinding of pepper, and the thyme leaves.

SERVES FOUR TO SIX

New Potatoes and Garlic Baked in Parchment

The idea for making little packages of potatoes came from Alice Waters at Chez Panisse. Held taut with fragrant steam, the fragile paper packages contain tender new potatoes and whole cloves of garlic and are opened at the table. We have often served them with a fresh herbed goat cheese, bowls of olives, and a plate of radishes or young carrots. The crackling sounds and aromatic smells that come from opening the packages, and the pleasure of putting together different tastes and textures, always seem to lift people's spirits. This recipe makes one parchment package; multiply by the number of people to be served.

1 sheet baking parchment, approximately 11 by 16 inches
4 to 5 small new potatoes (about 5 ounces total)
4 to 5 large cloves garlic, unpeeled
Small branch of rosemary or several thyme branches
1 tablespoon virgin olive oil
Salt
Pepper

If the potatoes are really small, an inch across or less, keep them whole; otherwise cut them into pieces that are more or less the same size, slightly smaller than an inch square. Leave the skins on if the potatoes are fresh.

Preheat the oven to 400°F. Fold the paper in half to make a crease; then open and lay the potatoes on the lower half. Tuck in the garlic cloves and the rosemary or thyme, pour the olive oil over all, and season well with salt and freshly ground black pepper. Bring the top side of the paper back down; then roll tightly along the edges to form a pouch, giving a firm final twist at the end to hold the package closed.

Bake the packages for 30 minutes, and serve immediately, while they are hot and inflated. Instead of individual packages, you can also make a single large one, from which people may help themselves.

MAKES ONE PACKAGE; SERVES ONE

Winter Squash and Leeks Baked in Parchment

Folded in parchment, the squash and leeks steam in their own moisture, and none of the sweet flavors are lost. The squash is cut into tiny cubes so that it cooks before the paper gets too dark. The squash pieces will hold their angular geometric shape, but collapse to a purée when picked up with a fork. Fresh sage leaves are used for the seasoning here, but you could also use a small dried red chili or chopped Italian parsley. The recipe is for a single parchment package; multiply by the number of people to be served.

½ cup winter squash (butternut is very good), cut into ¼-inch cubes
2 to 3 tablespoons leeks, chopped into ½-inch squares or smaller
¼ teaspoon garlic, finely chopped
1 teaspoon virgin olive oil
Salt
Pepper
1 piece baking parchment, about 12 by 15 inches
1 to 2 teaspoons butter
2 fresh sage leaves

Toss the squash, leeks, garlic, and olive oil together, and season with salt and freshly ground black pepper.

Preheat the oven to 425°F. Fold the parchment paper in half to make a crease. Open it up and generously butter the bottom half, covering all but an inch from the edge. It is important to coat the surface thoroughly, or the sugars in the squash will stick to the paper and burn. Heap the vegetables into the center of the buttered area and tuck in the sage leaves. Lay a few small pieces of butter on top. Fold the top half of the paper down and tightly roll the edges over onto themselves to make a half-circle. Give the paper a good twist at the end to hold the packet firmly closed. Bake for 25 minutes.

MAKES ONE PACKAGE; SERVES ONE

White Beans with Shallots, Chervil, and Cream

This can be served as a side dish, alongside a filo pastry, for example, or covered with bread crumbs and baked as a gratin. The use of light cream will keep it from being too rich or cloying, and a few tiny diced vegetables add cheerful color. Pale green flageolet beans are also delicious treated this way.

1 cup navy beans
1 bay leaf
½ teaspoon salt
1 tablespoon butter
1 to 2 shallots or 2 tablespoons onion, finely diced
1 small carrot, cut into tiny, even cubes
1 small celery stalk, cut into tiny, even cubes
½ cup light cream or half-and-half
3 branches thyme, chopped, or a pinch dried thyme
1 tablespoon chervil or parsley, chopped
Pepper

Sort through the beans and remove any chaff or small stones. Rinse them well, cover them generously with water, and set them aside to soak 5 hours or overnight. Pour off the soaking water, cover the beans with fresh water, and bring to a boil. Add the bay leaf and the salt, lower the heat, and simmer gently until the beans are tender, about 1 hour. Drain and set aside, saving the broth for another use.

Just before serving, melt the butter and add the shallots or onion, carrot, and celery, and cook over low heat for about 2 minutes. Add the cream, or half-and-half, and thyme, bring to a boil, and simmer for 1 minute. Then add the beans and cook until they are heated through. Stir in the chervil or parsley, season with salt and freshly ground black pepper, and serve.

Variation

WHITE BEAN GRATIN

To make a gratin, prepare the bean mixture according to the recipe and put it in a lightly buttered baking dish. If it is at all dry, add a little extra cream or cooking liquid. Toss ½ cup fresh bread crumbs with a good olive oil or melted butter and press them over the top. Bake in a preheated 425°F oven until the top is browned and the beans are hot, about 20 minutes. Served with a green salad, this can make a simple and satisfying meal.

MAKES 3 CUPS

Vegetable Brochettes with Marinated Tofu

These brochettes of seasonal vegetables and marinated tofu, grilled over a wood or charcoal fire, are colorful and handsome. Prepared in this way, they take on the wonderful flavor of the wood smoke. Certain vegetables are always good to include—mushrooms, cherry tomatoes, boiling onions, and green peppers—to provide contrasting colors and textures, but others can be included when in season. In summer try rounds of sweet corn, zucchini, eggplant, and new potatoes. In winter include winter squash, slices of yams or sweet potatoes, or fennel. Remember that you will need to marinate the tofu at least a day before making this dish.

At the restaurant, we serve the brochettes with the Brown Rice and Herb Butter. You could serve them with pasta as well, or with the Wild Rice and Brown Rice Pilaf. Use 10-inch-long wooden skewers, or long branches of rosemary, stripped of all but a tuft of their leaves. Rosemary or other herbs thrown on the fire while the brochettes are grilling make the smoke even more aromatic, and flavor the vegetables. Allow two brochettes per person for a main course.

Brochette Marinade (see below)
16 medium mushrooms
1 green bell pepper, or pepper of any color, cut into squares or wedges
8 cherry tomatoes
16 boiling onions, parboiled and peeled
Choose two or three of the following:
    Zucchini and yellow squash, cut into rounds
    Sweet corn, sliced through the cob into ½-inch rounds
    Winter squash, cut into 1-inch cubes
    Small new potatoes, or potatoes cut into 1-inch cubes
    Sweet potatoes, or yams, cut into rounds
    Japanese eggplant, cut into ¼-inch rounds
    Fennel, thickly sliced
16 to 24 ounces Marinated Tofu (page 304), cut into 1-inch cubes
8 bay leaves
Salt
Pepper

Prepare the brochette marinade and set it aside.

Clean and trim the vegetables. If boiling onions are not available, use 2 or 3 red or yellow onions, cut into wide wedges, the root ends left intact. Some of the vegetables need to be parboiled: 2 to 3 minutes for the corn; 6 to 8 minutes for the winter squash; 10 to 12 minutes for the potatoes, yams, and sweet potatoes. Cook the vegetables until they are done but still firm enough not to fall off the skewers, keeping in mind that they will cook about 10 minutes over the coals. Toss the eggplant slices in oil.

Gather all the vegetables and the tofu. Plan to place a mushroom on either end (they work well as an anchor for the rest of the vegetables); then skewer an assortment of vegetables and the tofu, including the bay leaves, to make a colorful, attractive brochette. Put the finished brochettes on a baking sheet, and brush them generously with the brochette marinade, turning them so that all sides are well coated.

Grill the brochettes 6 to 8 inches over the coals, turning every few minutes to expose all the surfaces to the heat. When the vegetables are nicely browned and hot, after 5 to 10 minutes, depending on the heat of the fire, remove them to a serving platter. Brush them with extra marinade, season with salt and freshly ground black pepper, and serve.

BROCHETTE MARINADE

2 tablespoons red wine vinegar or sherry vinegar
1 clove garlic, finely chopped
1 tablespoon Dijon mustard
1 tablespoon herbs: parsley, thyme, marjoram, finely chopped
¾ cup olive oil
Salt
Pepper

Mix the vinegar with the garlic, mustard, and herbs. Whisk in the oil, and season with salt and pepper.

MAKES EIGHT 10-INCH BROCHETTES; SERVES FOUR

Marinated Tofu

Tofu, bland by nature, is given character with this strong marinade. Prepared in this fashion, the tofu is used in the Vegetable Brochettes and the Grilled Tofu Sandwich. Use firm (Chinese-style) tofu, rather than the soft or regular tofu, because it can be easily handled without breaking. The tofu tastes best if it has been marinated for several days, and should be marinated at least one full day before using.

1 or 2 packages firm tofu, 14 to 18 ounces each
½ ounce dried wild mushrooms, porcini or shiitake
1 cup water
2 teaspoons dried oregano or marjoram
2 cloves garlic, sliced
½ cup olive oil
½ cup sherry vinegar or red wine vinegar
½ cup red wine
½ cup tamari soy sauce
4 cloves
½ teaspoon salt
Several twists black pepper

Cut the tofu into slabs 1 inch thick—firm tofu often comes in pieces that size—and drain them: Set them on a bread board or the back of a baking sheet and raise one end; point the lower end toward the sink to let the water drain off. Cover the tofu with another tray and weight it down with something heavy, such as a few cans of tomatoes. Let the tofu drain for about ½ hour. This will remove excess water and allow the marinade to penetrate without being diluted.

While the tofu is draining, prepare the marinade. Simmer the mushrooms in the water for 15 minutes. Heat a small heavy skillet and toast the oregano or marjoram slowly until it is fragrant. Add the oregano and the remaining ingredients to the pot with the mushrooms, bring to a boil, and simmer slowly a few minutes more.

Remove the tofu from the draining board and arrange it in a single layer in a square or rectangular non-corrosive pan. Strain the marinade through a coffee filter or paper towel and pour it over the tofu. Cover with plastic or a lid and refrigerate at least one day, preferably longer.

The tofu can marinate 4 to 5 days. The marinade can be boiled, strained, and reused, if the tofu was well drained.

MAKES 2½ CUPS MARINADE (ENOUGH FOR 2 PACKAGES TOFU)

Charcoal-Grilled Leeks

Serve these garnished with finely diced hard-cooked eggs, olive oil, and herbs, or as part of a plate containing other grilled vegetables, a garlic mayonnaise or green sauce, olives, grilled bread, and fresh garden vegetables.

4 large or 8 to 12 small leeks
½ teaspoon salt
3 tablespoons light olive oil
Pepper
A few tablespoons extra virgin olive oil, for garnish
1 tablespoon Italian parsley or chervil, finely chopped, for garnish

Cut most of the greens off the leeks and remove the roots, keeping their bases intact. If the leeks are larger than an inch across, halve them lengthwise. Rinse the leeks well, allowing the water to run down inside the many layers.

Fill a wide skillet (one that will comfortably hold the leeks) with water, bring it to a boil, and add the salt. Lower the heat, add the leeks, and simmer gently for 4 to 6 minutes, until they can be pierced with a knife but still offer a little resistance. Remove them from the water, and set them aside on a clean kitchen towel to drain.

When it is time to grill the leeks, brush both sides with the light olive oil, and put them over the coals. Turn them once 45 degrees, to make a crosshatching of grill-marks, and cook on both sides until they are nicely colored. Remove them to a serving plate. Season with salt and freshly ground black pepper, and garnish with a spoonful of extra virgin olive oil and the chopped herbs.

SERVES THREE OR FOUR

Grilled Zucchini with Herb Butter

Young zucchini, simply grilled and brushed with butter aromatic with fresh herbs, make an uncomplicated and flavorful accompaniment to a summer gratin or timbale. They can also be served with the Grilled Tomato Sauce with Basil or the Ancho Chili Sauce to make a lively appetizer.

Herb Butter (page 325)
8 to 12 small green or golden zucchini
¼ cup light olive oil
Salt
Pepper

Prepare the Herb Butter and set it aside.

Use small green or golden zucchini with firm flesh and undeveloped seeds, allowing 2 or 3 per person. Slice them in half lengthwise, brush them with olive oil, and season them with salt and freshly ground black pepper. Grill the zucchini on both sides, 6-8 inches above the coals, turning them once 45 degrees on the cut side to make a cross-hatching of grill marks. Serve brushed with the Herb Butter.

SERVES FOUR TO SIX

SAUCES

RELISHES *and*

BUTTERS

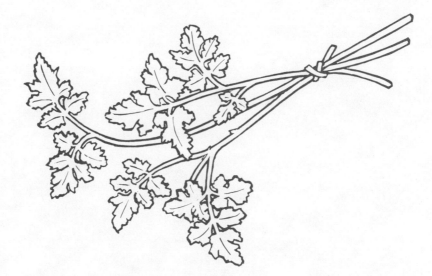

Often it is a sauce, relish, or flavored butter that takes a dish, or even a meal, out of the ordinary and makes it something complete and special. Their flavors, colors, and textures can contrast with or accentuate the foods they accompany. The preparation of these enhancements is neither difficult nor time consuming—they are well worth considering when planning a meal.

Aromatic White Sauce

A sauce to serve with crepes, roulades, and timbales, the milk is simmered with aromatics to give it depth and flavor. Thickened with a small amount of flour, it has the texture of cream but is much lighter than a sauce made of reduced cream.

2½ cups milk
1 tablespoon chopped onion or leek
1 bay leaf
6 peppercorns
4 branches thyme or a generous pinch dried thyme
1 small branch marjoram
2 tablespoons parsley, coarsely chopped
1 tablespoon butter
1 tablespoon flour
½ cup heavy cream
Salt

Combine the milk, onion or leek, and herbs in a saucepan and slowly bring to a boil; then lower the heat and simmer as slowly as possible for about 20 minutes. A flame-tamer may be helpful here. Turn off the heat, and let the milk sit, covered, until needed; then strain. There should be about 2 cups.

Melt the butter, stir in the flour, and cook the roux over medium-low heat for about 1 minute while stirring. Whisk in the warm milk all at once, and stir in the cream. Season with salt. Set the sauce on a flame-tamer or in a double boiler and simmer for 25 minutes, stirring frequently.

Variations

HERB BÉCHAMEL

Prepare the Aromatic White Sauce. Close to the time you want to serve it, stir in fresh herbs, using a selection that will best complement the dish it is to accompany. Use 3 tablespoons finely chopped parsley, chervil, or chives, plus 1 to 3 teaspoons of stronger herbs, such as basil, tarragon, fennel greens, various thymes, etc. One small clove of garlic, finely chopped, might be included as well.

BÉCHAMEL WITH LEMON AND LEMON THYME

Prepare the Aromatic White Sauce, but steep the milk with 3 large pieces of lemon peel, 6 to 8 branches lemon thyme, 1 small bay leaf, and 6 peppercorns. Strain the milk and proceed with the rest of the recipe.

MAKES 2½ CUPS

Cream with Shallots, Marjoram, and Chives

It takes less than 1 minute to cook this sauce of reduced cream and aromatic herbs.
It is well suited for all dried and fresh pasta dishes. Vary the herbs according to your
preferences and what is available. For a lighter herb sauce, make the Herb Béchamel.

2 cups light or heavy cream
1 shallot, finely diced
2 tablespoons marjoram leaves, finely chopped
2 tablespoons chives, sliced into narrow rounds
Salt
Pepper

Just before you want to use the sauce, heat the cream in a wide skillet with the shallot
and the herbs. Bring to a boil and cook for a half-minute or so, until it is as thick as
desired. Season to taste with the salt and freshly ground black or white pepper.

MAKES ABOUT 1¾ CUPS

Wild Mushroom Sauce

This is a deeply flavored sauce that does not use any milk, although crème fraîche or
cream can be added for enrichment.

2 tablespoons butter
2 tablespoons flour
3 cups Wild Mushroom Stock (page 66)
1 tablespoon tomato sauce or 1 teaspoon puréed sun-dried tomatoes
4 tablespoons cream or crème fraîche (optional)
Salt
Pepper

Melt the butter in a saucepan; then stir in the flour and cook over a low flame for
about 2 minutes, stirring frequently. Remove it from the heat to let it cool slightly.
Bring the mushroom stock to a boil; then whisk it into the cooled roux. Stir in the
tomato and the cream or crème fraîche, if using, and season with salt and freshly
ground black pepper to taste. Cook the sauce over low heat, stirring frequently, for
20 to 25 minutes.

MAKES 3 CUPS

Sorrel Sauce

This slightly thickened sauce goes particularly well with dishes made with spinach, mushrooms, and eggs, such as the Spinach and Ricotta Roulade and is used in the Mushroom Timbale with Sorrel Sauce.

2 cups Wild Mushroom Stock (page 66) or ½ ounce dried porcini mushrooms
2½ tablespoons butter
½ red onion, finely chopped
2 to 3 cups sorrel leaves, stems removed
1½ tablespoons flour
½ cup light cream
½ cup crème fraîche
Salt
Pepper

If you are not using the Wild Mushroom Stock, cover the dried mushrooms with 2½ cups boiling water, and set them aside to soak for at least ½ hour. Once they have soaked, squeeze them dry, and pour the liquid through a coffee filter or a strainer lined with a paper towel. It is fine to use the less expensive mushrooms imported from South America for this as the mushrooms themselves are not used in the sauce. If you are using better quality dried mushrooms, rinse them thoroughly after soaking to remove any sand or grit, squeeze them dry, and set them aside to use in another dish. As before, strain the soaking liquid.

Melt 1 tablespoon of the butter in a saucepan and add the onion. Cook it gently for 1 minute or so; then add the sorrel. Cover the pan to sweat the leaves for a few minutes; then remove the lid and stir down the sorrel, which will melt to almost nothing. Add the stock or mushroom liquid, bring to a boil, then simmer slowly, covered, for 5 minutes. Cool briefly, purée in a blender, and set aside.

Melt the remaining butter, stir in the flour, and cook over low heat for 2 minutes. Add the puréed liquid all at once, and whisk it into the roux. Add the two creams, and season to taste with salt and freshly ground black pepper. Bring to a boil; then cook gently, stirring occasionally, for 12 to 15 minutes.

MAKES 3 CUPS

Walnut Sauce

Use this sauce with pasta dishes. It is particularly good in the Cannelloni with Greens and Walnut Sauce.

½ cup fresh walnuts, chopped very fine
3 cups milk
2 cloves garlic, peeled and smashed with the flat side of a knife
2 small bay leaves
1½ tablespoons butter
1½ tablespoons flour
Salt
White pepper
Nutmeg

If possible, use new crop walnuts, freshly shelled and chopped very fine, either by hand or in a food processor. Slowly warm the milk with the walnuts, garlic, and bay leaves. When the milk is near boiling, turn off the heat, and set it aside for the flavors to steep. Melt the butter in a saucepan and stir in the flour to make a roux. Gently cook it for 2 minutes, stirring frequently, until it is lightly colored. Remove the bay leaves and the garlic cloves from the milk; then add the milk all at once to the roux, and stir with a whisk. Season to taste with salt, freshly ground white pepper, and a scraping of nutmeg; then slowly simmer the sauce, stirring frequently, about 25 minutes.

MAKES 3 CUPS

Fresh Tomato Sauce

This basic tomato sauce can be used in gratins or pasta dishes, or as a light accompaniment to roulades, crepes, or timbales. Make it in the summertime when tomatoes are ripe and full of flavor. Romas are the best sauce tomatoes because they are meaty and less juicy than most.

10 to 12 medium tomatoes (about 2½ pounds)
4 tablespoons olive oil
½ medium yellow onion, minced
2 cloves garlic, peeled
1 large bay leaf
3 branches parsley
4 branches thyme or ¼ teaspoon dried thyme
Salt
Sugar, if necessary
2 tablespoons basil, chopped
1 tablespoon virgin olive oil or butter
Pepper

Plunge the tomatoes into a pan of boiling water to a count of 10 seconds; then transfer them to a bowl of cold water. Cut out the cores, slip off the skins, halve them horizontally, and squeeze out the juice and seeds. Chop them finely.

Warm the olive oil; add the onion and the whole garlic cloves. After 30 seconds, add the bay leaf, parsley, and thyme branches; the herbs can be tied together if you like. Cook over medium heat for 8 to 10 minutes until the onion is soft; then add the tomatoes, raise the heat, and cook briskly.

When the tomatoes start to break down after 5 minutes or so, taste them and season with salt. If they are very acid, add a pinch or two of sugar, or more, to taste. Continue to cook until the sauce is no longer watery, 10 to 12 minutes, stirring occasionally, then remove the whole herbs and garlic cloves. The finished sauce will retain some texture, but if you want a smooth sauce, pass the tomatoes through a food mill. Check the seasoning, stir in the basil, the virgin olive oil or butter, and freshly ground black pepper to taste.

MAKES 2 CUPS

Grilled Tomato Sauce

Grilling tomatoes over a wood fire imparts a smoky fragrance that, aside from the tomato itself, is the main flavoring in this sauce. It goes beautifully with many dishes, particularly those made with corn.

With a grill going constantly in the restaurant, it is a simple matter to roast tomatoes whenever needed, but for the home cook it is more complicated. Take advantage of other grilling occasions to roast a number of good ripe tomatoes, and later make a sauce, which can be frozen or refrigerated for use within a day or two. Alternatively, the tomatoes can be broiled or roasted over a flame.

8 to 10 medium tomatoes (about 2 pounds)
2 tablespoons olive oil or corn oil
½ small onion, finely chopped
Salt
Sugar, if necessary

Wash the tomatoes and grill them over the coals, gradually turning them so that the entire surface of the skin blisters and chars slightly. Pull off any pieces of skin that have become blackened and hard, but leave on everything else. Roughly purée the tomatoes in a blender or food processor, leaving a little texture. Heat the oil, add the onion, and cook it gently until it is soft and translucent, about 8 minutes. Add the puréed tomatoes, and cook them over medium heat until they have thickened slightly and the excess water has evaporated, 5 to 10 minutes. Taste, and season with salt. If the tomatoes are very tart, add a pinch or two of sugar to correct the acidity.

For broiling the tomatoes: Lower your broiling rack to the lowest notch and line it with foil. Broil the tomatoes, turning them frequently with a pair of metal tongs, until they are blistered and lightly charred; then proceed with the recipe.

This sauce is lightly seasoned so that the flavor that comes from grilling or broiling can be appreciated. It can be used as it is, or as a basis for more complex sauces, such as the Grilled Tomato Sauce with Basil and the sauces used in the Mexican dishes.

MAKES ABOUT 2 CUPS

Grilled Tomato Sauce with Basil

This thick sauce with its faintly smoky background can be used with many things—warm pastas and pasta salads, grilled vegetables, as a flavoring in a vinaigrette, or as a dressing in a pita sandwich or pan bagnat. Covered and refrigerated, it will keep several days.

2 cups Grilled Tomato Sauce (page 315)
4 tablespoons virgin olive oil
1 cup basil leaves, loosely packed
2 cloves garlic
½ teaspoon coarse sea salt
Pepper
Balsamic vinegar to taste

Prepare the grilled tomato sauce, cook it until it is somewhat further thickened, and set it aside. Pour the oil into a blender jar, add half the basil, and blend until it is well incorporated. Gradually add the rest of the basil, and blend until it is fairly smooth but a little texture remains. Add this to the tomatoes.

Pound the garlic with the sea salt in a mortar until it forms a smooth paste. Stir it into the sauce, and season to taste with freshly ground black pepper, the vinegar, and some table salt if necessary.

MAKES 2 CUPS

Ancho Chili Sauce

This sauce has only a few ingredients, but it is robustly seasoned with roasted garlic and ancho chilies. We use it with the Crepas con Queso y Verduras, and it goes well in the Corn and Zucchini Timbale with Ancho Chili Sauce, and with grilled polenta and grilled vegetables.

2 pounds tomatoes, fresh or canned
20 large garlic cloves, unpeeled
3 to 4 ancho chilies or chilis negros
2 teaspoons dried oregano
Salt

If possible, grill the tomatoes over a charcoal or wood fire until they are soft but the skins have not blackened. Otherwise, broil them for 5 to 8 minutes, turning them frequently, until they are soft and the skins are blistered. Purée in a blender and set them aside.

Preheat the oven to 350°F. Roast the garlic cloves until they are soft inside and slightly browned on the outside, about 20 minutes. Let them cool briefly; then peel. Put them in a small blender jar, and blend them with some of the tomato purée.

Roast the chilies in the oven until they puff up and are fragrant, about 3 to 5 minutes. Remove the stems, seeds, and veins, tear into pieces, then blend in a small blender jar or spice mill. Roast the oregano in a dry skillet until it is aromatic, and remove it to a dish to stop the cooking.

Heat the tomatoes; season them with the garlic purée, chili, oregano, and salt, and simmer for 15 to 20 minutes.

MAKES ABOUT 3 CUPS

Tomatillo Sauce

Tomatillos, also called Mexican green tomatoes, have a pleasing, delicate tartness, but they can very greatly in acidity, and may require a little sugar for balance. They are commonly available in Mexican groceries, and in the West, in supermarkets. Choose fruits that are firm and yellow-green with split papery husks. This versatile sauce can be used with rice, in tacos, egg, and avocados, and will enliven rich Mexican-style stews and dishes. If fresh tomatillos aren't available where you live, try using the canned ones from Mexico, often labeled Mexican green tomatoes.

1 pound fresh tomatillos
½ small red onion, very finely diced
1 clove garlic, finely chopped
2 serrano or other hot green chilies, seeded and finely chopped
1 to 2 tablespoons cilantro leaves, chopped
Sugar, if necessary
Mild vinegar to taste
Salt

Bring a pan of water to a boil. After removing the papery husks from the tomatillos, add them to the pan, and lower the heat. Simmer them gently for about 20 minutes; do not let them split. As they rise to the surface, it will be necessary to turn them so that they cook all over. When the tomatillos are done cooking, drain them in a colander.

Mix together the onion, garlic, chilies, and cilantro in a bowl, either as they are or ground together in a mortar to make a coarse paste.

Blend the tomatillos to make a coarse textured purée. Or if you have a stone *molcajete*, a Mexican stone mortar, grind them by hand to break them up. Add the tomatillos to the rest of the ingredients, add a pinch or two of sugar, if they are especially tart, then season to taste with salt and a few drops to ½ teaspoon of vinegar. Allow the sauce to cool; then serve. It will keep in the refrigerator for several days, although the brightness of the fresh cilantro will fade after a few hours.

Variation: If you do not enjoy the taste of raw onion or plan to use this as an ingredient in a cooked dish, sauté the onions first in a teaspoon of corn oil or peanut oil for about 1 minute to take away the raw edge; then proceed with the rest of the recipe.

MAKES ABOUT 1 ½ CUPS

Sweet Pepper Relish

This colorful relish of tiny squares of peppers marinated in fruity olive oil and vinegar goes particularly well in the Eggplant and Zucchini Timbale with Sweet Pepper Relish. It also makes a bright garnish for frittatas, sliced avocados, potato fritters, pastas, and so forth.

1 small yellow pepper
1 small red pepper
¼ small red onion, finely diced
⅓ to ½ cup virgin olive oil
1 to 2 tablespoons balsamic vinegar, or more, to taste
Salt
Pepper

Trim the peppers, cut them into narrow strips, then into small, even pieces a little less than ¼ inch square. Combine the peppers and the onion, add enough olive oil to cover, and season with the vinegar, salt, and freshly ground black pepper. Marinate for 2 hours. Before using, strain off any excess oil if desired. The oil can be used in a vinaigrette or for cooking.

Variation: For a more elaborate relish, include finely chopped black olives, a little garlic, and fresh herbs. For a third color, include green peppers.

MAKES ABOUT 1½ CUPS

Green Sauce (Salsa Verde)

The flavor of this sauce can be constantly varied to reflect what is in the market and the garden. Use it with grilled or steamed vegetables and with hard-cooked eggs; in a frittata, or on fresh or grilled bread. Vary the tartness and the flavor to best complement what you are serving it with.

2 shallots or a small, freshly pulled onion, very finely diced
½ cup Italian parsley, finely chopped
⅓ cup finely chopped mixed herbs and herb blossoms: choose from the various thymes,
*   chervil, salad burnet, lovage, hyssop, summer savory, rocket (arugula) leaves, dill,*
*   tarragon, basil, marjoram*
Grated peel of 1 lemon
1 clove garlic, finely chopped
¾ cup virgin olive oil
Champagne vinegar or lemon juice to taste
Salt
Pepper
1 to 2 tablespoons capers, rinsed and chopped (optional)

Combine all of the ingredients, and season to taste with salt and freshly ground black pepper. For a sauce that is more tart, add the capers.

If the sauce is not to be used right away, wait until the last minute to add the vinegar or lemon juice so that the colors remain vivid and green. The herbs and oil can be combined well in advance of serving, covered, and refrigerated.

MAKES ABOUT ¾ CUP

Salsa Picante

Red, tangy, and tart, this sauce is an excellent condiment to serve with the Chilaquiles or the Crepas con Queso y Verduras. Use the smoked chilpotle chilies, or for a fresher taste, use serrano chilies, seeded and chopped.

4 medium tomatoes (about 1 pound)
½ small red onion
2 to 4 tablespoons cilantro leaves, coarsely chopped
3 cloves garlic, roughly chopped
1 to 2 canned chilpotle chilies or 1 to 2 serrano or jalapeño chilies
Salt
Rice wine vinegar to taste

Bring a small pan of water to a boil, immerse the tomatoes for a count of ten, and immediately set them in a bowl of cold water. Cut out the cores, then remove the skins and squeeze out the seeds. Or, for a more rustic salsa, simply wash the tomatoes and chop them.

Blend the onion, cilantro, and garlic together with a little of the tomato for about 20 seconds; then add the rest of the tomato and blend very briefly, retaining some texture.

Mince or purée the chili and add it, to taste, to the sauce. Season with salt and a ¼ teaspoon or more vinegar to bring up the flavors.

MAKES ABOUT 2½ CUPS

Banana and Yogurt Raita

This is a sweet and cool dish to serve with curried dishes.

1 tablespoon clarified butter (page 325)
2 teaspoons black mustard seeds
½ cup dried coconut, preferably unsweetened
1 cup yogurt
1 large banana, roughly chopped
1 to 2 tablespoons cilantro leaves, chopped, for garnish

Heat the clarified butter in a small pan or skillet, and when it is hot, add the mustard seeds. Have a lid handy and cover the pan as soon as the seeds begin to pop and fly about. Shake the pan back and forth a little so that the seeds don't burn. When they have finished popping, add the coconut, stirring constantly until it has turned a golden brown. Add these ingredients to the yogurt and stir in the banana. Chill and serve cold, garnished with the chopped cilantro.

MAKES 1½ TO 2 CUPS

Fresh Fruit and Mint Chutney

Fresh and lively, this chutney combines hot, sweet, tart, and cool tastes. Serve with any of the curry dishes.

½ cup raisins
1 cup lightly packed mint leaves
1 firm tart apple
1 orange
1 serrano or jalapeño chili, seeded and diced
Juice of 1 lemon
Salt

Cover the raisins with a cup of hot water; then set them aside to soften and plump up.

Wash and dry the mint leaves. Quarter the apple and remove the core. Slice the peel off the orange, and cut the orange into rounds. Finally, drain the raisins, and gently squeeze out the extra moisture.

Chop all the ingredients, separately or together, into small irregular pieces. Squeeze lemon juice over all, and add a little salt to bring up the flavors.

MAKES 2 CUPS

Basic Mayonnaise

Homemade mayonnaise is a tremendous improvement over store-bought, especially when using an oil of good quality. The oil should have pleasant, but not overly strong flavor. Herbs or garlic may be used to season the basic recipe.

1 egg
½ teaspoon salt
½ to 1 teaspoon Dijon mustard
1 tablespoon lemon juice or white wine vinegar
1 cup light olive oil, peanut oil, or vegetable oil
Hot water

Quickly bring the egg to room temperature by setting it in a bowl of hot water for two or three minutes, or until the egg no longer feels chilled when held in your hand. Then separate out the yolk.

Combine the egg yolk, salt, mustard, and lemon juice or vinegar in a bowl; set the bowl on a folded towel to keep it from moving around. Briskly whisk the ingredients together until they are thoroughly blended; then begin adding the oil, drop by drop at first, then in gradually increasing amounts. When the oil is completely incorporated, taste the mayonnaise, and add more salt or lemon juice or vinegar if desired. A very thick mayonnaise can be thinned by stirring in a spoonful or two of hot water until you get the consistency you want.

FOR MAYONNAISE MADE IN THE BLENDER OR FOOD PROCESSOR
When making mayonnaise this way, use the whole egg, not just the yolk, and the rest of the ingredients as listed in the recipe. Combine the egg, salt, mustard, lemon juice or vinegar, and ¼ cup of the oil in the blender jar or food processor. Blend together, and with the machine still running, add the rest of the oil in a steady stream until all of it is incorporated. Season to taste with more salt and lemon juice if needed.

MAKES I CUP

Clarified Butter

Clarified butter is butter from which the milk solids have been removed through heating and straining. It has a slightly nutty flavor that becomes more pronounced as the butter continues to cook. It is particularly good with dishes using Indian spices and is essential when frying in butter. Once the milk solids have been removed, the butter will not burn when heated.

One pound of butter will yield about 1½ cups clarified butter. Use unsalted butter, cut into small pieces, and melt it slowly in a heavy saucepan over low heat. Once it has melted, raise the heat to medium. A white foam will rise and cover the surface. Skim off the foam with a fine sieve, but don't worry about removing all of it. Cook the butter slowly for 10 minutes; then turn off the heat and let the butter cool to tepid. The milk solids will settle to the bottom. Pour the butter through a fine-meshed strainer or a strainer lined with cheesecloth. Let it cool completely; then cover and refrigerate, or not, as you prefer.

MAKES 1½ CUPS

Herb Butter

We serve this on brown rice, but it is good with many other foods as well—potatoes, pasta, and vegetables. A spoonful stirred into a cream soup makes a flavorful enrichment. The herb selection can be varied, and leftover butter can be frozen.

½ cup butter, softened
1 shallot, finely chopped
Small clove garlic, minced
1 teaspoon lemon juice
¼ teaspoon grated lemon peel
2 tablespoons parsley, finely chopped
1½ teaspoons thyme, finely chopped
1½ teaspoons marjoram, finely chopped

Combine all of the ingredients.

MAKES ½ CUP

Chili Butter

This spicy red butter is good on corn, polenta, fritters, warm tortillas, rice, and wherever else you might enjoy the combined flavor of chili and butter.

About 4 tablespoons Chili Powder (see below) or Ancho Chili Purée (page 327)
½ cup butter
Grated peel and juice of 1 lime
Salt

Prepare the chili powder or purée. Soften the butter by beating it with a spoon; then work in the chili to taste. Season with the lime peel and juice, and a pinch of salt. If you wish, add a little grated onion and chopped cilantro. Extra amounts can be stored in the freezer.

MAKES ½ CUP

Chili Powder

To make a pure chili powder, select several pasilla or ancho chilies, or use several kinds of dried chilies and blend them together after they are ground. (Any dried chili: pasilla, ancho, negro, New Mexico, or California may be used.) Preheat the oven to 350°F and roast the chilies until they puff up and are fragrant. This will take 3 to 5 minutes. Remove them from the oven and let them cool briefly; then break them open and remove the veins, seeds, and stems. The flesh should be dry and crisp. Crumble it into pieces; then grind it in a spice mill to make a powder.

Sometimes the thick-fleshed pasilla chilies will be damp even after roasting. In this case, lower the oven temperature to about 200°F and return the chilies to the oven until they are dried. Take care not to let them burn, or their flavors will be altered.

ONE LARGE CHILI WILL YIELD 1 TO 2 TABLESPOONS POWDER

Ancho Chili Purée

Use this purée to flavor sauces, stews, and soups. It can also be used spread on the bottom of a pizza crust or worked into butter to make a red chili-flavored butter.

Remove the stems, seeds, and veins from several ancho chilies and pour boiling water over them just to cover. If you like, you can toast the chilies first in a preheated 350°F oven, 3 to 5 minutes, or until they puff up. Let the chilies soak for 20 minutes; then blend to make a smooth paste.

Other dried chilies, such as pasilla, negro, New Mexico, and California, may also be prepared in this way. Keep the purée covered and refrigerated.

MAKES ½ CUP

Chilpotle Purée

This purée is also used to flavor soups and stews and it is also very good spread on the bread used for grilled cheese sandwiches. Puréeing these hot chilies makes it possible to season with them a little more precisely than if they were used whole or even roughly chopped. Because the dried chilpotle chilies are difficult to find, use the canned ones. Blend the chilies with enough light vegetable oil to make a smooth paste. Cover and store in the refrigerator.

Curry Powder

This curry powder can be used to flavor stews, sauces, and vinaigrettes. The aromas of freshly ground sweet and pungent spices are always tantalizing, so make curry powder in small portions and often.

2 teaspoons coriander seeds
2 teaspoons cumin seeds
1 teaspoon mustard seeds
1 teaspoon cardamom seeds
1 stick cinnamon, about 3 inches long
10 cloves
¼ teaspoon cayenne pepper
1 teaspoon turmeric

Grind the whole spices in an electric spice mill to make a fine powder; then stir in the cayenne and turmeric. Use soon after making, and store any that is left over in a cool place in a tightly covered jar.

MAKES ABOUT 3 TABLESPOONS

DESSERTS

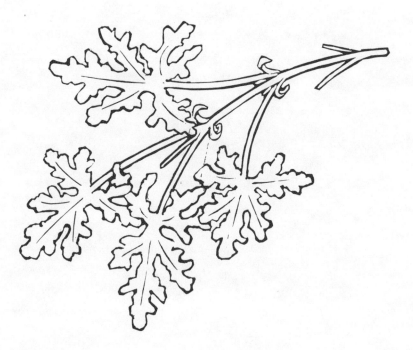

Desserts made with fruit are our favorites, especially variations on classic American crisps, cobblers, and Betties. Even when made with nontraditional combinations of fruits, there is something very familiar, even friendly, about these old-fashioned dishes. Fragrant and lush, they are both wholesome and inviting.

Fresh fruits, served alone or with simple embellishments such as honey, cream, or leaves of rose geranium and mint, make an ideal dessert; a really superb piece of fruit redolent with perfume, warm from the sun, and frosted with bloom is a rare treat. A plate of figs or a white peach makes a perfect end to a summer meal, as does a bowl of sliced oranges in winter served after a rich gratin or spicy stew. Fresh fruits are fragile, their seasons brief, and the appearance of each variety announces the incremental shifting of the year from spring to late spring to early summer. . . . As with vegetables, we are beginning to see a revival of old fruit varieties, as well as the introduction of new hybrids.

Creamy-textured desserts such as sherbets, ice cream, custards, and puddings are soothing and refreshing, particularly after a meal that is highly seasoned or complex with many colors, shapes, and tastes. The very uniformity of their texture helps carry the preceding diversity to a single, gentle conclusion.

Cakes and tarts can give the end of a meal a more resounding finality, but they are sometimes better when served with just coffee or tea.

Cherry-Apricot Crumble

This early summer dessert is friendly, old-fashioned, and luscious. Deep red and very sweet Bing cherries are the best variety to use. The crumble is also wonderful cold the next morning for breakfast.

THE FRUIT
2 pounds apricots
¾ pound Bing cherries
2 tablespoons sugar, or more, to taste
1½ tablespoons tapioca

Rinse the fruit; then slice the apricots in half and remove the pits. Cut the halves into thick slices or chunks. Apricots often ripen unevenly, but don't hesitate to include those parts that are soft to the point of being mushy. They will cook into a sauce as the crumble bakes. Pit the cherries, or slice them in two and pull out the seeds. Combine the fruit and toss them with the sugar and tapioca. If they are especially tart, add more sugar to taste. Make the crisp topping.

THE TOPPING
1 cup unbleached white flour
½ cup brown sugar
Pinch salt
½ cup plus 2 tablespoons unsalted butter, cut into small pieces

Combine the flour, sugar, and salt in a bowl; then add the butter. Work the ingredients together with your fingers until they are blended. Preheat the oven to 400°F. Pour the fruit into a pie plate or gratin dish with a 6-cup capacity. Cover it with the topping and bake for 45 minutes, or until the top is browned and there is a thick juice around the edge. Remove the crumble from the oven and let it rest; then serve warm with cream, the Cinnamon Crème Anglaise, or the Vanilla Ice Cream.

SERVES SIX

Individual Deep-Dish Fruit Pies

These special little pies are made with nectarines, plums, and berries—the essence of summer. This recipe will also make a single 10-inch pie.

1 recipe Tart Dough (page 236) or Cream Cheese Pastry (page 196)
2 pints blackberries, olallieberries, or raspberries
8 medium nectarines (about 1½ pounds)
2 plums, Santa Rosa or other flavorful variety
4 to 6 tablespoons sugar
2 tablespoons tapioca
2 tablespoons cream, mixed with 1 teaspoon sugar

Prepare the dough and divide it into the number of pieces needed to cover the pies. Roll them out into circles somewhat larger than the dishes; then stack them between waxed paper, and refrigerate until needed.

Preheat the oven to 400°F. Sort through and wash the berries. Wash the nectarines and plums, and slice them into pieces a little less than ½ inch wide. Put them in a bowl with the berries, sugar, and tapioca, and gently toss everything together. If the fruit is tart, use the larger amount of sugar. Pile the fruit into the baking dishes, and lay the circles of dough over them. If the dough is very cold, it will need a few minutes to soften. When it is pliable, press the dough lightly over the fruit, tuck in the edges, and crimp them prettily. Cut a vent in the top, or make several cuts in a star-shaped pattern. Brush the tops with the cream, and bake until the crusts have browned, about 45 minutes for individual pies, 50 to 60 minutes for a large pie.

If you are baking a large pie, the edges of the crust may brown before the center. To keep them from burning, cover them, once they are sufficiently browned, with strips of foil, after 25 to 30 minutes, and continue baking until the center is browned. Because the fruit is juicy and may bubble over, set the pies on a baking sheet, or lay a piece of foil in the bottom of the oven to catch any drips.

Serve warm with the Vanilla Ice Cream, or a pitcher of cream, or the Cinnamon Crème Anglaise.

MAKES SIX 3- TO 4-INCH PIES, OR ONE 10-INCH PIE

Peach and Blueberry Cobbler

The peaches are first heated on the stove to bring out the juices, then baked with the blueberries under a rich biscuit dough. Let the cobbler settle and cool a short while before serving with cold heavy cream, or the Peach or Vanilla Ice Cream.

THE FRUIT

2 pounds ripe, fragrant peaches
1 pint blueberries
¼ to ½ cup sugar, depending on the sweetness of the fruit
¼ teaspoon cinnamon
¼ teaspoon nutmeg
1 tablespoon lemon juice
2 tablespoons tapioca

Peel and slice the peaches. If the skins cling, place the peaches in boiling water for 10 to 15 seconds to loosen them. Remove the stems and leaves from the blueberries, rinse them, and set them aside. Combine the peaches with the sugar, spices, lemon juice, and tapioca. Set them aside in a saucepan while you make the biscuit.

THE BISCUIT

1 cup unbleached white flour
1 teaspoon baking powder
1 tablespoon sugar
⅛ teaspoon salt
1 vanilla bean or ½ teaspoon vanilla extract
4 tablespoons unsalted butter
1 egg
3 tablespoons light cream
Additional cream

Combine the dry ingredients and sift them together. If you are using whole vanilla, halve the bean lengthwise, scrape out the seeds with the tip of a knife, and add them to the flour, lightly rubbing the seeds between your fingers to distribute them, but don't worry if they clump together somewhat.

Cut the butter into small pieces; then cut it into the dry ingredients until the mixture resembles coarse meal. Beat the egg with a fork, and add the cream. If you are using vanilla extract, add it to the cream. Pour the liquid into the dry ingredients, and bring everything together with a few light, quick strokes of a fork.

Flour your work surface, and turn out the dough. Shape or roll it into a circle or rectangle about ⅜ to ½ inch thick. Cut out six 2½-inch circles, and make a seventh circle out of the scraps.

Preheat the oven to 400°F. Use a glass or earthenware baking dish with an 8-cup capacity—the top of the sides should be 1 inch above the fruit. Heat the peaches on the stove until the juices boil; then pour them into the baking dish and stir in the blueberries. Lay the biscuit rounds over the surface and brush their tops with cream. If desired, sprinkle them with sugar to make them sparkle. Bake the cobbler until the biscuits are browned, about 25 minutes.

SERVES SIX

Blackberries with Rose Geranium Leaves

The berries, layered with the rose-scented leaves, are left for several hours, or all day, in the refrigerator, so that the flavor of the leaves perfumes them. Nothing could be simpler than this dessert.

2 to 3 cups blackberries
6 rose geranium leaves
1 to 2 tablespoons light brown sugar
Rose geranium blossoms, for garnish
1 cup heavy cream

Sort through the berries, and remove any stems and leaves. Rinse the rose geranium leaves and crush them gently in your hands to release their perfume. In a serving dish make several layers of berries and leaves, with sugar sprinkled lightly over the berries. Cover the bowl and let the berries sit for several hours, or all day, in the refrigerator.

Bring the berries to room temperature before serving; remove the geranium leaves, and garnish the berries with the individual pink blossoms. Serve the cream separately in a pitcher.

SERVES FOUR

Blackberry Crisp

Blackberries have a long season and grow wild in many places throughout the country. They are delicious baked in a crisp. Olallieberries, Marion berries, and other types of blackberries can be used interchangeably. Serve with a pitcher of cold thick cream or the Vanilla Ice Cream.

THE FRUIT
About 4 cups blackberries
1 tablespoon flour
3 tablespoons white sugar or light brown sugar
1 teaspoon orange rind, finely grated

Preheat the oven to 375°F. Sort through the berries and toss them with the flour, sugar, and orange rind. Put them in an 8-inch glass pie pan or equivalent earthenware baking dish. Prepare the topping, and distribute it over the berries. Bake until the top is lightly browned, and the juices have risen around the edges, about 30 to 40 minutes.

THE TOPPING
½ cup unbleached white flour
6 tablespoons light brown sugar
¼ teaspoon cinnamon
⅛ teaspoon nutmeg
⅛ teaspoon salt
4 tablespoons unsalted butter

Combine the flour, sugar, spices, and salt. Cut the butter into small pieces; then work it into the flour with two knives or your fingers until the small pieces begin to hold together.

SERVES FOUR

Fresh Figs, Honey, Cream Cheese, and Mint

This is a fresh and easily prepared plate of fruit to serve for dessert, or for a summer afternoon snack with a glass of iced tea. Use any kind of fig as long as it is sweet and ripe. The beautiful Adriatic figs with their pale green skins and bright red-pink centers look especially handsome mixed with black mission figs. The cream cheese, lightened with ricotta, can be prepared well ahead of serving.

4 ounces fresh ricotta
3 ounces cream cheese
About 2 tablespoons milk, cream, or crème fraîche
About 18 ripe figs
1 to 2 teaspoons fresh mint, finely chopped
Honey

Beat the ricotta and cream cheese together with enough milk or cream to make the mixture soft and easy to work. Pass it through the fine screen of a food mill or sieve; then scrape it into a ball and wrap it in a dampened kitchen towel or piece of cheesecloth. Set aside in the refrigerator until needed.

When you are ready to make the dessert, wipe off the figs with a damp kitchen towel, as they are often dusty, and slice off the tough stems. Make two perpendicular cuts from the top down, stopping about ¾ inch from the base of the fig. Press each fig at the base, which will cause the top to open up in a flowerlike shape. Arrange the figs on a serving plate or plates, and slip a spoonful of the cheese mixture into each one. Sprinkle a little mint over the cheese and drizzle the whole with a thin thread of honey. Greek thyme honey, while not necessary, is most delicious with fresh figs.

SERVES FOUR TO SIX

Pear-Apple Crisp

This is perfect to make in midsummer when the Bartlett pears and Gravenstein apples are both in season and are full of flavor. Use pears that have ripened to yellow but are still firm. Later in the season, try other varieties of pears and apples.

THE FRUIT
4 medium apples
4 medium pears
1 tablespoon white sugar or brown sugar
1 to 2 teaspoons lemon juice

Preheat the oven to 400°F. Peel the fruit and slice it thinly. Toss it with the sugar and lemon juice; then lay it in a 9- or 10-inch pie plate, or similarly sized earthenware or porcelain gratin dish. Cover the fruit with the crisp topping, and bake it for 30 minutes, or until the top is nicely browned and the apples are cooked. Serve with cream whisked just enough to thicken it slightly, and flavored, if you like, with amaretto, or with the Cinnamon Crème Anglaise.

THE CRISP TOPPING
4 pairs of amaretti cookies
½ cup unbleached white flour
½ cup brown sugar
½ teaspoon cinnamon, freshly ground
Pinch salt
4 tablespoons unsalted butter

Crush the amaretti with a rolling pin, leaving them in the paper wrappings as you do so. Leave plenty of texture in the crumbs rather than reducing them to a powder. Combine the amaretti, flour, sugar, cinnamon, and salt in a bowl. Cut the butter into small pieces; then work it into the dry ingredients with 2 knives or your fingertips, until the texture is crumbly and beginning to hold together.

SERVES FOUR TO SIX

Rhubarb-Apple Betty

This is a variation on a classic dessert of fruit baked between layers of bread crumbs. The rhubarb will bake more evenly if the stalks are approximately the same width. Hothouse-grown rhubarb, which is thinner and more lightly colored than field-grown, will end up fairly sweet, whereas field-grown rhubarb will be a little tart. If using the latter, add a few extra spoonfuls of sugar, or not, as you prefer.

1 pound rhubarb
3 apples
1 cup brown sugar
½ teaspoon ground cinnamon
⅛ teaspoon ground cloves
¼ cup orange or tangerine juice
2½ cups fresh bread crumbs
6 tablespoons unsalted butter, melted

Wash the rhubarb and trim the stems, cutting off any leaf parts that still remain. Unless they seem tough and stringy, don't peel them. Halve any stalks that are extra wide, to make them approximately the same width as the narrower stalks; then cut the stalks into pieces about 1 inch long. Peel the apples, and thinly slice them. Put the two fruits together in a large bowl. Mix the sugar, cinnamon, and cloves together. Set aside 2 tablespoons of the mixture, add the rest to the fruit, along with the orange juice, and toss together.

Preheat the oven to 350°F. Add the 2 tablespoons of reserved sugar-spice mixture to the bread crumbs, and pour the melted butter over them. Lightly toss them together with your fingertips to combine. Use a non-corrosive baking pan—a glass pie plate or earthenware gratin dish—for the Betty. Pat half the buttered bread crumbs into the bottom, cover with the fruit, and top with the remaining crumbs. Bake, loosely covered, for 20 minutes, then uncover and bake another 25 minutes, or until the fruit is tender and the crust is browned. Serve the Betty warm with the Vanilla Ice Cream, the Cinnamon Crème Anglaise, or a pitcher of thick cream.

SERVES FOUR TO SIX

Rhubarb Fool

Serve this very cold in tall glasses with a crisp buttery cookie such as the Toasted Almond Butter Cookies.

1½ pounds rhubarb
1 cup light brown sugar or white sugar
¼ teaspoon powdered cloves
½ vanilla bean, cut lengthwise in half, or ½ teaspoon vanilla extract
Juice of ½ orange or 1 Meyer lemon
Several large pieces of orange or lemon peel
1 cup heavy cream
1 tablespoon sugar
Orange flower water or Grand Marnier to taste

If possible, choose narrow stalks of rhubarb that are red throughout and have a tender, unblemished surface. If the stalks are large and rough in spots, peel them: Use a paring knife to loosen the ends; then pull the strings off the stalks. Cut the rhubarb into roughly ½- to 1-inch pieces, and put it in a saucepan with the sugar, cloves, vanilla bean (but not the vanilla extract, if using), and the orange or lemon juice and peel. Cook over medium heat until the rhubarb has melted into a thick purée, and most of the water has cooked away, about 15 minutes. Stir toward the end of the cooking to make sure the fruit doesn't scorch. The fruit need not be perfectly smooth—a little irregularity in the texture makes it more interesting to eat. Once the rhubarb is cooked, scrape out the seeds of the vanilla bean with the tip of a knife and stir them into the fruit, or add the vanilla extract, if using. Transfer the whole to another container, cover, and refrigerate.

When the fruit is cold, whip the cream with the sugar until it holds its shape, and flavor it to taste with orange flower water or Grand Marnier. Fold it into the rhubarb somewhat imperfectly to give it an irregular, marbled texture. Pile the rhubarb into tall glasses and serve. It will hold in the refrigerator several hours before serving.

SERVES FOUR TO SIX

Honeydew in Ginger-Lemon Syrup

This is a cool dessert for hot weather. If you are serving it after a spicy dinner of Indian dishes, use the smaller amount of ginger. In the fall, a handful of pomegranate seeds makes a pretty garnish.

1 to 2 ounces fresh ginger root
1 lemon
2 cups water
²⁄₃ cup sugar
1 honeydew melon, weighing about 2 pounds
Mint leaves or pomegranate seeds, for garnish

Peel the ginger root and roughly slice two thirds of it into coin-shaped pieces. Remove several strips of peel from the lemon. Combine the water with the sugar, and add the ginger slices and lemon peel. Bring to a boil; then simmer for 7 minutes. Remove and discard the ginger and lemon peel.

Going with the grain, slice the remaining piece of ginger as thinly as possible; then cut the slices into fine threads. Remove another wide strip of peel from the lemon, and cut it into fine threads as well. Add both the ginger and lemon pieces to the syrup, and simmer slowly another 10 minutes. Transfer the syrup to a bowl, and set it in the refrigerator to cool.

Cut the melon in half, scoop out the seeds, and slice it into wedges about ¾ inch wide. Remove the skin; then cut the slices into pieces and put them in a serving bowl. Flavor the cooled syrup with lemon juice to taste, and pour it over the melon. Cover the melon and return it to the refrigerator for an hour or longer to chill thoroughly. Serve garnished with mint leaves or pomegranate seeds.

SERVES FOUR TO SIX

Pears Poached in Vanilla Syrup

Serve these classic poached pears with the Maple Mousse, the Vanilla Ice Cream and toasted pine nuts, or simply by themselves to make a light winter dessert.

6 Bosc or firm Comice pears
2½ cups water
¾ cup sugar
½ vanilla bean, slit lengthwise
3 ½-inch strips lemon peel

Peel the pears and cut them in half. Use a pear corer or a spoon to carefully remove the seeds and the narrow fibrous strip that goes up to the stem.

Bring the water to a boil with the sugar, vanilla bean, and lemon peel. Stir to dissolve the sugar; then lower the heat. Add the pears and cook them gently until they are translucent around the edges; then remove them to a bowl. Scrape the seeds out of the vanilla bean, and add the pods to the pears; then pour the syrup over the fruit. Cover and refrigerate until chilled.

SERVES SIX

Poached Dried Apricots with Ginger

The season for fresh, ripe apricots is extremely brief, but much of the apricot crop is dried. The concentrated flavor of the dried fruits can be enjoyed throughout the year and this is a fine dessert for fall and winter. The amber-colored syrup is dark and glistening. Because the flavors are strong, serve it very chilled.

3 cups water
1 cup sugar
1½ ounces peeled fresh ginger, cut along the grain into fine threads
6 to 8 ounces dried apricots
Peel of 1 lemon, cut into fine, narrow strips

Combine the water and sugar in a saucepan, and bring to a boil over moderate heat. Add the ginger and simmer for 5 minutes; then add the apricots and lemon peel. Lower the heat and cook the apricots gently until they are tender but not mushy, about 25 minutes. The time will vary depending on how the apricots were preserved and how dry they are.

When the apricots are done, remove them from the syrup with a slotted spoon and put them in a serving dish. Simmer the syrup until small bubbles appear all over the surface and it has thickened slightly, 5 to 6 minutes; then pour it over the fruit. Chill until very cold. Serve plain, with cream, or with crème fraîche, beaten and thinned to pouring consistency.

Variations
Roll several apricots inside a warm buckwheat crepe, and serve with the Vanilla Ice Cream and some of the syrup spooned over the ice cream and around the crepe.

MISSION FIGS IN GINGER SYRUP
Substitute dried black mission figs for the apricots. Remove the hard stems; then cook until they are tender, about 25 minutes. Reduce the syrup; then pour it over the fruit and chill. Apricots and figs can also be cooked together.

SERVES FOUR TO SIX

Sweet Tart Dough

This dough is used to line a 9-inch tart pan with a removable bottom. It can be made by hand or in a food processor. If well wrapped, it can be kept frozen for 4 to 6 weeks.

1 cup all-purpose flour
Pinch salt
1 tablespoon sugar
¼ teaspoon grated orange peel
4 ounces unsalted butter, room temperature
1 tablespoon water
½ teaspoon vanilla

To make the dough by hand, combine the flour, salt, sugar, and orange peel in a bowl. Cut the butter into small pieces, add it to the dry ingredients, and rub the mixture between your fingers to make a coarse meal. A pastry cutter or two knives can also be used. Combine the water and the vanilla, stir them into the flour-butter mixture with a fork, and then mix lightly with your fingers until the pastry comes together when pressed. Gather the dough into a ball, press it into a round disk, wrap it in plastic, and let it rest for a ½ hour. If it is a warm day and the butter is very soft, let it rest in the refrigerator.

To make the dough in a food processor, first combine the flour, salt, sugar, and orange peel. Then add the butter, cut into small pieces, and process until a coarse meal has formed, 10 to 15 seconds, depending on how soft the butter is. Combine the water and vanilla and pour it into the flour-butter mixture while the machine is running, and process for just 5 seconds. Do not let the dough form a ball. Instead, empty the contents of the bowl onto your work surface, gather them together with your hands, and press the dough into a ball. Flatten it into a disk, wrap it in plastic, and set it aside for ½ hour in the refrigerator, or freeze the dough for future use.

Because the dough is soft and buttery, use your hands to line the pan, rather than attempt to roll it out. Generally it seems to work best to shape the sides first, then the bottom. Press the dough into the pan, forming sides of even thickness that rise about ¼ inch above the rim. Using the heel of your hand, press the dough evenly over the bottom. Make it somewhat thinner closest to the rim because the sides will inevitably slump a little during the baking, filling in that area between the rim and the bottom. After the bottom is shaped, go back to the sides and reshape any sections that need it.

Cover the shell lightly with foil and put it in the freezer for at least ½ hour, or until the dough is firmly set in place. At this point the tart shell can be baked, or wrapped well and frozen for future use. Freezing the tart dough makes it unnecessary to line it with foil and pie weights while baking.

To bake the shell, preheat the oven to 400°F. Place the shell in the lower third of the oven. Check it after 5 minutes; use the point of a sharp knife to pierce any large air bubbles that may have formed. If the shell is going to be filled and baked further later, cook it until it is lightly browned, about 10 to 12 minutes. If it is not going to be baked again, bake a few minutes longer until it is well browned all over, about 15 minutes in all.

MAKES ONE 9-INCH TART

Blueberry-Cream Cheese Tart

The blueberries in this tart are fresh. To keep them from rolling away when the tart is sliced, some of the berries are cooked together with a little sugar to make a syrup. The separate parts of this dessert can be made well in advance, but put the tart together as close to serving time as possible to keep the shell crisp.

1 recipe Sweet Tart Dough (page 344)
4 ounces natural cream cheese
¼ cup sour cream
Grated peel of 1 small lemon
1 to 2 teaspoons sugar
Nutmeg
3 cups blueberries
¼ cup sugar
Powdered sugar

Prepare the tart dough. Press it into a 9-inch tart pan with a removable rim and freeze it for at least 30 minutes; then bake it until it is well colored all over, about 15 minutes. Set it aside to cool.

Beat together the cream cheese, sour cream, and lemon until they are well combined. Sweeten to taste with sugar and add a few scrapings of nutmeg.

Sort through the berries and remove any stems and leaves. Put ½ cup of the berries in a saucepan and heat them. As soon as they begin to release their juices, add the ¼ cup sugar, and cook until the juice feels smooth and syrupy when rubbed between your fingers. This should take just a minute or two. Pour the cooked fruit over the rest of the berries, and toss them all together.

To assemble the tart, spread the cream cheese mixture evenly over the crust; then carefully distribute the berries on top. Dust the edges of the tart with powdered sugar.

Remove the tart from its ring and carefully set it on a flat serving plate. Cut it into wedges and serve.

MAKES ONE 9-INCH TART

Almond-Pine Nut Tart

This is a three-layered tart, good to make when fresh fruit is not in season. The crust is spread with a sweet layer of jam, and the creamy almond filling is covered with a layer of pine nuts. This recipe is well suited to a food processor, but if you are not using one, grind the almonds in a hand-turned nut grinder or in the blender, and add the rest of the ingredients in the same order as given in the recipe, beating well with each addition.

1 recipe Sweet Tart Dough (page 344)
½ cup almonds
⅓ cup sugar
Pinch salt
2 eggs
1 teaspoon vanilla
A few drops almond extract
½ cup unsalted butter, room temperature
2 tablespoons flour
½ teaspoon baking powder
3 to 4 tablespoons raspberry or apricot jam
½ cup pine nuts
Powdered sugar

Prepare the sweet tart dough, line a 9-inch tart pan, and partially bake it according to the instructions.

Bring a small pan of water to a boil, add the almonds, turn off the heat, and let them sit for 1 minute. Drain them; then slip off the skins, and rub them in a clean kitchen towel to dry. Grind the almonds in a food processor fitted with a metal blade for about 45 seconds. Add the sugar, salt, eggs, vanilla, and almond extract, and process another 10 seconds; then add the butter, flour, and baking powder, and process long enough to make a smooth batter, about 10 seconds.

Preheat the oven to 375°F. Spread a thick layer of jam over the tart shell; then cover it with the almond filling. Set the pine nuts over the top, and bake the tart until the surface is firm and browned, about 30 minutes. Remove it from the oven and let it cool; then dust it with powdered sugar. Serve it by itself or with soft mounds of sweetened whipped cream.

MAKES ONE 9-INCH TART

Mince Cookies

This cookie, filled with spicy apples, raisins, and dates, is flavorful without being too sweet. The filling is enough for two batches and will keep covered in the refrigerator for several weeks.

POPPY SEED DOUGH
2½ cups unbleached white flour
1 teaspoon baking powder
¼ teaspoon salt
2 tablespoons poppy seeds
⅓ cup sugar
1 teaspoon grated lemon peel
1 cup unsalted butter, room temperature
1 egg
¾ teaspoon vanilla extract

Combine the white flour, baking powder, salt, poppy seeds, sugar, and lemon peel. Cut in the butter with 2 knives, or work it between your fingertips until the mixture resembles cornmeal. Make a well in the center and add the egg and the vanilla extract. Beat the egg with a fork, and incorporate it into the rest of the mixture with your hands. Press the dough together, wrap it in plastic or waxed paper, and refrigerate for 15 to 20 minutes, or longer. Prepare the filling.

MINCE FILLING
1 orange
1 lemon
½ cup apple juice
2 large apples
½ cup raisins
½ cup golden raisins
¼ cup dates, chopped
¾ cup brown sugar
¼ teaspoon salt
¼ teaspoon cinnamon
¼ teaspoon cloves
¼ teaspoon nutmeg, freshly ground
¾ teaspoon vanilla extract
1 tablespoon rum

Wash the orange and the lemon and slice them into sections (peel and all). Purée in a blender with the apple juice. Set the purée in a non-corrosive pan over low heat. Peel, core, and thinly slice the apples; then chop them into small pieces no larger than ⅜ inch, adding the cut pieces to the purée as you work. Add the raisins, dates, sugar, salt, and spices, cover, and let everything stew for 15 to 20 minutes, stirring occasionally. Continue cooking about 10 minutes longer, stirring more often until the mixture is quite thick. Add the vanilla extract and the rum, and breathe deeply. Set the mixture aside to cool.

To form the cookies, remove the poppy seed dough from the refrigerator, and roll it out on a floured board to ⅛-inch thickness. If the dough has been refrigerated for more than 30 minutes, let it sit for 10 minutes or so to soften before you try to roll it out.

Cut the dough into 3¼- to 3½-inch rounds with a cookie cutter. Put about 1 tablespoon of the filling on half the round, and fold over the other half. Press the edges together; then crimp them with a fork.

Preheat the oven to 375°F. Place the cookies on a buttered baking sheet and bake for about 20 minutes, until the bottoms and edges are lightly browned.

Variation
MINCE TART
Bake the mince filling in a 9-inch tart pan lined with the Sweet Tart Dough, and cover the top with a lattice of dough; or lattice the top with poppy seed dough. This would make a good choice of pie for Thanksgiving or Christmas dinner, served with whipped cream flavored with rum, or hard sauce.

MAKES ABOUT TWO DOZEN FILLED COOKIES

Toasted Almond Butter Cookies

These buttery cookies are filled with toasted ground nuts and dusted with powdered sugar. They make an excellent accompaniment to poached fruit desserts, or the Meyer Lemon Mousse or the Rhubarb Fool.

½ cup almonds
⅔ cup unsalted butter, room temperature
½ cup powdered sugar
Pinch of salt
½ teaspoon vanilla
Few drops almond extract
1⅓ cups unbleached white flour
Additional powdered sugar

Preheat the oven to 350°F. Coarsely chop the almonds; then bake them until they begin to smell toasted and the cut surfaces have browned slightly, about 7 to 10 minutes. Remove them from the oven and let them cool; then grind them in a nut grinder or a food processor. If you are using a food processor, some of the almonds will be reduced to a powder while others are still in small pieces, which is fine.

Cream the butter and the sugar together until they are well combined; then stir in the salt, vanilla, and almond extract. Gradually work in the almonds and the flour to make a smooth dough. Shape the dough into a cylinder 1 to 1½ inches across, wrap it in plastic, and chill for 30 minutes to make it easier to handle. When you are ready to bake the cookies, slice the dough into coins ¼ inch thick and set them on an unbuttered cookie sheet. Bake them in the center of the oven until they are lightly browned on top; then remove them to a cooling rack and dust them with powdered sugar, worked through a sieve.

If you don't want to bake all the cookies at one time, wrap the dough tightly and store it in the freezer until needed.

MAKES ABOUT FOUR DOZEN 1-INCH COOKIES

Brazilian Chocolate Cake

This chocolate cake is light and moist and has a distinct fine crumb rather than a fudgy, truffle-type texture. Baked in a tube pan, it comes out high and looks impressive with a dark red-brown center.

3 ounces semisweet chocolate
1 ounce unsweetened chocolate
1 cup plus 2 tablespoons hot strong coffee
½ cup unsalted butter, room temperature
1½ cups sugar
2 eggs
1 teaspoon vanilla extract
2 cups sifted cake flour
1 teaspoon baking soda
½ teaspoon salt

Preheat the oven to 350°F. Use a tube pan that is constructed in one piece because the batter is very thin and will flow through the seams of a two-piece pan. Butter it generously and coat it with flour. Tap out the excess flour.

Heat the chocolate with 2 tablespoons of the coffee in a double boiler over low heat, stirring constantly until it is melted and smooth. Set it aside.

Cream the butter; then gradually add the sugar and beat until the mixture is light. Add the eggs one at a time; then stir in the vanilla and the melted chocolate.

Sift the flour and measure 2 cups; then resift it with the baking soda and the salt. Gently stir it into the batter, alternating it with the rest of the coffee, until all is incorporated. Pour the batter into the tube pan, and bake the cake for 50 minutes, or until the cake pulls away from the sides and a toothpick inserted in the middle comes out clean. Let rest 5 minutes in the pan, then turn out onto a rack to cool.

CHOCOLATE ICING
3 ounces semisweet chocolate
3 tablespoons water or strong coffee
1 teaspoon vanilla
6 tablespoons unsalted butter, cut into small pieces

Put the chocolate and the water or coffee in a small heavy saucepan and heat slowly, stirring constantly until the chocolate has melted. Remove it from the heat and stir in the vanilla; then gradually add the butter, stirring continually. At first the icing will be quite thin, but it will thicken as it cools. The process can be speeded up by cooling it over a bowl of ice. When the icing has thickened, cut the cake in two, and spread it over the middle. Return the top and dust it with powdered sugar.

MAKES ONE 8-INCH TUBE CAKE

Maple Spice Cake

This is a well-spiced cake that is sweetened with maple syrup. Freshly ground whole spices are particularly aromatic; commercially ground spices may also be used, but may not be as fragrant or as strong. If the ground spices do not have a good strong smell, it is probably time to replenish your supply.

2 to 2½ inches stick cinnamon (2 teaspoons ground)
Scant ½ teaspoon cardamom seeds
½ teaspoon allspice nuts
12 cloves (¼ to ⅜ teaspoon ground)
3¾ cups sifted cake flour
2 teaspoons baking powder
1 teaspoon baking soda
1 teaspoon salt
1 cup unsalted butter, room temperature
¾ cup dark brown sugar
2 eggs
1 teaspoon freshly grated ginger (1 teaspoon ground)
¾ cup buttermilk
¾ cup maple syrup
2 tablespoons rum

Preheat the oven to 350°F. If possible, use a tube pan with a removable bottom. Butter it well, lightly flour it, and set it aside.

Combine the whole spices, and grind them in a spice mill to make a fine powder. Sift the flour and measure 3¾ cups; then resift it with the spices, baking powder, soda, and salt, and set it aside.

Cream the butter and the sugar, and add the eggs one at a time, beating well with each addition; then stir in the ginger. In another bowl, combine the buttermilk, syrup, and rum. Add the flour mixture and the liquids alternately to the creamed butter, beginning and ending with flour. Blend well after each addition.

Spoon the batter into the tube pan, and bake for 50 to 60 minutes, until the cake pulls away from the sides and a toothpick or a knife inserted in the middle comes out clean. If the cake is baked in 8-inch layers, the cooking time will be reduced to about 30 minutes. Let it cool in the pan for 5 to 10 minutes before removing. Serve with softly whipped cream or the Maple Mousse.

MAKES ONE 8-INCH TUBE CAKE

Maple Mousse

This is a versatile dessert that is quick to assemble and especially appropriate in fall and winter. Serve it either soft or frozen, dusted with praline, or use it to accompany poached pears or the Maple Spice Cake. If you enjoy a strong maple taste, use a darker grade of syrup.

6 tablespoons maple syrup
3 egg yolks
Pinch salt
1 to 2 teaspoons grated orange peel
1 cup heavy cream

Combine the syrup, yolks, and salt in a double boiler set over medium heat. Beat with a whisk until the mixture has thickened and the color has lightened from dark brown to tan, about 7 minutes. Take care not to let the mixture overcook or it will curdle. When it has thickened, remove it from the heat, stir in the orange peel, and set it aside to cool. To do this quickly, place the custard over a bowl of ice and stir it frequently until it is cool.

Whip the cream until it holds its shape; then fold it into the cooled custard. Refrigerate or freeze the mousse in dessert dishes or ramekins. If the mousse is frozen longer than 3 hours, let it soften for 20 minutes in the refrigerator before serving.

MAKES ABOUT 2½ CUPS; SERVES FOUR TO SIX

Meyer Lemon Mousse

Meyer lemons have a fuller, sweeter, more aromatic flavor and are less acidic than the commonly available Eureka lemon. If the latter variety is used, however, you might want to increase the amount of sugar by 1 or 2 tablespoons. Though not stabilized with gelatin, the mousse will hold well, refrigerated, for about 6 hours.

Grated peel of 2 lemons
3 egg yolks
½ cup lemon juice (3 to 4 Meyer lemons or 1 to 2 Eureka lemons)
½ cup sugar, in all
3 egg whites
¼ teaspoon cream of tartar
½ cup heavy cream

Grate the lemon carefully, avoiding the white area under the skin, which has a bitter flavor. Beat the egg yolks well and pour them through a strainer into a small non-corrosive saucepan. Then add the lemon peel, the lemon juice, and half the sugar. Cook over medium-low heat, stirring constantly, until the mixture thickens. Take care not to let it boil or the yolks will curdle. Set the lemon curd in the refrigerator to cool.

When ready to assemble, beat the egg whites with the cream of tartar until they form firm peaks; then gradually beat in the rest of the sugar. In another bowl, whisk the cream until it holds its shape. Using the same whisk used for the cream, break up the lemon curd and beat it until it is smooth. Fold in the meringue, then the whipped cream. Lightly spoon the mousse into dessert glasses and refrigerate until it is well chilled.

Garnish the mousse with rose geranium flowers, freshly candied violet blossoms, or rose petals, coarsely chopped. The mousse is also wonderful served with sweetened raspberries, blackberries, or red currants.

Variation
MEYER LEMON CURD

Follow the directions for making the lemon custard, but leave out the egg whites and cream. Use the curd right away, or cover and keep refrigerated. Use it to spread over the bottom of a prebaked tart shell; then cover it with fresh raspberries or blackberries for a delicious summer tart.

SERVES FOUR TO SIX

Semolina Pudding with Blood Orange Syrup

A soft sweet pudding of Greek origin, this can be served warm or cooled with the syrup. The blood oranges give it a rose-pink hue, but if they are not available, use regular oranges.

THE PUDDING

1 vanilla bean or 2 teaspoons vanilla extract
4 cups milk
1 cup sugar
¾ cup semolina, or Cream of Wheat
½ cup butter
2 teaspoons grated orange peel
5 eggs

Preheat the oven to 350°F and generously butter a 9-by-12-inch baking dish.

Split the vanilla bean in half lengthwise and scrape the seeds into the milk. Add the pods and the sugar and heat slowly, stirring to dissolve the sugar. When the milk is hot but not boiling, gradually pour in the semolina, stirring continuously. Cook the cereal, continuing to stir, until it has thickened, about 10 minutes. Remove it from the heat, take out the vanilla pods, and stir in the butter and the orange peel.

Separate the eggs. Beat the yolks with a little of the cereal to gradually warm them; then stir them into the pot of cooked semolina. Beat the egg whites in a large bowl until they form firm peaks; then add them to the semolina and gently fold everything together with a wide rubber spatula. Pour the batter into the baking dish and place it in the center of the oven. Bake for 1 hour and 10 minutes, until the center is firm and the top is browned. (If it seems that the top is browning too much, cover it loosely with foil.) Remove the pudding from the oven and let it cool.

BLOOD ORANGE SYRUP

Several pieces orange peel
1 cup blood orange juice, about 2 to 3 oranges
1 cup sugar
1 tablespoon Grand Marnier (optional)
3 cloves
1-inch piece of cinnamon stick

Remove the orange peel with a vegetable peeler and cut it into fine strips. Combine with the remaining ingredients and bring to a boil. Simmer slowly for 10 minutes.

Cut the pudding into diamond-shaped pieces, and serve it with some syrup and a few of the candied peels spooned over the top.

SERVES TEN

Coconut Crème Caramel

A delicate custard flavored with coconut and cinnamon, this is particularly good after a meal of spicy Indian or Mexican food. It is made without milk or cream, but for a richer version that includes cream, see the variation.

4 cups dried coconut, preferably unsweetened
4 cups boiling water
3 whole eggs
3 egg yolks
⅓ cup sugar
Pinch salt
Pinch cinnamon
½ cup sugar, for the caramel

Cover the coconut with the water and set it aside for ½ hour; then put the entire contents in a blender and blend at high speed for 3 minutes. Pour the blended coconut through a strainer lined with a piece of dampened cheesecloth or use a kitchen towel. After most of the liquid has dripped through, gather the corners of the cloth together and twist hard, to squeeze out the remaining coconut milk. (A second batch of milk can be made with the used coconut and additional water. It won't have as much flavor as the first, but it can be used for making Indian stews and soups.)

Combine the eggs and the egg yolks, and beat well; then add the sugar, salt, and cinnamon. Warm the coconut milk and stir it into the rest of the ingredients; then pour it through a strainer.

Make a caramel with the ½ cup sugar. Heat it in a heavy light-colored pan over medium heat until it is thoroughly dissolved and golden brown. Once the sugar begins to melt, stir it continually. Pour it into six custard dishes. Don't worry if it doesn't spread evenly—it will do so once the custard begins to bake.

Preheat the oven to 325°F. Pour the custard over the caramel, set the cups in a pan of hot water, and bake until the custard is set and a knife inserted comes out clean. Serve well chilled.

Variation: Make the coconut milk using 3 cups coconut and 3 cups water. Measure the resulting milk, add enough heavy or light cream to make 3 cups total, and proceed with the recipe.

SERVES SIX

Raspberry Sherbet

There is nothing but the pure flavor of raspberries in this sherbet. Serve it by itself, with cookies, or alongside the Peach Ice Cream or the Vanilla Ice Cream.

2 baskets raspberries (about 2¾ cups)
⅓ cup water
½ cup sugar

Sort through the berries and purée them briefly in a food processor or pass them through a food mill; then work them through a fine-meshed sieve, pressing with a rubber spatula to force out the thick juice. It takes about 10 minutes to do this. In the end the seeds should be fairly dry and you will have about 1¼ cups purée.

Boil the water with the sugar until it is dissolved; then pour it into the purée and whisk together. Set it over a bowl of ice or refrigerate until it is cool; then freeze it in your ice cream machine according to the instructions.

MAKES 1 PINT

Muscat Grape Sherbet

The flavor of the muscats is very pronounced in this sherbet. This is a light autumnal dessert. Serve it with the crisp Toasted Almond Butter Cookies.

1½ pounds muscat grapes
6 tablespoons sugar
2 tablespoons lemon juice

Rinse the grapes and pull them off their stems. Put them in a non-corrosive pan with about ¼ cup of water, cover, and bring to a gentle boil. Cook the grapes until they have given up their juices and have begun to fall apart, about 5 minutes. Put them through a food mill to make a smooth purée. Take care not to crush the seeds as you do so, as they are bitter.

Combine the sugar with ½ cup of the grape purée and heat it on the stove, stirring until the sugar is dissolved. Add this syrup back to the rest of the grape purée, and add the lemon juice. Chill; then freeze it in your ice cream maker according to the instructions.

MAKES 1 PINT

Peach Ice Cream

This is the quintessential summer ice cream. Use any kind of peach as long as it is ripe and full of flavor. The small white Babcocks that appear in late June are the most fragrant and delicate. Serve the ice cream with a handful of Alpine strawberries, puréed raspberries, or with a scoop of fresh Raspberry Sherbet.

1 vanilla bean
1 cup milk
2 cups heavy cream
3 egg yolks
½ plus ⅓ cup sugar
5 to 6 peaches (1 to 1½ pounds)

Slit the vanilla bean in half lengthwise and put it in a saucepan with the milk and ½ cup of the cream. Set it over a medium-low flame to heat, and while it is warming, beat the yolks and the ½ cup sugar together. Stir the hot milk slowly into the yolks and sugar, taking care not to create too many bubbles; then return the mixture to the pan and set it over low heat, stirring constantly with a wooden spoon. Check the back of the spoon frequently, and as soon as the custard is thick enough to coat it, remove it from the heat and pour it directly into a bowl. (If the milk was very hot when you poured it into the eggs, this may take only a short time—a minute or less. Do not let the custard come to a boil or it will curdle.) Pour the cooked custard through a strainer into a clean bowl; then stir in the remainder of the cream. Scrape the seeds out of the vanilla bean into the custard, put the pods back in, and set the custard over ice or in the refrigerator until it is thoroughly cooled. This can be done a day in advance.

Peel the peaches and slice them. Use either a potato masher or a food processor to break them into a very coarse purée that has plenty of small chunks of fruit. The chunks must not be too large, or they will be unpleasantly hard once frozen. Stir the remaining ⅓ cup sugar into the fruit, and let it sit until it has dissolved, about an hour. When the custard is well chilled, remove the vanilla pods, add the peaches, and freeze according to the instructions of your ice cream machine.

MAKES 5 TO 6 CUPS

Vanilla Ice Cream

Vanilla ice cream certainly is not original, but it always goes well with warm fruit desserts. Make the custard the day before so that the beans have a long time to steep and flavor the ice cream. Afterward, the pods can be wiped off, dried, and buried in a jar of sugar to make vanilla sugar.

2 vanilla beans
1½ cups milk
4 egg yolks
¾ cup sugar
Pinch salt
2 cups heavy cream

Slit the beans lengthwise in two and steep them with the milk in a pan set over a low flame. Beat the egg yolks and the sugar together; then once the milk is hot, whisk it slowly into the yolks, beans and all, taking care not to stir up too many bubbles or it will be hard to tell when the custard is cooked. Return the mixture to the pan and cook it over medium heat while stirring constantly with a wooden spoon. Check the back of the spoon frequently; as soon as the custard has thickened enough to coat the spoon, pour it back into the bowl. (Do not let the custard come to a boil or it will curdle. If the milk was very hot when you poured it into the eggs, it may take only a very short time to thicken, so check your spoon right away and watch carefully.)

Pour the custard through a strainer into a clean bowl. Wipe off the vanilla beans with your fingers, then scrape the seeds with the tip of a paring knife into the custard. Add the pods as well, a pinch of salt, and the cream. Cover and refrigerate the custard until the next day, or until you are ready to make the ice cream.

Just before freezing, remove the beans and run your fingers down them again, squeezing out the vanilla essence. Freeze the custard according to the instructions on your machine.

MAKES A GENEROUS QUART

Cinnamon Crème Anglaise

Serve this instead of cream or ice cream with various fruit desserts, such as the Pear–Apple Crisp or Individual Deep–Dish Fruit Pies.

2 cups light cream
1 cinnamon stick
4 egg yolks
¼ cup sugar
½ teaspoon cinnamon

Slowly warm the cream with the cinnamon stick to infuse the cream with the flavor of the cinnamon; 10 to 15 minutes should be sufficient. While the cream is heating, beat the egg yolks and the sugar together. When the cream is hot, remove the cinnamon stick, and gradually pour it into the yolks, gently stirring with a whisk to keep from creating too many bubbles, which would later make it difficult to see how the custard is cooking.

Pour the mixture back into the pan and return it to the stove. Keep the bowl close by. Cook the custard over medium heat, stirring constantly with a wooden spoon. As it cooks it will thicken slightly, but visibly, coating the spoon. Keep checking the back of the spoon to see how the cooking is progressing. When the custard no longer falls off the spoon, but coats it, immediately pour it into the bowl. (Do not let it come to a boil or it will curdle. If the cream was very hot when you poured it into the eggs, it may take only a very short time to thicken, so start checking right away.)

Stir in the ground cinnamon. The flavor will strengthen as it sits, so keep it a little understated. Pour the custard through a strainer into a clean bowl, cover, and refrigerate until cold.

Variation
CINNAMON ICE CREAM
Add 1 cup of heavy cream to the custard and an additional ½ teaspoon freshly ground cinnamon. When the custard is cold, freeze it in an ice cream machine according to the instructions. This is a perfect ice cream to serve with pear, apple, and peach desserts.

SERVES FOUR TO SIX

APPENDIX

Seasonal Menus

The following are some suggestions for seasonal menus formed around the recipes in this book. Each menu brings together dishes whose colors, textures, and tastes complement one another in a lively way, so that each meal will be a pleasure to serve and eat. Although these menus have been thought of primarily as dinner menus to be served in several courses, a simpler supper or a lunch can be made using two or three of the suggested dishes. Many of the recipes in this book are best accompanied by something that is simple and familiar, such as a steamed or sautéed vegetable; recipes are not always given in the book for these suggestions. Similarly, different combinations of seasonal greens have been suggested for salads that are not always included as recipes.

SPRING

Many foods we cook in the spring still draw upon winter produce, the root vegetables and winter squashes. But around February they begin to include fresh green vegetables—snow peas and artichokes, the first asparagus, bitter lettuces such as escarole, curly endive, and Belgian endive. Later come fava beans and sugar snap peas, beets, and tender herbs—mint, sorrel, chervil, and rocket (arugula). The spring fruits include all the citrus, notably blood oranges and Meyer lemons, rhubarb, and the first strawberries. As summer approaches, the menus become lighter, using more and more fresh vegetables and fruits.

Bresse Mushroom Soup
Leek and Mustard Pie; Warm Spring Vegetable Salad
Salad of Mixed Greens (including wild greens, rocket [arugula], and chervil)
Meyer Lemon Mousse

Fresh Pea Soup with Mint Cream
Artichoke and Fennel Stew Covered with Pastry
Wild Rice and Brown Rice Pilaf
Butter Lettuce Salad with Mint and Chives
Coconut Crème Caramel

Appetizer of Pizza with Escarole, Fontina, and Walnuts
Leek and Chervil Soup
Spring Pasta with Artichokes, Mushrooms, and Peas
Lamb's-Lettuce Salad with Walnut Vinaigrette and Sieved Egg Garnish
Almond-Pine Nut Tart

Taglierini, Zucchini, Lemon, Pine Nuts, and Herbs
Mosaic Timbale with Herb Béchamel
Chicory Lettuce Salad with Mustard Vinaigrette and Croutons
Poached Dried Apricots in Ginger Syrup

White Bean and Fresh Tomato Soup* with Parsley Sauce
Artichoke Tart
Salad of Mixed Greens (rocket [arugula], lettuces, and nasturtium leaves and flowers)
Strawberries and Cream

Potato-Sorrel Soup
Steamed Asparagus with Butter and Meyer Lemon Juice
Individual Turnip Gratins with Toast Fingers
Belgian Endive and Watercress with Roasted Walnuts
Rhubarb Apple Betty

Olive Oil Bread
Appetizer Plate of Grilled Leeks,** Hard-Cooked Eggs, Black Olives, and Green Sauce
Asparagus Crepes with Fontina Cheese served with Béchamel with Lemon and Lemon Thyme
Butter Lettuce and Watercress Salad with Citrus and Avocado
Poached Dried Figs in Ginger

Beets, Apples, and Cress with Walnuts and Curry Vinaigrette
Onion-Sorrel Tart; New Potatoes and Garlic or Winter Squash Baked in Parchment
Semolina Pudding with Blood Orange Syrup

SUMMER

Summer is the fullest, most generous season for produce. Every week brings new varieties of fruits and vegetables, a succession of familiar pleasures. Many of the foods that are available year-round are harvested in summer, such as red onions, garlic, new potatoes, and cucumbers, and they are especially delicious then. Herbs are most plentiful and there are crops of delicate tender fruits such as fragrant white peaches, figs, raspberries, and blackberries. Tomatoes and corn are absolutely at their peak, and colorful bell peppers are plentiful and sweet. This is the ideal season for meals of composed salads and light foods.

New Potatoes and Garlic Baked in Parchment
Many-Layered Crepe Cake; Sautéed Spinach
Salad of Summer Lettuces and Flowering Herbs with Champagne Vinaigrette
Raspberry Sherbet

Farm Salad of Late Summer Tomatoes with Herbs, Bush Beans with Tarragon,
   and Hard-Cooked Eggs
Green Ravioli with Ricotta, Marjoram, and Cream
Summer Lettuce Salad with Rocket (Arugula) or Land Cress
Cherry and Apricot Crumble

---

*It's early for good tomatoes, but you can replace the fresh ones with three or four sun-dried tomatoes cut into small pieces.
**Instead of grilling the leeks, which is risky in spring if you're depending on good weather, blanch or steam them. As the crepes are creamy with the cheese and sauce, you can omit the avocado from the salad if you wish.

Roasted Eggplant Soup with Saffron Mayonnaise
Summer Roulade
Charcoal Grilled Zucchini with Herb Butter
Green Salad; Goat Cheese and Sun-Dried Tomato Toasts
Blackberry Crisp

Zucchini Fritters, Corn Fritters, or Red Bell Pepper Fritters with Ancho Chili Butter
Black Bean Chili
Salad of Romaine Lettuce with Mint, Cilantro, and Roasted Pine Nuts
Peach Ice Cream with Fresh Raspberries

Olive Oil Bread with Green Olives
Composed Salad of Herb Cream Cheese (garnished with chopped herb blossoms),
    Grilled Peppers, and Marinated Eggplant
Corn Pudding with Dill and Parsley; Cherry Tomatoes Sautéed with Shallots
Summer Lettuces with Champagne Vinaigrette
Blueberry-Cream Cheese Tart

Crouton Appetizer of Herb Cream Cheese and Cucumbers on Toast and
    Goat Cheese and Sun-Dried Tomato Toasts
Spinach, Cheese, and Tomato Lasagne; Green and Yellow Bush Beans with Basil
Red Romaine Lettuce Salad
Peaches with Cinnamon Crème Anglaise

Wilted Spinach Salad
Filo Pastry with Zucchini and Ricotta; Summer Leeks and Yellow Peppers
Individual Deep-Dish Fruit Pies

Composed Salad of Rocket (Arugula) Salad with Rocket Blossoms, Shallots and Walnut
    Vinaigrette, Hard-Cooked Eggs, and Baguette Croutons
Charcoal-Grilled Leeks
Eggplant Gratin with Saffron Custard; Fresh Herb Pasta
Fresh Figs, Honey, Cream Cheese, and Mint

A Summer Picnic
Lentil Salad with Mint, Roasted Peppers, and Feta Cheese
Summer Squash Frittata with Green Sauce
Easy Onion Pickle
Assorted Olives
Eggplant-Garlic Purée
Cherry Tomatoes with Olive Oil and Herbs
Country French Bread or Pita Breads
Blackberries with Rose Geranium Leaves
Toasted Almond Butter Cookies

FALL

Fall, like spring, is a transitional season. It includes the last of the tomatoes, peppers, and beans and the beginning of winter squash, turnips, fennel, and the winter root vegetables. Walnuts are harvested in September and wild mushrooms start to appear in October. For fruits there are late melons and fresh figs, but more apples, pears, and grapes. With fewer fresh foods on the menu, these fall fruits make a perfect dessert. This is a time for foods with smoky flavors and rich colors.

Winter Squash Soup with Red Chili and Mint
Corn and Zucchini Timbale with Ancho Chili Sauce or Grilled Tomato Sauce
Potato Gordas or Corn Bread
Pear-Apple Crisp

Grilled Leeks with Sieved Egg Garnish, Olive Oil, and Herbs
Whole Baked Eggplant
Winter Squash Gratin
Curly Endive Salad with Walnuts and Walnut Vinaigrette
Poached Dried Apricots in Ginger Syrup or Fresh Figs

New Potatoes and Garlic Baked in Parchment
Tomato and Wild Mushroom Soup
Chard and Saffron Tart
Butter Lettuce and Watercress Salad
Muscat Grape Sherbet

Warm Red Cabbage Salad
Winter Squash Tart; Butter-Fried Onions with Vinegar and Thyme
Japanese Mountain Pears and Toasted Almond Butter Cookies

Escarole and White Bean Salad with Fennel and Gruyère Cheese
Spicy Red Pepper Soup
Whole Wheat or Rye Bread
Spice Cake

Wilted Endive and Potato Salad with Sieved Egg Garnish
Lentil-Spinach Soup
Winter Squash Ravioli
Fresh Fruits (melons, figs, and grapes)

Yellow Squash Soup with Curry Spices
Grilled Vegetable Brochettes; Brown Rice and Herb Butter
Belgian Endive and Watercress Salad with Roasted Walnuts
Pears and Gorgonzola Cheese

Appetizer Plate of Guacamole, Oven-Roasted Peppers, and Warm Tortillas
Squash Stew with Chilies, Spices, and Ground Nuts
Orange-Jicama Salad (prepared as a relish)
Cinnamon Ice Cream with Apple Crisp

Broccoli with Roasted Peppers, Capers, and Pine Nuts
Baked Polenta Layered with Tomato, Fontina, and Gorgonzola Cheese
Curly Endive and Lettuce Salad with Walnut Vinaigrette
Brazilian Chocolate Cake

WINTER

Winter produce includes firm sweet root vegetables—parsnips, celeriac, fennel, and tur-nips—wild mushrooms, pearl and boiling onions, mature leeks, and potatoes. Buckwheat, rosemary, lentils, mildly bitter chicories and the sweeter lamb's-lettuce, nuts and nut oils are winter flavors, and stews, hearty soups, and creamy crusted gratins are winter dishes. Sweet and refreshing, citrus fruits also come into season at this time—tangerines, blood oranges, ruby grapefruit, Meyer lemons, and kumquats, as well as navel oranges and tart Eureka lem-ons.

Farm Salad of Beets in Walnut Vinaigrette, Hard-Cooked Eggs, and Lamb's-Lettuce Salad
Potatoes and Chanterelles Baked in Cream
Green Chard with Slivered Carrots
Fennel and Blood Orange Salad
Coconut Crème Caramel

Wild Rice and Hazelnut Salad Wrapped in Lettuce Leaves
Fennel and Celeriac Soup
Sorrel-Onion Tart; White Beans with Shallots, Chervil, and Cream
Winter Fruits and Roasted Chestnuts

Red Onion and Red Wine Soup with Tomatoes and Thyme
Mushroom Lasagne; Steamed or Sautéed Carrots
Watercress Salad with Walnut Vinaigrette and Gorgonzola Cheese
Meyer Lemon Mousse

Beets, Apples, and Cress with Walnuts and Curry Vinaigrette
Leek and Chervil Soup
Wide Green Noodles, Cauliflower, Broccoli, and Mustard Butter
Poached Pears with Maple Mousse

Winter Vegetables with Parsley Sauce
Wild Mushroom Ragout; Grilled Polenta
Limestone Lettuce Salad
Almond-Pine Nut Tart

Lentil-Spinach Soup
Winter Vegetable Stew
Romaine Hearts with Buttered Croutons and Roquefort Vinaigrette
Mince Cookies and Vanilla Ice Cream

Spinach Soup and Indian Spices
Butter-Fried Potatoes with Curry Spices and Cream
Fresh Fruit and Mint Chutney
Lettuce Salad with Lemon Vinaigrette
Semolina Pudding with Blood Orange Syrup

Turnip Soup with Turnip Greens
Buckwheat Linguine with French Lentils and Carrots
Salad of Escarole, Curly Endive, Apples and Roasted Walnuts with Walnut Vinaigrette
Maple Mousse with Toasted Almond Butter Cookies

Fennel, Mushroom, and Parmesan Salad
Cheese and Nut Loaf with Aromatic White Sauce; Green Chard with Slivered Carrots,
    and Butter-Fried Onions with Vinegar and Thyme
Belgian Endive Salad
Poached Dried Apricots with Ginger

Kale and Potato Soup with Red Chili
Escarole Frittata
Broccoli with Roasted Peppers, Capers, and Olives
Pear-Apple Crisp

Wines with Vegetarian Food

Serving wine with food can add to the enhancement and enjoyment of any meal. At Greens we have a small, but select, wine list. We choose wines that are not only excellent in their own right, but are compatible with our food in particular. To help us select, a tasting panel meets for lunch once a month at the restaurant to try a group of wines with our menu. Sometimes we find that the full-flavored wines that often do well in tastings turn out to be overpowering with our cuisine, whereas a less distinctive wine may blend well with our food. Since we are located in California near some of the finest grape-growing country in the world, we concentrate on California wines, but still enjoy offering our customers a few French and Italian wines, especially when there is no real equivalent in California. Rather than having a house wine, we serve several wines by the glass so that people can have more of a choice and a chance to experiment.

Even more so than food, wines are a matter of personal taste. By their nature, wines encourage the language of poetry, of romance. If a wine strikes you "like the sound of a bell," no one can argue—you were the one struck by it. That a wine brings to mind peaches, autumn leaves, butterscotch, cigar boxes, raspberries, cut grass, or the hay on a summer evening is simply a matter of personal poetry. This becomes especially obvious when our tasting panel—a group of food and wine "experts"—gives the same wine both a first- and last-place vote. For some, that "hay on a summer evening" is seedy or musty, while others settle down and luxuriate in it.

Finding a wine merchant whose taste you trust is often the best way to discover wines you like. A serious and conscientious retailer tries hundreds of wines to find a few good ones for his store. Also, an aware retailer can help you in each price range and tell you more about the wine than what is on the label: whether or not the wine is dry, if it has an appealing crispness, what its flavor characteristics are, whether or not it was aged in wood, if it is suitable for drinking now, etc.

To consider how wines combine with various foods, several of the components of wine should be examined. Probably the most critical one, certainly in white wines, is the amount of residual sugar. Sugar is converted into alcohol in the fermenting process, and a wine that is "dry" is one that has no residual sugar after fermentation. Generally, dry wines make the best food wines, as any residual sugar can leave a cloying or syrupy taste in the mouth when it is being consumed with food. Exceptions are rieslings and gewurztraminers, where sweetness is balanced with appropriate levels of tartness, but even these can sometimes be too sweet to be refreshing with food.

There are several varieties of California wines where it is particularly important to note whether or not the wine is dry (the American palate likes sweet, so the wines are often made that way). These include chenin blanc, French colombard, white zinfandel, vin gris (white pinot noir), pinot blanc, and sometimes sauvignon blanc. When these wines have residual sugar they have a softer, more mellow quality and fruitier flavors, and are probably more attractive served without food for afternoon or evening get-togethers, or perhaps with light snacks. Sometimes these wines are referred to as "off dry," which means close to dry (1 or 2 percent residual sugar). When listed here as possible food wines, the dry version of these wines is intended.

Although people often ask which wine is "drier" (i.e., which wine has less residual sugar), they just as often overlook considering the amount of acid in the wine. When acid is lacking, the wine is "flat," "fat," or "flabby," and tastes sweeter than it would otherwise. The proper level of acid in a wine gives it a refreshing, palate-cleansing quality, particularly important with rich, creamy foods or spicy foods. A wine with good acidity is referred to as "crisp," and higher levels of acid make the wine "tart" or "lemony." So even among wines that are equally dry, there are variations in the level of acidity as well as variations of flavor. And also remember that wines that are too tart by themselves are often refreshing and clean-tasting with food.

In broad terms, the differences between California and French wines, and European wines in general, are in sugar and acid levels. French wines tend to be crisper (i.e., have higher acid levels) than California wines, while their flavor is more diffuse, or subtle. California wines tend to have a full, rich flavor, but are sometimes lacking in acid, and their strong flavor statement can be overwhelming, especially for vegetarian food. On the whole, cooler weather in France means that the grapes develop higher acid and lower sugar content and a lower flavor intensity than their California counterparts. Many people prefer French wines as food wines because their tartness is palate-cleansing and their flavors complementary; their best qualities come out with food. Others prefer California wines because they provide more of a contrast or additional flavor interest to food. As always, it is a matter of personal taste.

Considering the basic flavor characteristics of different wines will help determine which foods they best accompany. Wines can be divided into three main flavor categories (which correspond to the three basic plant parts): fruit or flower; herbaceous, or "stem"; and earth. An additional factor, though, is that some wines are aged in wood, and the flavors imparted by wood aging do not necessarily fit into these categories. Also, sometimes you may want a wine that complements the food, while at other times you may choose a wine that provides more of a contrast. Root vegetable dishes, for instance, can be complemented with an earthy wine or contrasted with a fruity one. An herbaceous pasta can be complemented with an herbaceous wine or contrasted with one that is earthy or fruity. The type of fruitiness, whether it is plum, berry, peach, raisin, apple, and so forth, should also be taken into account.

White Wines

CHARDONNAY

Chardonnay is the aristocrat of white wines. Those that have not been aged in wood have predominantly fruit flavors of a citrusy kind, particularly lemon or grapefruit, while those aged in French oak have a kind of sweet earthiness ranging from vanilla and butterscotch to cloves, and have a "toasty" or "buttery" quality. The wood aging also tends to bring out more of a peach or apple (rather than citrusy) fruitiness.

Chardonnays correspond to the French white Burgundies, and good ones can be expensive. Some inexpensive chardonnays with little or no aging in wood are available from France and Italy and are a good value, but the more inexpensive California chardonnays are generally not as good as other varieties in the same price range.

The chardonnays with citrusy flavors tend to combine well with a variety of dishes, except those that already have tart flavors. The chardonnays aged in wood can be more difficult to match. Their grainy sweetness—the toasty quality—makes them complementary with grain dishes and resonant with some cheeses. Goat cheese and chardonnay, for example, is a classic combination (although there are those who prefer sauvignon blanc). Chardonnays are also good with fairly simple vegetable preparations, whereas those dishes that are highly seasoned either with peppers or herbs may overly interfere with the exquisite flavors of a fine chardonnay. Also the California chardonnays tend to be slightly low in acid, so these may not be crisp enough for dishes rich with cream, butter, or cheese, but if you pick one with sufficient acidity, a chardonnay can work very well with these foods.

CHENIN BLANC

To be acceptable as a food wine, California chenin blanc must be fermented to dryness. When this is done and the wine is aged in oak, chenin blanc can be a wine of distinction. While the off-dry versions have pleasant honeylike fragrances, the drier versions tend to have an earthy nature, a certain stoniness, or flinty quality—a cleanness like water flowing over rocks—with just traces of fruit, flower, and stem.

Dry chenin blancs set off almost any food with a kind of "grounding," while the food brings out the hidden flavors in the wine. This is the one white wine that pairs especially well with mushroom dishes.

FRENCH COLOMBARD

This grape, when handled well and fermented to dryness, can produce a practical food wine, though not of the depth of chenin blanc. When it is dry, its flavors are mildly herbaceous.

PINOT BLANC

Similar to chardonnay, pinot blanc has a more delicate and subtle nature. It is earthy with hints of flowers and fruits. Mostly, people are familiar with this wine as being a little sweet, but some California wineries are producing it as a dry wine. When dry, it is a good food wine, with "clean" flavors that complement a wide variety of dishes, since it does not have dominant flavors of its own. But keep it away from strongly seasoned foods, for they will overwhelm it.

RIESLINGS AND GEWURZTRAMINERS

These wines are grouped together, since they have similar characteristics as food wines. Their flavor category is fruity, even flowery. Both are reminiscent of fragrant spring blossoms such as freesias. Rieslings tend to have the wonderful bouquet of white grapes: gewurztraminers are more blossomy and spicy. Of all wines these need to have some, but not an undue amount of, residual sugar. When there is too much, they can taste syrupy with food. When there is too little, the wines lose their beautiful bouquet and flavor. These wines correspond to those produced in Germany, where the sweetness in the wine is often well balanced with tartness.

Given that not everyone likes them, and that you need to find ones with a proper amount of residual sugar, rieslings and gewurztraminers are particularly good with simple vegetable preparations (especially spring and summer), where the fruitiness of the wine brings out the sweetness of the vegetables. In relation to curry dishes, they have an uplifting chutneylike quality. They also contrast well with the smokiness of grilled vegetables and the spiciness of chili dishes.

SAUVIGNON BLANC

Among white wines, sauvignon blancs are second in "class" only to chardonnays, and they have an important place, because of all white wines, they have a flavor characterized as herbaceous, even "grassy." They are sometimes made to minimize this quality, which some people find unattractive, but a well-made grassy sauvignon blanc makes an excellent complement to herbaceous foods and those dishes prepared with chili peppers.

Sauvignon blanc corresponds roughly to the whites from Bordeaux and the Loire valley in France, where they often have a more flinty character. In California they are frequently made with residual sugar, which produces a softer, fruitier wine. Some of these with very low residual sugar can be good food wines, but generally the dry ones are preferred.

Again, the herbaceous quality of the wine is particularly effective with cilantro and all the Mexican dishes that are prepared with cilantro. Their crispness (they have higher acid levels than chardonnays on the whole) makes them a good choice to serve with rich, creamy dishes.

VIN GRIS AND WHITE ZINFANDEL

The term vin gris refers to those wines made from pinot noir grapes that are fermented in the manner of white wines. On the market these go by a variety of names: vin gris, eye of the swan, eye of the peacock, and so forth. To make vin gris or white zinfandel, the juice is pressed out of the grapes and fermented separately from the skins, stems, and seeds so that the wines pick up just a blush of the color that they would get if the juice was fermented with the skins.

Most of these wines are too sweet to be considered good food wines, but those that are dry can be versatile and lively. Their clean, refreshing taste has hints of fruit—the zinfandel, of prunes or raisins; the vin gris, of peaches, apricots, or berries. While not providing a great deal of additional flavor interest, these wines will accent or enhance a wide variety of dishes: Mexican dishes, vegetables, grilled foods, and Provençal dishes with olives, capers, and onions. They have a tartness that makes them pleasing with filo pastries and creamy or cheese dishes.

Because they go well with so many foods and offer clear value for the money, good day-to-day white wines are dry chenin blanc, French colombard, vin gris, or white zinfandel, or a blend (again, dry or nearly so) of chardonnay and riesling or gewurztraminer. Investigation may turn up other inexpensive blends that are suitable food wines, including some containing sauvignon blanc.

Red Wines

BEAUJOLAIS AND BEAUJOLAIS NOUVEAU

Beaujolais wines are from the Beaujolais region of France. They have bold fruit qualities with just hints of earthiness. They very much resemble pinot noir, but they are lighter and brighter. When made in the "nouveau" style Beaujolais may take some getting used to, not because their flavors are unusual or unique, but for precisely the opposite reason—the wines are light, smooth, silky, easy to swallow, and very fruity, with predominantly strawberry flavors. Recently a number of California wineries have started making beaujolais (and other varieties) in the French fashion of carbonic maceration, and some are quite acceptable. These lively wines are good with grilled foods and appetizers, foods with olives and capers, Greek salads, spring dishes, vegetable pastas, and pizzas. Their lightness makes them suitable for lunch or warm evenings, when other reds would be too full-flavored. Beaujolais nouveau is also one red best served slightly chilled.

(Chinon, another French wine, somewhat resembles Beaujolais, only its softness and fruitiness is combined with a robust earthiness. At least one winery in California is making wine from cabernet franc, the same grape that is used in Chinon.)

CABERNET SAUVIGNON

Cabernets fall into the herbaceous or "stemmy" category. Their flavor is often described as reminiscent of green tea, coffee, tobacco, and, on occasion, green pepper, although this last is even more characteristic of merlot, the lighter cousin of cabernet. Cabernets have only a hint of fruitiness, which is plumlike, if anything.

Cabernets correspond to the French Bordeaux wines, although these are often made from two or more grapes. Cabernets, especially the California ones, tend to be big and bulky, and their strong flavors can overpower vegetarian food, but again the lighter ones or those with finesse can be attractive with dishes that feature nuts or whole grains, and complementary with some of the egg dishes: timbales, tarts, and frittatas, especially when the other ingredients are strong-flavored vegetables and herbs rather than those with more delicate flavors.

More sedate than zinfandels and pinot noirs, cabernets do not provide liveliness or contrast as much as they deepen and expand the flavors of a dish. These are not so much wines to have fun with, but serious wines to contemplate, and they need dishes of some weight to carry them along.

CHIANTI

This is a wine made from four grape varieties, giving it a rather unique blend of earthiness with traces of stem, fruit, and spice. These wines are from the Chianti region of Italy, and especially the Chianti Riserva can be warmly attractive and inviting, combining a harmonious range of flavors with a silky and soft feeling on the tongue.

With no dominant flavor characteristics, Chiantis, when not overly brash, make good food wines, especially suitable for the earthy grains and vegetables, but also combining well with grilled foods, cheeses, and frittatas.

PINOT NOIR

Along with a slight earthiness and smokiness imparted from aging in oak, pinot noirs have predominantly fruit flavors reminiscent of raspberries or blackberries, sometimes strawberries. Their counterpart in French wines are the reds from Burgundy, some of which are regarded as the best in the world. The quality of California pinot noir varies considerably, so to find those that are stylish, drinkable, and enjoyable with food may be problematic, but there are many available.

The smokiness of pinot noir makes it a fine complement to grilled foods, and the fruitiness is wonderful with preparations featuring vegetables. Pinot noirs have a characteristic lushness or fullness, which can be attractive with summer foods— squashes, eggplant, tomatoes—and can also give an uplifting feeling to winter squashes and potatoes. For some it is a favored red wine with cheeses.

RHÔNE WINES

These include a whole grouping of wines from the Rhône valley in France. Of particular interest are the large number of good Côtes-du-Rhône wines. An excellent value, these wines have an earthy quality with scant fruit and spice. Sometimes their flavor is referred to as being "cheesy." These are good food wines that go well with a wide variety of dishes, but they are especially compatible with mushroom dishes. Their earthiness complements root vegetable dishes and grains and gives contrast to the spicy Mexican foods. The Côtes-du-Rhônes can also be paired with cheese and egg dishes.

ZINFANDEL

This red wine grape is grown principally in California and does not have any clear counterpart among European wines, although Italian Barbera is probably the closest. The flavors are hearty, fruity—from berry to plum, prune, and raisin—and spicy. Although some are far too robust to be good food wines, light to medium zinfandels go well with almost any vegetarian dish, particularly those with tomatoes and cheese, and Mexican dishes. Zinfandels can also give a bright contrasting flavor to dishes with root vegetables or grains, which tend to be earthy—their inherent sweetness is brought out by the wine. The wine also matches up well with Provençal dishes and others with onions, olives, capers, or feta cheese.

For everyday drinking, the best values in red wines are the lighter zinfandels and the Côtes-du-Rhône wines. Of course there are many other good wines, including inexpensive blends, that can be discovered with a bit of a search.

Serving Temperature for Wines

This discussion of wines would not be complete without mentioning how serving temperature affects wine. The smell, and hence the taste, of a wine is greatly affected by temperature. Generally, it may be said that white wines are drunk too cold and reds are drunk too warm. When chilled, the aroma and taste of a wine will be reduced; as it heats up, more flavor molecules will be released. Red wines are not as volatile as whites, so they are served at higher temperatures to enhance their flavors, but above 65°F the alcohol and other elements of the wine begin to vaporize and detract from the wine's character.

Chill masks deficiencies in wines, particularly their sugar and acid levels, so inexpensive whites are best served very cold. Better quality whites, however, are most flavorful between 45 and 55°F, rieslings and gewurztraminers at the lower end and chardonnays at the higher. Beaujolais is best in this range also, at 50 to 55°F, while Côtes-du-Rhônes and lighter zinfandels are best at 55 to 60°F. A little planning is necessary to overcome our tendency to drink white wines straight from the refrigerator and red wines at a room temperature above 70°F: White wines may need to be left out of the refrigerator for a while and red wines put in. Of course, all this is much less important with everyday wines than a special bottle.

Serving Suggestions

In summary, here is a chart listing some suggestions for pairing wine with food:

FOOD CATEGORIES	WHITE WINES		RED WINES	
	complementary / *contrasting*		complementary / *contrasting*	
Grains	chardonnay chenin blanc	*sauvignon blanc*	cabernet Côtes-du-Rhône	
Spring Vegetables	French colombard	*riesling/ gewurztraminer chardonnay*	Beaujolais zinfandel	
Summer Vegetables	sauvignon blanc	*chardonnay pinot blanc*		*pinot noir Beaujolais*
Autumn Vegetables		*chardonnay pinot blanc*		*pinot noir Beaujolais*
Winter Vegetables	chenin blanc chardonnay	*riesling/ gewurztraminer*	Rhône	*pinot noir zinfandel*

FOOD CATEGORIES	WHITE WINES		RED WINES	
	complementary / *contrasting*		complementary / *contrasting*	
Mexican	vin gris sauvignon blanc	*riesling/ gewurztraminer*	zinfandel	*Rhône*
Provençal	vin gris sauvignon blanc	*chenin blanc*	zinfandel Beaujolais	*Rhône*
Cream, Butter	sauvignon blanc		zinfandel Rhône	
Cheese	chardonnay chenin blanc		Côtes-du-Rhône	*pinot noir*
Mushrooms	chenin blanc	*pinot blanc*	Rhône	*zinfandel Barbera*
Curries		*riesling/ gewurztraminer*		*zinfandel*
Grilled Foods	vin gris sauvignon blanc	*riesling/ gewurztraminer chardonnay*		*pinot noir Beaujolais zinfandel*
Herbaceous	sauvignon blanc vin gris	*riesling/ gewurztraminer*	cabernet	*Beaujolais*
Eggs	sauvignon blanc	*chardonnay*	cabernet Rhône	*pinot noir Chianti*
Nuts	chardonnay		cabernet	*pinot noir*

In weighing the various recommendations listed here, consider the overall tone or feeling of a dish, rather than the specific ingredients. However, one needn't look for the perfect combination. To experiment with new combinations of food and wine can be enjoyable and instructive. The combination does not have to be perfect to be a wonderful pleasure.

Bon appétit!

Glossary of Ingredients

Anaheim chilies: See CHILI PEPPERS.

Ancho chilies: See CHILI PEPPERS.

Basil: The familiar large-leafed basil is used throughout the summer in both cooked dishes and salads. It is always wonderful with tomatoes and is delicious with all summer vegetables—eggplant, squash, new potatoes, and beans. New varieties of basils are now available in nurseries and from seed catalogs. Opal basil, a smaller plant with deep purple leaves, has a more pungent flavor and makes a striking fresh garnish for salads, pastas, and eggs. Lemon basil has a clear lemon fragrance mingled with the familiar basil perfume, and the flavor is summery and refreshing. Cinnamon basil is intensely fragrant with sweet and spicy scents that are clearly redolent of cinnamon. It is especially good in spicy foods, such as curries. Regular basil may be substituted for any of the more exotic varieties.

Borage: Large plants up to four feet tall, borage is covered throughout the summer with clusters of bright blue star-shaped flowers that make a cheerful, pretty garnish in salads. The leaves have a pleasant cucumber taste, but they are generally too prickly to use raw. They do, however, contribute depth to the flavor of soup stocks. If you have plants in your yard, you can make a habit of adding five or six leaves to a stock. Borage grows easily from seeds and will self-sow.

Butter: At Greens we use unsalted butter, which is fresher and more flavorful than salted butter. However, we have specified its use only for desserts, where its delicate flavor is particularly important. Since unsalted butter can turn rancid more easily than salted, try to buy it frozen and keep it in the freezer until needed.

Chervil: An herb with a mild anise flavor and delicate feathery leaves, chervil can be used generously by itself or in combination with other herbs such as parsley, marjoram, and chives. Chervil leaves are pretty to look at and the taste is mild, so it is nice to use them broken into sprigs and scattered in a salad as well as chopped. Chervil is easy to grow from seed; in hot climates, it needs to be sown monthly. It is an herb that is best used fresh rather than dried. If it isn't available, substitute a mixture of parsley and a little tarragon, fresh or dried.

Chili negro: See CHILI PEPPERS.

Chili Peppers: A remarkable number of fresh and dried chilies give piquancy and heat and also contribute color and flavor to foods. The fresh green ones tend to have a grassy taste, while the dried ones are earthy and fruity. The seeds and veins of chilies are the hottest parts, as well as the least flavorful; they are usually removed so that more of the chili taste can come through. When working with chilies, take care not to touch your face or eyes because the pepper oils are potent and can burn. Even the hands and fingertips of people with sensitive skin can be affected by handling chilies. A pair of thin rubber gloves is very helpful in this case. Of the many varieties of chilies, we use but a few. For more information about chilies, their names and characteristics, see Diana

Kennedy's book, *The Cuisines of Mexico*. Be aware, however, that there is a certain amount of confusion surrounding the nomenclature of particular varieties of chilies, and in these cases we have used the names found in California markets rather than the names used in Mexico.

Fresh chilies:

Anaheim chilies are widely available in supermarkets, where they are referred to as mild green chilies. They are 5 to 7 inches long, a shiny light green, cylindrical, and about 2 inches in diameter. They can vary in piquancy from mild to fairly hot. Closely related are the New Mexico or California chilies. They also come in cans labeled as "green chilies." When you use canned chilies that have been packed in vinegar, rinse them well before using. Anaheims are used for cooking more than as a seasoning. Prepare them as you would bell peppers—stuffed or sautéed, roasted or grilled.

Jalapeño peppers are a dark, rich green, about 2 inches long and a bit wider at the stem ends than serrano chilies. Jalapeños are slightly less hot than serranos, but the two can be used pretty much interchangeably. New varieties have been recently introduced that are fairly mild and can be used when you want the flavor but not the heat.

Poblano chilies are generally 4 to 6 inches long, a glossy dark green, almost green-black on the shoulders, and heart-shaped. They are rich and flavorful—more flavorful than the Anaheims. Poblanos can also be used in the same ways bell peppers are. When dried, they are called pasilla or ancho chilies.

Serrano chilies are 2 to 3 inches long, a shiny light green, cylindrical, and about ½ inch in diameter. They are very hot—one or two are ample in most dishes. Serranos are used to season salsas and relishes, and can be cooked with vegetables or simmered in soups.

Chilis negros are about 5 to 7 inches long and an inch or so around with black, wrinkled skins. They have a pronounced earthy, almost muddy, flavor.

Dried Chilies:

The three preceding chilies can be dried in the oven and ground and blended together to make a fresh, pure chili powder that contains no other seasonings. New Mexican chili powder is one such type of powder that can be purchased already ground. Usually the name of the type of chili used is given on the label. Soaked and puréed, these dried chilies can be used to give wonderful depth and complexity to various red sauces.

Chilpotle peppers are jalapeño peppers that have been smoked. They are commercially available canned in vinegar or red adobo sauce (we use those packed in the sauce), and are intensely hot with an unmistakable smoky fragrance. They can be puréed and used to season soups and stews or as a spread on bread for sandwiches. Once the can is opened, the chilies will keep almost indefinitely if covered and refrigerated.

Pasilla or Ancho chilies are the dried form of the poblano type. Three to six inches long, they are broad at the stem end, 2 to 3 inches across, and taper to a point. The color of the wrinkled skins ranges from deep ruby red to dark brown or black. The term "ancho" refers to the smaller, redder chilies. The fragrance of both these chilies is reminiscent of prunes and raisins, and they can be used interchangeably.

Pepperoncini rossi are small, thin red chilies an inch or two long. They can be found in Italian markets, and in this book are referred to as small red chilies. Used whole, or crumbled into flakes and cooked with vegetables, they give a pleasant hot bite to foods.

Chilpotle peppers: See CHILI PEPPERS.

Cilantro (coriander): Fresh coriander leaves, or cilantro, as it is commonly called, is an essential seasoning in Mexican and Asian dishes. The delicate leaves have a strong, assertive flavor for which there is no real substitute. The dried coriander seeds are much sweeter and only vaguely reminiscent of the fresh leaves. Also called Chinese parsley because it is used so ubiquitously in Chinese cooking, it can be found in Asian as well as Mexican markets, and is becoming increasingly available in supermarkets. Cilantro can be grown from seeds or bought in nurseries as small plants. As it grows quickly and will flower quickly in warm weather, it is much more economical to sow small beds periodically rather than to buy individual plants. If, after flowering, the seeds are allowed to mature and dry, they can be stored and used in curries and in pastry making.

Corn oil: See OILS.

Cream cheese: We use a natural cream cheese, which has not been stabilized with gelatin. It is lighter, smoother, and less cloying than the regular commerical cream cheese.

Crème Fraîche: The advantages of using this type of soured cream are several—the lack of stabilizers and preservatives, the taste, and most important, the fact that when it is cooked it will not curdle as does commercial sour cream. It is costly to buy but relatively inexpensive and easy to make: Mix 2 cups cream with 1 tablespoon buttermilk and put it in a clean bowl or jar. Cover it and let it sit at room temperature or in a warm part of the kitchen for 24 hours, by which time it should have thickened. If it hasn't, let it go another 12 hours. Refrigerate the finished cream, and before using, stir it well. The flavor will sharpen as it sits. In place of buttermilk, reserve a tablespoon and use it to start your next batch. Use crème fraîche as you would sour cream.

Dried mushrooms: Dried mushrooms have an intensity of flavor that makes them an invaluable ingredient for the vegetarian cook. The oriental dried mushrooms (*pasania cuspidata*), known as shiitake in Japanese, are also available from Chinese grocers as dried black mushrooms or dried black forest mushrooms. European dried mushrooms (*boletus eduli*) are known as porcini in Italian and cèpes in French. There are also some dried mushrooms imported from South America that have excellent flavor for stocks and sauces even though their texture is not good for eating. Occasionally these mushrooms are available in supermarkets, but otherwise look for them at Asian markets.

Dry jack: This is Monterey Jack cheese that has been aged at least 6 months. It is a dry, hard grating cheese, similar to Romano or Asiago.

Fontina: Italian Fontina cheese is creamy and fruity and melts beautifully. Danish Fontina is more readily available and less expensive, but its flavor and texture are not as fine. Use the Italian variety in those dishes where it is especially featured. If it's not available, use the Danish.

Herbs: Since the generous use of fresh herbs adds greatly to the range and nuance of flavors in foods, we have called for fresh herbs throughout the book, even though we realize that many of them are not readily available in supermarkets. With a few exceptions they can be replaced with their dried forms, using about one third as much dried in place of the fresh. The actual relative strength will vary somewhat, depending on the herb, how long it has been stored, and in what form. Dried herbs lose their flavors, especially when stored over a year, and the rate of loss is accelerated if they have been powdered first.

When buying dried herbs, late autumn is when you are likely to find the most recent harvest. Try to buy herbs in bulk and in seed or leaf form, whenever possible. When using dried herbs, always rub them between your fingers as you add them to the pan, or bruise them in a mortar to release the aromatic oils. Rather than relying on a measuring spoon, use your nose to check how strong they are and whether you need to use more or less than the recommended amount.

As mentioned, not all herbs can be dried successfully. Delicate green herbs like chervil, parsley, cilantro, and fennel are all best when used fresh, as their flavors either disappear or are altered, becoming grassy and indistinct when dried. In such cases, when the fresh herb is not available, it may be better to replace it with an altogether different herb, even when the flavor is not comparable. Sometimes the dried seeds can be used to replace fresh leafy herbs; for instance, fennel seeds convey much of the flavor and scent of the fresh feathery greens, and celery seeds successfully replace celery leaves or approximate lovage. In other cases, however, the flavor of the seed is, at best, reminiscent of the fresh herbs. Coriander seeds, for example, though delicious in curries and certain pastries, are inadequate for replacing fresh coriander (cilantro) leaves. Experimenting and tasting are the best ways to gain familiarity in this somewhat complicated territory.

We have called for a number of uncommon herbs because they have contributed so much to our cooking at Greens and to encourage experimenting with new ingredients. If necessary other, more common herbs may be substituted. One thing to keep in mind, however, is that most herbs are easy to grow. They are beautiful plants to include among ornamental garden plantings, and the woody-stemmed varieties can be included as part of the permanent landscape. Herbs also do quite well when grown in containers. They can be started from seed or purchased as young plants from nurseries. Seeds can be found in the catalogs listed here, although not all the catalogs carry seeds of all the herbs.

The Cook's Garden, Box 65, Londonderry, Vermont 05148

Le Marché Seeds International, Box 566, Dixon, California 95620

Seeds for the World, Vermont Bean Seed Co., Garden Lane, Bomoseen, Vermont 05732

Shepherd's Garden Seeds, 7389 West Zayante Road, Felton, California 95018

Hyssop: A hearty shrub with blue, pink, or white flowers, hyssop is an intensely aromatic, strong-flavored herb, reminiscent of licorice. The leaves can be used sparingly in robustly flavored dishes and the flowers, strewn over salads, make a festive, pretty garnish.

Italian parsley: Italian, or flat-leafed, parsley has a sweet full flavor, and for this reason it is preferable to the more familiar curly-leafed parsley, although they can be used interchangeably. The flat surface of the Italian parsley leaf doesn't catch in the throat the way the ruffled hard leaves of the curly parsley can, making it more suitable when you wish to include whole leaves in a salad. Grown from seed or purchased as small plants, Italian parsley is not a difficult herb to grow. Both the leaves and the stems are used in stocks for their deep, earthy flavor.

Jalapeño peppers: See CHILI PEPPERS.

Jicama: This large, tuberous vegetable from Mexico has a thin brown skin and white flesh with a crisp, crunchy texture. Its flavor is mild and sweet, somewhat like a fresh water chestnut. It is especially good eaten raw in salads.

Lamb's-lettuce (corn salad, mâche): One of the first greens to appear in the spring, the tender spoon-shaped leaves of lamb's-lettuce are always welcome in green salads and vegetable salads. Seeds from Italy, France, and England are available through catalogs. The plants form small rosettes and can be used whole, but they must be washed very carefully, as fine soil often accumulates at the base of their leaves. Nut oils nicely complement the flavor of this green.

Land cress: Land cress, curly cress, broadleaf cress, and upland cress are all quick-growing, delicately textured greens that have the sharp, peppery flavor of watercress. They add a pleasant bite to salads and sandwiches and go well with sweeter, milder vegetables, such as beets or potatoes. As they can be grown indoors as well as outside, a fresh salad green can be made easily available even during the winter months of the year.

Lemon thyme: Like its better-known cousin, culinary, or common, thyme, lemon thyme is a hardy low-growing shrub. The tiny leaves are bright green with yellow markings, and the flavor is clearly a pleasing mixture of lemon and culinary thyme, though not as strong as culinary thyme. The branches can be steeped in hot milk to impart a lemon flavor, or tucked among potatoes and turnips in a gratin. The leaves, plucked from the branches, make a lovely addition to leaf and vegetable salads.

Lovage: Lovage leaves resemble a large version of Italian parsley, and they have a clean, strong, celerylike taste. Lovage goes well with tomatoes, corn, and potatoes, and is delicious in tossed salads, the leaves torn into small pieces. When simmered in soups and stews, the flavor mellows, but lovage should be used with a judicious hand. A handsome garden plant with its glossy bright green leaves, the stalks of mature plants can be chopped and used as a soup vegetable.

Miner's lettuce: A succulent, tender green that appears in the spring, miner's lettuce grows wild and can be found in city lots as well as in the country. Seeds can be found for it through *The Cook's Garden* (see page 381). This is a very mild-tasting salad green with an unusual configuration of disk-shaped leaves pierced through the middle by their stem.

Niçoise and Gaeta olives: These are small black olives from the South of France and from Italy. They have a pure olive taste and come packed with their pits. The pits can be easily removed by pressing on them with the bottom of a flat dish or the heel of your palm. Green Niçoise olives come already pitted. Their flavor is more tart than the black olives.

Oils: Mostly we use olive oil (see *Olive oils*) at Greens, both for cooking and for dressing salads. We also use walnut and hazelnut oils on leaf and vegetable salads, particularly in the winter months. The warm nutty flavors go particularly well with the bitter chicories and strong-tasting wild greens. Dark (toasted) sesame oil is very flavorful and aromatic, good to use with oriental foods as a dressing rather than a cooking oil. Light sesame oil is better for cooking. We also use corn and peanut oils for frying and sautéeing foods where the flavor of olive oil isn't appropriate to the dish.

Olive oils: Olive oil is referred to three different ways in this book, reflecting the different grades of oil. Extra virgin oil comes from the first pressing and is the most fragrant, soft, and flavorful of the olive oils. It is also the most expensive, and generally best reserved for use where its flavor will not be altered by cooking—on leaf salads, vegetable salads, and as a flavorful addition stirred into soups and pastas. Virgin olive oil comes from the second pressing and like the extra virgin, it is fruity and full-bodied, but not as fine or as soft. Use it as you would use extra virgin oil and cook with it when you want the flavor of the olive to come through. Pure olive oil (noted in the book simply as olive oil) comes from the third and any subsequent pressings. It is light-colored and mild in flavor and does not have a distinctive olive taste. It can be replaced with other oils, if you prefer.

Olive oil is produced in California, but most of that sold in America is imported from France, Italy, Greece, and Spain. There is considerable variation in the flavor and quality of these oils, and there is no one oil that we use all the time. Like wine, the quality of oil fluctuates from year to year, and even oils produced within miles of each other will vary. This means tasting various oils periodically to find out what you like. For flavorful virgin oils suitable for everday cooking we have used many kinds, but particularly Spanish and Italian oils. For extra virgin olive oil, those from Tuscany and from the South of France always have the best fragrance and flavor.

Parmesan and Parmesan Reggiano: Parmesan Reggiano is the true Parmesan cheese from Parma, Italy, which has a wonderful nutty flavor. A very special cheese, it's both hard to find and costly, so it is best used where its flavor can really be noticed and enjoyed. A true Parmigiano Reggiano will have those words stamped on the rind. Other Parmesan cheeses—domestic or imported—may be substituted for Reggiano. Whether you are using a Parmesan or any other hard grating cheese, it is always preferable to grate it freshly so that you may enjoy its fullest flavor.

Pasilla chilies: See CHILI PEPPERS.

Peanut oil: See OILS.

Pepperocini rossi: See CHILI PEPPERS.

Poblano chilies: See CHILI PEPPERS.

Purslane: A common garden weed that has been domesticated, purslane creeps along the ground and has thick, succulent leaves. When cooked, it turns a little bitter, but it has a delicate flavor when eaten raw. The texture of the leaves is crisp and crunchy, which makes it an interesting green to mix with soft, buttery lettuces.

Rocket (roquette, arugula): This is a salad plant that has become very popular in the last few years. It is one of the easiest greens to grow. The seeds germinate in about three days, and the leaves can be picked almost as soon as they begin to appear. As the plant matures, the flavor becomes increasingly hot and peppery. The flavor is strong and assertive and goes very well with nut oils and rich, fruity olive oil. Rocket is often mixed with other salad greens. The cream-colored blossoms of the mature plants are pretty tossed in salads or used to garnish a salad plate.

Rose geranium: The leaves of some geranium plants have a perfume that clearly brings to mind the scents of other flowers and some spices. The rose geranium is one of the best examples, for the leaves are unmistakably rose-scented. Steeped in milk or cream, layered with fruits, or placed on the bottom of a cake pan, the leaves impart their flavor to custards, compotes, and pastries. Plants can be found in nurseries and raised in pots or set in the ground. With its lacelike leaves and pink blossoms, the rose geranium is a pretty plant to include in the garden.

Serrano chilies: See CHILI PEPPERS.

Sesame oil: See OILS.

Sorrel: The tart, lemony leaves of the sorrel plant provide a high note in salads and have many uses in cooking. Even an enormous volume of leaves will melt within minutes into a strongly flavored purée that is very good combined with potatoes, stewed onions, or eggs, or in creamy soups and sauces. An established plant will last three to five years. Picking the leaves encourages new ones to grow.

Sun-dried tomatoes: Sun-dried tomatoes have an unusual and highly concentrated flavor best used in small quantities. They can be cut into very thin strips and tossed in pastas or with vegetables, or pureed and added to tomato sauces or spread over a baguette crouton or pizza crust. The best sun-dried tomatoes are those from Italy, which come packed in olive oil. The taste can vary, some being quite salty. Some farmers in this country have recently begun producing sun-dried tomatoes, which can often be found at farmers' markets or natural food stores. They are sold dry and can be softened in hot water and blended into a purée. Their quality is often uneven, but they are certainly worth experimenting with.

Vinegars: Unlike the limited choices of a not-too-distant past, there is now available an enormous variety of vinegars, providing the cook with great flexibility when seasoning or constructing a dressing. We use six or seven vinegars on a regular basis. For mild white wine vinegars we use Champagne vinegar, tarragon vinegar, and rice wine vinegar. For the more strongly flavored reds we use aged red wine vinegar, Spanish sherry vinegar, and balsamic vinegar. The latter is made in Italy, aged a number of years in wood, and is quite sweet, with lower than average acidity. We often use it in combination with a red wine vinegar. We have used Chinese black vinegars, which are also sweet with low acid, but their quality fluctuates, so we have replaced them with balsamic vinegar.

Useful Kitchen Tools

The kitchen at Greens is equipped with standard kitchen items. Here are some that are just as useful in the home.

Chinoise: Also called a China cap, this is a sturdy conical sieve that gives much the same results as a food mill. Chinoises, which are used with a conical wooden pestle, come with large or small holes, and are somewhat more expensive than food mills. One with finer holes is practical for making fine purées and straining out small particles, and one with large holes works well for general straining. For small quantities of food a regular kitchen strainer and wooden spoon or rubber spatula can be used with similar results.

Crepe Pans: These are lightweight for easy handling. Some come with a non-stick surface.

Earthenware Gratin Dishes: These beautiful 6- and 8-cup glazed dishes are perfect for baking. They hold heat well and always look handsome when brought to the table. They can be used for stews and gratins, and for fruit dishes, such as crisps and cobblers. The large oval ones convey a sense of hominess and abundance.

Food Mill: This old-fashioned device is often preferable to a blender when puréeing soups and vegetables because it does not overwork the food or incorporate a lot of air into it. Potatoes passed through a food mill will not be gummy, and soups will still have a little texture after they are puréed. A food mill is also very useful for separating seeds from berries, and the skins and seeds from apples and pears, and for screening out stringy particles of food. Food mills with interchangeable screens allow for a range of finer and coarser textures, but those with a single screen work extremely well and are easier to find. See also *Chinoise.*

Metal Tongs: Spring-loaded metal tongs come in different lengths and are available in hardware and cookware stores and restaurant supply houses. They are like having an extended and extremely dexterous hand, allowing you to pick things up and reach into hot places with ease. They are especially useful when cooking and serving pasta, and for grilling. In the kitchen shorter tongs are easier to manipulate, while the longer ones are especially practical for grilling.

Mortar and Pestle: A mortar and pestle is useful for crushing herbs and spices, for breaking garlic into a purée, and for making pastes of garlic, oil, and herbs and other malleable foods. Mortars come in different shapes and sizes—they can be wide and shallow or deep with high sides. They are made of various materials—marble, stone, ceramic, porcelain, and wood. If you buy a wooden one, choose one made of hardwood, such as olive, rather than soft fir or pine. A large mortar can be used for grinding even a small amount of material; the rough surface at the bottom helps keep things from flying about. Wooden mortars absorb and hold the flavors of foods, so if you use them frequently, it is a good idea to have two, one for dessert spices, the other for herbs and garlic.

Pasta Machine: For making pasta at home use one of the small stainless steel machines that clamp to a table. Choose one that is of good, solid construction. The number of settings, whether six or seven, is not important.

Pizza Stone and Peel: A large ceramic "stone" and peel, or wooden paddle, can be found in most cookware stores. If you enjoy baking pizzas and breads, using these will give you a great deal of pleasure. The pizza or bread is placed on the floured peel, then slid onto the stone, which has been preheated in the oven. Baking directly on the hot stone gives these foods a crisp, delicious crust.

Ramekins: These are individual casserole dishes, suitable for baking and then serving at the table—French onion soup is often baked and then served in this type of dish. Two sizes are useful: those with a 2-cup capacity can accommodate individual stews and casseroles, while 1-cup ramekins are a good size for individual timbales.

Skillet, 6-inch cast iron or enamel: A small heavy skillet made of cast iron or enamel is useful for toasting seeds and herbs, and for making caramel. Such a skillet warms gradually and holds the heat evenly. When making caramel, a skillet that is light colored is ideal because you can check the progress of the sugar as it darkens.

Skillet, 12-inch with a non-stick surface: Almost every stove-top recipe cooked in this book has been made in this size skillet—a common but remarkably useful piece of equipment. Most of the large stews will fit in it if necessary, although a cast iron or enamel casserole is more roomy and convenient.

Spice Mill: Actually a coffee mill, this is basically an electric version of the mortar and pestle, and it is especially useful for making your own powdered spices. Freshly ground herbs and spices have a great deal more flavor than those bought preground and stored for long periods of time. Spice mills are also useful for grinding small amounts of nuts, bread crumbs, and other foods for which a blender or food processor would be too large. Because the aromatic oils from the spices can linger even when the machine is cleaned after use, it is not recommended that you use the same mill for both coffee and spices.

Bibliography

Boni, Ada. *Italian Regional Cooking*. New York: Bonanza Books, 1969.

Brennan, Georgeanne. *The New American Vegetable Cookbook*. Berkeley: Aris Books, 1985.

Brown, Edward. *The Tassajara Bread Book*. Boston: Shambhala, 1970.

———. *Tassajara Cooking*. Boston: Shambhala, 1973.

———. *The Tassajara Recipe Book*. Boston: Shambhala, 1985.

Bugialli, Giuliano. *The Fine Art of Italian Cooking*. New York: Times Books, 1977.

Child, Julia; Bertholle, Louisette; and Beck, Simone. *Mastering the Art of French Cooking*. Vol. 1. New York: Alfred A. Knopf, 1970.

———. *Mastering the Art of French Cooking*. Vol. 2. New York: Alfred A. Knopf, 1970.

Clayton, Bernard, Jr. *The Breads of France*. New York: Bobbs–Merrill, 1978.

Dalí, Salvador. *Les Dîners de Gala*. New York: Felicie, 1973.

David, Elizabeth. *Classics: Mediterranean Food, French Country Cooking, Summer Cooking*. New York: Alfred A. Knopf, 1980.

———. *Italian Food*. London: Penguin Books, 1976.

———. *Spices, Salt and Aromatics in the English Kitchen*. London: Penguin Books, 1970.

Escoffier, Auguste. *Ma Cuisine*. London: Drury House, 1966.

The Fanny Farmer Cook Book. Revised by Marion Cunningham. New York: Alfred A. Knopf, 1982.

Fisher, M. F. K. *The Art of Eating*. New York: Random House, 1976.

Grigson, Jane. *Jane Grigson's Vegetable Book*. New York: Atheneum, 1979.

———. *The Mushroom Feast*. New York: Alfred A. Knopf, 1975.

Hughes, Phyllis, ed. *Pueblo Indian Cookbook*. Santa Fe: Museum of New Mexico Press, 1977.

Jaffrey, Madhur. *An Invitation to Indian Cooking*. New York: Random House, 1976.

———. *Madhur Jaffrey's World-of-the-East, Vegetarian Cooking*. New York: Alfred A. Knopf, 1981.

Johnson, Hugh. *The World Atlas of Wine*. New York: Simon and Schuster, 1971.

Johnston, Mireille. *Cuisine of the Sun*. New York: Random House, 1976.

Kamman, Madeleine M. *When French Women Cook: A Gastronomic Memoir*. New York: Atheneum, 1976.

Kennedy, Diana. *The Cuisines of Mexico*. New York: Harper and Row, 1972.

Larkcom, Joy. *The Salad Garden*. New York: Viking, 1984.

Mondadori, Arnoldo, ed. *Feast of Italy*. New York: Thomas Y. Crowell, 1973.

Olney, Richard. *The Good Cook: Technique and Recipes*. Alexandria, Va.: Time-Life Books, 1979.

———. *Simple French Food*. New York: Atheneum, 1974.

Root, Waverley. *The Food of France*. New York: Random House, 1977.

———. *The Food of Italy*. New York: Random House, 1977.

Ross, Janet, and Waterfield, Michael. *Leaves from Our Tuscan Kitchen*. New York: Vintage Books, 1975.

Sahni, Julie. *Classic Indian Cooking*. New York: William Morrow and Company, 1980.

Shere, Lindsey Remolif. *Chez Panisse Desserts*. New York: Random House, 1985.

Waters, Alice. *Chez Panisse Menu Cookbook*. New York: Random House, 1982.

———; Curtan, Patricia; and Labro, Martine. *Chez Panisse Pasta, Pizza, and Calzone*. New York: Random House, 1984.

Wolfert, Paula. *Couscous and Other Good Food from Morocco*. New York: Harper and Row, 1973.

Index